S104 Exploring science
Science: Level 1

The Open University

The Right Chemistry

Prepared by John Baxter and Ellen Heeley

D1470763

This publication forms part of an Open University course S104 *Exploring science*. The complete list of texts which make up this course can be found on the back cover. Details of this and other Open University courses can be obtained from the Student Registration and Enquiry Service, The Open University, PO Box 197, Milton Keynes MK7 6BJ, United Kingdom: tel. +44 (0)845 300 60 90, email general-enquiries@open.ac.uk

Alternatively, you may visit the Open University website at http://www.open.ac.uk where you can learn more about the wide range of courses and packs offered at all levels by The Open University.

To purchase a selection of Open University course materials visit http://www.ouw.co.uk, or contact Open University Worldwide, Michael Young Building, Walton Hall, Milton Keynes MK7 6AA, United Kingdom for a brochure. tel. +44 (0)1908 858793; fax +44 (0)1908 858787; email ouw-customer-services@open.ac.uk

The Open University
Walton Hall, Milton Keynes
MK7 6AA

First published 2008

Edited and designed by The Open University.

Typeset by SR Nova Pvt Ltd, Bangalore, India

Printed and bound in the United Kingdom at the University Press, Cambridge.

ISBN 978 0 7492 2669 5

1.1

Contents

Chapter 1   Introduction   1
1.1   Chemistry in our lives   1
1.2   How to study Book 4   5

Chapter 2   Where do materials come from?   7
2.1   Building blocks of the Earth   7
2.2   Summary of Chapter 2   11

Chapter 3   Atoms, molecules and ions   13
3.1   What are atoms?   13
3.2   The structure of the atom   15
3.3   Molecules   17
3.4   Ions and crystals   19
3.5   Summary of Chapter 3   22

Chapter 4   Groupings of atoms, molecules and ions   23
4.1   Introduction   23
4.2   Intermolecular forces   23
4.3   Solids   27
4.4   Melting   31
4.5   Liquids   32
4.6   Solutions   34
4.7   Vaporisation   36
4.8   Gases   37
4.9   Summary of Chapter 4   41

Chapter 5   Organising the elements   43
5.1   More on atoms   43
5.2   Electronic configuration   44
5.3   Atomic structure and the Periodic Table   47
5.4   Using the Periodic Table   52
5.5   More on covalent bonding   54
5.6   Summary of Chapter 5   56

Chapter 6   Chemical formulas and equations   57

6.1   Chemical formulas   57

6.2   Chemical equations   59

6.3   Using chemical equations to calculate quantities   62

6.4   Working with solutions: concentration   65

6.5   Summary of Chapter 6   67

Chapter 7   Metals   69

7.1   What is a metal?   69

7.2   Gold and silver   71

7.3   An atomic model for metals   73

7.4   Copper   74

7.5   Tin and bronze   75

7.6   The Iron Age and iron   78

7.7   Summary of Chapter 7   80

Chapter 8   Reactivity of metals   81

8.1   Metal ions in solution   81

8.2   Reactions of metals with acids   83

8.3   Oxidation and reduction   85

8.4   Metal ions and the Periodic Table   88

8.5   Corrosion of metals   90

8.6   Modifying metals   92

8.7   Summary of Chapter 8   94

Chapter 9   Chemical reactions and energy changes   95

9.1   Energy changes and internal energy   99

9.2   Chemical reactions that release or absorb heat   100

9.3   Introducing enthalpy   102

9.4   Thermochemical equations   104

9.5   Enthalpy changes: delving deeper   110

9.6   Summary of Chapter 9   113

Chapter 10   Rates of chemical reactions and chemical equilibrium   115

10.1   Chemical kinetics: how fast do chemical reactions go?   115

10.2   Varying the rate of a chemical reaction   118

10.3   Why reactions happen: molecular collisions and energy   119

10.4   Changing the energy barrier of a reaction   123

10.5   Chemical equilibrium: how far will a chemical reaction go?   123

10.6 Reversible reactions and dynamic equilibrium   124

10.7 Equilibrium: a quantitative approach   127

10.8 Equilibrium and response to change: Le Chatelier's principle   133

10.9 Summary of Chapter 10   141

Chapter 11 Acids, bases and equilibrium   143

11.1 Hydrogen ion concentration   144

11.2 The equilibrium constant for acid dissociation   153

11.3 The equilibrium dissociation of water   156

11.4 Measuring acidity: the pH scale; a quantitative method   160

11.5 Summary of Chapter 11   165

Chapter 12 Introducing carbon compounds: crude oil   167

12.1 Processing crude oil: fractional distillation   167

12.2 Hydrocarbons   170

12.3 Crude oil as a source of fuel   180

12.4 Summary of Section 12   183

Chapter 13 Further uses for crude oil   185

13.1 Important chemical feedstocks   187

13.2 Reactions of alkenes   189

13.3 Polymers   190

13.4 Summary of Chapter 13   193

Chapter 14 Functional groups and their reactions   195

14.1 The functional group approach   201

14.2 Characteristic reactions of functional groups   201

14.3 Crude oil: final thoughts   208

14.4 Summary of Chapter 14   210

Chapter 15 Applying the functional group approach: food chemistry   213

15.1 Fats and oils   213

15.2 Proteins   223

15.3 Carbohydrates   232

15.4 Summary of Chapter 15   238

Chapter 16 Organic molecules in action: pharmaceuticals   239

16.1 The discovery of aspirin   239

16.2 How drugs work   241

16.3 Summary of Chapter 16   250

Chapter 17 Summary of Book 4   251

17.1 Sustainable organic chemistry?   251

17.2 Looking back at Book 4   252

17.3 Looking ahead to Book 5   254

Answers to questions   255

Comments on activities   276

References   296

Acknowledgements   297

Index   298

Chapter 1
Introduction

The overall focus of this book is the link between the structure of matter on the small scale (submicroscopic) and its large-scale (macroscopic) properties. You will explore how changes at the submicroscopic level, involving atoms, ions and molecules, result in changes at the macroscopic level – the observable properties of matter.

You will look in some detail at the way matter undergoes change, the importance of the rate at which change occurs and how ideas about energy can inform our understanding of such changes. This is what chemistry is about. As this course progresses, you will find yourself building a bigger and more complete picture of the scope and influence of science. Many ideas from the earlier books underpin the later parts of the course; this book is no exception. Materials from the Earth which you met in Book 2 are examined with a focus on their underlying structure, and aspects of energy which you studied in Book 3 play a key role here, when the role of energy in chemical change is addressed.

1.1   Chemistry in our lives

It is surprising how quickly we accept changes to our lives, not just the landmark changes but those changes that creep up on us and yet have a major impact on the way we live. It was only in the 1960s that package holidays really began to take off, and today a holiday that involves flying is the norm for many people in the western world. This is due in part to increasing prosperity, but over the past 50 years the real cost of air travel has dropped tenfold.

More efficient work practices, economies of scale and changes in the price of oil have reduced the cost of flying, but there have been major improvements in the design of the aeroplanes themselves. New lightweight metal alloys, the replacement of metals with plastics, better tyres and engine parts made from new materials are all aspects of the aeroplanes that have helped bring down costs (Figure 1.1). These are all areas where chemistry plays a major role.

The microwave oven has changed cooking habits, and in line with this there has been a notable increase in the range and quality of ready-prepared meals available from food stores. It is not just the application of science and technology to food preparation that has moved forward but the packaging for these meals owes much to the skills of the chemist. The idea of a disposable food container made of plastic that could be used both in a microwave oven and in a conventional oven at a temperature of 200 °C would have seemed fanciful just a few decades ago. The transparent film which covers the container has to act as a sterile seal while the pack is on the store's shelf but it must peel off easily even after it has been heated in the oven (Figure 1.2).

In 1969, the world watched in awe as Neil Armstrong and 'Buzz' Aldrin became the first humans to set foot on the Moon. The on-board computers that helped guide the NASA *Apollo 11* mission on its 800 000 km return journey

Figure 1.1   Today, flying is within the realm of many people.

Figure 1.2   A ready-prepared meal with packaging that can be used in a microwave oven or heated to 200 °C in a conventional oven.

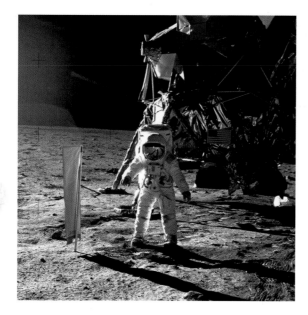

Figure 1.3 'Buzz' Aldrin on the Moon during the 1969 *Apollo 11* mission.

Figure 1.4 Breathable yet waterproof outdoor clothing. The secret is in a synthetic layer which allows passage to the exterior of water vapour but excludes liquid water.

(Figure 1.3) were *far* less powerful than the personal computers (or even most calculators!) that are used in almost every office and home today. The heart of the modern computer is the microchip based on the element silicon, although other materials such as gallium arsenide provide the means for even faster-operating machines. At the time of writing (2007), a good desktop PC will outperform many 'supercomputers' from the early 1990s.

Synthetic fabrics have revolutionised the clothing industry, from the appearance of nylon around 1940 through to the specialist fabrics of today. A commonly used and effective fabric for waterproof clothing is woven nylon coated with a thin layer of another synthetic material, polyurethane. This is completely waterproof and certainly protects the wearer from the rain. However, the body produces a large amount of moisture during periods of exertion. The waterproof nature of this fabric means that this moisture cannot escape and the wearer gets wet with condensed perspiration. What was required was a fabric penetrated with microscopic holes, so small that liquid water could not pass through while allowing water vapour to pass from the inside of the garment to the outside. Research produced a synthetic material that satisfied these criteria, and this is marketed under the name Gore-Tex®. This material has transformed foul weather clothing for hikers and climbers (Figure 1.4), and today there is a range of breathable fabrics based on different polymer materials.

■ Take a moment to look at Figure 1.5, a fuel filling station; then make a list of everything that appears in the picture in which you think chemistry may have played a part.

☐ The building itself is made of brick, with tiles for the roof, steel for window and door frames and, of course, glass in the windows. The production of all these materials involves processes that bring about chemical changes. Even the paint used for the various signs on the building has been formulated by chemists. The pumps themselves are made from metal, the displays involve polymers and the fuel hoses are synthetic rubbers. What about the vehicles? The steel and many other metals and alloys from which they were constructed, the paint and wax used for rust protection, plastics, glass, tyres and lubricants all owe much to the chemist. Of course, what you cannot see in the picture is the reason for the existence of the filling station itself – the fuel. Both petrol and diesel fuels are stored in underground tanks and

Figure 1.5 A fuel filling station.

pumped through a metering system into vehicles. These fuels are obtained from crude oil, which you will learn more about in Chapter 12.

Now let us go back over a much longer timespan and see what combination of need, knowledge and inspiration has led to changes in the way people have lived throughout history. Take a look at Figures 1.6–1.9, which represent aspects of life in Europe over a span of about 3500 years.

Figure 1.6 An artist's impression of Bronze Age metalworking.

Figure 1.7 16th century village life depicted by the Flemish painter Pieter Bruegel the Elder, in his 1559 painting *Netherlandish Proverbs*.

Figure 1.8 London street scene in 1894.

The scenes in the pictures are very different; you would expect to see some dramatic changes over this period. Spend some time looking in detail and try to focus on the changes that have occurred over this period. Analyse each picture

Figure 1.9   Chemistry in the early 21st century.

under the following headings: materials for building, tools used, transport, clothing, colour and food. (You will not be able to extract information under all the headings from each picture.)

The picture of the Bronze Age village in Figure 1.6 is based on archaeological evidence from around 3400 years ago. Information that can be gleaned from the picture is limited but it is clear that the materials used in the construction of the dwellings are not highly processed. Roofs are thatched with grasses and reeds on a crude wooden frame. Wood, stone and earth are used for building walls. Clothing is roughly woven plant material or animal skin and food probably comes from small cultivated plots around the village. There is evidence of small-scale processing of materials from the bronze tools and fired-clay cooking pots. Needless to say, colour and transport do not feature strongly, with the inhabitants striving to maintain what seems to be a somewhat drab lifestyle in their settlement.

A gap of about 3000 years separates the Bronze Age village from the picture of a Flemish village in Figure 1.7, painted in 1559. This picture gives a good indication of village life in northern Europe in the 16th century but it must be regarded as something of a caricature. It might seem incredible but over 50 proverbs, sayings and customs of the time have been identified in the picture. Our immediate interest is not with these maxims but with the evidence that the picture presents of the way materials were used in the 16th century. Look first at the building materials: wood, stone, brick, tile, glass and lead in the windows.

Many of the tools are metal. The shovel and shears are probably iron or steel and it appears that there are metal hinges on window shutters. Transport is depicted by a sailing boat constructed of wood with a sail made of woven cloth, probably a canvas of flax from the fibre of the linseed plant. There is also a wooden cart wheel with a metal rim. Villagers are dressed in a range of woven clothing, some of which may be wool from domesticated sheep. Bleach must have been used to achieve the whiteness of shirts and headgear, and dyes have given a range of colours to other clothing. The colours are soft and muted, which suggests that the dyes may have been extracted from plant materials. However, this is a picture that was painted over 400 years ago when the availability of painting pigments was limited. It may be, too, that the colours of these paints have faded with time. Food is represented by the crops, possibly wheat, shown growing in a field and from the sheep, pigs and the calf. The scene is of a relatively self-sufficient village but with longer distance travel and communication afforded by the sailing ship.

Another 300 years or so and we are in the latter part of the Industrial Revolution (Figure 1.8). Buildings are of brick, stone and tiles, not so different from today. The range of clothing available to people has moved on since the 16th century and there is evidence of the use of metals in the lamp post and the carriage. At this time, many people worked in factories and mills where there were machines such as the looms and carding machines of the cotton industry. The age of steam had arrived with railways and steam-powered machinery in factories. During the Industrial Revolution, there was a movement of population from the countryside into towns and cities.

And then we move on to today (Figure 1.9) where there are manufactured materials in which chemistry has played a major role wherever we care to look: in communication, health, transport and clothing. The two centuries since the onset of the Industrial Revolution have seen a huge number of changes, far more than were achieved over the previous 3500 years. The real difference is that now we can develop materials with almost whatever properties we require.

1.2   How to study Book 4

This book contains a great deal of material to engage with, and many new concepts to learn. This is reflected in the course Study Calendar, which suggests that you allow rather longer to study this book than indicated for the earlier ones. The amount of material may well seem daunting at this stage, but if you follow the strategies you developed to organise your study of Books 1–3, you should find it possible to study all the material in the time available.

We strongly suggest that you spend a little time planning your study, and that you use the timetable template available on the course website to generate your own personal study timetable. The chapters in the book are of uneven length, and you may find, as in the earlier books, that the length of a chapter doesn't necessarily give a good indication of how long it will take to study. The online study calendar gives a broad guide to help you plan your study time.

You should note that Chapters 3, 4, 8, 9, 10, 12, 14, 15 and 17 all include activities that require you to work at your computer. Chapter 11 includes a practical activity using household liquids – we suspect that in most instances you will need to be at home to do this activity and you will need to ensure that you have the necessary materials available. There are also two minor practical activities in Chapters 3 and 4. Please do make time to do all these activities, as the assessment material will be designed assuming that you have undertaken all of them. Finally, in constructing your plan don't forget to allow time to answer the assessment questions associated with this book.

In studying this book, you will come across many new concepts, but you will also be developing new skills. Many of these skills will develop and reinforce those you used in the earlier books, but some will be new. You will find that there are a number of places where you can develop further the mathematical skills you first practised in Book 3. (While some mathematical skills are essential to the study of chemistry, you may be relieved, or perhaps disappointed, that there is rather less mathematics in this book.) Additionally, your problem-solving skills will be tested and developed in a number of places. Indeed, when you have finished studying this book, it may be useful to reflect on the problem-solving strategies you have used.

Finally, it is likely that this book will contain words and symbols that are new to you. We would encourage you to maintain the glossary of symbols you started in Book 3, adding new symbols as you come across them.

Chapter 2
Where do materials come from?

Figures 1.6–1.9 reflect two characteristics of humans: the use of tools and the need for shelter. During the Bronze Age, stone for building was simply taken from the Earth; in other parts of the world, building bricks were produced from clay. Similarly, the only metals available in the Bronze Age were gold, silver and bronze (actually a mixture of two metals, copper and tin). In the 16th century, the major metal used was iron (or steel) but as we get closer to today that range of metals has increased greatly. Most of the materials that are in use today, and that have been used over history, have been processed. The way that resources are distributed on Earth can help us understand how materials have influenced history and how humans can use resources to design materials for a better future.

2.1   Building blocks of the Earth

In Book 7, you will look in some detail at how the Universe began and developed. The widely accepted view is that the Universe arose from the Big Bang about 14 billion years ago. The first two of these building blocks (which are known as **elements**) to be formed in the aftermath of the explosion were hydrogen and helium. These gases eventually condensed under gravitational forces to form galaxies and the stars within them. The extraordinarily high temperatures inside stars (and the even higher temperatures when super-massive stars collapse to form supernovae) resulted in the formation of many of the elements that we know today. These are the building blocks of all the materials around us. Even so, much of the matter in the Universe is in interstellar gas clouds of hydrogen and helium, and this is reflected in the distribution of the elements shown in Figure 2.1. The Earth was formed from material that condensed around the Sun and contains a range of elements.

As you saw in Book 2, Section 10.3, the Earth has a diameter of about 12 700 km but the crust is relatively thin, being between 20 and 80 km deep on land. (The thicker parts tend to be under the major mountain ranges.) Under the oceans, the crust is about 7 km thick. Even with modern technology, we can only extract materials from the upper part of the crust. Figure 2.2 indicates just how much of the Earth is inaccessible to direct exploration. The deepest extraction is for oil; commercial wells have been drilled to depths of up to 7 km.

Figure 2.1 Distribution of elements by mass in (a) the Universe, (b) the Earth overall and (c) the Earth's crust. (Note that these figures can vary according to the source of the data and methods of measurement.)

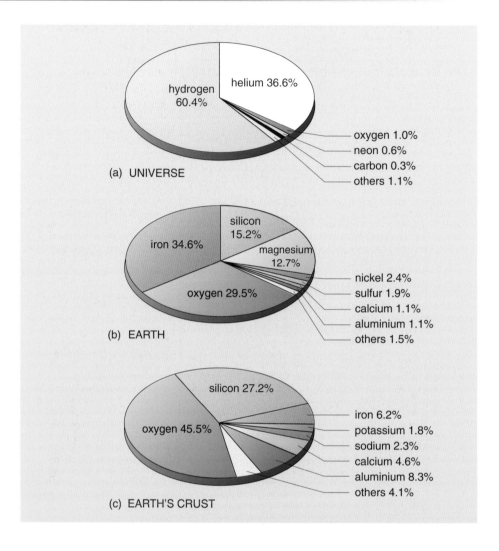

Figure 2.2 The structure of the Earth. The Earth's crust is a thin skin on the surface of the planet, while the bulk of the Earth comprises a rocky mantle enclosing a central core. The inner core is solid but the outer core is liquid.

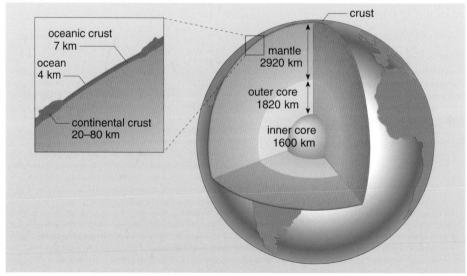

■ Look again at Figure 2.1. What is the first thing that you notice about the distribution of elements in the Universe and in the Earth overall?

☐ An obvious point is that the distributions are different. For example, the element hydrogen comprises 60.4% of the mass of the Universe, yet in the Earth overall it is iron that is the most common element at 34.6%.

These elements are not evenly distributed in the Earth itself, as you can see from Figure 2.1. Compare the relative proportions of the elements in the whole Earth (Figure 2.1b) and in just the outer layer, the Earth's crust (Figure 2.1c).

■ What element shows the greatest difference in proportion in the whole Earth and the Earth's crust distributions?

☐ Iron. In the whole Earth, almost 35% of the mass is iron, yet in the crust the proportion is about 6%.

In its very early history, when the Earth was much hotter and probably molten, the more dense elements such as iron tended to sink towards the centre of the Earth under the influence of gravity. Today, the Earth has a core comprised largely of iron (with some nickel), while the solid crust is relatively depleted in iron but rich in silicon and oxygen. Consequently, near the surface of the Earth, most of the iron and other metals are found in silicates (compounds of the elements silicon and oxygen). Gold is unusual among the metals in that it is one of only a few that exists in the Earth's crust as the pure element. It is very resistant to chemical attack by air and water. Gold is a relatively rare element with an average abundance in the Earth's crust of only 4.0×10^{-7} % by mass. (This means that the average abundance is 4.0×10^{-7} kg of gold in 100 kg of the Earth's crust.)

■ Express the abundance of gold in terms of parts per million (ppm) and parts per billion (ppb) by mass. (Refer to Book 1, Section 5.2, for an explanation of ppm and ppb.)

☐ In 1.0 kg of the Earth's crust, there is 4.0×10^{-9} kg of gold. So in 10^6 kg of the crust, there is 4.0×10^{-3} kg of gold which represents 4.0×10^{-3} parts per million (4.0×10^{-3} ppm). In 10^9 kg of the crust, there is 4.0×10^0 kg of gold, which represents 4.0 parts per billion (4.0 ppb).

Some idea of what the calculation in the answer to this question implies can be seen from Figure 2.3.

Figure 2.3   If gold were evenly distributed through the Earth's crust, the amount of rock that would be needed to extract 20 g of the element would fill 250 twenty-tonne trucks.

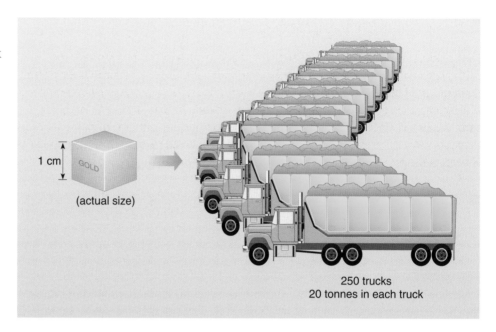

Question 2.1

If all the elements in the Earth's crust were evenly distributed, what mass of rock (in kg) would be needed to extract 20 g of gold? (This mass is approximately represented by a cube of gold of side of about 1 cm.)

Gold is not, however, distributed evenly throughout the crust of the Earth and neither are the other elements. The 19th century gold rushes of California (1849) and the Klondike in western Canada (1897) would certainly never have happened had there been an even distribution of the elements. In both areas, the rush for gold started with the chance finding of gold nuggets weighing several grams (Figure 2.4).

■ Look again at Figure 2.1c. What are the two most common elements (by mass) in the Earth's crust?

☐ Oxygen and silicon are the most common elements. Oxygen is 45.5% and silicon is 27.2% abundant by mass.

The element silicon is a lustrous, grey solid, whereas elemental oxygen is a colourless gas.

It is important to know that masses and not volume are being compared here. The mass of a cube of silicon of side 1.0 cm is about 2.3 g, but the same volume of the gaseous element oxygen would have a mass of just over 0.0013 g under normal temperatures and pressures.

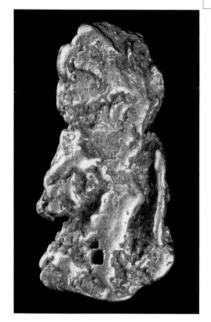

Figure 2.4   A gold nugget.

Question 2.2

Use the data in Figure 2.1 to express the average abundance of carbon in the Universe in parts per million.

2.2   Summary of Chapter 2

The elements are not evenly distributed through the Universe, nor through the Earth. The core, mantle and crust of the Earth all have different distributions of the elements and values quoted are average distributions. The relative concentration of elements such as gold makes it possible to extract these materials from the Earth's crust. Element concentrations should be expressed in terms of mass, as elements have different densities. Typically, element concentrations are expressed as percentage by mass, parts per million or parts per billion.

Chapter 3
Atoms, molecules and ions

Is it possible to get to the ultimate structure of matter by continuously dividing a sample of a material into ever smaller pieces? Try to imagine what would happen if you were able to take, say, a lump of gold and keep dividing it into two pieces. At each stage, you examine the newly divided sample and ask if it is the same substance as the one with which you started. Is a point reached where you can no longer subdivide without losing the character that makes gold what it is, or can it be subdivided for ever? In other words, is there a particle that is the smallest possible thing that can still be called gold, or is there not? The first few divisions will be straightforward. There will just be less of the gold to see each time. As the dividing continues, there will come a time when the piece of gold becomes too small to see. Now what?

There are (at least) two possibilities. One is that there is no limit to the extent to which the dividing of the gold can continue without changing the nature of the gold. This is the hypothesis that matter is continuous. The other option is that eventually a point is reached where no more subdivision can occur without destroying the essential character (whatever that is) of gold. (The assumption is made that there is a 'magic' knife available that will enable divisions of ever smaller pieces of gold to be made.) The logical conclusion in this case is that there is something, some entity, which is the smallest possible component that retains the characteristics of gold. If that entity is further divided, then you no longer have 'gold' but something else. This is the hypothesis that ultimately the elements are composed of **atoms**.

3.1 What are atoms?

A starting point to work through this idea is a cube of gold with each side measuring one centimetre. This cube of gold has a precise mass of 19.3 g. (The same volume of water has a mass of just 1.00 g.) Now cut the gold in half. At this point, there is no question that each half cube is still 'gold'. Take one half and cut that in half and continue this process. After about 18 divisions, the piece of gold is hardly visible to the unaided eye. After 64 divisions or so, the gold would take on a distinctly grainy look; about two thousand or so particles of some kind make up the block. If these particles could be 'seen', they would appear to be perfectly spherical; furthermore, they would not be jumbled together but arranged in a regular way. After about 11 more cuts (that is about 75 or 76 in total) there would be one single gold sphere (Figure 3.1), an atom, the fundamental building block of chemistry.

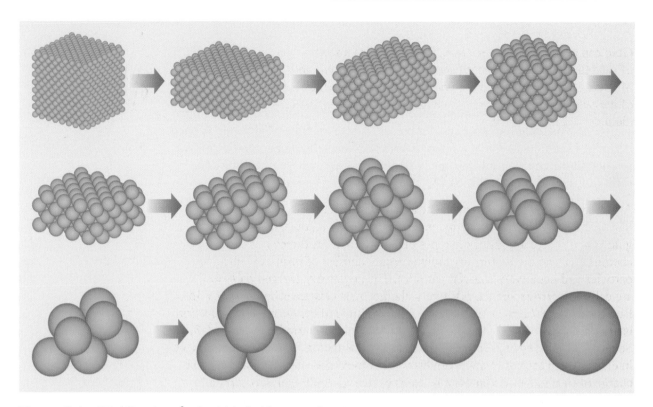

Figure 3.1 Dividing 1 cm³ of gold in half repeatedly: the last divisions needed to reach a single atom.

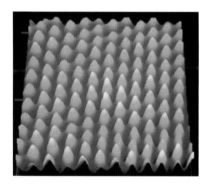

Figure 3.2 An image of a layer of gold atoms on the surface of a crystal obtained by scanning tunnelling microscopy.

That gold atom is unique to gold and identical to all other atoms of gold. (This comment needs some qualification which will be addressed in the next section.) Compared with atoms of most other elements, it has a large mass. But on an everyday scale of things it is very tiny indeed, and one can never see an atom with the unaided eye or even with the best optical microscope. In recent years, the development of a technique known as scanning tunnelling microscopy has enabled images to be obtained that are the closest we can get to a picture of an atom. Figure 3.2 shows such a picture of a layer of gold atoms. It really isn't surprising that some people believed that matter was continuous, because on the normal scale of things it looks as if it is.

Around 75 divisions have moved us right away from any scale that belongs to our direct experience. (To get an idea of how fast things change when you double or half progressively, work out how much money you would have if you had been given £1 at birth which was then invested in a scheme that guaranteed to double your money every year. You would have been a millionaire by the time you reached your 21st birthday!) One of the problems facing the early practitioners of chemistry is that changes happen on such a small scale. To understand chemical changes in terms of 'this thing reacts with that thing', this tiny scale has to be addressed.

The mass of a gold atom is 3.3×10^{-25} kg and its diameter is about 2.9×10^{-10} m. Elements and their atoms are represented by **chemical symbols**: the symbol for hydrogen is H, oxygen is O and gold is Au (from *aurum*, the Latin word for gold).

Question 3.1

Gold can be beaten into very thin, flexible sheets known as gold leaf. Just 1 g of gold (a cube of side a little less than 4 mm) can yield gold leaf with an area of about 1.0 m². What would be the approximate thickness of the sheet in terms of the number of gold atoms? (The mass of a gold atom is 3.3×10^{-25} kg and its diameter is 2.9×10^{-10} m.)

3.2 The structure of the atom

Atoms are actually divisible but once an atom of gold, for example, is divided into smaller particles, the identity and distinctiveness that makes that atom gold is lost. There are just three types of particle that are directly of concern to chemistry. There are within any atom an equal number of positively charged particles and negatively charged particles. The negatively charged particles are called **electrons** and the positively charged particles are called **protons**. In Book 3, Section 7.2, you learned that the magnitude of the charge on an electron is -1.602×10^{-19} C. (C is the abbreviation for coulomb, introduced in Book 3, Section 7.1.) The charge on the proton is $+1.602 \times 10^{-19}$ C. It is often convenient in chemistry to look at relative values, which would give the electron a relative charge of -1 and the proton $+1$. All atoms except for hydrogen also carry a certain amount of 'ballast' in the form of a third type of particle known as a **neutron**, which has zero electrical charge but has a mass almost exactly equal to that of the proton. The mass of the electron is very much less than that of the proton or neutron (Table 3.1). Again, it is helpful to use relative values. Relative mass data are valuable for making comparisons between atoms but do not represent the actual mass of the atom.

Table 3.1 Properties of protons, neutrons and electrons.

Name	Actual mass/kg	Relative mass	Actual charge/C	Relative charge
proton	1.7×10^{-27}	1	$+1.602 \times 10^{-19}$	$+1$
neutron	1.7×10^{-27}	1	0	0
electron	9.3×10^{-31}	5.4×10^{-4}	-1.602×10^{-19}	-1

One element is distinguished from another only by the number of protons that the atom of the element contains. An atom has no overall electrical charge, so the number of protons and electrons in an atom is the same; thereby ensuring that the total positive charge from the protons is exactly balanced by the total negative charge from the electrons. The number of protons in an atom is called the **atomic number** and given the symbol Z. There are about 116 elements known to date, of which 92 are found in nature. Those not found in nature have been made by nuclear physicists from high-energy collisions of subatomic particles but several exist in only submicrogram quantities. There is a continuing quest to make new elements.

All matter is built from this relatively small set of building 'bricks'. Just as from a child's set of building blocks, many structures can be created from relatively few different types of blocks, so the huge variety of material on Earth is built from this relatively small set of elements.

In Section 3.1, it was suggested that the idea that all atoms of a particular element were identical warrants some qualification. This now needs to be examined further.

■ What is it that distinguishes an atom of one element from an atom of another element?

☐ The number of protons in an atom of the element.

It is possible for different atoms of one element to contain different numbers of neutrons. Atoms that differ only in the numbers of neutrons they contain are called **isotopes** of the element in question. For example, most hydrogen atoms contain just one proton and one electron; they have no neutrons. However, there are hydrogen atoms that contain one proton, one neutron and one electron. These are still hydrogen atoms because elements are defined by the number of protons, not the number of neutrons. Note that the number of electrons in the hydrogen atom is one, the single negative charge balancing the positive charge on the proton. The addition of a neutron does not affect the charge balance of the atom.

You may have come across isotopes in a number of contexts. They are used in medical studies as tracers to investigate the biological processes going on in the body; they are used in the testing of new drugs before they are made available to the general public; and they are used for archaeological dating, the most familiar being an isotope of carbon (carbon-14) used for radiocarbon dating. You will learn more about isotopes later, in Books 6 and 7. However, chemistry is dominated by protons and electrons and, in general, this book will not be concerned with isotopes of elements.

■ An atom of gold comprises 79 protons, 118 neutrons and 79 electrons. What is the relative mass of an atom of gold? (The tiny mass of the electrons is usually ignored in these calculations.)

☐ From Table 3.1, both the proton and the neutron have a relative mass of 1. The gold atom then has a relative mass of $79 + 118 = 197$.

For the gold atom, this relative mass of 197 is known as the **relative atomic mass** (sometimes abbreviated to **RAM**) and is represented by the symbol A_r. The relative atomic mass of an element can be calculated simply by the adding the number of protons to the number of neutrons in the atom.

The relative atomic mass of many elements is not a whole number. A case in point is the element chlorine, which has a relative atomic mass of 35.5. How can this happen in the light of our simple model of the atom, and the relative masses of protons and neutrons? Naturally occurring elements, more often than not, comprise atoms of a number of isotopes in varying proportions. Sometimes, as in the case of hydrogen or helium, the element is almost completely a single isotope; in others, as in the case of chlorine, there is more than one isotope present in a significant proportion. Naturally occurring chlorine consists of two isotopes. Chlorine-35 has 17 protons and 18 neutrons and represents 75% of naturally occurring chlorine. The remaining 25% of chlorine is chlorine-37 with again 17 protons but with 20 neutrons. The average relative mass of chlorine atoms is therefore $(0.75 \times 35) + (0.25 \times 37) = 35.5$.

Finally in this look at the structure of the atom, the question arises as to how the protons, neutrons and electrons are arranged in the atom. The atom is constructed of a very dense core of protons and neutrons, the **atomic nucleus**. In the nucleus there are protons packed very closely together. They are positively charged and so they would be expected to repel one another. However, when they are as close together as they are in a nucleus, a very short-range force, a sort of atomic 'superglue', holds the nucleus together. (This is examined further in Book 7.) Compared with the overall size of the atom, the nucleus is very tiny. A gold atom has a diameter of about 3×10^{-10} m. However, the nucleus is very much smaller, being about $\frac{1}{10\,000}$ of the diameter of an atom, or around 1×10^{-14} m. A simple model of the atom is one in which the electrons surround the nucleus, like a cloud of tiny charged particles moving around the nucleus (Figure 3.3).

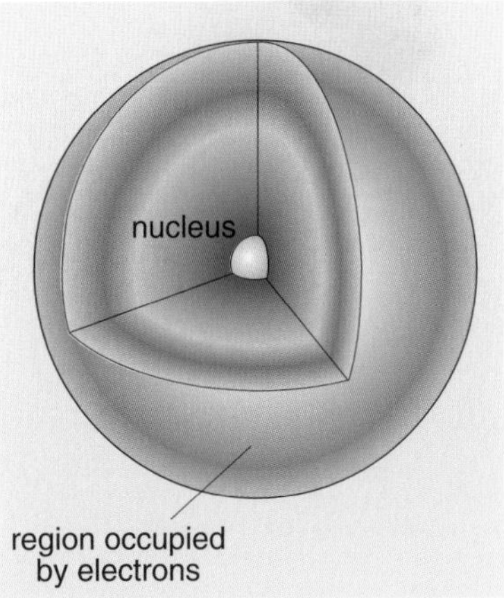

One implication of this model of the atom is that when atoms interact, the immediate contact is between the electrons of one atom with those of the other atom. This model is key to being able to build up a picture of materials that are, in some cases, made from atoms of a single element, and, in many others, from combinations of atoms of different elements.

Figure 3.3   A representation of the atom.

3.3   Molecules

If you were able to divide a drop of water 70 or so times in the same way that you did for the cube of gold, what would you finish with? Instead of the identical atoms of gold, at this scale there would be atoms of two elements, hydrogen and oxygen, joined together so that in each unit there are two hydrogen atoms and one oxygen atom. Further division would result in separate atoms of hydrogen and oxygen but you would no longer have water. This grouping of two hydrogen atoms and one oxygen atom is called a water **molecule**. 'Molecule' is a general term for a group of atoms that are joined together in fixed proportions with a particular geometric arrangement around each atom.

It is important to note that the atoms in a molecule are joined together. They are held together by **chemical bonds** which arise from the interaction of the electrons of one atom with those of another. The atom has a positively charged, small nucleus surrounded by electrons. Negative and positive charges attract each other, so the electrons stay around the nucleus. When two atoms are brought close together, the nuclei repel each other because they both are positively charged. This repulsion is reduced by the negatively charged electrons coming between the nuclei. The details of the interactions of the nuclei and electrons are complex but the overall effect is for there to be an attractive force between an oxygen atom and the two hydrogen atoms of the water molecule. This type of linking of atoms where electrons are shared between two nuclei is known as a **covalent bond** and is represented by a solid line. The covalent bond linking the two hydrogen atoms in a molecule of hydrogen, H_2, is represented as H—H. The distance between the centres of the two nuclei which are bonded together is called the **bond length** (Figure 3.4). In a water molecule, the distance between the centre of the oxygen

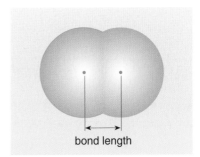

bond length

Figure 3.4   A covalently bonded molecule made up of two identical atoms showing the bond length.

atom and the centre of each hydrogen atom is about 1×10^{-10} m. This very small distance between the hydrogen and oxygen atoms is the same in every water molecule.

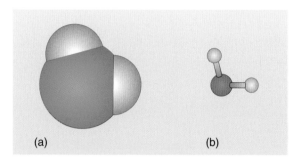

(a)   (b)

Figure 3.5 (a) Space-filling model of a water molecule. (b) Ball-and-stick model of a water molecule.

In Figure 3.5, the water molecule is represented in two different ways. The first (Figure 3.5a) is a space-filling view. It shows the space occupied by the clouds of electrons surrounding the atoms in the molecule. Note that the central oxygen atom is larger than the hydrogen atoms. This is reasonable as hydrogen has just one electron whereas oxygen has eight, and hence the space occupied by the electrons (and hence the size of the atom) is that much larger. The second view (Figure 3.5b) is called a ball-and-stick model. It is perhaps less 'realistic' but it has the major advantage that the relative positions of the centres of the atoms in the water molecule can be seen more easily. It also represents the geometry of the molecule. The angle between the three atoms in the water molecule is about 104°. This is called the **bond angle**.

The 'bent' nature of the water molecule is an essential part of the molecular structure of water, and helps to determine the structure and properties of liquid water and ice. The fixed geometric relationships in molecules are what ultimately give everything its form and structure.

The **chemical formula** of water is H_2O. In writing a chemical formula, the number of each type of atom in the molecule is indicated by a subscript after the symbol for the element. So for water, the formula H_2O means that there are two hydrogen atoms and one oxygen atom in each molecule. (The subscript '1' is assumed if no other number is written.) A **compound**, such as water, is a substance made up of a large number of molecules of the same kind, and the molecules of which are made up of atoms from more than one element. Just as the idea of relative atomic mass can be used for atoms, molecules likewise have a relative mass. The **relative molecular mass** (abbreviated to **RMM** and given the symbol M_r) for water is 18. Each of the two hydrogen atoms in the water molecule has a RAM of 1 and the RAM for oxygen is 16, giving $(1 + 1 + 16) = 18$, the RMM for water.

■ What is the relative molecular mass of the carbon dioxide molecule CO_2 (the relative atomic mass of carbon, C, is 12).

☐ Since the relative molecular mass is simply the sum of the relative atomic masses of all the atoms in a molecule, for carbon dioxide CO_2, the RMM is given by $(12 + 16 + 16) = 44$.

Oxygen in the air is not present as separate oxygen atoms, but as molecules of oxygen, in which two oxygen atoms are joined together, written as O_2. Oxygen is an element, so this illustrates that elements can exist as molecules. Many elements do exist in molecular rather than atomic forms. Hydrogen is also an element and exists as molecules in which two hydrogen atoms are joined by a covalent bond, written as H_2. In contrast, the noble gas helium, He, comprises single atoms. We will discuss covalent bonding in more detail in Section 5.5.

Question 3.2

The molecule ammonia contains one nitrogen atom and three hydrogen atoms. How would you write its chemical formula?

3.4   Ions and crystals

Covalent bonds are not the only way in which chemical compounds can be held together. One of the most startling demonstrations of the power and effects of chemical change is the reaction between the metallic, shiny element sodium, Na, and the toxic, pale green, gaseous element chlorine, Cl_2. They react together violently to form the white, water-soluble solid called sodium chloride, NaCl, which is best known as common salt. Salt is an essential part of the human diet, yet the elements sodium and chlorine of which it is composed could cause death or serious injury if ingested.

A sodium atom in sodium metal has 11 protons (and 12 neutrons) in its nucleus which is surrounded by 11 electrons.

■   If the sodium atom loses an electron, how many protons and electrons are left, and what is the overall electrical charge?

☐   In losing one electron, the sodium atom reduces its number of electrons from 11 to 10, but the number of protons in the nucleus stays unchanged. The overall charge on what is left is therefore $(+11 - 10) = +1$ as there is one more proton than there are electrons.

The entity that remains after electrons are lost from or gained by atoms is called an **ion** (pronounced 'eye-on'). An ion is an atom or a group of atoms bonded together that carries an electrical charge. Positively charged ions are called **cations** (pronounced 'cat-eye-on') and ions with a negative charge are known as **anions** (pronounced 'an-eye-on'). The sodium cation is written Na^+, where the superscript plus sign indicates one positive charge on the ion. A negative sign is used for anions. A common anion is the sulfate anion, SO_4^{2-}, a group of five atoms (one sulfur and four oxygen) covalently bonded together with an overall charge of −2.

■   How would you write the anion derived from chlorine, in which each chlorine atom gains one electron? (Note that the anion derived from the chlorine atom is called chloride.)

☐   By analogy with the sodium cation, the way to write the chloride anion is Cl^-.

When sodium metal reacts with chlorine gas, the electron that is lost from a sodium atom is added to a chlorine atom to give the chloride anion. The opposite electrical charges on the cations and anions are responsible for holding these ions together to give sodium chloride.

As you will see in Activity 3.1, solid sodium chloride occurs as regularly shaped grains known as **crystals**. In the case of sodium chloride, the crystals are cubic,

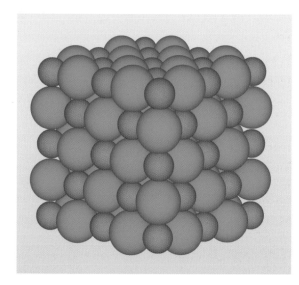

Figure 3.6   A model of a small part of a sodium chloride crystal. The ions are shown in their space-filling representation. The sodium cations are grey (smaller spheres) and the chloride anions are green (larger spheres).

Figure 3.7   Crystals of calcite (left), quartz (centre), pyrite (centre front) and amethyst (right).

reflecting the internal structure in which the ions themselves are arranged in a cubic array. Sodium chloride crystals are made up of a regular array of positively charged sodium cations and negatively charged chloride anions (Figure 3.6). The crystal is held together by the attraction between the oppositely charged ions; because of the arrangement of the ions, this attraction is greater than the repulsion between ions with like charge. This is known as **ionic bonding** and is a different kind of bonding from the covalent bonding discussed earlier. Even in the smallest crystal there are billions of ions present. But whatever the size of the crystal, it has no overall charge because the number of negative charges is always exactly balanced by the number of positive charges.

Note that there are no individual molecules in this structure. Each sodium cation is surrounded by six chloride anions, each of which is exactly the same distance away from the sodium cation as the other five. The same is also true for the chloride anions, which are surrounded by six sodium cations. This is a very efficient way to pack the oppositely charged ions. It is much more efficient than having the ions randomly distributed. When you pack a suitcase, you can get much more in it by packing it carefully than by just throwing everything into it at random.

Crystals of other compounds come in a huge variety of shapes and sizes (Figure 3.7), but each compound usually has only one crystal form. It is possible to make a salt crystal grow bigger by putting it in a concentrated solution of salt and allowing the water to evaporate slowly. More sodium chloride crystallises from the solution and attaches itself to the starting crystal. When this happens, the enlarged crystal tends to stay the same shape. The shape of a crystal is characteristic of the particular substance from which it is made, and is often a reflection of the internal order within that crystal.

Crystals are efficiently and regularly packed 'suitcases' of ions (or molecules or atoms). The defining characteristic of a crystal is that the building blocks are stacked in a regular and repeated way. The way in which the components of a crystal are packed is usually the most efficient way of packing those components into a regular pattern.

Activity 3.1   Common salt: examining an ionic solid

We expect this activity will take you approximately 30 minutes.

In this activity, you will examine the properties of the most common ionic solid: sodium chloride. You will need the hand lens from the Practical Kit, a glass jam jar, a pinch of table salt, and some coarse sea salt (often available from a supermarket) or rock salt (available from a roadside grit container). You will also need to access the computer-based resource *Minerals Gallery*.

Safety Warning

Read the whole of this section before starting the activity and make sure that you have read the section on 'Practical activities' in the *Course Guide*.

When carrying out practical activities, you should always take care to observe the simple safety precautions highlighted in the course book. Very often, as in the case of this activity, these precautions will seem quite obvious and just a matter of using common sense. However that does not mean that you should ignore the safety instructions. The Open University has a duty to give advice on health and safety to students carrying out any activities that are described in the course. Similarly, *you* have a duty to follow the instructions and to carry out the practical activities having regard for your own safety and that of other people around you. Whenever you do practical activities you should think about the hazards involved, and how any risks can be minimised.

Important safety precautions

Take note of the following safety precautions, which apply to all practical activities:

- Keep children and animals away while you are working.
- Clear your working area of clutter. Put all food away. Ensure there is nothing to trip on underfoot.
- Always wash your hands thoroughly after a practical activity.
- Any household items should be thoroughly cleaned before returning them to domestic use.

In addition, you should note the following precautions specific to this activity:

- Avoid getting salt in your eyes, as this will be painful. For this reason, you should keep your face well away from the rock salt when you are crushing it. If you do get salt in your eye, wash it out with copious amounts of water. If irritation persists, seek medical advice.
- Do not use excessive force when crushing the sea salt or rock salt, as this may break the jam jar.

Task 1

Table salt is refined from naturally occurring salt by evaporating brine (salt water) very rapidly, to produce small grains which are all around the same size. Use the hand lens from your Practical Kit to closely examine a pinch of table salt (against a dark background if you can). Write a short description of what you see.

Task 2

Examine the largest of your grains of sea salt or rock salt with the hand lens and write brief notes to describe what you see. Now gently roll a jam jar over one of the larger grains to crush it slightly. Tip the fragments onto a dark surface and look at them with the hand lens, again making brief notes about what you observe. Suggest why the grains break in the way that they do.

Task 3

The mineral halite is the form taken by sodium chloride in nature; it is the main constituent of the rock salt used to clear ice from roads. In the *Minerals Gallery*, select 'halite' and examine the three-dimensional model. Rotate the model in space and compare the structure with that given in Figure 3.6.

Now look at the comments on Tasks 1 and 2 of this activity at the end of this book.

Question 3.3

What is the difference between a hydrogen cation and a proton?

Question 3.4

The element magnesium forms ions with two positive charges, Mg^{2+}. Magnesium has an atomic number of 12 and a relative atomic mass of 24. How many protons and how many neutrons are there in the nucleus of the cation and how many electrons surround the nucleus?

3.5   Summary of Chapter 3

Atoms comprise a tiny, dense nucleus surrounded by one or more negatively charged electrons. There are protons with a positive charge and neutrons with zero charge in the nucleus. The neutral atom has the same number of protons in the nucleus as there are electrons. One element is distinguished from another by the number of protons in the nucleus. In some cases, atoms of the same element can have different numbers of neutrons in the nucleus and these atoms are isotopes of that element.

Molecules are groups of atoms linked together usually by covalent bonds. Ionic bonding occurs where cations and anions come together in an ordered array to form a solid. The relative molecular mass can be calculated by adding together the relative atomic mass values of all the atoms in the molecule.

In studying this chapter, you have practised drawing conclusions from careful observations.

Chapter 4
Groupings of atoms, molecules and ions

4.1   Introduction

All matter which humans experience is constructed of atoms, molecules or ions in some combination or another. These are truly the foundations of all structures, from a molecule of hydrogen gas to the rocks of the Himalayas. With the exception of crystals, in which many millions of ions or molecules are incorporated, the focus so far has been on single entities and their structures. The characteristic shape of crystals is a result of the packing of ions or molecules in the most efficient way. To illustrate that crystal formation is spontaneous, it is useful to look at how crystals can be grown. Materials, such as sodium chloride, that dissolve in water do so to different extents with temperature and are usually more soluble at higher temperatures. When ionic compounds dissolve in water, the regular, organised array of ions in the crystal is destroyed as the ions move from the solid crystal to a more random arrangement in the water. It is important to note that ions exist in the solid and in the solution of the solid in water; they are not changed (except in the context of their organisation) when the solid dissolves.

Sodium chloride dissolves to the extent of 36 g in 100 cm^3 of cold water and 39 g in 100 cm^3 of boiling water, so the difference in this case is relatively small. However, the related compound, potassium chloride, shows a greater difference. It dissolves to a lesser extent in cold water than sodium chloride, 24 g in 100 cm^3 of water at 20 °C, but about 57 g of potassium chloride dissolves in 100 cm^3 of water at 100 °C. (Potassium chloride, KCl, has a potassium ion, K$^+$, in place of the sodium ion in sodium chloride.)

■   What do you think would happen if you took 57 g of potassium chloride, dissolved it in 100 cm^3 of boiling water, and then let the resulting solution cool slowly?

☐   As the temperature falls, the amount of potassium chloride that can stay in solution becomes smaller, eventually reaching only 24 g in 100 cm^3 at 20 °C. The result is that 33 g of potassium chloride must come out of solution as it cools and appear as a solid, spontaneously forming crystals. The apparently random distribution of the ions in the solution changes to the ordered array of the crystals.

4.2   Intermolecular forces

The forces between ions are such that ionic compounds can form crystalline solids. It is also possible to have crystals made from molecules. What are the forces between molecules that cause some of them to form crystals? The strength of the different types of forces between molecules determines whether a molecular substance is normally a solid or whether it is a liquid or a gas. The key here is the different types of forces there are *between* molecules – **intermolecular forces** – as distinct from the forces or chemical bonds that hold atoms together *within* a molecule – **intramolecular forces**.

Figure 4.1 Solid iodine showing its colour, lustre and crystalline form.

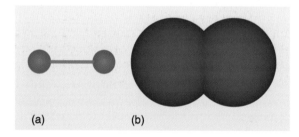

(a)   (b)

Figure 4.2 Two views of the iodine molecule, I_2: (a) ball-and-stick; (b) space-filling.

4.2.1 Van der Waals forces

The element iodine is a dark purple shiny solid at normal temperatures (Figure 4.1). Iodine is an element with chemical properties somewhat similar to those of the element chlorine. Under normal conditions, chlorine is a gas and iodine a solid. However, just as chlorine exists as molecules containing two chlorine atoms joined together, Cl_2, iodine similarly has molecules containing two iodine atoms, I_2 (Figure 4.2). Iodine molecules are not ionic as they do not carry an overall positive or negative charge. What, then, is the 'glue' that holds them together in a crystal of iodine? We need to delve further into the structure of molecules to address this question.

In an atom, the centre of positive charge is the nucleus. As the electrons are symmetrically arranged around the nucleus, the centre of the negative charge is centred on the nucleus. However, it is possible for the centres of positive charge and negative charge to be separated. Given that the electrons are moving around the nucleus, at any given moment it is possible for there to be more electrons on one side of the nucleus than on the other. If this happens, the resulting separation of electrical charge is known as a **dipole**. It is important to realise that this is a temporary or transient feature, as the next moment could see relatively more electrons around the other side of the atom (Figure 4.3). You can think of a dipole as the electrical equivalent of a magnet. Just as one magnet attracts another (because the north pole of one attracts the south pole of the other and vice versa), the positive end of a dipole attracts the negative end of another and vice versa (Figure 4.4).

Figure 4.3 The momentary imbalance of charge as the electrons move around the two nuclei in a molecule of iodine at one instant (a) and the next (b). To simplify matters, only a single positive charge and a single electron are considered for each atom, but in fact each iodine atom has 53 protons in its nucleus with 53 electrons surrounding it. The direction of the transient dipole at the instant represented in (b) is shown in (c).

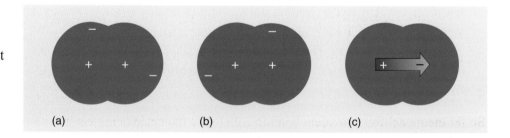

(a)   (b)   (c)

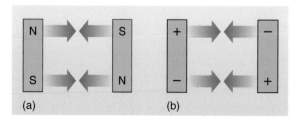

(a)   (b)

Figure 4.4 The attraction between (a) the north and south poles of two magnets and (b) the positive and negative ends of two dipoles.

Consider now two iodine molecules side by side. The presence of a **transient dipole** in one molecule has the effect of distorting the arrangement of the electrons in an adjacent molecule. Electrons in the adjacent molecule will be attracted to the positive end of the dipole and move away from the negative end. The effect is to create, or induce, a dipole in the second molecule (Figure 4.5a). As the electrons move around the first molecule, the transient dipole will change direction. However, this will induce a corresponding dipole in the second molecule and again the two will attract one another (Figure 4.5b).

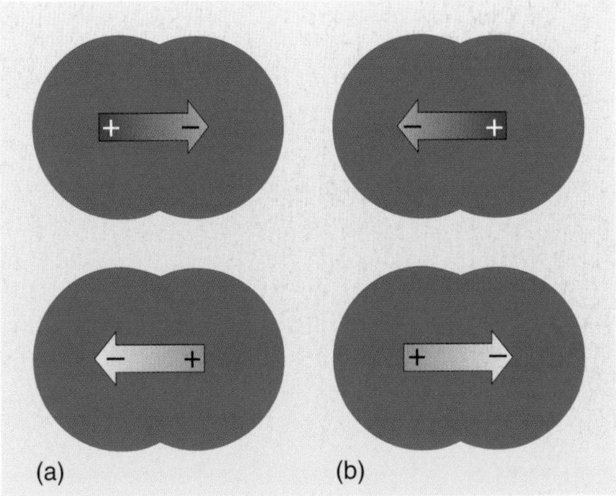

The relationship between the two transient dipoles results in the attractive forces not cancelling as you might have expected. Adding all these momentary attractions between each pair of molecules, the result turns out to be an overall net attraction. The strength of the attractive forces between molecules – intermolecular forces – depends on how easily the molecules form transient dipoles. Molecules containing atoms with many electrons form transient dipoles more easily (they are said to be more easily **polarised**), and hence give rise to stronger intermolecular forces. The stronger the forces between molecules, the more difficulty they have in separating; in other words, the more likely the material is to be a solid rather than a liquid, or a liquid rather than a gas. There are other types of forces between molecules, but those arising from transient dipoles are known as **van der Waals forces**. These forces are much weaker than the chemical bonds between atoms in a molecule.

Figure 4.5 (a) The transient dipole in one molecule (pale arrow) induces a dipole in an adjacent molecule (dark arrow). The two dipoles then experience an attractive force. (b) The transient dipole in the first molecule has changed direction, which causes the induced dipole in the second molecule also to change. The two dipoles still experience an attractive force.

■ Can van der Waals forces provide an explanation as to why chlorine, Cl_2, is a gas at normal temperatures and not a crystalline solid like iodine?

☐ Compared with an iodine atom (with 53 electrons), a chlorine atom (with 17 electrons) is less easily polarised. Transient dipoles do not form as readily, which means the intermolecular van der Waals forces are weaker, so the molecules of chlorine are more easily separated.

4.2.2   Dipole–dipole attractions

So far the model for a covalent bond in a diatomic molecule (a molecule with two atoms) has simply implied that the electrons that are shared between the nuclei to form the bond are shared equally. This is only true for bonds between the same type of atom, as in hydrogen, H_2, chlorine, Cl_2, or iodine, I_2. For bonds between different types of atoms, electrons forming the chemical bond are not shared equally. Some atoms in molecules attract electrons towards themselves more strongly than others; they have more than their 'fair' share of the electrons forming the bond. Elements that are effective in attracting electrons to themselves include fluorine, chlorine, oxygen and nitrogen. In the hydrogen chloride molecule, HCl, the chlorine atom attracts the electrons forming the chemical bond (the **bonding electrons**) more strongly than does the hydrogen atom. The result is that these bonding electrons spend more

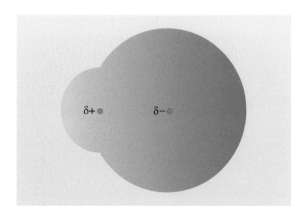

Figure 4.6   The unequal distribution of the electrons in the bond between two dissimilar atoms such as a hydrogen atom and a chlorine atom in hydrogen chloride.

time nearer the chlorine atom than near the hydrogen atom. Overall there is effectively more negative charge towards the chlorine end of the molecule than there is at the hydrogen end (Figure 4.6). The hydrogen chloride molecule has a dipole but it is there all the time, a **permanent dipole**, as distinct from the transient dipoles that give rise to the attractive van der Waals forces between molecules.

It is important to note that hydrogen chloride is not ionic; it is a neutral molecule with no net overall charge. The number of protons in the nuclei of the two atoms is exactly balanced by the number of electrons surrounding them.

In Figure 4.6 the symbols $\delta+$ and $\delta-$ appear (δ is the lower-case Greek letter *delta*), and this is a way of indicating that that there is an uneven distribution of the electrons in the bond connecting the two atoms: $\delta+$ indicates that there is a slight positive charge, $\delta-$ that there is a slight negative charge. Bonds that have a permanent dipole are known as **polar bonds**.

There is an attraction between the permanent dipoles that are present in the hydrogen chloride molecule. These attractive forces are called **dipole–dipole forces**. They are additional to the attractive forces due to the transient dipoles. A consequence of molecules of a particular substance having a permanent dipole is that the molecules stick together more strongly than those that do not.

You should be clear that both dipole–dipole forces and transient dipole attractions ultimately derive from the electrical attraction between the negatively charged electrons and the positively charged protons, but arise in different ways. Dipole–dipole forces arise from the presence of permanent dipoles in a molecule; transient dipoles result from the fluctuation in the electron distribution in the molecules. Both types of force are essentially short-range and weaken very rapidly with molecular separation.

4.2.3   Hydrogen bonds

Water is a liquid at normal temperatures. The related molecule hydrogen sulfide, H_2S, has a sulfur atom replacing the oxygen atom in water. Oxygen atoms have eight electrons and sulfur atoms have 16 electrons.

■   On the basis of what you have learned about intermolecular forces, would you expect hydrogen sulfide to be a solid, liquid or a gas?

☐   Atoms with more electrons are more easily polarised so there ought to be stronger van der Waals forces between hydrogen sulfide molecules than there are between water molecules. The expectation is that hydrogen sulfide could be a liquid or even a solid at normal temperatures.

Hydrogen sulfide is in fact a gas with a boiling temperature of $-60.7\ °C$. The implication of this is that there must be attractive forces additional to the van der Waals forces between water molecules which are not present between hydrogen sulfide molecules. There is a particularly strong dipole–dipole interaction between the water molecules. Hydrogen atoms in such circumstances form directional bonds to similar strongly electron-attracting atoms in other molecules. Although rather weaker than normal covalent bonds, they are different enough in character to be given a special name; they are called **hydrogen bonds**.

In the water molecule, the hydrogen atoms are bonded to oxygen atoms and these are therefore able to form hydrogen bonds with oxygen atoms in other water molecules (Figure 4.7). The hydrogen bond is often represented by a dashed line rather than the solid line that is normally used to represent a covalent bond. Only nitrogen, oxygen and fluorine atoms attract electrons sufficiently to be able to form hydrogen bonds.

Hydrogen bonds come about because oxygen and nitrogen attract the electrons in the O—H and N—H bonds so strongly. Hydrogen in one water molecule is positively charged and is attracted by the oxygen atom in another molecule. The four types of hydrogen bond that are most common are shown in Figure 4.8. Despite the very restricted number of elements that can form hydrogen bonds, the fact that oxygen and nitrogen atoms are present in many molecules means that hydrogen bonding is of great importance in the types of interaction that occur between molecules of a very wide range of compounds.

This brief examination of the attractive forces (chemical bonds) that link atoms together to form molecules and of the attractive forces between molecules provides a basis for a consideration of solids, liquids and gases and what happens at the molecular level when a substance changes from one state to another.

4.3   Solids

The description given earlier of ionic crystalline solids, and by extension molecular crystals, implies that the components of a solid have a fixed geometric relationship to each other. Crystals made from ions are held together by the attraction of opposite charges on the ions. Not all solids are ionic, so what holds crystals together that are made of uncharged molecules such as those of sugar? There is not a single answer to that question; several different types of solids are known. A few examples will illustrate the sort of forces that hold solids together, and the different types of solids that there are.

The only forces between iodine molecules in a crystal of iodine are those between transient dipoles. These are sufficiently strong that iodine is solid at normal temperature and pressure. However, these forces between molecules are much weaker than those between ions. This is apparent when the normal melting temperature of iodine (114 °C), a molecular solid, is compared with that of sodium chloride (801 °C), an ionic solid. As a general rule, **molecular crystals** melt at lower temperatures than ionic crystals.

Another example of a molecular solid is solid water, ice. The crystalline appearance of snowflakes seen under a microscope suggests an underlying ordered arrangement (Figure 4.9).

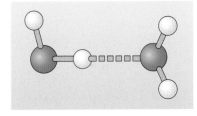

Figure 4.7   A hydrogen bond (dashed line) formed between a hydrogen atom of one water molecule and the oxygen atom of another. Note that hydrogen bonds are directional and the three atoms are in a straight line.

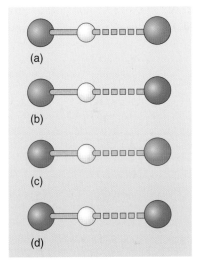

Figure 4.8   Four common types of hydrogen bond: (a) O—H⋯O (b) O—H⋯N (c) N—H⋯O (d) N—H⋯N.

Figure 4.9   Photograph of snowflake crystals.

Hydrogen bonds between the molecules of water account for the fact that water is a liquid at normal temperature and pressure. But hydrogen bonds are also present in ice. The regular and directional nature of these bonds is illustrated in Figure 4.10, which shows part of an ice crystal structure. Two hydrogen bonds can form to each oxygen atom. Each oxygen atom is then surrounded by four hydrogen atoms.

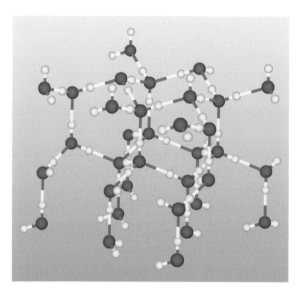

Figure 4.10   Model of the structure of ice. The water molecules are shown as a ball-and-stick representation to allow the relative orientations of adjacent molecules to be seen more easily. In ice the O—H covalent bond length is 1.01×10^{-10} m while the O—H hydrogen bond length is 1.75×10^{-10} m, which is considerably longer.

The last type of crystal is one in which all the atoms are joined by covalent bonds. Each crystal is therefore a single (but enormous) molecule. The mineral quartz, which featured in Book 2, Chapter 5, is a crystalline solid comprising an extended array of covalently bonded atoms of the elements silicon and oxygen. The structure is based on the silicon atoms being attached to four oxygen atoms with the O—Si—O bond angle at silicon of 109.5° (Figure 4.11). This is the angle at the centre of a tetrahedron and will assume considerable importance in the discussion of carbon compounds in Chapters 12–16 of this book.

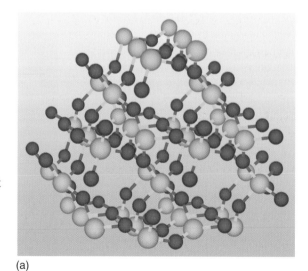

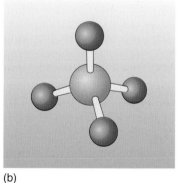

(b)

Figure 4.11   (a) Model of part of a quartz crystal. The ball-and-stick representation allows the crystal structure to be seen more easily. (b) The tetrahedral 'SiO$_4$' unit.

(a)

How should the chemical formula for the mineral quartz be written? The whole crystal is, in effect, a single molecule in which there are twice as many oxygen atoms as there are silicon atoms. It would just not be possible to write a formula that expressed the precise number of atoms in the crystal. Even if this were possible, another crystal of quartz of a different size would have a different number of atoms although the relative numbers of oxygen and silicon atoms would be the same in each case. To have different chemical formulas for the same substance would be nonsense. The way round this is to write a formula that expresses only the ratio of the number of atoms of one type to the number of the other. The formula to be used in this case is SiO_2. The chemical substance of quartz is silicon dioxide (which is also known as silica). The formula SiO_2 is an **empirical formula**. This is the formula that is obtained from an experiment designed to determine the ratio of the numbers of atoms of each type. The simplest ratio is used, so it is SiO_2 rather than Si_2O_4 or even $Si_{100}O_{200}$.

Solid water or ice comprises a crystal in which there are discrete identifiable water molecules linked to one another by hydrogen bonds which are weaker than the covalent bonds that link the individual atoms in the molecule. So H_2O is the **molecular formula** for water as it represents the formula of the individual molecules in the structure. For water, H_2O is also the empirical formula as it conveys the simplest ratio of the relative numbers of hydrogen and oxygen atoms.

■ The chemical formula for sodium chloride is written NaCl. Is this an empirical formula, a molecular formula or both?

☐ Sodium chloride is an extended array of sodium cations and chloride anions, each crystal comprising millions of atoms. It would not be possible to write a formula representing the precise numbers of each type of ion in a crystal, so the formula can only represent the ratio. The formula NaCl is an empirical formula, indicating that there are the same number of sodium cations and chloride anions in sodium chloride.

Every atom in a crystal has a fixed spatial relationship to every other. With some crystals, the application of considerable pressure can change the structure. In the case of minerals, this is one of the several processes in metamorphism (Book 2, Activity 5.1). For example, under high pressure, silicon dioxide forms the mineral coesite, which has a different structure from quartz.

There are solids that are not crystalline. Many plastics come into this category. Polythene (or polyethene to give it a proper chemical name) is a solid. Polythene comprises long molecules or chains of carbon atoms with many thousands of atoms joined together, with hydrogen atoms attached to the carbon atoms. These chains are not spatially ordered like the components of a crystal but are somewhat intermingled, similar to the strands in a bowl of spaghetti.

■ Carbon–carbon and carbon–hydrogen bonds are not very polar. What type of forces hold polythene molecules together?

☐ The attraction must be due to transient dipoles, giving rise to van der Waals forces.

As a carbon atom has only six electrons and hydrogen just one, the forces arising from the transient dipoles between one atom in one chain and an adjacent atom in another chain will be quite weak. However, the effect of weak forces is considerably magnified when the molecular chains are long and therefore have a large surface area. Think about gluing two spheres together and two matchsticks together. To get two spheres to stick together, you need a powerful glue because the area of contact is small. To stick two matches together side-by-side, you do not need such a powerful glue as there is a large area where the two sticks are in full contact. Even though the forces between individual atoms in adjacent chains are weak, the overall attractive force between the long molecules is considerable and polythene is a solid. This is a general effect – the longer non-polar molecules are held together more strongly than smaller non-polar molecules.

Activity 4.1   Quartz: examining a natural molecular crystal

We expect this activity will take you approximately 30 minutes.

In this activity, you will examine the properties of a natural molecular crystal: quartz. You will need a jam jar, some sea or rock salt, and the hand lens and Specimen 1 from the Practical Kit. You will also need to access the computer-based resource *Minerals Gallery*.

Important safety precautions

Take note of the following safety precautions, which apply to all practical activities:

- Keep children and animals away while you are working.
- Clear your working area of clutter. Put all food away. Ensure there is nothing to trip on underfoot.
- Always wash your hands thoroughly after a practical activity.
- Any household items used should be thoroughly cleaned before returning them to domestic use.

In addition, you should note the following precautions specific to this activity:

- Avoid getting salt in your eyes, as this will be painful.
- Do not use excessive force when assessing the strength of the quartz, as this may break the jam jar.

Task 1

Examine Specimen 1 (the mineral quartz) while turning it slowly. You may wish to use your hand lens. Make brief notes on the ways in which the appearance of the quartz is different from that of rock or sea salt. You may wish to refer to the notes you made for Activity 3.1.

Task 2

In Activity 3.1, you saw that the crystal structure of rock or sea salt was relatively easy to break. Assess whether the quartz is any stronger than the common salt. You should not bash it, but just drag the broken end over the surface of a glass jam jar. What happens? Try the same with some sea salt.

Task 3

Now examine the broken end of the quartz crystal through the hand lens. Is there any sign of a cleavage?

Task 4

In the *Minerals Gallery*, select 'quartz' and thoroughly explore the molecular properties of this mineral.

Now look at the comments on this activity at the end of this book.

4.4 Melting

All solids undergo internal motion in which ions, atoms or molecules are vibrating. In a crystal, at the molecular, ionic or atomic level, there is always motion. The ions, atoms or molecules are jiggling or oscillating around their 'normal' position. From an imaginary viewpoint inside the crystal, you would witness frantic motion all around but nothing would be going anywhere. Increase the temperature and the motion gets more violent. Eventually, the forces that were acting to restore the molecules, ions or atoms to their original positions are no longer adequate to hold the structure together against the temperature-dependent oscillation forces. For a crystalline material, at a precise temperature a **phase change** takes place. There are three possibilities: a change from a solid to a liquid (**melting**); a change from a solid to a gas (**sublimation**); or a change from one crystal structure to another (structural phase transition).

The most familiar of these changes is the melting of a solid to give a liquid, which is what happens to a cube of ice taken from the freezer. When the temperature of the ice rises to 0 °C molecular vibrations get more violent and some of the hydrogen bonds that held the crystal together break and the ice melts. At a pressure of one atmosphere (i.e. 10^5 Pa), ice always melts at 0 °C.

Water is unusual in that it increases in volume on freezing. Ice has a highly ordered and somewhat open structure with two hydrogen bonds linking an oxygen atom of a water molecule to two other water molecules. However, this degree of order cannot be maintained in a liquid. On melting, some of the hydrogen bonds are disrupted. In liquid water, the hydrogen bonds are constantly breaking and reforming between different molecules. This allows the water molecules to come closer together than in the more open ice structure. The result is that liquid water at 0 °C has a greater density than ice at 0 °C (1000 kg m^{-3} as compared with 920 kg m^{-3}). In contrast, with most substances the components are packed more closely together in the solid than they are in the liquid, so the solid is more dense than the liquid. Here, melting is accompanied by an increase in volume.

Ionic solids melt to give liquids if sufficient energy is supplied to overcome the net attraction between ions. Ionic solids generally have high melting temperatures because the net attraction between the ions is so strong. A great deal of energy is required to separate the ions and break down the highly ordered structure.

Not all solids melt at atmospheric pressure to give liquids when they gain enough energy. Some, such as solid carbon dioxide, change directly into gas, although this is relatively uncommon. Carbon dioxide is a gas at normal temperatures. Solid carbon dioxide, commonly known as 'dry ice', is solid only at temperatures below −78 °C. (Touching dry ice with unprotected hands can lead to frostbite as the water in your fingers freezes.) At temperatures higher than that, such as room temperature, dry ice disappears in front of your eyes (albeit rather slowly), being transformed *directly* to gaseous carbon dioxide (that is why it is called *dry* ice). Liquid carbon dioxide does exist, but only at high pressures.

Apart from the change from a solid to a liquid (melting) or the direct change from a solid to a gas (sublimation), the third possibility mentioned earlier was a change from one crystal structure to another. You may not be aware of a change in crystal structure unless it is accompanied by some visible or measurable physical change. A well-known example of this phenomenon is the metal tin. Tin has one structure known as white tin that is stable above 13 °C; below this temperature, it changes to another form called grey tin with quite different properties.

Non-crystalline solids such as the plastic polyethene do melt but not usually at a precise temperature. The way in which the chains are intertwined and aligned will be slightly different from place to place in the solid. The attractive energy between the chains is not therefore uniform throughout the solid. There is not a single temperature at which the forces holding the solid together are overcome by thermal motion. So a typical plastic such as polyethene softens as the temperature rises and it melts over a wide temperature range. This contrasts with the behaviour of a pure crystalline solid which would melt at a specific temperature.

4.5   Liquids

Liquids are materials that flow, have a fixed volume (at a given temperature) and take the shape of their container. If you try to compress a liquid, you will have very little success. Hydraulic devices, in which a force is transmitted from one point to another by means of a fluid, rely on the relative non-compressibility of liquids.

The structure of liquids is quite different from that of solids. The regularity, order and fixed geometric relationships in solids are replaced by randomness, disorder and lots of movement in liquids. In a liquid, molecules are able to move from place to place. An indication that molecules in a liquid are not motionless can be gained by adding a small drop of ink to a glass of water. At first, the ink moves through the water leaving a trail; after a while, the trail gets very fuzzy and eventually the colour becomes uniformly spread throughout the liquid.

If molecules are moving rapidly, it may seem surprising that the ink drop is not instantly dispersed to all corners of the glass. But imagine a molecule in a sea of other molecules; if it moves in one direction then the chances are that it will collide with one of its neighbours and bounce back towards its original position.

Just because the molecule is moving fast does not necessarily mean that it will rapidly travel long distances from its starting point. If you are in a crowd that is milling around, even if you can move quickly, you would have to change your path many times before reaching a specific target on the other side of the crowd.

When a molecular crystal such as ice melts to form a liquid, the individual molecules that made up the crystal still retain their identity although they are no longer arranged in an organised way. For ionic materials the result of melting is slightly different. Sodium chloride is represented by the empirical formula NaCl. When the thermal motion in the crystal is such that the ordered structure breaks down (at the melting temperature), the ions (sodium cations, Na^+, and chloride anions, Cl^-) stay as individual ions but are no longer uniquely associated with any other ions. The sodium and chloride ions in molten sodium chloride are free to move randomly through the liquid.

One of the main differences between the liquids that are produced from the melting of molecular solids and those produced from ionic solids is that the latter conduct electricity because the ions in the liquid are mobile and carry electrical charge (Book 3, Section 7.2). This can be illustrated with the diagram of a simple apparatus for passing an electric current through a liquid (Figure 4.12). In this simple arrangement, an electrical power source (in this case a battery) is connected to the two metal rods labelled anode and cathode. The **cathode** is the electrode attached to the negative terminal of the power source, and so electrons flow towards the cathode through the wire connecting it to the power source. The **anode** is the electrode connected to the positive terminal, and so electrons flow away from the anode towards the positive terminal of the power source. The effect of the movement of positively charged sodium cations and the negatively charged chloride anions in the molten salt is to complete an electrical circuit.

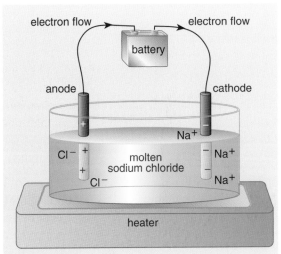

Figure 4.12   Diagram of a simple experimental arrangement for the electrolysis of molten sodium chloride.

■   In which direction do you think the ions will move?

☐   As opposite charges attract, it seems reasonable to suppose that the negative ions (anions) will migrate towards the anode and the positive ions (cations) will migrate towards the cathode.

That is exactly what does happen. But what will happen to the anions when they reach the anode and the cations arrive at the cathode?

If a circuit is to be completed, electrons must be accepted by the (positively charged) cations at the cathode. In other words, the sodium ions must accept an electron at the cathode. If they do so, the sodium ions form sodium atoms. To complete the circuit, electrons must be given up by the (negatively charged) anions at the anode so they can return to the power source. In other words, the chloride ions must give up an electron at the anode to form chlorine atoms. (These then combine in pairs to form chlorine molecules, Cl_2.)

The reaction that is described above is exactly what does happen and this process, called **electrolysis**, is the method used to make sodium metal. Metallic sodium, which is so reactive that it even reacts with water, is not found in nature and has to be made from compounds such as sodium chloride. The other product of the electrolysis of molten sodium chloride is chlorine gas.

It may not have escaped your notice that the production of sodium and chlorine in this way is the exact reverse of the reaction that was used to illustrate the formation of ions – the spontaneous reaction of chlorine gas with metallic sodium. The main difference between the two reactions is that salt forms spontaneously but to get the reaction to go in reverse requires a great deal of energy. The sodium chloride first has to be heated to over 800 °C to melt it and then an electric current passed through the liquid. Both of these processes are very energy-consuming. Electrolysis is a common method for the production of certain metals.

4.6   Solutions

Having examined the properties of a liquid in terms of its constituent particles, we can now go on to consider how pure liquids differ from solutions. The discussion will be confined to solutions in molecular liquids; little will be said about solutions involving molten ionic substances.

In a pure molecular liquid, the molecules that make up that liquid will either be non-polar or they will be polar to some extent. Water molecules are polar. The molecules are not completely independent of one another (as they would be in a gas) but they are not in a fixed relationship either (as they would be in a crystal).

When another substance dissolves in a liquid (and solids, gases and other liquids can all do so), the structure and order within the liquid is modified. The least amount of disruption will take place when two very similar liquids are mixed. Water and ethanol (alcohol) are soluble in each other; in other words, they mix completely whatever the proportions. They both have oxygen–hydrogen bonds in their molecular structure and so can form hydrogen bonds with like molecules and with each other (Figure 4.13). The properties of a solution of ethanol in water are related to the proportion of each that is present. For a solution involving two liquids, it is somewhat arbitrary as to which is regarded as being the **solvent**, but normally it is the liquid that is present to the greater extent.

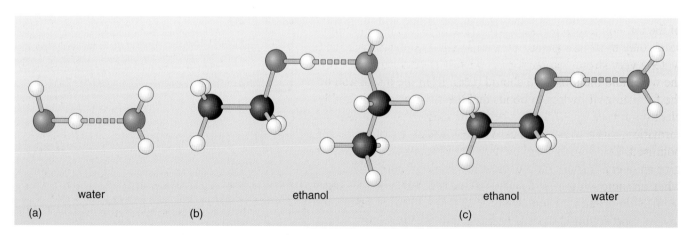

(a)   water   (b)   ethanol   (c)   ethanol   water

Figure 4.13   Water and ethanol both have oxygen–hydrogen bonds and so can form hydrogen bonds with like molecules (a) and (b), and with each other (c).

A property that is common to all solutions is that the temperature at which a solution freezes is always lower than that of the pure liquid. The amount of lowering depends on the quantity of material dissolved in the solvent. A bottle of gin will not freeze in a domestic freezer but wine will (and break the bottle as a result of the increase in volume that occurs when water freezes). Both gin and wine are solutions of ethanol (among other things) in water but the proportion of ethanol in gin is much greater than it is in wine.

Two rather different liquids are water and a vegetable oil, such as sunflower oil or olive oil. The oils are complex chemical compounds that are almost completely non-polar. A vegetable oil is made up of large molecules (with relative molecular mass some 25 times greater than that of water) which are rather stringy and are held together in the liquid mostly by van der Waals forces as the chains align themselves alongside other chains.

If oil and water are mixed, they eventually separate into two layers because they are almost completely insoluble in each other. The lower density of oil makes it float on water. Water molecules would have to break most of the intermolecular hydrogen bonds to accommodate the oil molecules into the liquid. In addition, the oil molecules would have to lose some of the benefit gained by lying alongside similar molecules. In a solution of oil and water (if such existed), both the oil molecules and the water molecules would be in a more 'alien' environment than in the individual single liquids.

Solids made from polar molecules tend to dissolve in polar solvents. Sugar is polar, with numerous O—H bonds, and is very soluble in water (one volume of water will dissolve more than three volumes of sugar). Hydrogen bonding between the sugar molecules and the water is very important. At the opposite extreme, our clothes tend to get soiled with stains that are greasy or oily in nature. These are non-polar, so they are not at all soluble in water. 'Dry-cleaning' processes use a non-polar solvent in which the non-polar grease stains will dissolve.

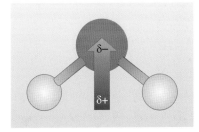

Figure 4.14 Polarisation of the oxygen–hydrogen bonds in a water molecule and the resulting combined dipole.

Ionic solids tend not to dissolve in non-polar solvents but often have solubility in the polar solvent, water. For an ionic solid to dissolve in a solvent, the ions have to be separated and the orderly arrangement of the crystal exchanged for the free-flowing form of a liquid. If the net attractive forces of the ion–ion interactions are to be lost in dissolving an ionic solid, they must be replaced by something else to compensate. In water a very strong interaction called **solvation** occurs between the water and the ions. You should recall from the discussion of the formation of hydrogen bonds that the oxygen atom is highly electron-attracting. As well as being the reason for hydrogen bond formation, this also means that the O—H bonds are permanently polarised. The dipoles from the two O—H bonds add together to give an overall dipole for the water molecule (Figure 4.14). So when an ionic substance dissolves, the water molecules arrange themselves around the ions with the appropriate end of the water dipole approaching the positive and negative ions. Figure 4.15 illustrates how this happens for sodium ions and chloride ions when dissolving sodium chloride in water.

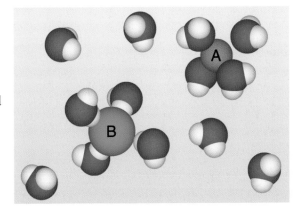

Figure 4.15 Solvation of a sodium ion (A) and a chloride ion (B) by water molecules.

4.7 Vaporisation

The expansion of a liquid as it is heated is a reflection of the increased internal motion within the liquid. Energy transferred on heating manifests itself at the atomic or molecular level with an increase in the motion of atoms and molecules. The higher the temperature, the more vigorous the movement of the atoms or molecules. As a result, the forces between the molecules are more readily overcome in hotter liquids. When a certain point is reached, the attractive forces are no longer sufficient to hold the agitated and energetic molecules together in the liquid state. At that point, the extra energy no longer goes into increasing the temperature of the liquid but into freeing the molecules from the attractive forces between them; however much the liquid is heated, the only effect is to increase the rate at which conversion to gas takes place. The temperature at which free vaporisation occurs is the **boiling temperature** of the liquid.

If you were to measure the temperature at which water boiled, it would be around 100 °C. The freezing temperature of water from your kitchen would be very close to 0 °C. It is not possible to be precise about the boiling temperature because it is much more susceptible to the local pressure of the atmosphere than is the freezing temperature.

If the external pressure is high, the temperature of the liquid has to be higher for it to boil. Conversely, if the pressure is very low then the temperature of the liquid can be relatively low for boiling to take place. An example (which is more often cited than attempted) is boiling an egg at the summit of Mount Everest (or Chomolungma, its Nepalese name). Pressure at the 8800 m summit is about one-third that at sea level and the boiling temperature of water is depressed below 100 °C; in fact, it's about 71 °C. An egg which takes 4 minutes to cook at sea level could take 30 minutes at this altitude. The inability to cook a decent boiled egg on Mount Everest does not appear to have diminished the number of climbers who attempt the ascent of the mountain every year.

Of more practical use in the home is the increased boiling temperature of water at high pressures. Food cooks faster at higher temperatures. No matter how much you heat your vegetable water in an open pan, the temperature will not rise above the normal boiling temperature of 100 °C or thereabouts. You may have a pressure cooker, which is a pan that can be closed and a weight placed over the only exit. The weight is connected with a valve so that the pressure inside the cooker increases to a fixed higher level as long as sufficient heat is supplied. If too much heat is supplied, the valve allows excess steam to vent from the pan. The increase in pressure inside the pan means that the water boils at a temperature above 100 °C and the pan is also filled with steam at the higher temperature. As the temperature is higher, the food cooks more quickly.

Question 4.1

Why do large molecules tend to have higher boiling temperatures than do small molecules?

4.8 Gases

4.8.1 Properties of gases

Liquids retain some order in their structure. The liquid flows and has a fixed volume. Both of these observations imply that there is some sort of interaction between the molecules (or ions) in the liquid state. Gases do not show either of these properties. A gas will fill all the available space in which there is a random distribution of molecules or atoms. A gas is the ultimate expression of disorder in the Universe. On average, matter is uniformly distributed throughout the space occupied by a gas.

To a good approximation, the individual atoms or molecules in a gas effectively behave as though they are independent of any of the other atoms or molecules in the surroundings until they collide with one another and bounce away (as if in a non-stop, three-dimensional snooker game). Compared with a liquid, the distances that molecules travel between collisions are very much greater. The expansion in volume in the change from a liquid to a gas can be any size, as a gas will fill all the space available, but at atmospheric pressure a volume of one decimetre cubed ($1 \, dm^3$) of liquid water yields more than $1000 \, dm^3$ ($1 \, m^3$) of gaseous water or steam. Recall that a decimetre is 10^{-1} m (Book 1, Box 3.3), so one dm^3 is $10^{-3} \, m^3$. One dm^3 is often referred to as a litre.

Liquids and solids are not readily compressed. In contrast, because a gas will expand to fill any space that is available, it must also follow that a gas can be compressed. When the volume of a fixed mass of gas is changed, the number of molecules remains the same, but the space the molecules occupy changes. This means that the pressure of the gas and its density must change. At a given temperature, the pressure of a gas is related to the number of molecules in each unit of volume, an idea that was introduced in Book 1, Chapter 5. Think of a pump for bicycle tyres. With each stroke of the pump, the volume of the air in the pump decreases. Since there is still the same number of molecules of gas in the pump at the beginning and at the end of the stroke, but now they are in a smaller volume, the pressure increases (so also does the temperature). As you continue to pump, the pressure eventually exceeds that of the air in the tyre, the valve opens, and more air is pumped in. Gases can be forced into a smaller volume by compression, but if the pressure increases beyond a certain point then there will be a change of state, usually to a liquid.

Question 4.2

Why is it necessary to specify the temperature and pressure of a gas if referring to the volume of the gas but this is generally not done for a solid?

4.8.2 Gases and relative molecular mass: a core hypothesis

The **Avogadro hypothesis** (named after Amadeo Avogadro, an Italian physicist; 1776–1856) asserts that equal volumes of different gases, at the same temperature and pressure, contain equal numbers of molecules. The simplicity of this hypothesis has far-reaching consequences, which is all the more remarkable when the very existence of atoms and molecules was hotly disputed by some of the scientific establishment when the hypothesis was proposed in 1811. The real value of the hypothesis to chemistry will become apparent in Chapters 5 and 6, but now it is worthwhile looking at the underlying rationale behind the hypothesis.

Activity 4.2   Verifying the Avogadro hypothesis

We expect this activity will take you approximately 45 minutes.

This activity should allow you to verify the hypothesis that equal volumes of different gases, at the same temperature and pressure, contain equal numbers of molecules. You will need a pencil, ruler and graph paper; or access to computer software that allows you to plot graphs.

Using simple apparatus and a chemical balance that can weigh very accurately, it is possible to demonstrate the validity of Avogadro's hypothesis. Avogadro would not have had the benefit of modern balances and so formulating the hypothesis in the first place was a considerable achievement. The test involves weighing a glass flask containing a number of different gases. The flask has a special stopper with a stopcock that allows gases to be let into the flask or pumped out (Figure 4.16).

The flask can be emptied of all gas by attaching a vacuum pump, and the stopcock closed. By weighing the evacuated sealed flask, the mass of the flask with no gas inside can be determined. One at a time, a number of different gases are then let into the flask in such a way that the gas is at atmospheric pressure each time. The flask is then weighed. By subtracting the mass of the evacuated flask from the mass of the flask with one of the gases inside, the mass of the gas can be determined. Finally, in order to determine the volume of the flask filled by the gas, the flask is filled with water to the stopcock tap, and the volume of water measured. Measurement of the volume of this flask shows it to be 150 cm^3. The temperature at which the measurement was taken is 25 °C.

Some typical results are given in Table 4.1, along with the relative molecular mass of each gas. If the Avogadro hypothesis is valid, the same number of molecules of gas will be in each sample, as the mass of the same volume is being measured in each case. The masses of the gases should then be directly proportional to their relative molecular masses. For example, oxygen, O_2, has a relative molecular mass of 32. The mass of the oxygen sample should be 16 times the mass of the hydrogen, H_2, sample because there is the same number of molecules of oxygen as there are atoms of hydrogen but each one has a mass 16 times that of a hydrogen atom. You should recall from Book 3 (Section 7.5.1) that when two quantities are directly proportional, a graph of one quantity against the other should be in the form of a straight line going through the origin. In order to test Avogadro's hypothesis, therefore, you will draw a graph of the masses of the gases against their relative molecular masses.

Task 1

The mass of the flask containing each gas and the mass of the evacuated flask are given. You should complete the fourth column of Table 4.1, by subtracting one value from the other as shown for hydrogen. Plot a graph with the mass of the gases (given in the fourth column) on the vertical axis and the relative molecular mass (from the fifth column) on the horizontal axis. If the Avogadro hypothesis is correct, you should see a series of points which fall on a straight line that passes through the origin. Draw a line of best fit through these points.

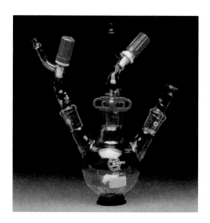

Figure 4.16   Flask sealed with a stopcock for testing the Avogadro hypothesis.

Table 4.1 Results from weighing gases.

Substance	Mass of flask containing fixed volume of gas/g	Mass of evacuated flask/g	Mass of gas/g	Relative molecular mass of substance
hydrogen, H_2	144.174	144.162	0.012	2
nitrogen, N_2	144.330	144.162		28
oxygen, O_2	144.354	144.162		32
fluorine, F_2	144.390	144.162		38
carbon dioxide, CO_2	144.425	144.162		44

Task 2

The experiment was repeated with an unidentified gas, Q, which is known to contain carbon and hydrogen atoms in the ratio 1 : 1. The mass of the flask when it contained this unknown gas was 144.314 g. You will use this data to find the molecular formula and relative molecular mass of Q. You may need to re-read Section 4.3 to remind yourself of the definitions of empirical and molecular formula. Relative molecular mass is defined in Section 3.3.

(a) Write down the empirical formula of Q.

(b) Write down some possible molecular formulas for Q (you can assume that Q has four or fewer carbon atoms in each molecule). For each possible molecular formula, calculate the relative molecular mass. (The relative atomic mass of carbon is 12; that of hydrogen is 1.)

(c) When the flask was filled with Q, the total mass was 144.314 g. Subtract the mass of the flask to find the mass of Q. Using this value should allow you to read off the value of the relative molecular mass from the graph you produced in Task 1. What is the molecular formula of Q?

Now look at the comments on this activity at the end of this book.

The establishment of Avogadro's hypothesis was a key moment in the history of chemistry. In order to explore why, you need to look again at the implications of the experiment described in Activity 4.2.

■ According to the results described in the activity, 150 cm^3 of a gas with a relative molecular mass of 20.0 has a mass of 0.120 g. What volume of gas would have a mass of 20.0 g? (Note that 1 dm^3 is equal to 1000 cm^3.)

□ Since 0.120 g of the gas has a volume of 150 cm^3, then 1.00 g will have a volume of $\left(\dfrac{1.00\text{ g} \times 150\text{ cm}^3}{0.120\text{ g}}\right) = 1250$ cm^3. So 20.0 g will have a volume of 20.0×1250 cm^3, which equals approximately 25 000 cm^3 or 25.0 dm^3.

More accurate measurements would give an answer of 24.5 dm^3, so the measurements from this simple experiment were not at all bad. The answer to this question has provided you with the volume of a gas with a relative molecular mass of 20.0 that has a mass of 20.0 g. In other words, it is the volume of gas that has the same mass as the relative molecular mass expressed in grams. So, according to the Avogadro hypothesis, 2 g of hydrogen, H$_2$, 28.0 g of nitrogen, N$_2$, or 32 g of oxygen, O$_2$, would all have a volume of 24.5 dm^3. (Note that this volume is appropriate at a pressure of 1 atmosphere and a temperature of 25 °C. The volume of a gas decreases with increasing pressure and increases as the temperature increases.)

The hypothesis also implies that a volume of 24.5 dm^3 of *any* gas contains the same number of *molecules*. The number is known as the **Avogadro constant** and has a value of 6.02×10^{23}, a very large number indeed. The number of molecules that are present in a mass of gas equal to the relative molecular mass of the gas measured in grams is given a particular name. It is the **mole** (the symbol for which is **mol**). Since there are 6.02×10^{23} molecules in one mole, the unit of the Avogadro constant is mol^{-1}.

■ How many moles are in 5.00 dm^3 of a gas at one atmosphere pressure at 25 °C?

☐ 24.5 dm^3 of the gas contains one mole, so:

$$1.00 \text{ dm}^3 \text{ contains } \frac{1.00 \text{ dm}^3}{24.5 \text{ dm}^3 \text{ mol}^{-1}}$$

$$5.00 \text{ dm}^3 \text{ contains } \frac{5.00 \text{ dm}^3}{24.5 \text{ dm}^3 \text{ mol}^{-1}}$$

which works out to be 0.204 mol.

The fact that one mole of any gas at one atmosphere pressure and 25 °C occupies a volume of 24.5 dm^3 is not only a remarkable observation but also a very useful one. It enables volumes of gases to be translated directly into numbers of molecules.

The concept of the mole takes a little getting used to, but once you realise that it is simply a way of counting molecules without the inconvenience of using very large numbers, you will appreciate its usefulness. The concept of the mole applies to all pure substances and not just to gases. A mole of any substance contains 6.02×10^{23} of the molecules (or atoms or ions) that make up that substance.

The mole concept is taken up again in Chapter 6, where there is a focus on chemical reactions, but the aim of the next chapter is to try to bring some order to the properties of the elements and their compounds.

Question 4.3

How many moles of helium atoms, He, will there be in a balloon that has a volume of 2.45 dm^3 at a temperature of 25 °C and a pressure of one atmosphere? How many moles of hydrogen molecules, H$_2$, will there be in another balloon of half the size at the same temperature and pressure?

Question 4.4

How many atoms of helium, He, and of hydrogen, H$_2$, would there be in each of the balloons featured in Question 4.3?

4.9   Summary of Chapter 4

Intermolecular forces can be of a number of types. Van der Waals forces are present in all molecular groupings and arise from the instantaneous (and temporary) uneven distribution of electrons in molecules. Additionally, some molecules have a permanent dipole and these interact to provide a net attraction. Molecules that have a hydrogen atom attached to nitrogen, oxygen or fluorine can also take part in hydrogen bonding which, although not as strong as covalent bonding, is stronger than the attractive forces arising from transient dipoles or permanent dipoles. The physical states of matter are, to a great extent, determined by the forces between the molecules (or ions).

The Avogadro hypothesis has far-reaching consequences in chemistry. One mole of any substance contains 6.02×10^{23} atoms, molecules or ions, whichever is the appropriate component.

One mole of any substance has a mass equal to the relative mass of that substance, expressed in grams.

In this chapter, you have applied your mathematical skills in a chemical context, specifically using proportionality and graphical representation.

Chapter 5
Organising the elements

5.1   More on atoms

Our model of the atom is that there is a tiny nucleus (comprising protons and neutrons and containing almost all the mass of the atom) with electrons arranged some distance from the nucleus. Electrons in multi-electron atoms are not all at the same distance from the nucleus but are arranged in shells which lie at different distances from the nucleus.

The element argon, Ar, can be used to explore this idea. Argon, atomic number $Z = 18$, is a minor component of the Earth's atmosphere. It is an atomic gas in that argon atoms exist as individual atoms and not as diatomic molecules like those of hydrogen, H_2, or fluorine, F_2.

Imagine moving outwards from the nucleus of an argon atom. At first, there is a region of empty space, then a narrow region where there is a good chance of meeting a set of two electrons. There is more empty space before another region in which electrons would be found. This time, the region is a home to a set of eight electrons. Finally, after more empty space, there is a further region that accommodates another set of eight electrons.

For argon, electrons are arranged in three **electron shells** at distances of about 5 pm, 20 pm and 70 pm from the nucleus (Figure 5.1). Recall that 1 pm (picometre) is 1×10^{-12} m (Book 1, Box 3.3). The shells are numbered 1, 2, 3 (and so on), moving outward from the nucleus. The number of the shell is known as the **principal quantum number**, and is given the symbol n.

Within each shell (with the exception of shell $n = 1$) there are subshells. The number of subshells in any shell is equal to the principal quantum number of that shell. The first subshell in a shell is given the symbol s; if there is a second, it is given the symbol p; if a third, the symbol d, and if a fourth, the symbol f. So a subshell can be identified by writing down the principal quantum number of its shell, followed by its characteristic letter. Thus, the f subshell of the shell of principal quantum number 4 is written 4f.

Electrons in specific shells and subshells have particular associated energies. In general, the further the electron is from the nucleus, the higher the energy. This is shown in

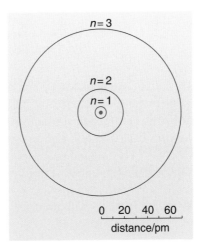

Figure 5.1   Representation of where electrons are likely to be found in the argon atom. The three circles identify three distances from the nucleus of an argon atom where the chances of finding an electron are at a maximum.

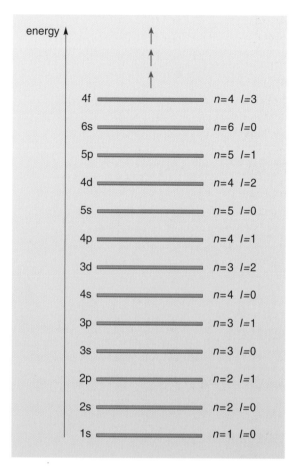

Figure 5.2   Electronic subshells and associated energy. (Note that the energy axis is not to scale.)

Figure 5.2, which also indicates the subshell corresponding to each of the principal quantum numbers.

■ Into how many subshells are the shells with principal quantum numbers 1 and 2 divided and what symbol should each subshell be given?

☐ There is one subshell in the shell with $n = 1$, so this is given the symbol s. In the shell with $n = 2$, there will be two subshells, so these are given the symbols s and p. These subshells can be written 1s, 2s and 2p respectively.

Subshells form the centre of this description of the arrangement of electrons in an atom. The arrangement is known as the **electronic configuration**, which tells us what subshells are occupied, and how many electrons there are in each one.

5.2   Electronic configuration

The electronic configuration of an atom is obtained by writing down the occupied subshells, and specifying the number of electrons in each one by a superscript number. Consider, for example, atoms of hydrogen, helium and lithium, which contain 1, 2 and 3 electrons, respectively. The electronic configurations of the hydrogen atom, $1s^1$, and the helium atom, $1s^2$, tell us that the hydrogen atom contains just one electron in the 1s subshell, and the helium atom contains two in the 1s subshell.

■ What information does the electronic configuration of the lithium atom of $1s^2 2s^1$ convey?

☐ In the lithium atom, both the 1s and 2s subshells are occupied; the former contains two electrons and the latter one.

This raises two questions. First, why can't the three electrons of the lithium atom all go in the 1s subshell? The answer is that there is an upper limit on the number of electrons that each subshell can hold. Just as each shell has its principal quantum number, each subshell also has its own quantum number, l, for the s, p, d and f subshells. This second quantum number takes the values 0, 1, 2 and 3, respectively. The maximum number of electrons for each subshell is equal to $2(2l + 1)$.

■ What is the maximum number of electrons that can be accommodated in the s, p, d and f subshells?

☐ The values are:

- for the s subshell ($l = 0$), $2[(2 \times 0) + 1] = 2$
- for the p subshell ($l = 1$), $2[(2 \times 1) + 1] = 6$
- for the d subshell ($l = 2$), $2[(2 \times 2) + 1] = 10$
- and for the f subshell ($l = 3$), $2[(2 \times 3) + 1] = 14$.

So in total, the s subshell can contain no more than 2 electrons, the p subshell 6 electrons, the d subshell 10 electrons and the f subshell 14 electrons. Helium, with an electronic configuration of $1s^2$, has a full 1s subshell. With lithium, a third electron must be accommodated so it must go into a new subshell (2s).

The second question is this: why, going from hydrogen, through helium, to lithium, is the 1s subshell occupied before the 2s? The answer is that the arrangement of the electrons in an atom is usually that of lowest energy, an arrangement known as the **ground state**. The lower-energy states of atoms are those in which the negatively charged electrons spend more time closer to the positively charged nucleus and, in general, the lower the principal quantum number of a shell, the closer to the nucleus are its electrons likely to be found.

There are about 116 elements in all, of which 92 are naturally occurring. The naturally occurring elements have a huge range of properties. The element potassium reacts with water with the evolution of hydrogen, and sodium behaves in a similar manner. Both chlorine and bromine react with sodium to give white crystalline compounds. Given the range of properties of the elements, are there patterns and similarities? Is there a way to classify and bring some order to the elements?

This is the question asked by the Russian chemist Dmitri Mendeléev (1834–1907) who based his work, in the best scientific tradition, on empirical observation. Beneath the pattern of the chemical properties of the elements, Mendeléev was able to discern an underlying rationale.

In classifying the elements, one of the more obvious divisions that can be made is between those elements that are gases, those that are liquids and those that are solids. But this classification depends on the physical properties of the elements (and physical conditions). In terms of their chemical properties, a more useful classification is to divide the elements into those that are metals, and those that are not metals (referred to as non-metals).

■ Write down the names of as many elements as you can that you think might be metals. Exactly what is a metal is explored in Chapter 7, but for the moment use your own ideas.

☐ Some that you might have thought of are iron, silver, gold, tin, lead, zinc, copper, aluminium, sodium and potassium. Slightly more exotic ones are chromium, nickel, cobalt, cadmium, titanium and manganese.

■ What substances can you recall that you think might be non-metallic elements?

☐ Some that have been mentioned earlier are hydrogen, nitrogen, oxygen, and chlorine. Others you might have thought of are bromine, sulfur and phosphorus.

In answering the question on metals, you might have written down bronze, steel, brass or pewter. These are not elements but mixtures of more than one element, often called **alloys**, in which the proportions of the different metals can vary over a wide range in contrast to compounds where the ratio of the atoms forming the compound is fixed. Bronze is an alloy of copper and tin. Steel is mainly iron but also contains some carbon and small amounts of other elements; stainless steel also contains a sizeable proportion of nickel and chromium. Brass is an alloy of copper and zinc. Pewter used to be made of 80% tin and 20% lead, but modern pewter used for household items consists largely of tin, with small amounts of antimony and copper.

■ What characteristics do metals have in your experience that distinguish them from other substances?

☐ Metals tend to be shiny and good conductors of heat and electricity.

The use of metals in structural applications (bridges, reinforcement for concrete, hoists and cranes, aeroplanes, ships, etc.) depends primarily on their strength and the ease with which they can be fashioned into complex shapes.

In the presence of oxygen in the atmosphere, sometimes helped by water, many metals form compounds containing the metal combined with oxygen. Such compounds are called **oxides**. Steel (which is largely made from iron) reacts with air and water to form just such an oxide, known commonly as rust. The rusting of iron to give the iron oxide is a chemical reaction, and a rather complicated one.

The metal magnesium will slowly become dull on contact with air at normal temperatures as it becomes coated with a layer of magnesium oxide, MgO, a compound of oxygen and magnesium. If heated sufficiently strongly, magnesium burns in air with a brilliant white flame and produces clouds of white 'smoke' of magnesium oxide.

In general, you might expect metals to be rather inert towards oxygen and towards water or at least to be affected only slowly. However, there are metals that could never be used to build a bridge or construct a submarine. Sodium is such a metal. It is silvery and shiny if kept away from oxygen, but it is soft enough that you can cut it with a knife. On exposure to air, it rapidly becomes dull and covered with a white bloom, which is sodium oxide, Na_2O. With water a more spectacular reaction is observed. A piece of sodium dropped into water skids around the surface fizzing and gets so hot that it melts into a ball (sodium melts at about 98 °C) and sometimes catches fire. The chemical reaction produces hydrogen gas from the water, which can be ignited by the heat evolved in the process. Sodium hydroxide, $NaOH$, is formed in solution in the water.

One metal that resists attack by air and moisture even over a period of centuries is (our favourite element) gold. Gold artefacts that have been buried in the ground or submerged in water for hundreds of years can usually be restored to their former glory by gently brushing off the grime and giving them a light polish.

■ Look back at the descriptions of the reactivity of gold, sodium, iron and magnesium with air and water and list them in order of decreasing reactivity.

☐ The order is: sodium, magnesium, iron, gold. Sodium reacts rapidly with water and air; magnesium is slightly reactive but much less so than sodium; iron only oxidises slowly; gold is essentially inert.

All of the reactions of metals with water or oxygen have a common feature. They involve the loss of one or more electrons from the metal atom. Much of chemistry is concerned with electrons being transferred from one atom or group of atoms to another. Metals, in general, share the tendency to lose electrons when they react, and pass them on to other atoms or molecules. Some atoms, like sodium, lose one electron very readily, but no more. Elemental magnesium atoms will lose two electrons, no more, no less. Gold atoms can lose electrons but that is more difficult to achieve. The number of electrons that a metal loses in certain spontaneous chemical reactions is very characteristic and, as you will now see, was one of the properties used by Mendeléev in his classification of the elements which is known as the **Periodic Table** of the elements.

5.3   Atomic structure and the Periodic Table

One of the fundamental questions of chemistry is why different elements react at varying rates with different substances. Related to this are the questions 'Why should some elements lose electrons readily and why should some gain electrons?' and 'What determines how many electrons are gained or lost?' Chemistry can't exactly say *why* these things happen but, after centuries of observation, it can propose a convincing rationale for such observations and predict what is most likely to happen in new situations.

Mendeléev's great achievement was to make a classification based on the properties of the elements known at the time, which also had great predictive power. Not only did it organise the elements in patterns based on their properties, but it also allowed Mendeléev to predict the existence of certain elements, at the time undiscovered, to fill vacancies in his Periodic Table. Not only was he able to predict their occurrence but also he was correct in the prediction of their relative atomic mass, density, and the chemical formulas of their compounds with oxygen and chlorine. Mendeléev organised the elements into groups and periods, a model that has survived virtually unchanged to the present day (Figure 5.3, overleaf). A **group** is a vertical column of the Periodic Table in which there are elements with common chemical properties. For example, the elements sodium and potassium are in the same group. Both elements react rapidly with oxygen in the air to form a solid oxide and both elements react vigorously with water to produce hydrogen which often ignites during the reaction. A **period** is a horizontal row where there is general gradation or change of property along the row.

The chemical properties of the elements are related to the arrangement of electrons within atoms. Looking first at a group of gaseous elements that are almost completely unreactive chemically may seem perverse, but it can give useful clues to why other elements are more reactive. The elements are known as the **noble gases**. (It has been said, perhaps unfairly, that it is because these elements share with the nobility a tendency to do almost nothing.) These elements are all in the same group of the Periodic Table situated on the extreme right-hand side of it (Figure 5.3). It is difficult to add electrons to the atoms of the noble gases to form negative ions; it is also difficult to take electrons from them to form positive ions. Equally, they do not readily share electrons to form covalent bonds. Indeed, they do not even form bonds with themselves and exist as separate atoms unlike diatomic molecules of the elements chlorine, Cl_2, oxygen, O_2, or nitrogen, N_2. They seem to have particularly stable arrangements of electrons – that is, particularly stable electronic configurations.

There is a rationale for this stability by looking at the way the electrons fill the various shells and subshells. The way this is done is by a 'building-up' process in which, for any given element, you carry out a thought experiment in which

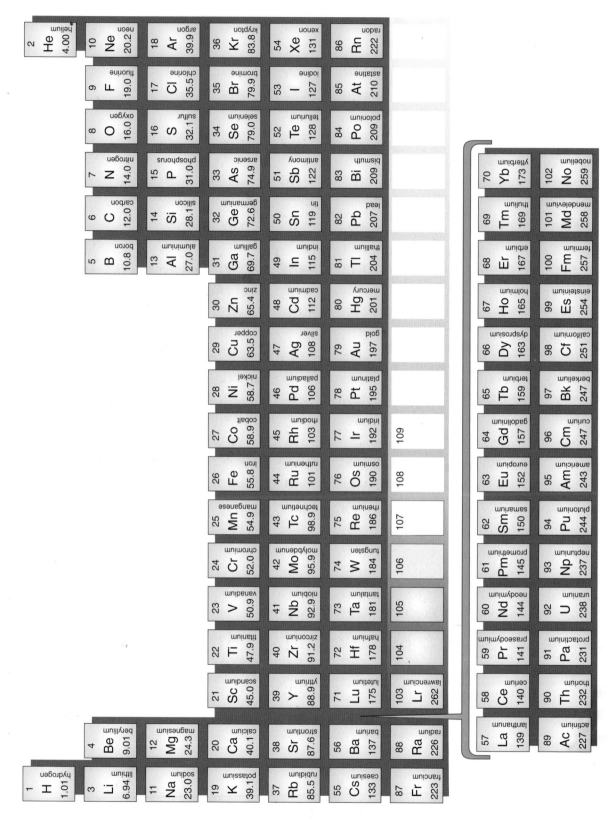

Figure 5.3 The Periodic Table of the elements. There are many variations of the Periodic Table in use. This is probably the clearest and most useful for use in this course. Note that the upper figure in each rectangle is the atomic number of the element and the lower one is the relative atomic mass.

you take the electrons in the atom and use them to fill the electron shells one at a time, beginning with the lowest-energy one first.

■   What information is needed in order to be able to do this?

☐   You need to know the sequence of the various shells and subshells in terms of increasing energy.

The order in which electron shells and subshells are filled is shown in Figure 5.4, which matches the layout of the Periodic Table.

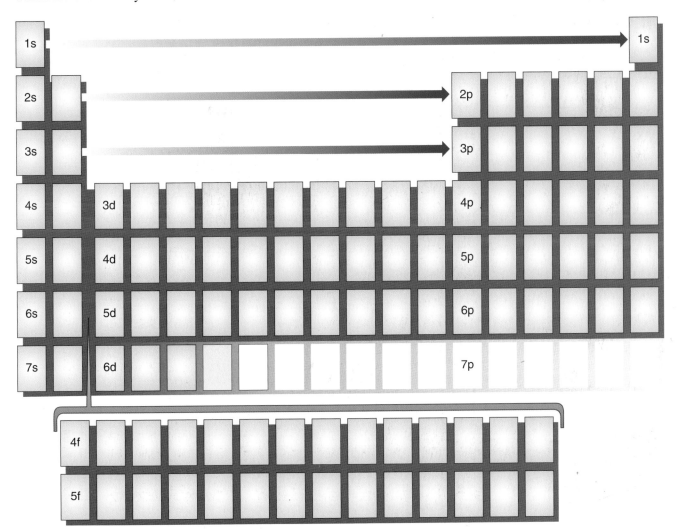

Figure 5.4   The order in which electron subshells are filled in the 'building-up' process. You need not be concerned with why the subshells are filled in this particular order.

The first member of this group is helium, He (atomic number $Z = 2$), with a nucleus containing two protons. There are just two electrons surrounding the nucleus. The first shell ($n = 1$) has only one subshell – an s subshell – which is capable of containing a maximum of two electrons. The electronic configuration of helium is written as $1s^2$, signifying that there are two electrons in the 1s subshell.

The element below helium in the noble gas group is neon, Ne, a gas used in the tubes of 'neon' advertising signs. Neon has an atomic number of 10, and so must have 10 protons in its nucleus and also have 10 electrons surrounding the nucleus. In neon, the first two shells are completely filled. As you have just seen, the first shell can contain just two electrons. The second shell has both s and p subshells, and so can hold a total of 8 (2 + 6) electrons, making a total of 10 for neon. The electronic configuration of neon is $1s^2 2s^2 2p^6$, where $2p^6$ indicates that there are six electrons in the p subshell that has the principal quantum number 2. Six is the maximum number of electrons that can be accommodated in a p subshell.

■ The third noble gas is argon, Ar. Argon has an atomic number of 18. Use Figure 5.4 to arrange the electrons in the argon atom.

☐ Since an atomic number of 18 means that argon has 18 protons in the nucleus, it will have 18 electrons. The first two electrons will go into the 1s subshell; two will go into the 2s subshell and 6 into the 2p subshell; then the remaining 8 electrons will be divided with 2 in the 3s subshell and 6 in the 3p subshell.

So the electronic configuration of argon is $1s^2 2s^2 2p^6 3s^2 3p^6$. This can be written in an abbreviated way as $[Ne]3s^2 3p^6$. The symbol [Ne] is used to indicate that the electronic configuration of argon is that of neon with additional electrons, these being represented by $3s^2 3p^6$. For atoms with high atomic numbers, this is a much shorter way of writing electronic configurations. It is most useful for chemists because generally when elements react, it is the outer electrons that are involved in compound formation. The outermost shell is often called the **valence shell** and the electrons that occupy it are the **valence electrons**.

■ Adopting the same procedure, write the electronic configurations for the noble gases krypton, Kr, and xenon, Xe.

☐ The electronic configurations are $[Ar]4s^2 4p^6$ for krypton and $[Kr]5s^2 5p^6$ for xenon.

■ Is there a pattern in the electronic configurations of these five noble gases?

☐ They all have full s and p subshells in their outer shell.

Given the link between the general lack of reactivity of the noble gases and this feature of their valence shell, it seems that this particular outer electronic configuration confers chemical stability (or lack of reactivity). Each of the noble gases represents the completion of a period, with the next element requiring the beginning of a new electron shell. Adding an additional electron to a noble gas requires considerable energy; similarly, removing an electron also requires considerable energy since the p subshell would then be incomplete.

Both lithium, Li, and sodium, Na, are very reactive elements. Lithium, like sodium, is also very reactive towards water, although not quite to the same extent as sodium. Lithium has an atomic number of 3 and so its nucleus contains three protons; there are therefore three electrons in the lithium atom. In terms of the electron shells, lithium has the first shell completely full and the second shell contains one electron only in the 2s subshell.

- ■ What is the electronic configuration of lithium written in full and using the shorthand notation?

- ☐ In full it is $1s^2 2s^1$; in the abbreviated form it is $[He]2s^1$.

Sodium has an atomic number of 11 and so has 11 protons and 11 electrons in the atom. The first and second shells are therefore completely full with electrons and the third contains a single electron in the 3s subshell; its electronic configuration is $1s^2 2s^2 2p^6 3s^1$ or $[Ne]3s^1$.

- ■ What is the similarity in terms of electronic structure between lithium and sodium?

- ☐ They both have a single electron in the valence shell, in an s subshell.

The chemistry of sodium is dominated by the relative ease with which it can lose an electron. When it loses an electron to form the sodium cation, Na^+, there are ten electrons surrounding the nucleus and the electronic configuration is the same as in neon. (Note that there is no change in the number of protons in the nucleus, so the cation Na^+ is still a sodium ion and not one of any other element.) This electron arrangement represents a particularly stable state. Lithium also loses one electron readily to form the lithium cation, Li^+, and it achieves the electronic configuration of the noble gas helium. So, as a first and very useful approximation, the attainment of an electronic configuration corresponding to one of the noble gases can be considered to be one of the main driving forces for bond formation.

The elements Li, Na, K and the others in the same group have one 'extra' electron over the number required for a noble gas configuration, so they can lose an electron with relative ease. In the dramatic reaction between sodium and chlorine to make common salt (sodium chloride), the sodium atom loses an electron to form the ion Na^+ and the chlorine atom gains an electron to become the chloride ion, Cl^-. Chlorine atoms have a nucleus that contains 17 protons surrounded by 17 electrons. Note that the two ions Na^+ and Cl^- and the atom Ar all have the same electronic configuration. They are said to be **isoelectronic**. Although the number and arrangement of the electrons is the same in the three isoelectronic species, they are different in that they have different nuclei, respectively the nuclei of sodium, chlorine and argon.

- ■ How can 17 electrons be arranged in the first three shells?

- ☐ Filling the first shell with two electrons leaves 15 electrons. The second shell will take eight electrons, so that leaves seven electrons. Of the seven electrons left, two will go into the 3s subshell and five into the 3p subshell.

So chlorine has an electronic configuration of $1s^2 2s^2 2p^6 3s^2 3p^5$ or, in other words, it has one less electron in its third shell than argon, the nearest noble gas. The obvious way to attain the noble gas configuration is for the chlorine atom to pick up an extra electron – which is what it does in the reaction with sodium. So the chloride ion has the same electronic configuration as argon, $1s^2 2s^2 2p^6 3s^2 3p^6$.

■ The potassium ion, K^+, argon, Ar, and the chloride ion, Cl^-, all have the same electronic configuration. Why do the K^+ and Cl^- ions have a charge but the argon atom has not?

☐ Although all three have the same number of electrons (18), the chloride ion has only 17 protons in the nucleus, potassium has 19 in its nucleus, whereas argon has 18.

Question 5.1

Using the abbreviated notation, write down the electronic configuration of nitrogen, N. (You will need to consult the Periodic Table (Figure 5.3) to find out the atomic number in each case, and use Figure 5.4 for the order of the electron subshells.)

Question 5.2

Using the abbreviated notation, write down the electronic configuration of the calcium cation, Ca^{2+}.

5.4 Using the Periodic Table

The Periodic Table certainly provides a convenient means of rationalising the atomic structures of the elements but, if that were all it did, it would be of limited value to the practising scientist. The value of the Periodic Table is that it brings together the multitude of the chemical properties of the elements in a simple and organised manner. The reason for this is that the main influence on how atoms of the elements interact chemically is their electronic structure and specifically the electrons in the valence shell. These electrons, being at the outer limits of the atom, are the electrons that first interact when two atoms come together. It would be impossible to list all the information that is brought together by the Periodic Table, but a few examples may emphasise its value.

The elements of Group 1 all form cations with a single positive charge. They all form white ionic solids with the element chlorine and these compounds have the empirical formula MCl, where M is the Group 1 element. Elements of this group all react with water to give hydrogen gas and the reaction becomes progressively more violent from lithium at the top of the group down to caesium near the bottom. The elements of Group 2 again form cations, but this time with a charge of +2, and form compounds with chlorine of empirical formula MCl_2. The elements in the group headed by carbon all form compounds with chlorine with the formula MCl_4 (tin and lead can also form compounds MCl_2). Hydrogen sulfide has the formula H_2S. Oxygen sits above sulfur in the same group and forms a compound with hydrogen, H_2O, i.e. water. Not surprisingly the formula of the compound of hydrogen with the element below sulfur is H_2Se, hydrogen selenide.

Elements have a tendency to form compounds with other elements in fixed ratios. It is almost as though atoms have a number of 'hooks' that can be used to hook on to other atoms. Of course, there are no hooks and the bonds between atoms are formed from the valence electrons (the outer electrons) of the atoms. Carbon forms many compounds with hydrogen and their formulas are consistent with carbon having four 'hooks'.

■ How many valence electrons does carbon have?

☐ The electronic configuration of the carbon atom is $1s^2 2s^2 2p^2$. So, in the valence shell (in this case corresponding to the principal quantum number 2), there are four electrons. Here the number of valence electrons corresponds directly to the number of hooks, but the link is not always so simple, as we shall see.

The simplest compound of carbon and hydrogen is the gas methane, CH_4: a formula that would be obtained if it were assumed that carbon had four 'hooks' and hydrogen had one. The chlorine atom has one 'hook', so the prediction for the formula of the compound from carbon and chlorine is CCl_4. This tendency for atoms to behave as though they have a specific number of 'hooks' (although it is the effect of interaction of electrons between the two atoms) is known as **valency**. The usual valency values of some elements are shown in Table 5.1. You should note the pattern here and compare it with the layout of the Periodic Table. These ideas are taken up again in Chapters 6 and 8 where the focus is on ions.

Table 5.1 Valency of some more common elements.

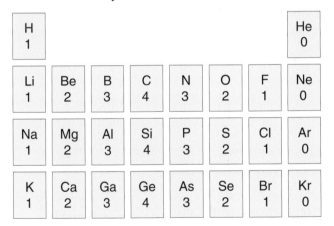

A huge quantity of information can be deduced about the chemistry of the elements from the Periodic Table. The principles that have been sketched out in this chapter are necessarily simplified but they do form the basis for an understanding of the nature of chemical reactivity. In the modern Periodic Table, there are large areas on the left- and right-hand sides where the simple rules described above work very well. In the centre, a modified and more complex set of rules applies to electron transfer and the electronic structures are not quite so simple.

Question 5.3

Aluminium forms a solid compound with the element sulfur. What would you expect the chemical formula for aluminium sulfide to be?

5.5   More on covalent bonding

In Section 3.3, you learned that a covalent bond is formed when two atoms share electrons, and that you can predict how many covalent bonds an atom is likely to form from its valency. However, armed with an understanding of electronic configuration (Section 5.2), you can learn a little more about how and why covalent bonds are formed.

Let's start by looking at chlorine gas, a molecular substance made up of Cl_2 molecules. One way in which a chlorine atom can reach a stable electronic configuration is by picking up an extra electron to form a Cl^- ion. Imagine, for a moment, that one of the two chlorine atoms in the Cl_2 molecule is indeed a Cl^- ion with the electron structure of argon.

■ What charge and electron structure will the other chlorine ion have?

☐ To maintain neutrality, it must be present as Cl^+. This ion does not have a noble gas structure; it has the electron structure of the sulfur atom, the element *preceding* chlorine in the Periodic Table.

5.1

In fact, the two chlorine atoms in Cl_2 both achieve noble gas electronic configuration – not from electron transfer as in ionic compounds, but from *electron sharing*. The key point is that the electrons are shared in *pairs*, and each shared pair constitutes a covalent bond. Thus two chlorine atoms can be represented by structure **5.1**. Here the seven dots on one atom and the seven crosses on the other represent the seven outer electrons of the shell structure. Remember that a chlorine atom has the electronic configuration $1s^2 2s^2 2p^6 3s^2 3p^5$; it has 7 electrons in the outer, $n = 3$, shell. Here we will find it helpful to use a simplified electronic configuration, indicating the number of electrons in each shell. In the case of chlorine the simplified electronic configuration is 2,8,7, meaning that there are 2 electrons in the $n = 1$ shell, 8 electrons in the $n = 2$ shell and 7 electrons in the $n = 3$ shell. The chlorine molecule, Cl_2, is represented in structure **5.2**.

5.2

Structure **5.2** is called a **Lewis structure**, named after the American chemist G.N. Lewis (1875–1946), who first proposed this theory of bonding. By convention, the outer electrons around each atom are grouped in pairs. The pair of electrons that falls between the two chlorines is counted towards the electron structures of both. The electron pair thus shared between the atoms is equivalent to a chemical bond.

■ What electron structure is thereby achieved by the two chlorine atoms in the Cl_2 molecule?

☐ Because the shared electron pair is counted towards the shell structure of both atoms, both atoms gain access to an extra electron. In this sense, each gains one electron and attains the shell structure of argon; that is, they both have eight outer electrons (2,8,8).

Because just *one* pair of electrons is shared in the Lewis structure of Cl_2, the bond is a *single* bond. The Cl_2 molecule can be represented using a **structural formula** in which the single covalent bond is represented by a single line, as in structure **5.3**.

Cl——Cl

5.3

As further examples, consider the molecules NCl_3 and H_2O. Nitrogen has five outer electrons (its abbreviated electronic configuration is 2,5), hydrogen has one (abbreviated electronic configuration 1) and oxygen has six (abbreviated electronic configuration 2,6). Suppose that the outer electrons on the nitrogen and oxygen atoms are represented by crosses, and those on the hydrogen and chlorine atoms by dots. Then each atom attains a noble gas structure in Lewis structures **5.4** and **5.5**.

5.4

In NCl_3, the nitrogen atom gains one electron from each of the three electron pairs that it shares with the three chlorine atoms. It thus achieves the electron structure of neon (2,8). Note that the three shared electron pairs needed to give nitrogen this structure explain why the valency of nitrogen is three. The neon structure is also attained by oxygen in the water molecule. Each hydrogen atom gains one electron from the single electron-pair bond that it forms with the oxygen atom, and attains the electron structure of helium (2).

5.5

■ Now draw a Lewis structure for the methane molecule, CH_4.

□ Carbon has four outer electrons (2,4). It can attain the electron structure of neon (2,8) by gaining four electrons from four electron pairs. Each hydrogen atom again attains the helium structure. The Lewis structure for methane is shown in **5.6**.

5.6

So far, any two atoms in the Lewis structures have been held together by just one electron-pair bond. But sometimes two or even three shared pairs may be involved. The Lewis structures and structural formulas for CO_2 and N_2 are shown in Figure 5.5.

The *two* electron *pairs* between each oxygen atom and the central carbon atom are an interpretation of each carbon–oxygen *double* bond. As the examples of CO_2 and CH_4 show, carbon has a valency of four because, when it exercises that valency, it attains the electron structure of neon. Likewise, the *three* shared *pairs* in the N_2 molecule are equivalent to a *triple* bond.

These Lewis structures tell us why hydrogen, carbon, nitrogen, oxygen and chlorine have the valencies they have. When atoms are forming covalent bonds, the valency is the number of shared electron-pair bonds that the atom must form if it is to attain the electron structure of a noble gas. Thus hydrogen and oxygen form water, H_2O, rather than HO or HO_2, because this molecular formula enables both elements to attain the electron structure of a noble gas.

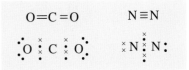

Figure 5.5 Lewis structures (bottom) and structural formulas (top) for CO_2 and N_2. All atoms have eight outer electrons.

Question 5.4

Oxygen gas and sulfur dichloride contain the molecules O_2 and SCl_2, respectively. Draw a Lewis structure for each molecule. Which noble gas structure is achieved by each atom in the molecules?

Write down the structural formula and a Lewis structure for the gases ammonia (NH_3) and fluorine (F_2).

5.6   Summary of Chapter 5

The Periodic Table organises the elements on the basis of electronic configuration. Electrons orbit the nucleus in electron shells which are identified by a principal quantum number ($n = 1, 2, 3, \ldots$). Each shell can have subshells which can accommodate a fixed number of electrons (s shell 2, p shell 6, d shell 10, $\ldots$).

Elements with similar valence shell electronic configurations are gathered into the same group of the Periodic Table. They tend to have similar chemical properties because their chemistry is dominated by the outer electrons of the atom. Properties of compounds of the elements of a single group, although similar, tend to change progressively from the top to the bottom of the group. Along the periods, there is a change in the chemical properties of the elements. An indication of this can be seen in the formulas of simple compounds reflecting the valency of the elements.

The common valencies that the non-metallic elements show in molecular substances are equal to the number of covalent bonds they form when they attain noble gas electron structures. Each shared electron pair constitutes a covalent bond. Each double bond, as in CO_2, requires two shared pairs; a triple bond, as in N_2, requires three.

Chapter 6
Chemical formulas and equations

Chemical formulas and equations are part of the language of chemistry but can appear rather complex. A little effort in coming to terms with these representations can open the door to so much. The word 'formula' has a Latin origin meaning 'form' or 'shape'. The plural is formulae if you adhere to the Latin, and this is much used in scientific writing. However, this book uses the form that is becoming increasingly common: formulas.

6.1 Chemical formulas

A number of chemical formulas have already appeared in this book. It is worthwhile just to recap on key features of the representation of chemical compounds by the chemical formulas. The water molecule comprises two hydrogen atoms attached to an oxygen atom. The formula is written as H_2O. The atoms of the molecule are represented by their chemical symbols: H for hydrogen and O for oxygen. The subscript 2 indicates that there are two hydrogen atoms in the formula. A subscript applies to whatever element comes immediately before the subscript. Where there is no subscript shown there is assumed to be a subscript 1. So in the formula H_2O for water, two hydrogen atoms and one oxygen atom are represented.

A more complex formula is that of barium nitrate, $Ba(NO_3)_2$. The chemical symbol for the element barium is Ba. (Note that some elements have an upper-case letter as their chemical symbol and others have an upper-case letter followed by a lower-case letter.) There is no subscript following Ba, so the assumption is that there is just one barium atom represented in the formula. The unit $(NO_3)_2$ needs a little unravelling. The subscript 2 again indicates that there is two of everything that comes before it. However, in this case there are brackets before the 2 so there are two lots of the contents of the brackets. Within the brackets there is an NO_3 unit. The symbol for the element oxygen O appears immediately before the subscript so there are three oxygen atoms and one nitrogen atom N (no written subscript so assumed to be 1) in the NO_3 unit. There are two of these units (remember the brackets followed by the subscript 2). So the formula represents one barium atom, two nitrogen atoms and six oxygen atoms. The reason for writing $Ba(NO_3)_2$ rather than BaN_2O_6 is that, in the compound barium chloride, each of the two nitrogen atoms is attached to three oxygen atoms. Thus the chemical formula can convey some structural information too. This is explored further in Chapters 12–16 where compounds of carbon take centre stage.

Activity 6.1   Using valency to predict chemical formulas in ionic compounds

We expect this activity will take you approximately 30 minutes.

In this activity you will use your knowledge of valency to predict the chemical formulas of some ionic compounds.

The valency of an atom can be described as the number of 'hooks' each atom has. In covalent compounds, the valency gives an indication of the number of covalent bonds an atom will form. (Covalent bonding was discussed in Sections 3.3 and 5.5.) In ionic compounds, it gives an indication of the charge an ion formed from a particular element will carry. For example, magnesium, Mg, has a valency of two and tends to form ions carrying two positive charges, Mg^{2+}. Note that the valency does not tell us whether an ion will carry a positive or negative charge: oxygen, O, also has a valency of two, and forms negative ions, O^{2-}. You can predict whether an atom will form negative or positive ions from its position in the Periodic Table: elements to the left (metals) will tend to form positive ions; those on the right (non-metals) will tend to form negative ions.

When oppositely charged ions combine to form compounds, there must be the same number of positive and negative charges, so that the compound carries no overall charge. Thus, when Mg^{2+} and O^{2-} combine to form the ionic compound magnesium oxide, there have to be equal numbers of magnesium cations and oxide anions. Magnesium oxide has the formula MgO. (Note that charges do not appear in the chemical formulas of compounds: you don't write $Mg^{2+}O^{2-}$.)

Similarly, when magnesium cations, Mg^{2+}, combine with chloride anions, Cl^-, there must be twice as many chloride anions as magnesium cations in order for the charges to balance each other. The chemical formula of magnesium chloride is $MgCl_2$.

Task 1

Using Table 5.1, predict the ions that will be formed from the following atoms: K, Ca, Al, S, F and Br.

Task 2

Give the formulas of the compounds that will be formed when the following pairs of elements combine to form ionic compounds:

(a) potassium and fluorine

(b) calcium and bromine

(c) potassium and oxygen

(d) aluminium and bromine

(e) aluminium and oxygen.

Task 3

Table 6.1 Some common ionic groups.

Charge	Name and formula
+1	ammonium, NH_4^+
−1	hydroxide, OH^- nitrate, NO_3^-
−2	sulfate, SO_4^{2-} carbonate, CO_3^{2-}

A number of covalent molecules also carry charges and are found in ionic compounds. These are often referred to as ionic groups. You have met the nitrate group (NO_3^-), a molecule carrying a single negative charge, consisting of three oxygen atoms covalently bound to a nitrogen atom. Table 6.1 gives the formulas and charges on some other ionic groups.

Give the formulas of the ionic compounds that comprise the following pairs of ions:

(a) potassium and hydroxide

(b) potassium and sulfate

(c) calcium and nitrate

(d) ammonium and fluoride

(e) ammonium and sulfate.

Now look at the comments on this activity at the end of this book.

6.2   Chemical equations

A chemical equation can at first sight appear to be unintelligible, something apparently written in a foreign language. In many ways, that is just what the problem is. The chemical equation is written in a different language from that used for everyday communication. Symbols are used to represent the nature and numbers of atoms in formulas. This is done in chemical equations too but the symbolic language is carried further. The chemical equation is a shorthand way of presenting lots of information.

Chemical equations are representations of chemical reactions, processes in which chemical substances are transformed into new chemical substances. The substances that are present at the beginning are known as the **reactants** and those that are produced in the reaction are the **products**.

Natural gas is almost pure methane whose molecules are made up of carbon and hydrogen atoms. Methane burns in (reacts with) oxygen in the air with the evolution of heat to yield the molecules carbon dioxide and water. In writing a chemical equation to represent this process, the first step is to put down what is present at the beginning of the reaction and what is there at the end. The reactants (starting materials) are written on the left and the products (final materials) on the right to give, initially, a word 'equation':

methane *and* oxygen *go to* carbon dioxide *and* water

Even the simple word equation carries much useful information in a relatively concise form but you can go further. You know that a formula tells us much more about a particular substance than does a name. The molecular formula of methane is CH_4 and this immediately indicates that the methane molecule comprises one carbon atom and four hydrogen atoms.

The next step is to replace the names of the compounds in the equation with appropriate formulas. The formula of carbon dioxide is CO_2.

CH_4 *and* O_2 *go to* CO_2 *and* H_2O

The word *and* can be replaced by the plus sign, +, and the reaction representation becomes:

$CH_4 + O_2$ *go to* $CO_2 + H_2O$

Even at this early stage of development of the equation, there is useful information being represented. Hydrogen atoms of the methane molecules in the reaction end up as part of the product water molecules and the carbon atoms end up as part of the product carbon dioxide molecules. It is important to note that the relationship provides information about the overall reaction. It does not say anything about how the reaction actually occurs, such as the way in which bonds are broken and formed to give the final products.

With the formulas in place, can you see a problem with the equation? On the left, there is one molecule of methane with four hydrogen atoms. Hydrogen appears on the right of the equation in the water molecule but the one water molecule contains just two hydrogen atoms. There are different numbers of oxygen atoms on each side: two on the left and three on the right. In going from the left to the right, there is a change in the numbers of atoms. In chemical reactions, atoms are neither created nor destroyed. There must always be the same number of atoms of each type in the products and in the reactants.

This information must be represented in the equation. The relative number of each of the formula units that is required is written immediately in front of that formula in the equation:

$$CH_4 + 2O_2 \; \textit{go to} \; CO_2 + 2H_2O$$

To represent two water molecules, the number 2 is placed immediately before the formula for water. This number indicates there is two of everything that comes after the number. So above there are two water molecules, i.e. two H_2O units. Where a number is not shown (such as in front of CH_4), you should assume (as with formulas) that a number 1 is implied.

Now a final check on the numbers of atoms: on the left side of the representation, there are 4 hydrogen atoms, 4 oxygen atoms and 1 carbon atom; on the right side, there are 4 hydrogen atoms, 4 oxygen atoms and 1 carbon atom. There is a balance in the numbers of atoms of each type on each side. The words 'go to' can be replaced with an equals sign to give:

$$CH_4 + 2O_2 = CO_2 + 2H_2O$$

The equals sign has a specific meaning in a chemical equation. It indicates that the representation is an equation with the same numbers of atoms of each element on each side. That is, it is a **balanced chemical equation**. This is why the words *go to* were retained earlier because, at that stage, the reaction representation was not balanced. Chemical equations are just a shorthand way of representing information about a chemical reaction. They are favoured because they save lots of words and, with a little practice, you will be able to 'read' an equation just as easily as you can read prose.

Note that you cannot balance equations by changing chemical formulas. For example, methane molecules always contain one carbon atom and four hydrogen atoms, CH_4. It is only the relative numbers of formula units in the equation that are changed in the balancing process.

An additional piece of information that is often included in chemical equations is an indication of the physical states of the species. Gas is represented by (g) coming immediately after the species, (l) represents liquid and (s) solid. At 25 °C, methane, oxygen and carbon dioxide are gases and water is a liquid.

$$CH_4(g) + 2O_2(g) = CO_2(g) + 2H_2O(l) \tag{6.1}$$

The skills of writing balanced chemical equations can be developed with practice. In this course, you are expected only to be able to balance relatively simple equations such as the one for the reaction of methane with oxygen. However, you do need to be able to decide whether an equation is balanced or not.

Many substances react with oxygen and one that is important biologically is the reaction of the simple sugar glucose with oxygen. Basically, this is a reaction that is core to the generation of energy within the body. Glucose has a complicated molecular structure but it can be represented by the formula $C_6H_{12}O_6$.

The chemical equation for the reaction between glucose and oxygen to give carbon dioxide and water is:

$$C_6H_{12}O_6(s) + 6O_2(g) = 6CO_2(g) + 6H_2O(l) \tag{6.2}$$

Even though this equation looks complicated, you should be able to check that it is balanced. On the left, there are 6 carbon atoms, 12 hydrogen atoms and 6 oxygen atoms from glucose and a further 12 oxygen atoms from oxygen molecules, a total of 6C, 12H and 18O. On the right, there are 6 carbon and 12 oxygen atoms from carbon dioxide plus 12 hydrogen atoms and 6 oxygen atoms from water, a total of 6C, 12H and 18O. This is a balanced chemical equation.

The balanced equation embodies a lot of information. It not only identifies the reactants and products and their respective formulas but also indicates the relative numbers of each reactant molecule and the relative numbers of each product molecule. It also shows, in the example above, that carbon from the glucose molecules ends up in carbon dioxide molecules, the hydrogen produces water and the oxygen in the product molecules comes both from the glucose molecules and from molecular oxygen. The physical states of the reactants and the products are also represented.

Many reactions involve charged species – ions. The rules for balancing equations representing reactions involving ions are exactly the same as they are for the reactions of neutral species. When the gas sulfur trioxide, SO_3, dissolves in water, hydrogen ions, H^+ (hydrogen atoms that have lost an electron) and the sulfate anions, SO_4^{2-}, are produced. The sulfate anion comprises four oxygen atoms covalently bonded to a sulfur atom and the whole unit has two negative charges from two additional electrons represented by the superscript $^{2-}$.

The balanced chemical equation for the reaction is:

$$SO_3(aq) + H_2O(l) = 2H^+(aq) + SO_4^{2-}(aq) \tag{6.3}$$

(Note that the symbol (aq) – for aqueous – is used to indicate species that are dissolved in water.) There are equal numbers of atoms of each type on either side of the equation: 1 sulfur, 4 oxygen and 2 hydrogen atoms. For **ionic equations** such as this, there is one more test that must be applied to ensure satisfactory balancing; that is, the total charge on each side of the equation must be the same. In this instance, there are only uncharged species on the left. On the right, there are two hydrogen ions each with a single positive charge and a sulfate anion with a double negative charge. The total charge on the right is $2 - 2 = 0$. The total charge on each side is zero. It is not necessary for the total charge on each side of an ionic equation to be zero; it is just that it must be the *same* on each side.

Question 6.1

Write balanced equations for the reactions represented in (a)–(d).

(a) $FeO + H_2$ *go to* $Fe + H_2O$

(b) $Fe_2O_3 + H_2$ *go to* $Fe + H_2O$

(c) $N_2 + H_2$ *go to* NH_3

(d) $CH_4 + Cl_2$ *go to* $CH_2Cl_2 + HCl$

Question 6.2

Indicate which of (a)–(c) represent balanced chemical equations.

(a) $Ag^+ + Cl^-$ *go to* $AgCl$

(b) $BrO_3^- + Br^- + 6H^+$ *go to* $Br_2 + 3H_2O$

(c) $2Ag^+ + Sn$ *go to* $2Ag + Sn^{2+}$

6.3   Using chemical equations to calculate quantities

The concept of the mole gives an alternative interpretation to chemical equations.

$$CH_4(g) + 2O_2(g) = CO_2(g) + 2H_2O(l) \tag{6.1}$$

This equation represents an overview of a chemical change in which molecules of methane and oxygen are converted to molecules of carbon dioxide and water. This is the molecular interpretation of the equation. The equation can also represent a process in which one mole of methane molecules and two moles of oxygen molecules react together to form one mole of carbon dioxide and two moles of water. This is a molar interpretation of the equation.

Using the mole, it is possible to calculate quantities of reactants and products from a chemical equation. Methane is the major component of natural gas. The average house in the UK burns about 1000 kg of methane each year. How much carbon dioxide enters the atmosphere from this source?

It is essential to ensure that the equation is balanced. In calculating quantities of reactants and products, the molar interpretation of the equation is the one to use.

The chemical equation indicates that one mole of methane molecules is converted into one mole of carbon dioxide molecules.

The first step is to calculate the relative molecular mass of methane and carbon dioxide. If there are substances present that are not molecular, the method is still valid. However, rather than the relative molecular mass, the term **relative formula mass** is used. For the ionic compound sodium chloride, NaCl, the relative formula mass is $(23.0 + 35.5) = 58.5$.

The relative molecular mass of methane is 16.0 (i.e. $12.0 + (4 \times 1.01)$) and that of carbon dioxide is 44.0 (i.e. $12.0 + (2 \times 16.0)$). So the mass of one mole of methane molecules is 16.0 g and the mass of one mole of carbon dioxide molecules is 44.0 g.

> One mole CH_4 is converted to one mole CO_2
>
> So 16.0 g CH_4 are converted to 44.0 g CO_2
>
> 1.00 g CH_4 is converted to $\dfrac{44.0}{16.0}$ g CO_2
>
> 1.00 kg CH_4 is converted to $\dfrac{44.0}{16.0}$ kg CO_2
>
> 1000 kg CH_4 is converted to $1000 \times \dfrac{44.0}{16.0}$ kg $CO_2 = 2.75 \times 10^3$ kg

So, on average, each house adds 2750 kg or 2.75 tonnes of carbon dioxide to the atmosphere each year.

Activity 6.2   Practising calculations using the mole

We expect this activity will take you approximately 45 minutes.

The concept of the mole is very important in chemistry, and it is important that you are confident to undertake simple calculations using moles. This activity allows you to have a go at a number of calculations. You will need to refer to the Periodic Table (Figure 5.3). The activity has two parts.

Part 1: From mass to moles and back again

It was stated in Section 4.8.2 that the mass of one mole of a substance is the relative mass of that substance expressed in grams. This is true whether you are talking about relative atomic masses for elements, relative molecular masses for covalent compounds, or relative formula masses for ionic compounds. The mass of one mole of a substance is called the **molar mass**; it has units of grams per mole ($g\ mol^{-1}$). The difference between a molar mass and the relative mass is that a molar mass has units, while the relative mass does not. The actual number is the same. Thus helium has a relative atomic mass of 4 (no units), meaning that a helium atom is, relatively speaking, 4 times heavier than a hydrogen atom. Helium has a molar mass of $4\ g\ mol^{-1}$, meaning that each mole of helium atoms has a mass of 4 g.

The definition of molar mass leads to two simple mathematical equations which help in performing calculations involving moles (they are in fact two forms of the same equation):

$$\text{mass of a substance} = (\text{number of moles of substance}) \times (\text{molar mass of substance}) \quad (6.4)$$

$$\text{number of moles of a substance} = \frac{\text{mass of substance}}{\text{molar mass of substance}} \quad (6.5)$$

If you were asked to find the number of moles of water in 100 g, this is one way you might go about it.

Step 1

Choose which form of the equation you need to use. As you want to find the number of moles, you should use the equation:

$$\text{number of moles of water} = \frac{\text{mass of water}}{\text{molar mass of water}} \quad (6.5)$$

Step 2

In order to use this equation, you need to find the molar mass of water (H_2O). This is simply the relative molecular mass expressed in $g\ mol^{-1}$:

$$RMM\ (H_2O) = [2 \times RAM\ (H)] + RAM\ (O)$$
$$= (2 \times 1.01) + 16.0$$
$$= 18.02$$

Molar mass of $H_2O = 18.0\ g\ mol^{-1}$

Step 3

Put the numbers and units in the equation:

$$\text{number of moles of water} = \frac{100 \text{ g}}{18.0 \text{ g mol}^{-1}}$$

$$= 5.56 \text{ mol}$$

A note on units: you may recall from Book 3 (Activity 4.2) the importance of using the correct units in your answers. Can you see how you ended up with the unit mol in the above calculation? The units can be found using the following sequence:

$$\frac{\text{g}}{\text{g mol}^{-1}} = \frac{1}{\text{mol}^{-1}} = \text{mol}$$

Now have a go at the following calculations. You will need to refer to the relative atomic masses given in Figure 5.3.

Task 1

How many moles are there in the following masses of substances?

(a) 10.0 g of He

(b) 54.0 g of H_2O

(c) 85.5 g of NaCl

(d) 0.769 g of CaF_2

(e) 26.5 g of H_2SO_4

Task 2

What are the masses of the following substances?

(a) 0.350 mol of Ar

(b) 6.90 mol of KF

(c) 1.55 mol of Na_2O

(d) 0.320 mol of SnI_4

(e) 0.140 mol of $C_6H_{12}O_6$ (glucose)

Part 2: Moles and chemical equations

You have seen that using the concept of the mole in conjunction with balanced chemical equations allows the masses of reactants and products to be calculated. You looked at the amount of carbon dioxide emitted as a result of burning methane. Here you will look at the calculations involved in designing a mission to send people into space.

People breathing in a confined space gradually increase the carbon dioxide concentration in the air around them. If this rises from its normal level of 0.038% by volume to above 6%, headaches and dizziness ensue. In spacecraft and spacesuits, this problem is tackled with chemicals that absorb carbon dioxide. One possibility is caustic soda or sodium hydroxide. This has the formula NaOH. However, the metal lithium also forms such a hydroxide with the very similar formula LiOH. Both of these solids absorb carbon dioxide, producing sodium carbonate, Na_2CO_3, and lithium carbonate, Li_2CO_3, respectively. The balanced chemical equations are:

$$CO_2(g) + 2NaOH(s) = Na_2CO_3(s) + H_2O(l) \tag{6.6}$$

$$CO_2(g) + 2LiOH(s) = Li_2CO_3(s) + H_2O(l) \tag{6.7}$$

In both these equations, one formula unit of CO_2 reacts with two of the metal hydroxide. So one mole of CO_2 reacts with two moles of the metal hydroxide.

Task 1

What mass of (a) NaOH and (b) LiOH is needed to absorb one mole of carbon dioxide? Which of the two metal hydroxides do you think the US space program uses?

Task 2

It is estimated that each crew member will exhale 1.0 kg of CO_2 per day. On that basis, if you were planning a 10-day mission with three crew members, what is the minimum mass of the metal hydroxide that would have to be provided?

Now look at the comments on this activity at the end of this book.

6.4   Working with solutions: concentration

Many of the reactions studied by chemists take place in solution (Section 4.6). The chemicals involved are dissolved in a liquid which is referred to as the solvent. The most common solvent is water, but in the laboratory a chemist may choose to work with any one of a number of different solvents.

It is important to begin to appreciate the properties of solutions and, in particular, how to measure the quantities of substances dissolved in solvents.

A given substance may dissolve more easily or less easily in a given solvent, and the **solubility** of a substance is defined as the maximum amount of **solute** (a substance that is dissolved in solution) that will dissolve in a given amount of solvent. For example, when common salt (sodium chloride, the solute) is dissolved in water (the solvent) this gives a solution of sodium chloride. The solubility of a substance varies with temperature and is usually expressed as the maximum amount of a substance that will dissolve in 100 g of water at a particular temperature. However, it is often more usual (and more useful) to express the amount of solute that is dissolved in a *specific volume of solution* at a particular temperature. This is known as the **concentration** of a solution, which is expressed as the amount of solute in 1 dm^3. Thus, if 10.0 g of sodium chloride is dissolved in water to give 1 dm^3 of solution, the concentration would be 10.0 g per dm^3 and so we would write 10.0 g dm^{-3}.

It is essential to define concentration as the amount of solute in exactly 1 dm^3, that is in 1 dm^3 of the final solution rather than the amount of solute dissolved in 1 dm^3 of water. If we did dissolve 10.0 g of sodium chloride in 1 dm^3 of water then the final volume would in effect be greater than 1 dm^3. Therefore to make up a solution with a particular concentration of a solute, the required amount of solute is firstly dissolved fully in a suitable amount of water (less than 1 dm^3) and then sufficient water is added to achieve the correct final volume of 1 dm^3.

However, it is often more practical in the case of concentrations of solutions to express them as the number of *moles* of solute that is dissolved in a specific volume (1 dm^3) at a given temperature. Thus, if we have 10.0 g of sodium chloride dissolved in 1.00 dm^3 of water, we can calculate the concentration of that solution in moles per dm^3 (mol dm^{-3}).

First, we need to calculate the molar mass of sodium chloride (NaCl). The relative atomic masses of Na and Cl are 23.0 and 35.5, respectively, so:

relative mass of 1 mole of NaCl = (23.0 + 35.5) g = 58.5 g

Thus the molar mass of NaCl is 58.5 g mol^{-1}.

Second, we calculate the number of moles of NaCl, using Equation 6.5. How many moles are there in 10.0 g of NaCl?

$$\text{number of moles of NaCl} = \frac{\text{mass of NaCl}}{\text{molar mass of NaCl}}$$

$$= \frac{10.0}{58.5} = 0.171 \text{ mol}$$

Therefore, 0.171 mol of NaCl is dissolved in 1.00 dm^3 of water, so the concentration of the solution is 0.171 mol dm^{-3}.

When sodium chloride dissolves in water, the resulting solution will contain equal numbers of sodium and chloride ions:

$$NaCl(s) = Na^+(aq) + Cl^-(aq) \tag{6.8}$$

Thus, if 1.0 mole of sodium chloride is dissolved in water to form 1 dm^3, giving a 1 mol dm^{-3} solution, the solution will contain 1.0 mol dm^{-3} of Na$^+$(aq) ions and 1.0 mol dm^{-3} Cl$^-$(aq) ions. However, if we dissolve calcium chloride in water:

$$CaCl_2(s) = Ca^{2+}(aq) + 2Cl^-(aq) \tag{6.9}$$

The resulting solution has two chloride ions for every calcium ion. So if we have a 1 mol dm^{-3} solution of calcium chloride, this time we have a concentration of 1 mol dm^{-3} of Ca^{2+}(aq) ions and 2 mol dm^{-3} of Cl$^-$(aq) ions. In this example, we multiply the concentration by 2 for the chloride ions as we have twice as many.

Question 6.3

(a) 20.0 g of sodium chloride (NaCl) is dissolved in water to give 1.00 dm^3 of solution. What is the concentration of Na$^+$(aq) in mol dm^{-3}?

(b) 30.0 g of calcium chloride (CaCl$_2$) is dissolved in water to give 1.00 dm^3 of solution. What is the concentration of Cl$^-$(aq) ions in mol dm^{-3}?

(c) 25.0 g of glucose (C$_6$H$_{12}$O$_6$) is dissolved in water to give 0.5 dm^3 of solution. What is the concentration of glucose in mol dm^{-3}?

6.5   Summary of Chapter 6

The focus of this chapter is on the representation of chemical compounds using formulas, the representation of chemical reactions using chemical equations and the calculation of quantities of reactants and products from chemical equations.

In chemical formulas, elements are represented by their chemical symbols. A subscript applies to the element appearing immediately before the subscript. If there are brackets before the subscript, the subscript applies to the whole contents of the brackets.

Chemical equations must balance if the two sides are linked by an 'equals' sign; there must be equal total numbers of atoms of each type on each side of the equation. To balance an equation, you cannot change the formulas of the species in the equation as these represent the particular chemical constitution of the species. However, the relative numbers of the formula units can be adjusted by placing a number immediately before the formula. This number then applies to everything that follows it, i.e. the whole of the formula unit. The physical states of the reactants and products are sometimes indicated in the chemical equation by the letters s, l, g or aq.

To calculate quantities of reactants and products, it is essential to start with a balanced chemical equation that is viewed from a molar rather than a molecular perspective. The relative molecular mass values for the substances involved must be calculated and, from this information, the masses of the substances involved in the reaction can be determined.

Concentration is a measure of the amount of solute dissolved in a solution and is measured in mol dm^{-3}.

After studying this chapter, you should be more confident about interpreting chemical equations and formulas. You have also developed your mathematical skills in a chemical context.

Chapter 7
Metals

The materials that have probably been the most influential in shaping society over the past two to three millennia are the metals. Go back to Figures 1.6–1.9 and note the way in which metals are being used in these pictures.

There is archaeological evidence in the UK of simple gold jewellery dating back beyond 4500 years ago. Bronze brought about many changes to society, but it was the development of iron technology that has had a continuing influence. The painting of 16th century Flanders (Figure 1.7) shows a range of roles for metals such as tools, horseshoes, and wagon wheel rims and nails for carpentry. There is a dramatic increase in the use of metals over the 3000-year timespan represented by the pictures, certainly through to Victorian times (Figure 1.8). Here, metals seem to be very much part of the fabric of life and, without metals (and supplies of energy), it is unlikely that the Industrial Revolution could ever have taken place. However, in the early 21st century, other materials are being used to replace metals (Figure 1.9).

You probably looked for uses of metals in these pictures without asking yourself just what is a metal. We all have an idea as to what is metallic and what is not, but this chapter pursues the distinction a little further.

7.1   What is a metal?

The fact that you have been able to identify some metals in the pictures suggests that you associate certain properties with metals. You would have little hesitation in distinguishing, say, the blade of a metal kitchen knife from the handle (which would probably be plastic or wood). What are these criteria and are there others that distinguish metals from other materials?

Scientists have tended to formalise metallic characteristics (as distinct from non-metals) by suggesting that metals are dense, lustrous (shiny), malleable (shaped by physical force) and good conductors of heat and electricity. There are also chemical criteria that help distinguish metals from non-metals.

Metals such as bronze, brass, pewter or stainless steel are not pure elements but alloys, blends of one metallic element with one or more others. Table 7.1 includes data for a range of metals (and the non-metallic element sulfur for comparison).

Table 7.1 Typical data for some common metallic elements and the non-metal, sulfur, at 25 °C.

Element	Chemical symbol	Proportion in Earth's continental crust by mass/%	Cost/ $ kg^{-1} (2006 estimate)	Annual world production/ 10^3 tonnes (2006 estimate)	Melting temperature/ °C	Density/ 10^3 kg m^{-3}	Heat conduction (1, best; 11, worst)	Electrical conduction (1, best; 11, worst)
aluminium	Al	8.2	2.64	33 100	660	2.70	4	4
chromium	Cr	0.012	7.73	20 000	1857	7.19	7	9
copper	Cu	0.0068	6.81	15 300	1083	8.96	2	2
gold	Au	0.000 000 4	19 300	2.5	1064	19.3	3	3
iron	Fe	5.6	0.05	1 700 000	1535	7.87	8	7
lead	Pb	0.0013	1.26	3360	328	11.4	10	10
magnesium	Mg	2.3	2.54	650	649	1.74	5	5
silver	Ag	0.000 008	360	19.5	962	10.5	1	1
sulfur	S	0.034	0.03	66 000	113	1.96	11	11
tin	Sn	0.000 21	7.98	273	232	7.31	9	8
zinc	Zn	0.0076	3.09	10 700	420	7.13	6	6

Cost and annual production from US Geological Survey (2007).

Activity 7.1   Exploring the properties of metals

We expect this activity will take you approximately 30 minutes.

This activity will allow you to explore the link between the properties and the uses of metals.

Use the data in Table 7.1 to arrange the metals and sulfur in a rank order for each property. Do this in Table 7.2 by inserting the symbols for these elements in the rows, ranked high to low from left to right for each property (the first row has been completed for you). Use the data in your table to answer the following questions.

(a) Which three metals are the best conductors of electricity? Why is just one of these three metals used much more than the other two?

(b) Why is aluminium used extensively in the construction of civil aeroplanes?

(c) Cans for food are made of steel (iron containing a small quantity of carbon) with a thin coating of tin. How could a thin and even coating of tin be put on an iron can?

(d) What connection is there between the abundance of a metal in the Earth's crust and its cost?

Table 7.2 Comparison of properties of some metals and the non-metal, sulfur.

Property	High										Low
	Al	Fe	Mg	S	Cr	Zn	Cu	Pb	Sn	Ag	Au
abundance in Earth's crust											
cost											
annual world production											
melting temperature											
density											
heat conduction											
electrical conduction											

Now look at the comments on this activity at the end of this book.

The non-metal, sulfur, is the poorest electrical and heat (thermal) conductor of the elements in Table 7.1 by some distance. For example, sulfur conducts electricity about 10^{22} times less effectively than even the worst metallic conductor in Table 7.1, lead. Sulfur is such a poor conductor that it is not regarded as a conductor at all. It is an effective insulator, being as good as the plastic insulation that surrounds electrical cables in the home. The metals are generally good conductors of both heat and electricity. A factor of only about 13 separates the best (silver) and worst (lead) electrical conductors.

7.2   Gold and silver

Most of the metallic objects recovered from archaeological sites are fashioned from either silver or gold and these were the first metals to be used by humans. Examples of gold ornamentation from Britain and ancient Egypt are shown in Figures 7.1 and 7.2. Gold has remained bright, shiny and lustrous whether it has

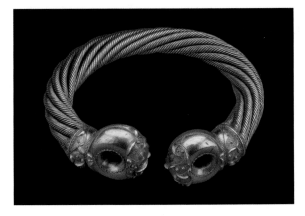

Figure 7.1   Iron Age torc (neck ring) made from an alloy of gold, silver and copper.

Figure 7.2   Gilded Egyptian mummy mask of Satdjehuty.

71

Figure 7.3 The Golden Buddha at Wat Traimit, Bangkok, Thailand. The solid gold statue, which is thought to date back to the 13th century, is 3.1 m tall and has a mass of 5500 kg.

spent thousands of years in the dry atmosphere of an Egyptian tomb or in the cool damp of an early British burial site.

One obvious reason why gold was used is that it is a highly attractive metal that does not tarnish. It is ideal for jewellery and has the lure of exclusiveness. It is one of the rarer metals of the Earth's crust. Gold was highly prized and could be used by powerful people as an indicator of social position. Gold also has a special place in religious ornamentation as evidenced by the Golden Buddha in Figure 7.3.

Silver is another metallic element that stands the test of time in that it does not significantly corrode although the surface can blacken with time. However, the main reasons why gold and silver were used in ornamentation by early civilisations, apart from the attractive appearance of the metals, is that these metals (and occasionally copper) can be found as pure elements in nature. Gold is sometimes found in veins of calcite and other minerals or in rivers where the flow of the water has washed away the rock (Figure 7.4). Only rarely is it found as the classic nugget (Figure 2.4) and much of the gold from the gold rush days of California and the Klondike was panned from river silt.

Figure 7.4 Gold embedded in the mineral calcite.

Figure 7.5 Panning for gold in the American West of the 19th century.

Small particles of the metal are separated from mud and rock by washing repeatedly with water (Figure 7.5). Eventually, the unwanted material is washed away and (with luck) a few glistening particles remain in the pan.

■ Look at Table 7.1. What property of gold makes this method of separation possible?

☐ Of all the metals in Table 7.1, gold has the highest density at 19 300 kg m^{-3}. By comparison, the density of rock is in the range 1500–3500 kg m^{-3}, so when the mixture of rock and gold particles is agitated in water, gold tends to settle more rapidly.

Today, the process of extracting gold is much more difficult. The proportion of gold is so low in many goldfields that it cannot be extracted by simple physical separation and chemical methods have to be used.

■ From what you know about gold and silver, what can you infer about their chemical reactivity compared with iron?

☐ Iron, unless it is protected by paint, oil or other covering, rusts away. Gold and silver do not. Iron is rather more reactive than silver or gold.

Gold and silver are very unreactive with respect to air and water. The other metals in Table 7.1 will react with air and water and are not generally found in nature as the metallic elements. Iron usually occurs combined with oxygen (iron oxide) and sometimes with sulfur (iron sulfide). The production of elemental iron from iron oxide represents one of the major chemical process industries.

7.3 An atomic model for metals

Metal atoms pack closely together in a similar way to bubbles on a liquid surface (Figure 7.6). Note how most of the bubbles are in contact with six neighbouring bubbles.

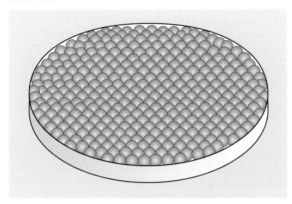

Figure 7.6 Bubbles packed together on a liquid surface. Note that there are very small irregularities in the arrangement. Similar flaws in the structure of metals represent weakness areas and are sometimes responsible for the appearance of cracks.

But metals are three-dimensional. The layer of atoms represented by the bubbles would be covered by other layers and have layers underneath in a solid metal. This three-dimensional structure can be seen in the way fruit is sometimes stacked on market stalls (Figure 7.7).

Each metal atom in the three-dimensional structure is in contact with 12 others: six in its own layer, three in the layer above and three in the layer below. Many metals adopt this kind of structure although some metal structures are such that each metal atom is in contact with just eight neighbouring atoms.

Figure 7.7 Fruit stacked on a market stall.

Metals are good conductors of electricity. Can this be explained by this model of metal structure? Each metal atom comprises a nucleus with a positive charge and surrounded by electrons. A feature of metals is that they tend to lose electrons to form cations. This model can be regarded as a structure of regularly arranged metal cations in a 'sea' of electrons (Figure 7.8). The movement of one electron

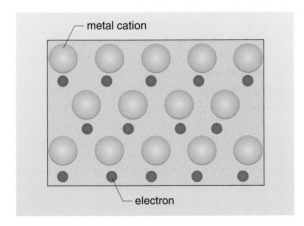

metal cation

electron

Figure 7.8 Metal ions in a 'sea' of electrons.

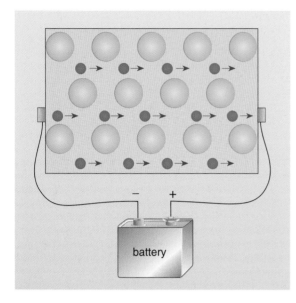

Figure 7.9   Conduction of electricity in a metal.

creates a hole that can be filled with a neighbouring electron, another electron moves into that hole, and so on. The effect is the movement of electrons through the metal when an electrical potential is applied with a battery (Figure 7.9).

7.4   Copper

Occasionally copper is found in nature in its elemental form. In 1857, the largest single lump of so-called 'native' copper was unearthed in Minnesota, USA. It had a mass of 420 tonnes. Native or elemental copper is not often found and has no commercial significance today. Nevertheless, it had a significant impact on early civilisations, as did silver and gold.

Copper is arguably the most beautiful of all metals with an almost salmon-pink sheen. It is a soft metal and can be beaten into shape. Usually, the surface is dulled in air but a transparent lacquer can be applied to keep the surface shiny. Unfortunately, lacquering changes the colour of copper slightly. In most houses, the water pipes and central heating pipework is copper. If you take metal polish and give a small area a good rub, you may be surprised at the delicate hue.

The usefulness of minerals as sources of metals depends on three factors: the ease of extraction of the mineral, the proportion of metal in the mineral and the ease with which the pure metal can be chemically produced. There are over 160 copper minerals known but only about a dozen or so are common. Many of these are brightly coloured, as you can see from Figure 7.10.

Figure 7.10   Native copper (lower centre), chalcopyrite (left) and malachite (right).

■ Malachite can be regarded as having a composition represented by the empirical formula $Cu_2CH_2O_5$. What is the proportion by mass of copper in malachite?

☐ The first step is to calculate the 'relative molecular mass' corresponding to the empirical formula (the formula mass) by adding the relative atomic mass values for the atoms in the empirical formula.

For $Cu_2CH_2O_5$, the relative atomic mass values are:

$(2 \times 63.5) + 12.0 + (2 \times 1.01) + (5 \times 16.0) = 221.0$

A mass of 221.0 g malachite contains 63.5 g copper.

The proportion of copper by mass in malachite is:

$$\frac{2 \times 63.5}{221.0} = 0.575 \text{ or } 57.5\%.$$

The fact that copper is occasionally found as the metal indicates that, like silver and gold, it is not particularly reactive. The converse is that when copper is in a chemical compound, it should be relatively easy to convert back to the metal.

Malachite, $Cu_2CH_2O_5$, is only one of several commercially valuable copper minerals. The first step is to heat the mineral (in air). Carbon reacts with oxygen and forms carbon dioxide and the hydrogen is removed as water, leaving copper oxide, CuO:

$$Cu_2CH_2O_5(s) = 2CuO(s) + CO_2(g) + H_2O(l) \qquad (7.1)$$

The next step is to heat the copper oxide with carbon, which is converted initially to carbon monoxide, CO, removing oxygen from the copper oxide:

$$CuO(s) + C(s) = Cu(s) + CO(g) \qquad (7.2)$$

The solid metal is known as blister copper because it contains bubbles of air and other impurities. This reaction occurs at the temperatures that can be achieved using charcoal as a source of carbon. The technology is relatively simple and copper was one of the very first metals to be chemically extracted from its ores.

7.5   Tin and bronze

Although gold, silver and copper were available to civilisations several thousand years ago, these metals did not change how people lived in a significant way. Indeed, it was only wealthy people who benefited from jewellery, decorations and vessels made from these metals. What was needed was a much harder metal, one that could be used for the heads of arrows and spears, for knives and other tools. Copper is a relatively soft metal and certainly could not be used as an effective cutting tool. Throughout the Stone Age, the best cutting tools were made from flint.

Tin does not occur as the pure metal like gold and silver but often as an oxide as in the mineral, cassiterite (Figure 7.11). Just how this material, which is dull black, was recognised as containing a useful metal is not known, but the extraction of tin from cassiterite represented the start of a metal extraction industry that has changed little in its chemistry to the present day.

Figure 7.11   Cassiterite, a source of tin.

75

Although it is not documented how methods were developed for producing tin, it is likely that it started with a chance observation. Imagine a large cooking fire in a Stone Age village perhaps somewhere in Cornwall. The location is not an accident as this part of Britain had (and still has) deposits of cassiterite, SnO_2, and other tin-bearing ores. Maybe there was a little cassiterite in the stone forming the base of the fire. The fire may have been used hundreds of times until someone raking through the ashes noticed a few, tiny silver–grey spheres. This would be metallic tin. Unfortunately, tin, like copper, was not a metal that could be sharpened. The keenness of the edge was soon blunted and it turned out to be not as good as flint for cutting tools.

The chemical reaction in the fire occurs in a number of stages but, overall, it can be represented by the equation:

$$C(s) + SnO_2(s) = CO_2(g) + Sn(s) \qquad (7.3)$$

Tin can exist in three different structural forms. Several elements have different structural forms, which are known as **allotropes**. Diamond and graphite are allotropes of the element carbon. The physical properties of the three forms of tin are different and each form is stable over a particular temperature range. White tin is the normal metallic form and this silvery metal is stable between about 13 °C and 161 °C (Figure 7.12). Between this range and 232 °C, the temperature at which tin melts, there is another form, rhombic tin.

Figure 7.12   Ingots of white tin.

Grey tin is the form that is stable below 13 °C and crumbles easily to a grey powder. Fortunately, it takes a considerable time for one form to turn into another. Tin that is used to plate metal food cans does not immediately become grey and powdery as soon as the temperature falls below 13 °C. However, prolonged exposure to very low temperatures may bring about this change. Tin pest, as this change to crumbly grey tin is known, limits the use of metallic tin and is said to have changed the course of European history.

Napoleon's campaign to take Moscow in 1812 proved to be a disaster. The city was stoutly defended, and did not fall. As the French troops retreated, the Russian winter closed in. Extreme cold and a shortage of food led to the deaths of many men and animals. Buttons on the soldiers' uniforms were made of tin and the low temperatures caused a change to the grey form of tin. The soldiers' buttons just crumbled away and made the clothing even less able to withstand the rigours of the winter.

However, the real value of tin in the progress of civilisation is as a component of bronze. Again, we do not know just how it came about that bronze was made from copper and tin, but it was probably a serendipitous observation. Tin and copper ores are sometimes found together and bronze may have been first produced in the normal production of copper with a fortuitous mixture of copper and tin ores.

The relative proportions of tin and copper can be varied over a wide range and the melting temperature of the alloy changes, as shown in Table 7.3.

Table 7.3 Composition and melting temperature of bronzes (copper–tin alloys).

Proportion of copper by mass/%	Proportion of tin by mass/%	Melting temperature/°C
100	0	1084
90	10	1005
80	20	890
70	30	755
60	40	724
50	50	680
40	60	630
30	70	580
20	80	530
10	90	440
0	100	232

■ Do the data in Table 7.3 indicate why bronze may have been a more useful material to early civilisations than copper?

□ As the proportion of tin in the alloy is increased, the melting temperature decreases. The melting temperature of copper is in the upper range of what can be achieved with a charcoal fire. By producing copper with tin together from a mixture of ores, bronze that can be melted in a fire is obtained. The liquid metal can be cast into sand or clay moulds, making a whole new array of objects possible. Before this, the only way to fashion copper was to beat it into shape.

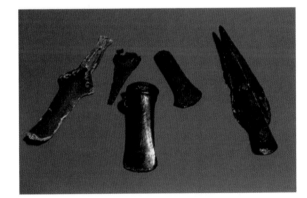

Figure 7.13 Bronze Age artefacts.

If it were only for this ease of casting, it is doubtful that bronze would have made a significant impact on civilisation. Certainly, there would not have been the long period in Britain, the so-called Bronze Age, where life was transformed through the properties of bronze (Figure 7.13). However, bronze turned out to be much harder than tin or the rather soft copper and it could be sharpened to a reasonably good cutting edge. Given the technology to cast the alloy into a range of shapes, hunting, warfare, farming, building, cooking and decoration were all transformed.

By experimenting, it was found that the most useful properties were obtained with a tin content between 5% and 20%. The lowering of the melting temperature of copper compared with a 20% tin bronze (by 194 °C) is not great, but it does bring the temperature down to within the working temperature of a wood fire. However, this composition gives excellent hardness properties too. How can a relatively small amount of tin increase the hardness of copper to such an extent?

The structure of metallic copper is shown in Figure 7.14 and comprises a regular array of copper atoms.

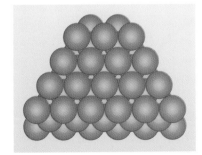

Figure 7.14 Structure of metallic copper.

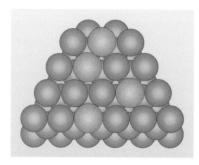

Figure 7.15   Structure of bronze.

When copper is squeezed or beaten, layers of copper atoms can easily slide over one another. Look at Figure 7.15 which shows the inclusion of the larger tin atoms into the copper structure.

The larger tin atoms disrupt the layers of copper atoms and prevent them from sliding smoothly over one another. This, together with attractive forces between copper and tin atoms, results in bronze being a much harder metal than copper.

Gold jewellery is rarely made from pure gold but from an alloy of gold and other metals, notably silver or copper. The effect is to harden the soft metal gold and make it more wear-resistant. Alloying also affects the colour of the metal. Pure gold is given a rating of 24 carats. If you have jewellery that is 9 carats you may not be pleased to learn that it is only 37.5% by mass of gold $\left(\frac{9}{24}\right)$ and the rest is probably copper.

The low reactivity of gold, silver and copper is one reason why these metals have been used for so long in coinage (Figure 7.16). There would be little value in a coinage that slowly reacted to form compounds.

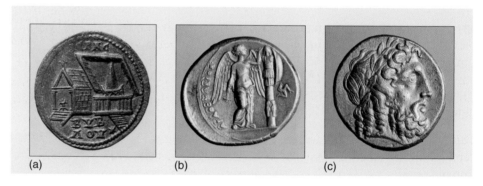

Figure 7.16   (a) Copper, (b) silver and (c) gold coins.

7.6   The Iron Age and iron

The Bronze Age represented a culture with a major dependency on a single working metal. True copper, silver and gold were known but they were not as useful as bronze (or, in the case of silver and gold, as available) for making cooking and storage vessels or axe and arrow heads. Comparison of the scene in the Bruegel painting (Figure 1.7) shows numerous changes, one of which is that many of the tools were made from iron. Iron is the element upon which the development of society was made from the beginnings of the Iron Age around 3000 years ago and upon which the Industrial Revolution was founded. Even today, it is the most widely used metal. Why was it that iron ousted bronze as society's metal?

At first, it seems easier to find reasons why iron should *not* have superseded bronze. There are many examples of gold, silver, copper and bronze artefacts preserved from antiquity but there is hardly anything left that was made from iron. The fact that iron rusts is no great surprise as evidenced by the way that car bodies tend to corrode (Figure 7.17). In recent years, the protection of steel against rusting has been much improved.

Figure 7.17   Corrosion of the steel body of a car.

Iron is widespread in the Earth's crust and, like tin, commonly exists as an oxide found in sedimentary rocks. There are major deposits of iron oxide ores in Sweden, France, Australia and in the USA (particularly Minnesota). Iron ore deposits of the east Midlands and Lincolnshire in Britain provided the base for the iron and steel industry of that area. It is not easy to persuade iron to release its hold over oxygen with which it is chemically combined. Like tin oxide, iron oxide has to be heated with carbon to win the metal, but the temperature required to carry out the reaction is higher and beyond that achievable with a wood or charcoal fire.

However, two small developments that were to make a big difference occurred during the Bronze Age. It was found that if wood, instead of being burned directly on a fire, was partly burned in a limited supply of air, charcoal was formed. Charcoal is mainly carbon and proved to be a much better and hotter fuel than wood and made the manufacture of bronze so much more convenient. Indeed, the production of charcoal was a significant industry up to the early 19th century (Figure 7.18).

Figure 7.18   Charcoal burning at the Weald and Downland Open Air Museum, Singleton, West Sussex, UK.

The temperature could be further raised by blowing air into the base of the charcoal fire with bellows. Even so, the real working limit of the fire of about 1150 °C is well below the melting temperature of iron, 1535 °C. Heating iron oxide in a charcoal fire through which air was blown resulted in metallic iron, but only because of a fortunate coincidence.

Carbon reacts with oxygen in the air and raises the temperature of the fire. In the centre of the fire, where there is little air, carbon begins to extract oxygen from iron oxide. As soon as the first iron is formed, carbon dissolves in it, lowering its melting temperature. The effect on the melting temperature of iron of even small quantities of dissolved carbon is dramatic. The melting temperature of iron containing just 4% by mass of carbon is 1150 °C, quite a fall from the 1535 °C melting temperature of pure iron. So it was the development of Bronze Age technology that helped move culture forward to the Iron Age.

Iron as produced from an Iron Age furnace contained about 4% by mass of carbon. Carbon atoms disrupt the regular arrangement of iron atoms to make it hard but brittle. If the iron is heated to about 850 °C, it becomes malleable and can be hammered into shape. Hammering iron at this temperature can help expose some of the carbon so that it can be removed by reaction with oxygen in the air.

Removal of carbon makes iron much less brittle but also reduces its hardness, the very qualities one needs for tools, farm implements and weapons. The outcome was a compromise where some of the carbon was removed to give a resilient steel. It was found that if such steel were cooled rapidly, its properties of toughness and strength are retained but the steel becomes hard and will retain a sharp cutting edge. But simply plunging steel into cold water is not enough. Water around the steel immediately boils and the resulting steam protects the steel and slows down cooling. The problem is that the water hardly touches the steel and heat is not conducted away quickly. It is not unlike the situation of a drop of water fizzing around on a layer of steam on an electrical hotplate. Years ago, urine was used to overcome this problem. Crystals of the compound urea in the urine are formed on the steel surface and break up the steam barrier. The properties of the metal are also modified by carbon diffusing into the surface layers when steel was heated in a blacksmith's fire.

Today iron is produced in basically the same way as it was in the Iron Age. The scale and technology have changed but the basic reaction is still the same, the reaction of iron oxide, FeO, with carbon:

$$FeO(s) + C(s) = Fe(s) + CO(g) \tag{7.4}$$

The process is carried out in a blast furnace which produces hundreds of tonnes of iron at a time. Iron ore and coke (coal heated in the absence of air) are added through the top of the furnace, air is blown in lower down and liquid iron runs off from the bottom of the furnace. Limestone is also added, which combines with silicate impurities in the ore to give a liquid waste (slag) which can be run off from the furnace.

Question 7.1

Why have the metals copper, silver and gold been used for coins through history?

Question 7.2

What can be said about carbon in terms of its tendency to form an oxide, relative to that of metals?

7.7   Summary of Chapter 7

The use of metals through history is intimately tied up with the chemical properties of these elements. In particular, the least reactive metals were the first to be used historically, as they were found either as the metal (gold) or as ores (copper and tin) from which the metal could be extracted relatively easily. The more reactive metals such as iron came later, as iron oxides are more difficult to process to give elemental iron. Metals tend to be identified by good thermal and electrical conductivity (and by a certain lustre).

Chapter 8
Reactivity of metals

Some metals that feature in earlier chapters are listed in Table 8.1 together with comments that relate occurrence and extraction of these metals.

Table 8.1 Metals and their occurrence and extraction.

Element	Comment
gold	found as metal
silver	found as metal
copper	occasionally found as metal but more usually as sulfide, carbonate or oxide
tin	found as oxide but can be converted to metal with carbon at relatively low temperature
iron	found as oxide but can be converted to metal with carbon (or carbon monoxide) at high temperature

■   What can you say about the relative reactivity of the metals in Table 8.1?

☐   The least reactive are gold and silver as they are found as the elements. Copper is the next least reactive as it is occasionally found as the metal but usually found combined with oxygen. Tin is a little more reactive, as its oxide is converted to the metal at relatively low temperatures. The most reactive metal in the table is iron, as higher temperatures are required for its extraction.

Activity 8.1   Reactivity of metals

We expect this activity will take you approximately 45 minutes.

You should now work through the computer-based activity *Metal Reactions*, which allows you to view the reactions of metals with water and with acids. In viewing the video sequences, you should try to assess the relative reactivities of the metals – which are most reactive, and which are least reactive.

To help you gather the data that you observe during the sequences, it would be useful to make notes about what you see. You may find it useful to draw a simple table to record the results of your observations prior to starting the video sequences. Based on your notes and observations, construct a table that arranges the metals in order of reactivity, starting with the most reactive. You will also need to refer to the information in Table 8.1. You will find further instructions within the computer-based activity.

When you have completed this activity, look at the comments at the end of this book.

8.1   Metal ions in solution

Another way of comparing the reactivity of metals is to look at reactions of metals in aqueous solution. A characteristic of atoms of the metals is that they tend to lose electrons to form positively charged cations. A copper cation dissolved in water can be represented by $Cu^{2+}(aq)$.

If a piece of iron is put into an aqueous solution containing copper cations, Cu^{2+}, a deposit of metallic copper is formed on the surface of the iron. What does this indicate about the reactivity of copper relative to iron?

Copper cations in solution have been converted to copper metal and to do this they have had to gain two electrons. The reaction can be represented by an equation in which an electron is denoted by 'e⁻'. Just as the negative charge on an ion is shown by a superscript (Section 3.4), the single negative charge on the electron is indicated in the same way:

$$Cu^{2+}(aq) + 2e^- = Cu(s) \tag{8.1}$$

The next question is, 'Where have the electrons come from?' Iron dissolves in the solution to form positively charged ions, Fe^{2+}, releasing two electrons:

$$Fe(s) = Fe^{2+}(aq) + 2e^- \tag{8.2}$$

In forming ions, the iron atoms lose electrons and it is these electrons that are transferred to adjacent copper cations in the solution to form elemental copper that coats the iron. In this reaction, iron appears to be more reactive than copper. You know that iron reacts more readily with oxygen than does copper from your observations on the ease of rusting of iron.

Similar experiments can be done with other metals and an **activity series** built up representing the tendency of metal ions to react with metals just as was done in Activity 8.1. The remarkable thing is the consistency of the activity series irrespective of whether they are developed from reactions in which one metal displaces another from solution or from reactions of metals with other elements.

There is a limit to the range of metals that can be used in these displacement reactions. Some metals (calcium is an example) react with water directly rather than displacing a metal from a solution, giving the metal cation, hydrogen and the hydroxide anion:

$$Ca(s) + 2H_2O(l) = Ca^{2+}(aq) + 2OH^-(aq) + H_2(g) \tag{8.3}$$

but there are methods of placing these elements in an activity series. With calcium, the reaction proceeds at a steady rate, but metals such as potassium, rubidium and caesium react violently with water. These metals are so reactive that they have to be stored under oil to protect them from oxygen and water.

$$2Cs(s) + 2H_2O(l) = 2Cs^+(aq) + 2OH^-(aq) + H_2(g) \tag{8.4}$$

During the reaction of caesium with water, enough heat is produced to ignite the hydrogen gas evolved and cause an explosion.

An order of reactivity of metals can be developed that holds for a wide range of reactions. Such an activity series for a range of metals is shown in Table 8.2, with high reactivity at the top.

Table 8.2 Activity series for a range of metals.

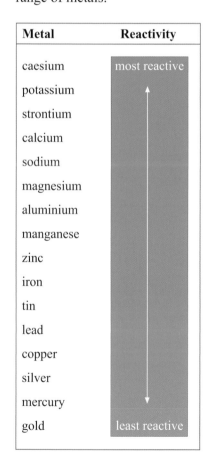

Metal	Reactivity
caesium	most reactive
potassium	
strontium	
calcium	
sodium	
magnesium	
aluminium	
manganese	
zinc	
iron	
tin	
lead	
copper	
silver	
mercury	
gold	least reactive

8.2 Reactions of metals with acids

At the end of the 19th century, the Swedish chemist Svante Arrhenius defined an **acid** as a substance that contains hydrogen and releases hydrogen ions, $H^+(aq)$, in water. The covalent molecule hydrogen chloride, HCl, dissolves easily in water. In this case, the dissolving process results in a chemical reaction in which the covalent bond linking the hydrogen and the chlorine atoms in the molecule is broken. Hydrogen cations and chloride anions are the products:

$$HCl(g) + H_2O(l) = H^+(aq) + Cl^-(aq) \qquad (8.5)$$

Although gaseous hydrogen chloride is a discrete molecule and does not contain hydrogen cations, it produces hydrogen cations in water and is therefore an acid according to Arrhenius's definition.

Many of the substances that can be classified as acids are of industrial importance (Table 8.3). Their greatest use is in the manufacture of agrochemicals and in the detergent and food industries.

These acids dissolve in water to give hydrogen cations, $H^+(aq)$; for example:

$$H_2SO_4(l) + H_2O(l) = 2H^+(aq) + SO_4^{2-}(aq) \qquad (8.6)$$

Equations 8.5 and 8.6 may seem to be slightly odd in that, at first glance, they do not balance. The equations represent the dissolving of acids in water. There is water implied in the aqueous state of the ions without a specific amount being specified. So in such reactions, the water part is not quantitative and is often omitted from the chemical equation.

A distinguishing feature of the chemistry of many metals is that they react with acids to form cations and liberate hydrogen gas. The addition of hydrochloric acid, which contains the ions $H^+(aq)$ and $Cl^-(aq)$, to zinc metal yields hydrogen and the ion $Zn^{2+}(aq)$:

$$Zn(s) + 2H^+(aq) = Zn^{2+}(aq) + H_2(g) \qquad (8.7)$$

You should note that in the above equation the chloride ion $Cl^-(aq)$ has not been included. This is because the chloride anion is unchanged in the reaction and is present at the beginning and at the end of the reaction.

■ What would you expect to happen if the metals magnesium and tin were treated with hydrochloric acid? Write appropriate equations to describe the reactions.

☐ As metals, magnesium and tin would be expected to react with hydrogen cations in the acid to form hydrogen and the metal cation:

$$Mg(s) + 2H^+(aq) = Mg^{2+}(aq) + H_2(g) \qquad (8.8)$$

$$Sn(s) + 2H^+(aq) = Sn^{2+}(aq) + H_2(g) \qquad (8.9)$$

There is another observation that could be made if you carried out reactions of metals with acids but you may be able to guess what it is. Look at the activity series for the metals in Table 8.2. This activity series holds for the reaction of metals with hydrogen cations. Magnesium lies above zinc in the series, which in

Table 8.3 Some acids of major industrial importance.

Name	Formula
sulfuric acid	H_2SO_4
phosphoric acid	H_3PO_4
nitric acid	HNO_3
hydrochloric acid	HCl

turn is above tin. The reaction of magnesium with hydrogen cations is more rapid than is the corresponding reaction for zinc or for tin. It is not always the case that the speed of a reaction is a guide to relative reactivity. However, for the reactions of metals with acids, it does work reasonably well.

Arrhenius also defined a **base** as a compound that gives hydroxide anions $OH^-(aq)$ in water. Sodium hydroxide, NaOH, is a white solid comprising the ions Na^+ and OH^-. It dissolves in water to give a basic solution, a solution containing $OH^-(aq)$ ions:

$$NaOH(s) = Na^+(aq) + OH^-(aq) \tag{8.10}$$

■ So what happens when an acid and a base are mixed?

☐ Mixing solutions of hydrochloric acid and sodium hydroxide might be expected to give a mixture of the four ions in solution: $H^+(aq)$, $Cl^-(aq)$, $Na^+(aq)$ and $OH^-(aq)$. However, there is a very rapid reaction between the hydroxide and hydrogen ions to give water molecules, a reaction that can be represented by the equation:

$$H^+(aq) + OH^-(aq) = H_2O(l) \tag{8.11}$$

This is **neutralisation**, a process in which hydrogen cations and hydroxide anions react together to form water molecules.

■ The mixture contained not just the hydrogen and hydroxide ions but sodium and chloride ions, too. What has happened to them?

☐ The simple answer is nothing. The sodium and chloride ions were there at the moment of mixing the two solutions and are there after the hydrogen and hydroxide ions have reacted. That is why they are not represented in the equation. A solution containing equal numbers of sodium and chloride ions is simply a solution of sodium chloride in water.

You could write the overall equation as:

$$H^+(aq) + Cl^-(aq) + Na^+(aq) + OH^-(aq) = H_2O(l) + Na^+(aq) + Cl^-(aq) \tag{8.12}$$

But why bother? The whole point of a chemical equation is to show just what is happening, which substances are reacting and being changed into new substances. The sodium and chloride ions are not reacting so they do not feature in the equation.

■ A solution of sulfuric acid contains the ions $H^+(aq)$ and $SO_4^{2-}(aq)$ and a solution of the base potassium hydroxide comprises the ions $K^+(aq)$ and $OH^-(aq)$. Try to write an equation for the reaction that occurs when these two solutions are mixed.

☐ You know that hydrogen and hydroxide ions react to give water molecules so the equation for the reaction is:

$$H^+(aq) + OH^-(aq) = H_2O(l) \tag{8.11}$$

The potassium ions and sulfate ions are present at the moment of mixing the two solutions and are there, unreacted, in solution at the end.

■   What is striking about the two reactions between hydrochloric acid and sodium hydroxide and between sulfuric acid and potassium hydroxide?

☐   The two reactions are the same. They can both be represented by the equation:

$$H^+(aq) + OH^-(aq) = H_2O(l) \qquad\qquad (8.11)$$

These are ionic equations. They must balance as normal chemical equations in terms of the relative numbers of atoms on each side of the equation and they must also balance in terms of charge.

8.3   Oxidation and reduction

The term **oxidation** originally had the simple meaning of 'combining with oxygen'. The definition of **reduction** was that combination with hydrogen had occurred. Today, the meaning is rather wider.

Solid copper oxide, CuO, is an ionic compound comprising a lattice of copper cations, Cu^{2+}, and oxide anions, O^{2-}. The reaction between elemental copper and oxygen molecules to form the oxide can be described as an oxidation:

$$2Cu(s) + O_2(g) = 2CuO(s) \qquad\qquad (8.13)$$

Copper has combined with oxygen to form the oxide and so copper is said to be oxidised. Look at the reaction a little more closely. The reaction product is the ionic compound, copper oxide. In the reaction, copper atoms have been converted into cations, two electrons have been lost from each copper atom. Copper has been *oxidised* in this reaction.

Oxygen has gone from the elemental form to the oxide ion, O^{2-}. There has been a gain of two electrons; reduction has occurred. Whenever there is an oxidation, there is always a parallel reduction; copper has been oxidised and oxygen reduced.

Loss of electrons represents oxidation. Gain of electrons represents reduction. (A convenient way to remember this is through the mnemonic 'OILRIG': oxidation is loss, reduction is gain.)

The importance of the idea of oxidation and reduction can be seen by looking at the activity series of metals. The metals higher in the series are those that are more easily oxidised; they lose electrons most easily. The addition of a metal higher in the series to a solution of the cations of a metal lower in the series will result in the reduction of the cation of the metal lower in the series. For example, if manganese metal is added to a solution containing $Cu^{2+}(aq)$ ions, the copper cations will be reduced to the metal according to Equation 8.14:

$$Mn(s) + Cu^{2+}(aq) = Mn^{2+}(aq) + Cu(s) \qquad\qquad (8.14)$$

The reverse reaction, in which elemental copper is added to a solution of $Mn^{2+}(aq)$ ions, does *not* take place. Manganese is more easily oxidised than copper.

The activity series can help in rationalising the ease with which metals are obtained from their ores. Copper is towards the bottom of the table, indicating that the metal is not very reactive. It is sometimes found in nature as the element and can be produced from oxides and sulfides by heating with carbon at the relatively modest temperature of 1000 °C. Iron is a tougher proposition. It is never found naturally as the metal (except in meteorites). The blast furnace process which produces iron from its oxides and carbon needs a temperature of over 1500 °C. This is a reflection of the tenacity with which iron as the oxide hangs on to oxygen, and the reactivity of the metal is indicated by its mid-table position. Higher in the table are metals like aluminium, sodium and potassium.

■   Under what conditions might you guess that aluminium metal could be extracted from its oxide, Al_2O_3?

☐   Given that aluminium is higher in the activity series than iron, the metal is likely to be more difficult to obtain from its oxide. It would be reasonable to guess that heating the oxide with carbon at a temperature greater than 1500 °C would be required.

It is possible for aluminium oxide to be reduced by carbon to aluminium but a temperature of over 2300 °C is needed. An 'aluminium blast furnace' could not be built and operated economically at this temperature. There would be problems with finding heat-resistant materials to line the furnace that would not melt at this temperature and the additional expense of operating the plant at such high temperatures.

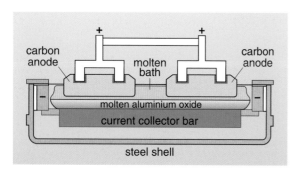

Figure 8.1   Representation of an electrolytic cell for the production of aluminium.

A clue to how aluminium may be obtained is seen if aluminium oxide, Al_2O_3, is regarded as comprising the ions Al^{3+} and O^{2-}. What is needed is a way of supplying electrons to the aluminium cations. An electric current is simply electrons moving through a conductor, so why not use these electrons to reduce the aluminium cations? The reaction is carried out in a vessel made from steel with a carbon lining (Figure 8.1). The vessel is known as an electrolytic cell and contains molten aluminium oxide, Al_2O_3, at a temperature of 1000 °C. The melting temperature of the pure oxide is 2045 °C but the addition of a naturally occurring fluoride of aluminium, cryolite (K_3AlF_6), to aluminium oxide lowers the melting temperature of the mix. The circuit is completed with carbon rods dipped into the melt. Electrons are fed into the cell via the carbon lining to bring about the reduction of Al^{3+} to the element.

Industrial electrolytic cells are about 10 m long and 3 m wide and a typical plant will have up to 1000 cells. Huge quantities of electricity are consumed and it is no surprise that the major aluminium plants are located close to sources of cheap electricity. For example, Jamaica has large deposits of aluminium oxide (the mineral bauxite) but has no aluminium production plants. Much of the country's bauxite goes to Canada where cheap electricity from hydroelectric schemes is exploited. The metals above aluminium in the activity series are extracted by similar electrolytic methods.

Aluminium used to be regarded as a 'luxury' metal. In 1855, the cost of aluminium metal was over £60 per kilogram, more expensive than gold. Emperor Napoleon III used aluminium cutlery at his banquets and even had a gold and aluminium baby rattle made for his son. The reason for this was not that aluminium is a rare metal; you have seen that it is one of the more common elements in the Earth's crust. Aluminium is a reactive metal and found naturally as the oxide. It proves particularly difficult to reduce the aluminium cations in the oxide to elemental aluminium and this can only be done electrolytically. In 1855, electricity was not available in the quantities required.

Electrolysis can be used to purify metals as well as to win them from their ores. As you saw earlier, the output of the extraction of copper is a material known as blister copper. Many of the uses of copper depend on its excellent qualities as an electrical conductor but only when it is of high purity. Electrical conductivity is much diminished by the presence of impurities in the metal, so there is a need for high-purity copper. This is obtained by the electrolysis of blister copper.

An electrolytic cell is set up with one electrode being an ingot of impure blister copper and the other a thin rod of the pure metal. These electrodes are dipped into an aqueous solution containing copper ions $Cu^{2+}(aq)$ (usually a solution of copper sulfate in water). The circuit is completed by connection to an electricity supply (Figure 8.2).

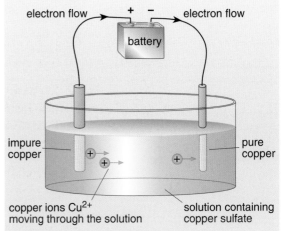

Figure 8.2   Schematic diagram for the electrolytic purification of copper.

Electrons are generated at the left electrode which is the ingot of impure blister copper. These electrons are produced when the copper atoms are oxidised. The resultant copper cations go into solution:

$$Cu(s, blister) = Cu^{2+}(aq) + 2e^- \qquad (8.15)$$

The electrons are driven through the external circuit to the right electrode which is in contact with copper cations in solution. At this electrode, reduction occurs. Copper cations in solution are reduced to the metal which is deposited on the electrode:

$$Cu^{2+}(aq) + 2e^- = Cu(s, pure) \qquad (8.16)$$

Only copper atoms are deposited and so the build-up of pure copper on the cathode increases. The blister copper electrode (which acts as the anode) is constantly losing copper. Copper atoms of the anode lose electrons and enter the solution as $Cu^{2+}(aq)$ ions, replacing those that are removed from solution at the cathode. The overall result is the transfer of pure copper from the blister copper electrode to the pure copper electrode. The impurities drop to the cell floor as the impure copper disappears.

Question 8.1

What would you expect to happen if:

(a) the metal tin, Sn, was added to an aqueous solution of copper chloride, $CuCl_2$, which contains the ions Cu^{2+} and Cl^-? Write a balanced chemical equation to represent any reaction that might occur but only include those species that actually take part in the reaction.

(b) the metal copper, Cu, was added to an aqueous solution of lead nitrate, $Pb(NO_3)_2$, which contains the ions Pb^{2+} and NO_3^-?

(c) the metal sodium, Na, was added to an aqueous solution of iron chloride, $FeCl_2$, which contains the ions Fe^{2+} and Cl^-?

8.4   Metal ions and the Periodic Table

Most of the elements in the Periodic Table are metals and these are identified by the pale grey boxes on the left-hand side of Figure 8.3. The non-metals on the right-hand side are represented by the green boxes. The semi-metals, which have intermediate properties, are in between, in orange.

As you have seen, metals are distinguished chemically from the non-metals in that the metals tend to form cations rather than anions. Metals are more easily oxidised than are non-metals. But how do we know what is the appropriate charge for a particular metal cation?

The question is really how many electrons does a metal lose in becoming a cation or what is the value of n in the equation where the metal is represented by the symbol M?

$$M(s) = M^{n+}(aq) + ne^- \tag{8.17}$$

Table 8.4 gives the charges on a range of common metal and non-metal ions. The ions have been arranged in the table in groups corresponding to the groups of the Periodic Table into which the elements fall. Look carefully at Table 8.4 and see if there are any generalisations to be drawn.

Table 8.4 Charges on some common cations and anions.

Group	Element	Ion	Charge on the ion
1	lithium	Li^+	+1
	sodium	Na^+	+1
	potassium	K^+	+1
	caesium	Cs^+	+1
2	magnesium	Mg^{2+}	+2
	calcium	Ca^{2+}	+2
	barium	Ba^{2+}	+2
13	aluminium	Al^{3+}	+3
15	nitrogen	N^{3-}	−3
	phosphorus	P^{3-}	−3
16	oxygen	O^{2-}	−2
	sulfur	S^{2-}	−2
17	chlorine	Cl^-	−1
	bromine	Br^-	−1
	iodine	I^-	−1

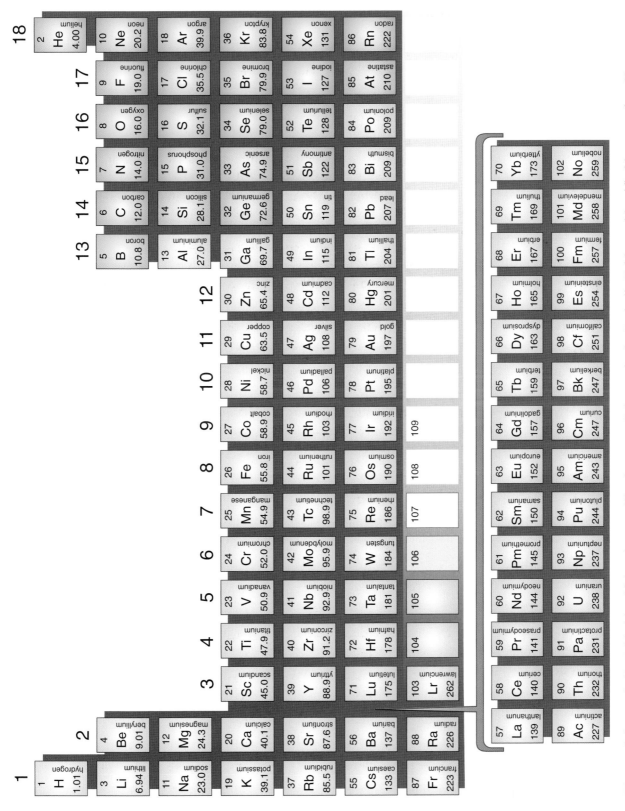

Figure 8.3   Periodic Table identifying the metallic elements. Columns in the Periodic Table are identified by a number. Here, metals are shown in grey, non-metals in green and semi-metals in orange.

The charge on the cations is the same as the group number of the element from which they are formed for Groups 1 and 2. For other groups you have to subtract 10 from the group number to get the magnitude of the charge on the ions. For example, aluminium is in Group 13 and the charge on the cation is +3 (i.e. 13 − 10), Al^{3+}. Sodium is in Group 1 and gives the ion Na^+ with a charge of +1. (Note that lead and tin are exceptions to this rule; they are in Group 14 but do form the ions Pb^{2+} and Sn^{2+}.)

Charges on non-metal ions are negative and are related to but not equal to the Group number. The relationship is that the charges are equal to the Group number minus 18 (although there are some exceptions). Chlorine is in Group 17 and the charge on the chloride ion, Cl^-, is (17 − 18) = −1. Sulfur is in Group 16 and the charge on the sulfide ion, S^{2-}, is (16 − 18) = −2.

■ Use the activity series to predict what would happen if:

(a) iron is added to an aqueous solution containing Sn^{2+} cations

(b) aluminium is added to an aqueous solution containing Fe^{2+} cations

(c) zinc is added to an aqueous solution containing Mg^{2+} cations.

☐ The prediction is that there would be a displacement reaction in (a) and (b) but not in (c).

If these experiments were undertaken, the predictions for (a) and (c) would prove to be valid but in (b), where the prediction was that aluminium metal would be oxidised to Al^{3+}, no reaction would be observed. So what has gone wrong with the activity series? This is the question we will now attempt to answer.

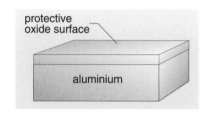

protective
oxide surface

aluminium

Figure 8.4   Aluminium protected by a layer of oxide.

Figure 8.5   Corrosion-resistant aluminium body of a 1950s Land Rover.

8.5   Corrosion of metals

According to the activity series, aluminium should react with oxygen more readily than iron, which is easily oxidised in the presence of water and oxygen. How is it then that aluminium can be used for aeroplanes which are in constant contact with water and oxygen from the air?

In reality, aluminium does react with oxygen very rapidly and forms aluminium oxide, Al_2O_3. The oxide has the ability to adhere to the surface of the underlying metal with great tenacity (Figure 8.4). This thin but robust layer of oxide then protects the underlying metal from further oxidation (Figure 8.5).

If the oxide becomes scratched and aluminium metal exposed, more oxide is formed and the protective layer renewed. The reason that no reaction is observed in part (b) of the question above is that the oxide film protects the aluminium and prevents reaction with Fe^{2+}(aq) ions. Even if aluminium metal is cleaned with emery paper, a protective oxide layer would form before the metal could be put into the solution containing Fe^{2+}(aq) ions.

The situation with iron is very similar in the sense that iron becomes oxidised to the familiar red–orange rust. However, rust takes up a greater volume than the iron from which it is formed and consequently splits and cracks. The rust is also porous to water and oxygen so that more rust can be formed from the underlying metal and eventually the oxidation process is complete. Rust is not the simple oxide Fe_2O_3 but is a compound that actually contains water molecules. It can be represented as $Fe_2O_3.nH_2O$ where n can vary according to the conditions under which the rust forms. The 'dot' in the formula indicates that the water molecules are incorporated into the array of iron cations and oxide anions.

■ Write a balanced chemical equation to represent the formation of rust on iron.

☐ $4Fe(s) + 3O_2(g) + 2nH_2O(l) = 2Fe_2O_3.nH_2O(s)$ (8.18)

By using n, it is possible to write a balanced equation even though the formula for rust is not known precisely.

Iron and steel are not weather-resistant, yet they find widespread use because of their relative cheapness and their mechanical properties. Try to think of ways in which steel can be prevented from rusting.

Perhaps the most obvious one is to protect the metal surface with a coating of something that does not rust. The most widely used coating is paint and it is very effective provided that the paint does not become damaged. If this happens, or the metal surface is not completely free of rust when it is painted, further rusting can occur.

The situation is made worse because rusting can spread under the paintwork and is often at an advanced stage when signs of blistered paint become apparent. Where a hard paint surface is not required (such as the inside of car body panels), waxes and paints that do not set completely are useful. If such a surface gets a small scratch, the paint will flow a little and effectively self-heal the scratch.

Another coating that protects steel is to use a metal that is further down the activity series: a metal that does not oxidise in the air. The ideal metals are gold, silver and copper which are towards the bottom of the activity series in Table 8.2. However, as you can see from Table 7.1, the cost of these metals precludes them except for small-scale specialised uses.

Galvanised buckets and dustbins, which used to be commonplace, did not rust even though they were made from steel. The metal surface of these containers appears to have irregular shiny crystals (Figure 8.6).

Galvanising is the process by which a metal surface is given a coating of zinc. Zinc melts at 420 °C, and objects to be galvanised are chemically cleaned and then dipped into a bath of molten zinc. Galvanising is more expensive than conventional paint protection but it is effective in protecting the underlying metal.

Figure 8.6 Galvanised steel dustbin.

Where does zinc come in the activity series? To coat steel with a metal that does not oxidise in air makes sense, so it seems odd to use a metal that oxidises even more readily than iron.

Zinc, like aluminium, oxidises easily. It also has an oxide that clings well to the metal and is not porous to water or oxygen. So the surface of the steel is protected by zinc metal overlain with zinc oxide. But there is a further advantage to using zinc. If the zinc coating is damaged and iron exposed, you might expect

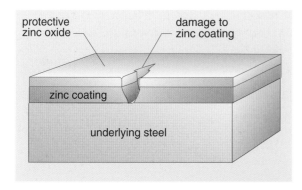

Figure 8.7   Representation of the protection of a galvanised surface. Electrons produced when zinc is oxidised to Zn^{2+} inhibit further oxidation of the underlying iron to the metal cations.

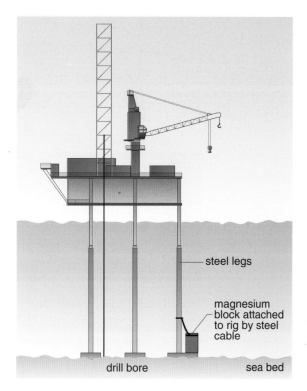

Figure 8.8   Protection of the steel in an oil rig platform with a block of magnesium.

the iron to rust, just as if a protective paint surface had been damaged. However, as zinc is more easily oxidised than iron, zinc is oxidised in preference and the iron remains in the metallic form (Figure 8.7).

A related protective method is used for larger steel structures such as buildings, oil rigs, ships and underwater or underground pipelines. For such large structures, it would not be practical to provide a covering of zinc. What is done is to attach a block of an easily oxidised metal (magnesium is often used) to the structure by a steel cable (Figure 8.8).

Magnesium preferentially oxidises to form the Mg^{2+} ion:

$$Mg(s) = Mg^{2+}(aq) + 2e^- \qquad (8.19)$$

The electrons produced can flow along the steel cable and give the oil rig a small negative charge. This makes it difficult for iron in the structure to oxidise and form positively charged ions as this would add even more electrons to what is an already negatively charged structure, and the steel rig remains intact. In time, the block of magnesium, which acts as a **sacrificial metal**, corrodes away and has to be replaced. This is much easier and cheaper than carrying out repairs on the structure of the rig.

The corrosion of metals is essentially the opposite process from that involved in producing metals from their ores. Smelting essentially involves a reduction process in which electrons are gained by metal cations to yield the elemental metal. With corrosion, metals lose electrons in an oxidation process to become metal cations.

8.6   Modifying metals

In the previous section, you saw that the resistance to corrosion of a metal could be changed by providing a surface coating of paint or other metal, but there is another way of changing the properties of the metallic elements that has been known for thousands of years. Bronze is an alloy of copper and tin and, like copper, its major component, it is resistant to corrosion. Bronze is also much harder than copper and it can be used in engineering. It finds particular use in the manufacture of propellers for ships where corrosion resistance is paramount. Here, there is a further advantage: copper is toxic to molluscs and is effective in inhibiting the growth of barnacles and other organisms on the propeller.

An alloy is different from a chemical compound which has a fixed ratio (and usually a very simple one) of one element to another. You have seen that the relative proportions of copper and tin in bronze can be varied over a wide range. For any ratio, atoms of the two metals are evenly distributed through the structure and the properties of the overall structure are very dependent on that ratio. The hardness, strength and corrosion resistance of metals can often be 'tuned' by carefully adjusting the proportions of elements in the alloy.

Steel is an alloy of carbon and iron where small changes in the proportion of carbon can have large changes in the hardness of steel. The addition of other metals to iron can improve corrosion resistance. Stainless steel contains up to 15% chromium by mass, often with some nickel. Rusting is prevented in part by a protective layer of chromium oxide. If you look at Table 7.1, you will see that chromium is an expensive metal, so stainless steel will never be an economic (although it might be a desirable) alternative to regular carbon steel, except for specialised uses. Table 8.5 shows the composition of some of the more common alloys.

It is difficult to predict just what will be the effect of alloying a metal with one or more other elements. There are two main factors to take into account. One is the effect of the different size of the atoms in the alloy and the second is related to the strength of attraction of the atoms of one element to another.

An interesting alloy is formed from copper with about 3% by mass of the element beryllium, Be. Beryllium atoms are rather smaller than those of copper. They seem to effectively 'glue' the copper atoms together to make a hard alloy which has found particular use in fire-sensitive areas such as oil refineries. This alloy will not spark when struck and so lessens the risk of fire.

Another property that is affected by alloying is melting temperature. Solder is an alloy of mainly tin and lead (Table 8.5) and has a melting temperature of about 180 °C. This is usefully lower than the corresponding temperature for pure tin (232 °C) and lead (328 °C). Intimate contact between the metal atoms in solder and those of the surfaces to be soldered is essential. The metal surface should be cleaned mechanically (with emery paper or steel wool) and then flux applied. Any trace of metal oxide left on the metal surface is reduced to the metal by the flux, improving the quality of the soldered joint.

■ Using normal methods, it is not possible to solder aluminium but copper is consistently easy to solder. Why should this be the case?

☐ Aluminium is a much more reactive and easily oxidised metal than copper. The surface of aluminium is covered with a thin layer of oxide. It can be removed by rubbing with emery paper but as soon as the metal surface is exposed, the oxide reforms. It is also difficult to reduce aluminium oxide to the metal, and soldering flux is not able to do this. The intervening aluminium oxide surface prevents solder from adhering to the metal. Copper is relatively unreactive and, should there be any oxide on the surface, it will be easily reduced to the metal by hot flux.

It is not only whether chemical reaction occurs, but also how quickly it occurs, that is important in deciding to what use elements and compounds can be put. Although iron and steel react with air and water, the rate of reaction is

Table 8.5 Composition of some common alloys.

Alloy	Composition by mass
bronze	Cu with up to 20% Sn
brass	Cu with up to 35% Zn
stainless steel	Fe with up to 15% Cr and often some Ni
solder	Pb with 40% Sn

relatively slow so that the metal can be used in the construction of many things. The next two chapters explore the rates at which chemical reactions occur in more detail and also examine energy changes in chemical reactions.

Question 8.2

Given that aluminium is higher in the activity series than iron, why does aluminium not rust in a manner similar to iron?

Question 8.3

Which metal could be used instead of magnesium as a sacrificial metal to protect a steel structure from corrosion?

8.7   Summary of Chapter 8

The activity series represents the ease with which metals can be oxidised. Metals such as sodium, potassium and aluminium are near the top of the series and are easily oxidised. Zinc, iron and tin lie near the middle of the activity series, and the least easily oxidised metals – gold, silver and copper – are near the bottom.

Oxidation is loss of electrons and reduction is gain of electrons. Extraction of metals from their ores involves reduction of the metal ions in the ores and metals are oxidised when they form compounds.

Problems associated with the rusting of metals may be minimised by coating the surface of the metal with a protective coating such as painting, galvanising with zinc or using a sacrificial metal.

Acids are compounds which release $H^+(aq)$ ions when dissolved in water. Many metals react with acids to form metal ions and hydrogen gas.

In this chapter, you have developed the skill of making observations and drawing inferences from them.

Chapter 9
Chemical reactions and energy changes

You have been introduced to a huge variety of materials: the elements of the Earth, metals and minerals, oil and plastics. You have seen how these are assembled from molecules, which in turn, are assembled from their basic building blocks, atoms. So, from the chemistry of these materials you were able to build up a description of chemical reactions in the form of balanced chemical equations. These balanced chemical equations are full of information, which includes the identification of the reactants and products from their formulas and the proportions in which they react. For example, the reaction between aluminium metal and bromine liquid can be written in the form of a balanced chemical equation:

$$2Al(s) + 3Br_2(l) = 2AlBr_3(s) \tag{9.1}$$

Figure 9.1   The materials described in Equation 9.1: aluminium metal (left), bromine liquid (centre) and aluminium bromide solid (right).

From Equation 9.1 you can see that the reactants, 2 moles of aluminium and 3 moles of bromine molecules, form the product: 2 moles of aluminium bromide. Figure 9.1 shows the reactants and product materials in their basic form. However, from the balanced chemical equation and the materials in Figure 9.1, you see a very 'static' type of chemical reaction and imagery of just the reactants and products. The picture and equation do not give any indication of how the reaction actually occurs in practice. If you were to do the experiment in a laboratory from the starting materials, you would observe a very different situation. Figure 9.2 shows you a snapshot of the reaction just seconds after a few shreds of aluminium metal were added to a beaker of bromine liquid.

This reaction, seen in Figure 9.2, is very vigorous and the mixture actually sets on fire, releasing heat and clouds of vapour. The reaction is in complete contrast to Figure 9.1 and

Figure 9.2   The vigorous reaction of aluminium metal and bromine liquid when mixed together.

the balanced Equation 9.1, which don't convey the reality of the rather violent reaction. So, a chemical reaction can easily be represented by a balanced equation but does this really convey what is 'physically' happening during that reaction? We think you would agree that, from the simple example shown here, a balanced chemical equation provides only a limited amount of information. From real observations of chemical reactions, you can see that they are not always a tranquil addition of reactants to give the products, but can be accompanied by physical changes such as the production of heat. However, this is not always the case, and not every chemical reaction will burst into flames like the example above. In fact, some chemical reactions do the opposite and actually absorb heat. So a key point about a chemical reaction is that it can be accompanied by a release or an absorption of heat, which cannot be inferred from its balanced chemical equation. An alternative way of expressing the possible release or absorption of heat in a chemical reaction is to state that *chemical reactions involve energy changes*.

Figure 9.3   A pre-dawn view of the oil refinery at Teesmouth, UK.

In the rest of this chapter, you will take a more detailed look at chemical reactions and the energy changes that accompany them. The energy changes that occur as a chemical reaction proceeds can have considerable practical benefits. For instance, most of our present daily energy needs are provided, in one way or another, by burning fossil fuels in air. These are chemical reactions that provide energy in our homes in many forms from lighting to heating, and energy to run cars and other forms of transport. It must be remembered, however, that these fuels – for example, natural gas and oil – are non-renewable energy sources and one day these reserves will be exhausted. Figure 9.3 shows an oil refinery, where fuels such as natural gas and oil are refined for our direct or indirect consumption, for example in transport fuels and consumer materials. Figure 9.4 shows the predicted growth in the world's energy consumption including fossil fuels and other energy sources. The remaining fossil fuel energy reserves therefore must be used as efficiently as possible and alternative energy sources need to be developed for the future if our consumption is to rise at the predicted levels. Chemistry has a major role to play in achieving these aims.

Modern lifestyles require the direct or indirect use of fossil fuels. The energy release that takes place when burning fossil fuels is a good example to help in investigating at a molecular level what processes occur. However, in this chapter you will not just concentrate on the energy released with respect to burning fossil fuels, but will investigate a number of chemical reactions that have a variety of associated energy changes. This will enable you to see how changes in energy occur in different ways in a chemical reaction and that the actual energy change is, in some cases, not always completely obvious!

To begin your investigation, you should attempt Activity 9.1. In this activity, you will observe several different chemical reactions. At various times you are asked to record your observations.

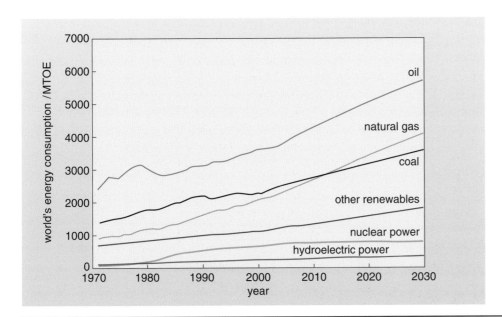

Figure 9.4 Predicted growth of the world's energy consumption with respect to energy source. MTOE, million tons of oil equivalent, is a unit of energy, equivalent to the energy released on burning one million tonnes of crude oil.

Activity 9.1   The properties of chemical reactions

We expect this activity will take you approximately 30 minutes.

You should now work through the computer-based activity *Features of Reactions*, which shows a number of chemical reactions. These reactions are not only visually interesting but also illustrate some of the properties of chemical reactions that you will study in more detail in this chapter. To help you gather the data that you observe during the video sequences, we have provided some simple tables to record the results of your observations. This will also make it easier to refer back to as you continue with your study of this chapter and Chapter 10.

Task 1   Observing the energy changes in chemical reactions

Record your observations of the changes that take place for reactions 1–3, as you work through the video sequence. (You do not need to know the details of the chemistry of reactions 1–3.)

You can now record the energy changes that you observe for these reactions in Table 9.1.

Table 9.1 The changes taking place in reactions 1–6.

Reaction number	Observation
1	
2	
3	
Reaction number	**Energy changes observed**
4	
5	
6	

Task 2 What effects do temperature and concentration have on a chemical reaction?

The next table for the activity is for reaction 7 (Table 9.2). Here, you will be asked to record the colour changes that take place on heating and cooling the liquid. During the reaction, a pink solution indicates the presence of mainly reactant, a blue solution indicates the presence of mainly product, and a violet solution indicates a mixture of reactant and product. The reasons why this reaction can be seen to be 'reversible' is investigated in the next chapter but, for now, you should record your results and keep them to refer back to.

Table 9.2 The colour changes for reaction 7 that take place on heating and cooling.

Conditions	Colour at start	Chemicals present at start	Colour at end	Chemicals present at end
beaker of ice	violet	reactant and product		
beaker of hot water	violet	reactant and product		
test tubes are then swapped over				
beaker of ice				
beaker of hot water				

For the next reaction, you will be asked to record the time taken for the colour change to occur. In this particular reaction, the solutions go from colourless to black over different periods of time. In the set of beakers in the video sequence, the concentration of reactants is varied. Use Table 9.3 to record the time taken for the colour change to occur.

Table 9.3 The time taken for the colour change to occur.

Beaker	Concentration of reactants	Time/s
left-hand	highest	
2nd from the left	high	
centre	intermediate	
2nd from the right	low	
right-hand	lowest	

Task 3 What effect does a catalyst have on a chemical reaction?

Finally, the last set of reactions show the effect of a 'catalyst'. Again, you will meet the details about catalysts and their effects on reactions in Chapter 10, but for now simply write out a short paragraph about what you 'observed' in the reactions with respect to the different catalysts used.

Now look at the comments on this activity at the end of this book.

9.1   Energy changes and internal energy

The concept of energy was discussed in detail in Book 3, and you should remember that the transformation of one form of energy into any other form is governed by the law of conservation of energy (Book 3, Chapter 2).

■   What is the law of conservation of energy?

☐   The total amount of energy is always constant, i.e. energy cannot be created or destroyed, but is transformed from one form into another.

■   In the computer-based activity *Features of Reactions*, you saw that various reactions release energy in different forms. What, apart from heat, were these forms?

☐   Light energy (reactions 2 and 4) and electrical energy (reaction 5).

Two reactions in the activity involved the release of energy in the form of heat. One was the volcano-like burning of an orange–red solid, ammonium dichromate, during heating as it decomposes to chromium oxide (Figure 9.5).

The second reaction involved the mixing of two colourless liquids at room temperature with the result that the temperature of the mixture increased significantly. It is important to note that this rise in temperature was not caused by any external heating of the reaction mixture.

Where does the energy released by these chemical reactions come from? The law of conservation of energy tells us that chemical reactions cannot create energy, and so there must be a transformation of one form of energy into another. Energy is released by these reactions because there is a change in internal energy.

Figure 9.5   Ammonium dichromate volcano reaction.

You should recall from Book 3 (Section 6.1) that there are two important components to the internal energy of a substance. One of these is kinetic energy, which is associated with random motion at the molecular level in a substance. The other component is potential energy. This is associated with the forces between particular atoms in a substance that result in the formation of chemical bonds, and also, if appropriate, with the forces between molecules that hold the substance together. In a chemical reaction, chemical bonds in the reactants are broken and new bonds are formed to give rise to the products. The reactants and products are chemically different, and this means that their respective potential energies will be different. This difference in potential energy is the source of the change in internal energy. It is sometimes referred to as a change in **chemical energy**.

So far, the discussion has focused on chemical reactions that release energy. However, in Activity 9.1, you saw an example of a reaction that absorbed energy from its local environment (Figure 9.6). In reaction 6, as the two solids (these are ammonium thiocyanate and barium hydroxide octahydrate, but the details of the chemistry need not concern you here) were mixed, they reacted to form a liquid product, and the puddle of water in which the beaker was standing was turned to ice. For this reaction, therefore, the change in internal energy is in the direction that results in heat being absorbed from the puddle of water, cooling it enough to cause the water to freeze. This reaction is by no means unique; many other chemical reactions absorb energy.

Figure 9.6   A reaction in which energy (in the form of heat) is absorbed from the local environment. The glass is attached to the beaker by ice.

You are now in a position to draw two important conclusions:

- All chemical reactions involve changes in internal energy.
- These changes can result in either a release of energy into, or the absorption of energy from, the local environment.

9.2   Chemical reactions that release or absorb heat

The fact that a large proportion of chemical reactions involve either the release or the absorption of energy in the form of heat suggests that it is worthwhile classifying reactions on this basis. Before doing so, however, it is useful to introduce two terms: **system** and **surroundings**. For the present purposes, you can think of the system as being the contents of a reaction mixture. The surroundings are literally everything else, but to be more practical it could simply be a beaker and the air (or water) in the immediate vicinity. This situation is shown in Figure 9.7, where the system is the contents of the beaker and the surroundings are the beaker and everything beyond. Both of these terms will be used in due course but, for now, only the term 'surroundings' is used explicitly.

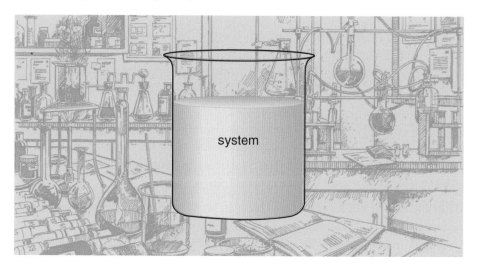

Figure 9.7   Schematic view of a system and its surroundings. Note that the beaker is part of the surroundings and the reaction mixture is the system.

If a chemical reaction releases energy into the surroundings, it is described as being **exothermic**. Conversely, a chemical reaction that absorbs energy from its surroundings is described as being **endothermic**. In each case, the internal energy of the system changes; Figure 9.8 shows how the internal energy changes in an exothermic and an endothermic reaction with respect to the initial and final amounts of energy in the system. Here you can see that the internal energy of the system (vertical axis) in an exothermic reaction is reduced; in other words, the products have a lower internal energy than the reactants. Conversely, in an endothermic reaction, the internal energy of the products is greater than that of the reactants.

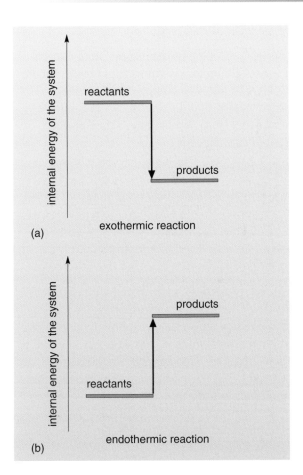

Figure 9.8 Change in internal energy of (a) an exothermic and (b) an endothermic process. The vertical axis represents the increasing internal energy of the reaction system. In an exothermic process, the reactants have greater internal energy than the products, and in an endothermic process, the reactants have lower internal energy than the products.

A chemical reaction that releases heat into the surroundings is called an **exothermic reaction**.

A chemical reaction that absorbs heat from the surroundings is called an **endothermic reaction**.

The terms exothermic and endothermic come from the Greek: *thermo* meaning heat, *exo* meaning outside, and *endo* meaning within. Hence *exo*thermic conveys the idea that heat is given *out* and *endo*thermic that heat is taken *in*. You should note that this classification takes no account of the timescale of a chemical reaction. Some reactions, for example rusting, occur so slowly that the heat released is hardly noticeable. However, rusting is classified as exothermic in exactly the same way as a reaction that bursts into flames.

In Chapter 8, the corrosion of metals was discussed and you saw that the rusting of iron involves the formation of iron oxide which contains a number of water molecules.

■ What is the chemical equation for the rusting of iron?

☐ The balanced chemical equation is:

$$4Fe(s) + 3O_2(g) + 2nH_2O(l) = 2Fe_2O_3.nH_2O(s) \tag{8.18}$$

n is used in the equation to indicate the number of water molecules, where n can vary depending on the conditions in which the rust forms.

Figure 9.9   A typical disposable cold pack.

Question 9.1

Immediate first-aid for a strain or sprain caused by playing sport often consists of cooling the damaged area. One way of doing this is with a 'cold pack' which effectively consists of a plastic bag divided into two compartments – one containing a soluble solid and the other water, like the one shown in Figure 9.9. The partition in the bag is broken (by squeezing) and the bag is then placed against the injury to achieve the desired cooling effect.

(a) Briefly explain how you think that the pack works.

(b) Suggest a design for a 'hot pack' that sports fans might appreciate on a cold winter's afternoon.

9.3   Introducing enthalpy

So far, only qualitative aspects of the energy changes associated with chemical reactions have been considered. However, quantitative information concerning the amount of energy released or absorbed by a chemical reaction under a given set of circumstances is of considerable practical interest. For example, the ability to compare the merits of different fuels in terms of the energy they release when they are burned is clearly important. To begin the discussion, the reaction between magnesium metal and fluorine gas will be taken as an example. When a stream of fluorine gas is blown over magnesium metal, magnesium fluoride is produced. This reaction is very vigorous and the reaction mixture bursts into flames. It can be described qualitatively as follows:

$$Mg(s) + F_2(g) = MgF_2(s) + energy \qquad (9.2)$$

Equation 9.2 indicates that the reaction is exothermic. This is because energy in the form of heat is transferred to the surroundings, as the mixture bursts into flames. This is because the product – solid magnesium fluoride – has a *lower* internal energy than the combined internal energies of the reactants – magnesium metal and fluorine gas. A schematic view of the energy changes in the reaction is shown in Figure 9.10.

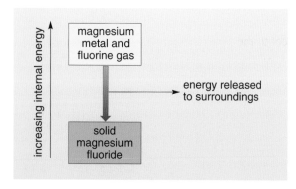

Figure 9.10   Schematic view of the energy changes that occur when magnesium metal reacts with fluorine gas. Note that the vertical axis represents internal energy, increasing upwards.

In practice, when an exothermic reaction occurs it normally raises the temperature of the reaction mixture, i.e. the system. However, after a time, heat will flow from the system to the surroundings until the products are at the same temperature as the reactants were at the start. For example, when the solid magnesium fluoride in Figure 9.10 has cooled to the same temperature as the magnesium metal and fluorine gas were at the start, *all* of the energy released in the form of heat will have been transferred to the surroundings. The overall effect is exactly the same as it would have been if the reaction had occurred throughout at a *constant temperature* equal to that of the reactants at the start of the reaction. This observation suggests a useful and unambiguous way to do energy accounting. If it is stated that an exothermic reaction has occurred at constant temperature, this indicates that all of the energy released in the form of heat has been transferred to the surroundings.

Question 9.2

Read the last paragraph again and then, without further reference, try to develop a similar account for an endothermic reaction in your own words.

More often than not, chemical reactions are carried out in containers that are open to the atmosphere. Therefore, in effect, the reactions are said to be carried out at *constant pressure*. This was the case, for example, for all of the reactions you viewed in Activity 9.1. The condition for constant pressure is very important when trying to understand and follow the changes in the internal energy of a reaction system. This can be further appreciated by considering a simple example. Acetylene gas, C_2H_2, can be produced by pouring water onto solid calcium carbide, CaC_2, expressed chemically by the following equation:

$$CaC_2(s) + 2H_2O(l) = C_2H_2(g) + Ca(OH)_2(aq) \qquad (9.3)$$

This reaction is exothermic and involves the formation of a gaseous product and so will also be accompanied by a net increase in volume. In other words, part of the internal energy change for this reaction will be expended in pushing back the atmosphere in order to 'make space' for the acetylene gas formed. So, if the reaction is exothermic, the energy released as heat will be less than the overall internal energy change for the reaction. In general, for any reaction that occurs at constant pressure and involves a volume change, there will be a difference between the change in internal energy and the energy released (or absorbed) as heat.

In most practical situations, it is the energy released, or absorbed, in the form of heat by a chemical reaction that is of direct interest. For any chemical reaction occurring at *constant pressure* this particular form of energy transfer can be identified with a change in a property called **enthalpy**. For a given substance the enthalpy can be thought of as a kind of energy store that provides, or accepts, energy in the form of heat. This idea is reflected in the derivation of the term – it comes from the Greek words for 'heat inside'.

The symbol for enthalpy is *H*, and an **enthalpy change** is written as ΔH, where Δ (the upper-case Greek letter *delta*) means 'change of'. (You met this notation in Book 3, Section 3.4.) Since an enthalpy change represents the heat transferred, the appropriate SI unit is the joule. For a chemical reaction occurring at constant pressure and constant temperature, describing this in words with respect to the change in enthalpy of the system:

change in enthalpy = enthalpy of products − enthalpy of reactants

or using the notation for enthalpy, *H*, you can write:

$$\Delta H = H(\text{products}) - H(\text{reactants}) \qquad (9.4)$$

Equation 9.4 says that the heat released, or absorbed, by the reaction is equal to the difference between the enthalpy of the products and the enthalpy of the reactants. Although no details are given here, such enthalpy changes can be measured experimentally.

The enthalpy change for any chemical reaction occurring at constant pressure and constant temperature can be taken as a direct measure of the energy released, or absorbed, in the form of heat alone.

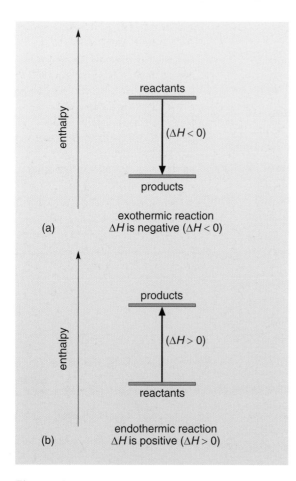

Figure 9.11   Enthalpy diagrams for (a) an exothermic reaction, where ΔH is negative, and (b) an endothermic reaction, where ΔH is positive. The vertical axes represent enthalpy (H), increasing upwards, and the enthalpies of reactants and the enthalpies of products are represented by different levels on the axes.

Now, from Equation 9.4, the sign of ΔH (+ or −) can be determined. The sign of ΔH reflects what is happening to the system, i.e. the reaction mixture itself. Therefore, for an exothermic reaction the system releases energy in the form of heat *to* the surroundings and so, in effect, ends up *minus* some energy. In contrast, for an endothermic reaction the system gains energy in the form of heat *from* the surroundings and so, in effect, ends up *plus* some energy.

For an exothermic reaction, ΔH is negative.

For an endothermic reaction, ΔH is positive.

An alternative way of depicting enthalpy changes for chemical reactions occurring at constant pressure and constant temperature is via enthalpy diagrams, as shown in Figure 9.11.

9.4   Thermochemical equations

You are now in a position to look at the energy changes associated with chemical reactions, and with changes in physical state in a more quantitative manner. Since it is the heat that is released or absorbed that is of most practical interest, the discussion will focus on enthalpy changes in reactions. You will start by considering enthalpy changes associated with changes of state.

9.4.1   Changes of state

The main example that you will be looking at in detail will be that ever-present substance: water. Picturing the events of the changes of state of water (solid ⟶ liquid ⟶ gas) at a molecular level will prove valuable in accounting for the enthalpy changes that occur in that particular system. As you will already be aware, we see the three states of water (gas, liquid and solid) all around us. In Figure 9.12, the three states of water are depicted in an everyday scene: water vapour in the air, liquid water in the lake and solid ice floating on top of the water. The packing structures of the water molecules are also given in the figure: a closely packed, regular arrangement in ice (the molecules vibrate in their fixed positions); more mobile molecules in liquid water (the molecules are not arranged in a regular way and can move around); and highly spaced, fast-moving molecules in the gas state (molecules move around rapidly in a chaotic manner).

The first process you will look at is the vaporisation of water; that is, changing from a liquid to a gas – for example, when you boil a kettle. The vaporisation of water, at atmospheric pressure and at its boiling temperature of 100 °C, can be represented by a chemical equation:

$$H_2O(l) = H_2O(g) \qquad (9.5)$$

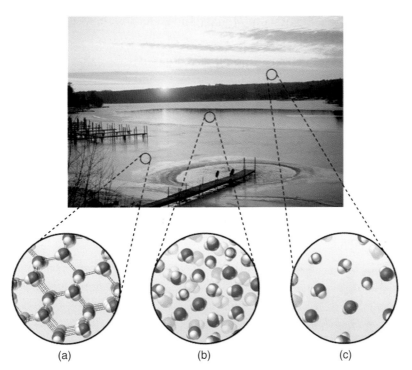

Figure 9.12 The three states of water in a partially frozen lake scene and the molecular structure of the water molecules in these states. (a) Ice (solid), where the molecules are arranged in a regular, close-packed, three-dimensional array. (b) Water (liquid), where the molecules are not in a regular repeating array and can move about, but must still be close together. (c) Vapour (gas), where the molecules are spaced well apart and are rapidly moving around in a chaotic manner.

(a)   (b)   (c)

■ Is this change of state an exothermic or endothermic process?

☐ Boiling a kettle requires the input of energy in the form of heat that has to be supplied (usually electrically) to vaporise the water. In other words, the change of state requires absorption of heat from the surroundings at constant temperature (100 °C). Therefore, vaporising a liquid is an endothermic process; energy has to be supplied.

■ In Book 3, a particular term was used to describe the energy required to vaporise a unit mass of a liquid at its boiling temperature. Can you remember what this term is?

☐ The energy required to vaporise a unit mass of a liquid at its boiling temperature is termed the specific latent heat of vaporisation, symbol L (Book 3, Section 6.5).

The latent heat of vaporisation of water is 2.26×10^6 J kg^{-1}. This quantity refers to the change of state occurring not only at constant temperature, but also at constant (atmospheric) pressure. It is therefore equivalent to an enthalpy change. This particular enthalpy change is often referred to as the **enthalpy of vaporisation** and is represented as $\Delta H_{\text{vaporisation}}$, or just ΔH_{vap} for short. Hence, we can write $\Delta H_{\text{vap}} = +2.26 \times 10^6$ J kg^{-1}, where the positive sign has been included because the change is endothermic. It is generally the case that enthalpy changes are reported in kilojoules, kJ, rather than joules; 1 kJ = 1.0×10^3 J. Thus, to be more conventional, we write $\Delta H_{\text{vap}} = +2260$ kJ kg^{-1}. This means that an enthalpy change of +2260 kJ occurs when 1 kg of liquid water, at 100 °C and at atmospheric pressure, is completely converted into water vapour (steam).

It is also useful to express enthalpy changes in molar terms, because a direct link can then be made with the corresponding chemical equation interpreted on a molar basis.

■ How would you interpret Equation 9.5 on a molar basis?

☐ It can be interpreted as indicating that one mole of water molecules in the liquid state is converted into one mole of water molecules in the gaseous (or vapour) state.

Question 9.3

Calculate a value for the enthalpy of vaporisation for one mole of water molecules, given that $\Delta H_{vap} = +2260$ kJ kg^{-1}. (You will need first to work out the mass of one mole of water molecules. Take the relative atomic masses of hydrogen and oxygen to be 1.0 and 16.0, respectively.)

The enthalpy of vaporisation of water calculated in Question 9.3 can be combined with the chemical equation (Equation 9.5) to give a **thermochemical equation** for the vaporisation of one mole of water:

$$H_2O(l) = H_2O(g) \quad \Delta H_{vap} = +40.7 \text{ kJ mol}^{-1} \tag{9.6}$$

This thermochemical equation conveniently combines the chemical equation, *which is to be interpreted on a molar basis*, with a statement of the corresponding enthalpy change. This type of equation will be used throughout the remainder of this book.

A thermochemical equation can also be written for **condensation**, which is the reverse of vaporisation. Since vaporisation involves the *absorption* of a given amount of energy in the form of heat, then it follows from the law of conservation of energy that this same amount of heat will be *released* on condensation. Hence, condensation is an exothermic process.

■ Write down the thermochemical equation that describes one mole of water molecules in the gaseous state condensing to give liquid water at 100 °C and atmospheric pressure.

☐ The thermochemical equation is:

$$H_2O(g) = H_2O(l) \quad \Delta H_{condensation} = -40.7 \text{ kJ mol}^{-1} \tag{9.7}$$

Question 9.4

Scalding by steam is extremely painful. Give a brief description of what happens in energy terms when steam comes into contact with skin.

9.4.2   A molecular description of change of state

Since vaporisation is an endothermic process, as energy has to be supplied, this can be simply related to the molecular process taking place in the system. From Figure 9.12, you can see that the molecules of water are more closely held together in the liquid than in the gaseous state. The strong attractive forces between the water molecules in the liquid are due to hydrogen bonding and this type of bonding needs to be broken to allow the molecules to escape one another into the gaseous state. (You met hydrogen bonding in Section 4.2.3.) Energy has to be supplied to break the hydrogen bonding present in liquid water to produce water vapour.

An enthalpy change also accompanies the change of state when a solid melts to give a liquid. Again water will be taken as the example, where at normal atmospheric pressure ice melts at 0 °C to give liquid water at the same temperature. This transition from a solid to a liquid is known as **fusion** and the related enthalpy change is usually referred to as the enthalpy of fusion (ΔH_{fus}). For water, the ΔH_{fus} at 0 °C is 6 kJ mol^{-1}; again, this is positive, indicating that the melting of ice is an endothermic process. You should note that the enthalpy of fusion is much less than the enthalpy of vaporisation. This can be explained at a molecular level. When a solid melts to a liquid the molecules are not separated completely but still have some interactions, whereas on vaporisation the molecules are completely separated. The reverse of melting is **freezing** and this is an exothermic process.

Finally, one other change of state that can occur is that of **sublimation** (Section 4.4). This is when a solid changes directly to gas. You can see this on a cold, frosty morning when the frost seems to vanish and yet no liquid is left behind. Again, sublimation is an endothermic process and the associated enthalpy change is termed the enthalpy of sublimation (ΔH_{sub}). The reverse of this process is known as vapour deposition. The thermochemical equation for this process can be written as:

$$H_2O(s) = H_2O(g) \quad \Delta H_{sub} = +46.7 \text{ kJ mol}^{-1} \tag{9.8}$$

The relatively large enthalpy of sublimation is a reflection of the fact that the water molecules in ice are securely locked together and require quite a lot of energy to separate them into the gaseous state. The changes in enthalpy of all the changes of state of water are depicted in Figure 9.13.

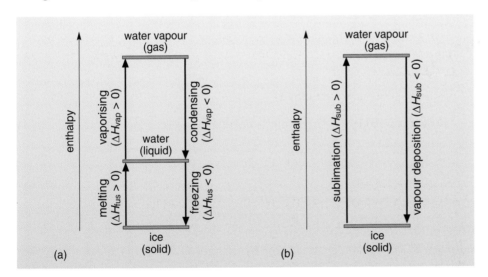

Figure 9.13   The enthalpy changes associated with changes in state for water. (a) The enthalpy changes associated with changes between gas, liquid and solid. (b) The enthalpy changes associated with direct change between gas and solid.

■ What do you notice from Figure 9.13 about the magnitude of enthalpy of fusion and vaporisation compared with that of sublimation for water?

☐ In Figure 9.13, the sum of both the enthalpy of fusion and vaporisation are equal to the enthalpy of sublimation for water and are all endothermic processes. Thus it can be written that:

$$\Delta H_{fus} + \Delta H_{vap} = \Delta H_{sub} \qquad (9.9)$$

9.4.3   Thermochemical equations and chemical reactions

The idea of a thermochemical equation is quite general. The reaction between magnesium metal and fluorine gas, for instance, gives rise to the following thermochemical equation:

$$Mg(s) + F_2(g) = MgF_2(s) \quad \Delta H = -1123 \text{ kJ mol}^{-1} \qquad (9.10)$$

This equation can be read as follows: when one mole of magnesium atoms in solid magnesium reacts with one mole of fluorine molecules in the gaseous state at constant pressure to form solid magnesium fluoride at the same temperature, 1123 kJ of energy in the form of heat are transferred from the system to the surroundings. Although expressed in molar terms, the thermochemical equation can be used to calculate the heat released when any amount of magnesium metal reacts with fluorine gas.

■ How much energy in the form of heat will be released when 5.00 g of magnesium metal reacts with fluorine gas at constant pressure? (The relative atomic mass of magnesium is 24.3.)

☐ According to Equation 9.10, the reaction of one mole of magnesium atoms, i.e. 24.3 g of magnesium, results in the release of 1123 kJ of energy in the form of heat.

So 1 g of magnesium will release $\dfrac{1123}{24.3}$ kJ. If 5.00 g of magnesium reacts, the energy released in the form of heat will be:

$$\frac{1123 \times 5.00}{24.3} \text{ kJ} = 231 \text{ kJ}$$

Thermochemical equations are particularly useful for comparing chemical reactions of the same type. An important set of reactions are those in which different fuels are burned in oxygen (usually from the air). For example, the thermochemical equations for burning hydrogen gas and methane gas are as follows:

$$2H_2(g) + O_2(g) = 2H_2O(g) \qquad \Delta H = -484 \text{ kJ mol}^{-1} \qquad (9.11)$$
$$CH_4(g) + 2O_2(g) = CO_2(g) + 2H_2O(g) \quad \Delta H = -802 \text{ kJ mol}^{-1} \qquad (9.12)$$

Comparing the two equations, you can see that completely burning *one* mole of methane gas releases significantly more energy in the form of heat than does burning *two* moles of hydrogen gas. However, fuel is not bought by the mole – it is often more useful to compare the heat released by different fuels on a mass-for-mass basis.

Table 9.4 Fuels and the energy they release as heat.

Fuel	Chemical equation	Enthalpy change/ kJ mol^{-1}	Energy released as heat per kilogram of fuel/kJ kg^{-1}
carbon, C (as in coal)	$C(s) + O_2(g) \longrightarrow CO_2(g)$	$\Delta H = -394$	33 000
methane, CH_4 (as in natural gas)	$CH_4(g) + 2O_2(g) \longrightarrow CO_2(g) + 2H_2O(g)$	$\Delta H = -802$	50 000
octane, C_8H_{18} (as in petrol)	$2C_8H_{18}(l) + 25O_2(g) \longrightarrow 16CO_2(g) + 18H_2O(g)$	$\Delta H = -10\ 240$	45 000
methanol, CH_3OH	$2CH_3OH(l) + 3O_2(g) \longrightarrow 2CO_2(g) + 4H_2O(g)$	$\Delta H = -1277$	20 000
ethanol, C_2H_5OH	$C_2H_5OH(l) + 3O_2(g) \longrightarrow 2CO_2(g) + 3H_2O(g)$	$\Delta H = -1238$	
carbohydrates (sugars and starches)	products are $CO_2(g)$ and $H_2O(l)$		an average value of 17 000
animal fats	products are $CO_2(g)$ and $H_2O(l)$		variable; 40 000 a typical value
hydrogen, H_2	$2H_2(g) + O_2(g) \longrightarrow 2H_2O(g)$	$\Delta H = -484$	120 000

Table 9.4 provides the thermochemical equations for a wider selection of fuels: those used in our homes, motor cars, industry and our own bodies. Petrol is a complex mixture and so information for the 'representative' compound, octane, is given; the balanced chemical equation is quite complex in this case. The chemical formulas given in the table are written in a way that you will learn more about later in the book. The final column in the table gives, for each fuel apart from ethanol, a value for the energy released as heat when 1 kg of the fuel is fully burned in oxygen. For convenience, these values are expressed to the nearest thousand kilojoules.

Question 9.5

To complete the final column of Table 9.4, calculate the energy released as heat when 1 kg of liquid ethanol is fully burned in oxygen.

On a mass-for-mass basis, hydrogen gas is potentially a very good fuel and, in principle, it could be distributed via a pipeline system to where energy is needed. A further advantage is that it is the only fuel in Table 9.4 that does not give rise to carbon dioxide emissions and thus to concerns about global warming. However, there are also significant drawbacks. A major problem is that there is little hydrogen on Earth that is not tied up in chemical compounds. Hydrogen has to be treated as a synthetic fuel that has to be manufactured – for example, from water. This can be done only at significant cost. Combustion of hydrogen in air also occurs at temperatures at which nitrogen will react with oxygen to produce a harmful mix of nitrogen oxide gases; in environmental terms, it is not a 'clean' process. Other points can also be made with regard to safety; a spark in the wrong place could be disastrous (to which the *Hindenburg* disaster of 1937, in which an airship caught fire and was very rapidly destroyed, is testimony). It is also important to recognise that hydrogen has the lowest density of any gas and so a given volume will have a relatively small mass. It turns out that, on a *volume-for-volume* basis, the energy released as heat by burning hydrogen amounts to roughly one-third of that released by burning natural gas.

9.5   Enthalpy changes: delving deeper

The enthalpy changes that have been quoted in thermochemical equations so far have all been measured experimentally. However, *for reactions in which the reactants and products are all gases*, it is often possible to estimate the magnitudes of enthalpy changes without recourse to experiment. The method of estimation provides a means of delving deeper into the source of the enthalpy change for a given reaction.

Underlying the method of estimation is an important property of the enthalpy change for any reaction occurring at constant pressure and constant temperature. The enthalpy change is *independent* of the way in which the reaction occurs. The starting reactants have a certain enthalpy, and so do the final products. The change is simply equal to the difference. You can think of this as being rather like travelling between two places; there may be several different routes but you will always finish up the same distance, as the crow flies, from your starting point.

As an example of estimating an enthalpy change, consider the reaction between hydrogen gas and oxygen gas:

$$2H_2(g) + O_2(g) = 2H_2O(g) \qquad\qquad (9.13)$$

Imagine this reaction occurring in a simple two-step sequence. In step 1, you can imagine that the covalent bonds in the diatomic hydrogen and oxygen molecules are broken so that individual hydrogen and oxygen atoms are formed.

$$\text{Step 1: } 2H_2(g) + O_2(g) \longrightarrow 4H(g) + 2O(g) \qquad\qquad (9.14)$$

In step 2, the hydrogen and oxygen atoms combine to form water molecules.

$$\text{Step 2: } 4H(g) + 2O(g) \longrightarrow 2H_2O(g) \qquad\qquad (9.15)$$

Equations 9.14 and 9.15 should both be interpreted on a *molar basis*. The overall reaction, which you know is exothermic (Table 9.4), can be represented by the enthalpy diagram in Figure 9.14.

Figure 9.14   Enthalpy diagram showing the two-step sequence that was selected to represent how the reaction between $H_2(g)$ and $O_2(g)$ occurs to produce $H_2O(g)$. Two molecules of hydrogen (grey, smaller spheres) are shown reacting with one molecule of oxygen (red, larger spheres).

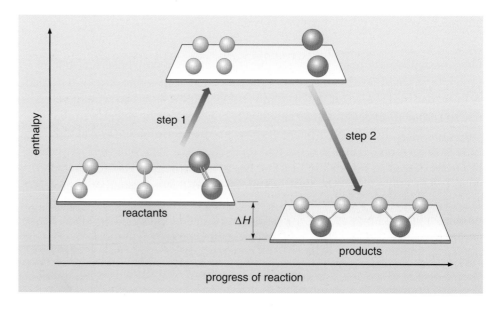

Remember that this two-step sequence need *not* represent how the reaction between hydrogen gas and oxygen gas actually occurs. In fact, it is known that this reaction occurs in a longer sequence of steps.

The breakdown of hydrogen, oxygen or indeed any diatomic molecule in the gaseous state into its constituent atoms is referred to as **dissociation**.

■ Would you expect dissociation to be an exothermic or endothermic process?

☐ If you imagine the process occurring at constant temperature, then energy in the form of heat will have to be supplied in order to break the covalent bonds. So dissociation is an endothermic process.

The thermochemical equations for the dissociation of hydrogen and oxygen are as follows:

$$H_2(g) \longrightarrow H(g) + H(g) \quad \Delta H = +436 \text{ kJ mol}^{-1} \tag{9.16}$$
$$O_2(g) \longrightarrow O(g) + O(g) \quad \Delta H = +498 \text{ kJ mol}^{-1} \tag{9.17}$$

The enthalpy change in each of these two equations is called the **molar bond enthalpy**. This term is general and applies to the dissociation of all diatomic molecules. Since the dissociation process is always endothermic, molar bond enthalpies are always positive.

■ What is the total enthalpy change for the process that is labelled step 1 in Equation 9.14?

☐ It is important to consider the number of bonds that are broken. Thus, there are 'two moles of hydrogen–hydrogen bonds' (each mole requiring 436 kJ) and 'one mole of oxygen–oxygen bonds' (requiring 498 kJ). Thus, for step 1, the total enthalpy change amounts to:

$$2 \times (+436 \text{ kJ}) + 498 \text{ kJ} = +1370 \text{ kJ}$$

You now need to consider step 2 (Equation 9.15), in which chemical bonds are formed.

■ Would you expect the formation of a chemical bond between two atoms to be an exothermic or endothermic process?

☐ Since bond breaking is endothermic, it must be the case that the reverse process – bond formation – is exothermic. (There are parallels here with the discussion of the vaporisation and condensation of water in Section 9.4.)

It is important to be clear about the details of the argument at this stage. The breaking of 'one mole of chemical bonds' is an endothermic process and has an enthalpy change given by the molar bond enthalpy. The reverse process – the formation of 'one mole of chemical bonds' – is exothermic and will have an enthalpy change that is simply the negative of the molar bond enthalpy.

■ The mean molar bond enthalpy for each of the two O—H bonds in the water molecule is 464 kJ. What is the total enthalpy change for step 2? (Consider the number of bonds that are formed.)

☐ In one mole of water molecules there are 'two moles of O—H bonds'. However, *two* moles of water molecules are formed. This is equivalent to the formation of 'four moles of O—H bonds', each mole of which releases 464 kJ. Thus, for step 2, the enthalpy change amounts to:

$$4 \times (-464) \text{ kJ} = -1856 \text{ kJ}$$

The water molecule contains two oxygen–hydrogen, O—H, bonds. In this case, the idea of bond enthalpy still holds but it refers to breaking *just one* of these bonds. In fact, the situation is a little more complex than it might seem. If the two O—H bonds in the water molecule are broken one after another, the enthalpy changes for these two processes treated separately are not equal. However, for the purposes of this calculation it is reasonable to take a mean of these enthalpy changes.

The calculations so far have been based on the separate reactions in Equations 9.14 and 9.15.

■ What happens if these equations are added together?

☐ The addition gives:

$$2H_2(g) + O_2(g) + 4H(g) + 2O(g) \longrightarrow 4H(g) + 2O(g) + 2H_2O(g) \qquad (9.18)$$

Cancelling out the species that are the same on both sides of this equation gives the equation for the overall reaction, i.e.:

$$2H_2(g) + O_2(g) \longrightarrow 2H_2O(g) \qquad (9.13)$$

In the same way, the overall enthalpy change for the reaction is found by adding together the enthalpy changes for the individual steps:

$$\Delta H = \Delta H(\text{step 1}) + \Delta H(\text{step 2}) \qquad (9.19)$$

■ What is the overall enthalpy change, in kilojoules?

☐ $\Delta H = +1370 \text{ kJ} + (-1856 \text{ kJ})$

$= +1370 \text{ kJ} - 1856 \text{ kJ}$

$= -486 \text{ kJ}$

This value is negative, indicating that the reaction is exothermic, and it agrees well with the experimental value in Table 9.4 of -484 kJ.

So, what can you now say about the enthalpy changes that occur during a chemical reaction? The two-step sequence for the reaction between hydrogen gas and oxygen gas was deliberately chosen to be simple. None the less, no matter how a chemical reaction occurs in practice, chemical bonds must always be broken and new ones formed between different partners. It is this 'breaking and making' of chemical bonds that makes a major contribution to the overall enthalpy change and, indeed, can determine whether a reaction is exothermic or endothermic. Estimates of enthalpy changes are generally restricted to reactions in which the reactants and products are all gases; i.e. to reactions that occur in the gas phase.

Question 9.6

Hydrogen gas reacts with chlorine gas as follows:

$$H_2(g) + Cl_2(g) = 2HCl(g)$$

The molar bond enthalpies for the H—H, Cl—Cl and H—Cl chemical bonds are 436, 242 and 431 kJ mol^{-1}, respectively. Use this information to estimate the overall enthalpy change for the reaction. Is the reaction exothermic or endothermic?

9.6   Summary of Chapter 9

Chemical reactions involve changes in internal energy.

A chemical reaction that releases heat into the surroundings is described as being exothermic; one that absorbs heat from the surroundings is described as being endothermic.

For a reaction that occurs at constant pressure and constant temperature, the enthalpy change, ΔH, can be taken as a measure of the exchange of energy in the form of heat with the surroundings. For an exothermic reaction the value of ΔH is negative, and for an endothermic reaction the value of ΔH is positive.

The enthalpy change for a chemical reaction can be represented using an enthalpy diagram.

A thermochemical equation combines the chemical equation, which is to be interpreted on a molar basis, with a statement of the corresponding enthalpy change.

Enthalpy changes for reactions occurring in the gas phase can be estimated using molar bond enthalpies.

You have used mathematical skills in a chemical context, and practised further the skill of making observations and drawing inferences.

Chapter 10
Rates of chemical reactions and chemical equilibrium

In Chapter 9, you learned how to describe, estimate and calculate the energy changes in a reaction and found that this can be done using thermochemical equations. However, these calculations only describe how the internal energy of a system changes in a particular reaction, and not whether the reaction will actually happen, or whether it will be slow or fast. When looking at a chemical reaction, the information provided by its balanced chemical equation does not provide any clues about the speed of the reaction. Here, 'speed' means how quickly the reactants are consumed or the products are formed. The speed of a chemical reaction depends on the substances involved and the conditions under which the reaction is taking place. This chapter now looks in detail at two other aspects of chemical reactions. First, we will examine how fast reactions happen, i.e. the 'rate of reaction' or, as it is generally referred to, **chemical kinetics**. Second, the chapter will explore **chemical equilibrium**.

10.1   Chemical kinetics: how fast do chemical reactions go?

First, looking at two chemical reactions that we often observe in our everyday lives, the burning of methane gas in oxygen and the rusting of iron (Figure 10.1), you would say that both reactions occur, but one is very fast and the other is relatively slow. The study of 'chemical kinetics' enables us to examine the rate of such reactions by determining how fast the reactants are used up to form the products and how the reaction responds to the changes in conditions, e.g. temperature or pressure. Everywhere, chemical reactions are occurring at

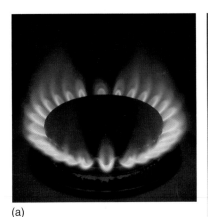
(a)

(b)

Figure 10.1   (a) Burning methane gas in the home on a gas stove: an example of a fast chemical reaction. (b) The rusting sculpture of the Angel of the North near Gateshead in the UK: an example of a slow chemical reaction.

varying rates, which enable us and our planet to exist. For instance, in our bodies many chemical reactions occur at different rates but are balanced and controlled, thereby allowing us to function. Understanding and controlling the rates of chemical reactions ultimately allows us to develop new chemical products, improve the efficiency of manufacturing processes and therefore chemical yields and determine many environmental processes. Therefore, not surprisingly, rates of chemical reactions influence all aspects of our lives!

10.1.1   The definition of the rate of a chemical reaction

If you want to investigate the rate of a chemical reaction and the way in which it proceeds, you need to be able to quantify it under certain conditions such as temperature and pressure. Following the rate of a chemical reaction implies that there is a passage of time during which the reaction proceeds. Therefore, to follow the rate of change of a reaction you would measure some physical quantity of that reaction which changes linearly with time. A basic definition for the rate of change can be written as follows:

$$\text{rate of change} = \frac{\text{change in physical quantity}}{\text{time interval}} \qquad (10.1)$$

For the interval of time, this could be seconds, minutes or hours, and the changing physical quantity could be the concentration of a reactant or product (Section 6.4) in a chemical reaction. So, if you were monitoring the change in the concentration of a product in a reaction the equation would now read:

$$\text{rate of reaction} = \frac{\text{change in product concentration}}{\text{time interval}} \qquad (10.2)$$

This equation tells you that the change in the concentration of the product divided by the time period in which the change occurs gives a measure of the rate of reaction, provided that the time interval is small compared with the duration of the overall reaction.

You can now relate this equation to a real chemical reaction. The example that will be used here is the 'clock' reaction (which you saw demonstrated in Activity 9.1), in which peroxodisulfate ions, $S_2O_8^{2-}(aq)$, react with iodide ions to produce sulfate ions and iodine, as shown in Equation 10.3. In the activity, you should recall from your tabulated observations that the reactants in the solution mixture went from colourless to black after different periods of time, depending on the concentration of reactants. The changing colour of the solutions is shown in Figure 10.2, where the left-hand beaker is most concentrated and the right-hand beaker is at the lowest concentration. In the activity, you observed the formation of the iodine product (black) with respect to time.

$$S_2O_8^{2-}(aq) + 2I^-(aq) = 2SO_4^{2-}(aq) + I_2(aq) \qquad (10.3)$$

The concentration of iodine is zero at the start of the reaction when solutions containing iodide ions and peroxodisulfate ions are mixed together. As the reaction proceeds, the concentration of iodine in the solution gradually builds to a constant value. Once this value is reached, no further change in the concentration is observed. The change in the concentration of iodine is shown graphically in Figure 10.3.

(a)

(b)

(c)

(d)

Figure 10.2 The iodine 'clock' reaction as seen in Activity 9.1. The most concentrated solution is in the left-hand beaker and the least concentrated in the right-hand beaker. (a) to (d) show the formation of the iodine product (black solution) as time progresses. The elapsed time is shown in seconds.

The curve in Figure 10.3 represents the progress of the reaction under a given set of reaction conditions. The slope of the curve at any point tells you how fast the reaction is going at that time. For a faster reaction, the curve will rise more steeply and then flatten out in a shorter time; for slower reactions, the initial rise will be more gradual and the time before the curve flattens out will be longer.

You can now write down an expression for the rate of the reaction in this early stage, when you follow the reaction with respect to the change in concentration of iodine:

$$\text{rate of reaction} = \frac{\text{change in iodine concentration}}{\text{time interval}} \qquad (10.4)$$

In Figure 10.3, the reaction takes place under certain conditions, that of fixed concentrations of reactants and a fixed temperature of 25 °C. Hence, the rate of that reaction relates specifically to those conditions only. If the conditions for a particular reaction are changed, the rate of reaction will change. One way to vary the rate of a chemical reaction is to change a certain condition: for example, the concentration of one or more of the reactants or the temperature. We can then monitor the change in the concentration of one of the products again with respect to time, and thus see how varying a particular condition affects the rate of that reaction. In the next section, we will look in more detail at how the rate of a reaction can be changed by varying a certain condition and therefore its overall effect: whether it increases or decreases the rate of reaction.

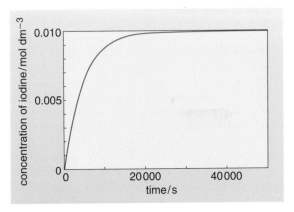

Figure 10.3 The increase in the concentration of iodine, $I_2(aq)$, as a function of time as the reaction in Equation 10.3 progresses at 25 °C.

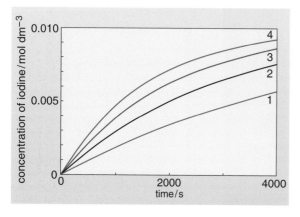

Figure 10.4   The progress of the reaction in Equation 10.3 as measured by the increase in iodine concentration at 25 °C for four initial concentrations of peroxodisulfate ions. The initial concentration increases in the order red, black, blue, green (labelled 1–4).

10.2   Varying the rate of a chemical reaction

From the reaction in Equation 10.3, we can now see how the rate of this reaction changes if we vary certain conditions. Again, you will follow the change in concentration of iodine molecules formed. The first condition that is varied is the initial concentration of peroxodisulfate ions, $S_2O_8^{2-}$(aq), in the starting solution. The rate of reaction is monitored from the change in iodine concentration and shown graphically in Figure 10.4, where the initial concentration of $S_2O_8^{2-}$(aq) increases in the order red (1) through to green (4) on the graph.

■   Look at the time taken for each of the reactions represented by the curves in Figure 10.4 to reach a particular concentration of iodine, say 0.002 mol dm^{-3}. Does the rate of reaction increase or decrease as the initial concentration of peroxodisulfate increases?

□   The curves in Figure 10.4 show that, as the initial concentration of peroxodisulfate ions increases, the time taken for the reaction to reach a particular concentration of iodine decreases, which means that the rate of reaction has increased.

The rate of this reaction, like many others, is increased by increasing the initial concentration of one of the reactants. Varying the concentration is thus one way in which the rate of reaction can be altered.

Another way to change the rate of a reaction is to vary the temperature. This is an effect you have probably come across in everyday life. Imagine that you left a carton of milk out on a hot summer's day; it would start to go 'off' or spoil quite quickly. The same would happen with a bowl of fruit in the hot weather, as in Figure 10.5; it will rot if left out too long. However, you know that if you keep the milk, fruit and other perishables cool then the spoilage tends to be slowed down. The deterioration of food is a chemical reaction which is affected by temperature, the rate increasing as the temperature increases. *In general, increasing the temperature of a chemical reaction increases the rate of reaction.*

If you go back to the reaction in Equation 10.3, you can now see how increasing the temperature affects the rate of the reaction while the concentrations of the initial reactants are kept the same in each case. Figure 10.6 shows the change in the concentration of the iodine molecules as the temperature is increased from the red curve to the green curve.

Figure 10.5   In the summer, fruit left in a bowl starts to rot quite quickly.

■ Look at the time taken for each of the reactions represented by the curves in Figure 10.6 to reach a particular concentration of iodine. Does the rate of reaction increase or decrease as the temperature increases?

□ The time taken for any chosen concentration of iodine to be produced decreases as the temperature increases; this means that the rate of reaction increases with increasing temperature.

You have now met two ways in which the rate of a reaction can be altered: changing the concentration of a reactant, and changing the temperature. The next section considers exactly *why* reaction rates depend upon concentration of reactants and the temperature.

10.3   Why reactions happen: molecular collisions and energy

A fundamental requirement for molecules to react is that they come into contact with each other. You would expect that the reactant molecules could form product molecules only if they collided with each other, and this is true for all molecules reacting in the gaseous state. Reactions of solids can be slow because of the difficulty that reactant molecules in the centre of a solid have in reaching other reactant molecules. Reactions can be speeded up by dissolving the reactants in solution, because the molecules can then encounter each other more easily. The more concentrated the solution, the greater the probability of reactant molecules encountering each other; consequently, reactions in solution often go faster as the initial concentrations of reactants increase. Figure 10.7 shows how increasing the concentration of molecules increases the chance of collisions and hence the

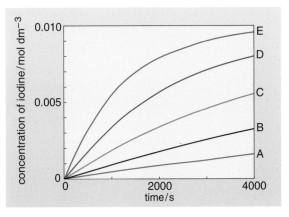

Figure 10.6   How the rate of the reaction in Equation 10.3 varies with temperature. The progress of the reaction is plotted as in Figure 10.4, but this time the initial concentrations of both reactants are fixed, and the different curves correspond to different temperatures; the temperature increases in the order red, black, brown, blue, green (labelled A–E).

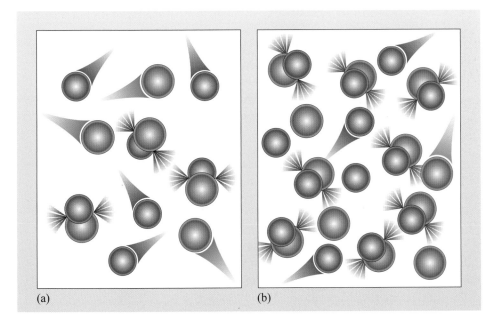

(a)   (b)

Figure 10.7   The effect of increasing concentration on the probability of molecules colliding and thus reacting to form products. (a) Collisions between the blue and the green molecules. (b) Increased collisions after the concentration is increased.

rate of reaction. Similarly, reactions in the gaseous state usually go faster if the pressure of the reactant gases is increased, because the molecules will collide more often.

You have also seen the effect of temperature on the rate of a reaction. As the temperature is increased, the rate of reaction also increases. Again, why is this so? If you think of how the reactant molecules move about in a gas or solution and the effect of heating the molecules, you have the answer. Heating the reactant molecules gives them more kinetic energy, so they move faster. This increased speed increases their chances per unit time to collide and so react with each other.

However, just increasing the concentration or the temperature of a system does not mean that all the reactant molecules that do collide will actually be successful in forming the products. So simply increasing the chance that the reactant molecules come together is not enough to ensure that a reaction will take place. In fact, only a small fraction of collisions will result in forming the final product. This is because the molecules colliding must have a certain amount of kinetic energy to make a successful reaction occur. Those without this amount of energy may collide but just 'bounce' off each other without reacting. This situation is easier to visualise in Figure 10.8, where the reactant molecules are shown to have varying degrees of kinetic energy. In zone 1, these reactant molecules don't have enough energy and if they collide they will not react to form products, but in zone 2, the molecules have the required amount of energy so will react to form products if they collide. You should note also that the number of molecules with sufficient energy to react is smaller than the number without sufficient energy (represented by the area under the curve) and this is why so few successful collisions actually occur.

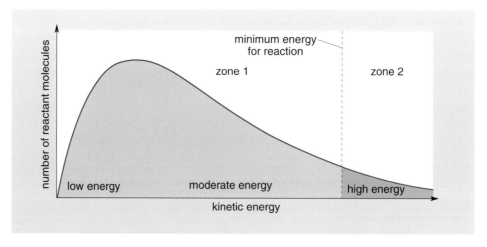

Figure 10.8 The kinetic energy of reactant molecules. The number of reactant molecules that have insufficient kinetic energy to react (zone 1) and those that have sufficient kinetic energy to react (zone 2).

You now need to consider how reactant molecules with the minimum amount of kinetic energy required actually react to form the products when they collide successfully, and why those that don't have the minimum amount of energy are unsuccessful. To do this, you will look at a simple reaction. In the lower layer of the atmosphere (the troposphere which you met in Book 1, Section 5.1), ultraviolet radiation from the Sun can break one of the O—H bonds in a water molecule to form a hydrogen atom, H, and a hydroxyl molecule, OH. The latter can react with an oxygen atom (formed by breaking bonds in other oxygen-containing molecules) to form an oxygen molecule and a hydrogen atom:

$$O(g) + OH(g) = O_2(g) + H(g) \qquad (10.5)$$

This reaction passes through an intervening stage, at the instant of encounter, in which the O—H bond in the hydroxyl molecule is partially broken and an O—O bond in the oxygen molecule is partially formed. This intervening stage is *not* a stable molecule: its internal energy is *higher* than that of either the products or the reactants. Figure 10.9 shows how the internal energy changes as the oxygen atom and the hydroxyl molecule react.

As can be seen from this diagram, before the products can form, the reactant molecules must gain enough energy to reach the intervening stage. In this case, the energy is supplied by the kinetic energy of the colliding oxygen and hydroxyl molecules. If, when they collide, the kinetic energy available is insufficient to enable the intervening stage to form, a reaction does not occur. The oxygen atom and the hydroxyl molecule simply bounce off each other. Thus, only encounters involving sufficient energy lead to reaction. Another way of describing this is to say that there is an **energy barrier** to a reaction, such that products can form only if reactant molecules gain enough energy to surmount the barrier.

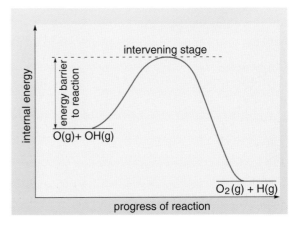

Figure 10.9   Schematic representation of how the internal energy changes during the process in Equation 10.5.

So, returning to the idea that an increase in temperature increases the reaction rate, you can now relate this to the energy barrier description. You know that the energy needed to surmount the energy barrier generally comes from the kinetic energy of the reactant molecules. However, only a fraction of encounters involve sufficient kinetic energy to overcome the energy barrier and lead to reaction. The molecules in a gas have a range of speeds, and their mean speed increases as the temperature increases.

■   How will the proportion of molecules with large amounts of kinetic energy vary with temperature?

☐   Molecules with high speeds will have high kinetic energies and so the fraction of molecules with high kinetic energy increases with increasing temperature.

If more molecules have high kinetic energy, the probability that an encounter involves sufficient energy to overcome the energy barrier will be higher and so the reaction will be faster. Figure 10.10 (overleaf) shows how the proportions of kinetic energy of the reactant molecules at two different temperatures ($T_2 > T_1$) differ; at T_2, a higher proportion have the minimum energy to react successfully. Molecules in solution also have a distribution of speeds and so similar arguments apply to reactions in solution. So, as the temperature is raised, the rate of reaction

Figure 10.10 The kinetic energy of reactant molecules at two different temperatures where $T_2 > T_1$. A greater proportion of reactant molecules at T_2 have enough kinetic energy to react successfully during a collision shown in zone 2.

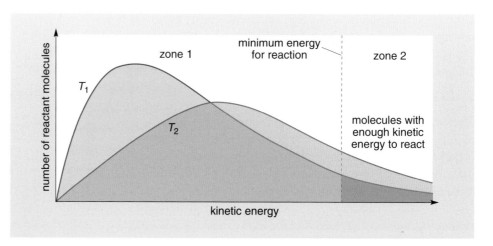

increases because more encounters have sufficient energy to overcome the energy barrier. You can draw a general conclusion about the effect of temperature on reaction rate:

> The rate of any chemical reaction can be increased by raising the temperature at which the reaction takes place.

Energy barriers exist for *every* chemical reaction, not just for simple reactions like the one in Equation 10.5. Therefore, it does not matter whether the reaction is exothermic or endothermic, the reactant molecules themselves must overcome the energy barrier to form the products. Knowing this, you can represent both exothermic and endothermic reactions using energy barrier diagrams as in Figure 10.11.

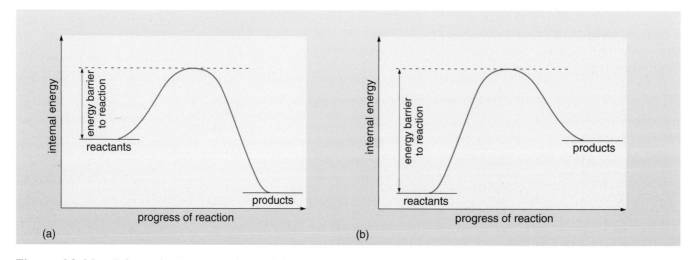

Figure 10.11 Schematic representations of the energy barriers that must be overcome for (a) a general exothermic reaction and (b) a general endothermic reaction.

> Every chemical reaction has an energy barrier that must be overcome before the reactant molecules can form products.

Question 10.1

The thermochemical equation for the reaction in Equation 10.3 is:

$$S_2O_8^{2-}(aq) + 2I^-(aq) = 2SO_4^{2-}(aq) + I_2(aq) \quad \Delta H = -341 \text{ kJ mol}^{-1} \quad (10.3a)$$

Sketch and label a schematic representation of the internal energy changes that occur in this reaction.

10.4   Changing the energy barrier of a reaction

If you have a particular reaction that has a large energy barrier, it may be useful to try to reduce the energy barrier so the rate of the reaction is increased. This is very important in industrial chemistry when you want to obtain the maximum amount of product as quickly as possible. This can be achieved using a *catalyst*. In Activity 9.1 you saw that the rate of decomposition of hydrogen peroxide at room temperature could be increased by the addition of small amounts of several substances, such as iron oxide, manganese oxide, and liver. In the demonstration, the hydrogen peroxide completely decomposed in each case, but the rate at which this happened varied considerably. However, at the end of the reactions, the added substances were still present in the same amount. So, the sole effect of these substances was to speed up the reaction but they were not used up in the reaction. This is essentially what a catalyst is. It increases the rate of a reaction but is not actually used up in the reaction and remains unchanged chemically at the end of the reaction.

A **catalyst** is a substance that increases the rate of reaction but is not itself used up during the reaction.

A catalyst increases the rate of a reaction by providing a new pathway for the reaction to take which, in effect, has a lower energy barrier. The internal energies of the reactants and products in energy profile diagrams are fixed, but the path in which the two are connected is not fixed. For example, you may want to walk from one specific place to another, but you can find several routes to do this and still arrive at the same place. One route may be over a mountain, which would be tough to climb compared with a simpler route by perhaps just going around the mountain to the same destination. Consider the reaction involving the decomposition of hydrogen peroxide, H_2O_2:

$$2H_2O_2(aq) = 2H_2O(l) + O_2(g) \quad (10.6)$$

The energy profile is given in Figure 10.12, for this reaction with and without a catalyst present. Without the catalyst the energy changes follow the profile in curve A but, in the presence of a catalyst, the intervening stage is of lower energy and thus the energy barrier is lower. Curve B shows what happens with

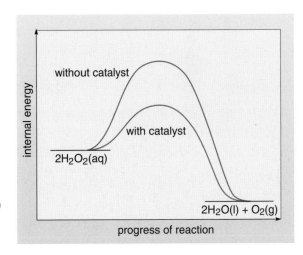

Figure 10.12   Energy profiles for the decomposition of hydrogen peroxide shown in Equation 10.6 with and without a catalyst present.

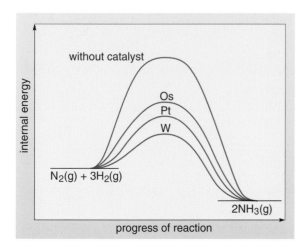

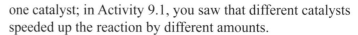

Figure 10.13 Internal energy profiles for the formation of ammonia (Equation 10.7) with different catalysts: osmium (Os), platinum (Pt) and tungsten (W), and without a catalyst.

one catalyst; in Activity 9.1, you saw that different catalysts speeded up the reaction by different amounts.

Another example of a catalysed chemical reaction is that of nitrogen and hydrogen to form ammonia:

$$N_2(g) + 3H_2(g) = 2NH_3(g) \qquad (10.7)$$

The effects of using three different metal catalysts on the magnitude of the energy barrier for this reaction are shown in Figure 10.13. Again, an important point to note is that the internal energies of the reactants and products are the same whichever catalyst is used.

The production of ammonia gas is of great practical importance and will be used in many further examples in this section. Finding a suitable catalyst was a determining factor in developing a viable commercial process for the production of ammonia, and catalysts are crucial ingredients in many other processes, not just in the chemical industry but in our bodies too. Biological catalysts in our bodies are known as 'enzymes' and you will study these in greater detail in Book 5.

10.5 Chemical equilibrium: how far will a chemical reaction go?

In the last section, you looked at the rates of reactions – how fast they go and how various conditions can be changed to increase the rate of a reaction. In the remainder of this chapter, you will be looking at chemical reactions with respect to how far they go, or the 'extent of a reaction'. At first glance, this seems a strange concept and you may think that in all reactions the reactants are completely converted to products and in some cases this is true, e.g. the burning of methane gas and the frying of an egg. However, for many reactions, all of the reactants do not go to form the products and so, in effect, they stop short of completion. With this type of reaction, the final system will be a mixture of both the products and the reactants. This is because many chemical reactions are actually reversible: for example, the thermal decomposition (the breakdown of a substance when heated) of solid ammonium chloride into ammonia and hydrogen chloride gas. This occurs when the ammonium chloride is heated strongly but, when cooled, the reaction is reversed and the solid ammonium chloride reforms. This is an example of both a reversible chemical reaction and a physical transformation of a solid to a gas (sublimation). Figure 10.14 shows an everyday example of an irreversible process (frying an egg) and a reversible process (an ice cube melting) where there is a change of state from a solid to a liquid.

(a)

(b)

Figure 10.14 (a) Frying an egg is an example of an irreversible process (the reaction goes to completion) and (b) melting an ice cube is an example of a reversible process.

10.6 Reversible reactions and dynamic equilibrium

In a reversible reaction, two processes occur: a forward reaction giving products, and a reverse reaction giving the reactants. If the rate of the forward reaction is equal to that of the reverse reaction, there is no net change in the reaction; the reaction is said to then be at a point of **dynamic equilibrium**.

Figure 10.15 shows graphically how the rate of reaction changes as a reaction mixture reaches equilibrium: initially, when the concentration of reactants is high, the rate of the forward reaction is fast, but then begins to decrease; simultaneously, the reverse reaction rate increases as the products begin to increase in concentration and are able to react together themselves to form the original reactants. Eventually, the decreasing forward rate of reaction equals the increasing rate of the reverse reaction and the system is said to be at equilibrium.

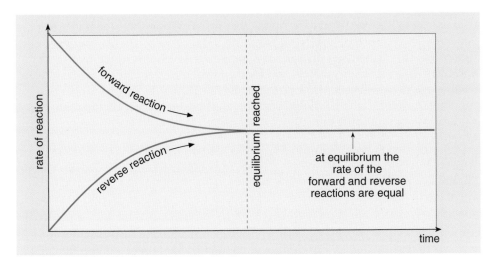

Figure 10.15   Graphical representation of the rate of reaction proceeding to equilibrium.

To highlight the two-way nature of equilibrium in chemical equations, two half-headed arrows pointing in opposite directions are used. So, for a chemical reaction that proceeds to equilibrium, you can write:

$$\text{reactants} \rightleftharpoons \text{products} \tag{10.8}$$

Dynamic equilibrium is the point when both the forward and reverse rates are equal.

For a chemical reaction that has reached dynamic equilibrium, the forward and reverse reactions are equal and it would seem that, because there is no net change, nothing is happening chemically in the reaction. This is not actually so; at a molecular level, the forward and reverse reactions are still taking place at a rapid pace, but this can't be physically observed. Therefore, equilibrium is a dynamic process with the forward and reverse reactions occurring at the same time and so the reactants and products coexist in the reaction mixture. It is important to realise that the rates for the forward and reverse reactions at equilibrium are equal, and the concentrations of the products and reactants are constant, i.e. they don't change. However, it should be noted that, even though the concentrations of the products and reactants are constant, it does not necessarily mean that they are present in equal amounts. You can look at this now in terms of the equilibrium reaction between hydrogen and iodine gases giving hydrogen iodide:

$$H_2(g) + I_2(g) \rightleftharpoons 2HI(g) \tag{10.9}$$

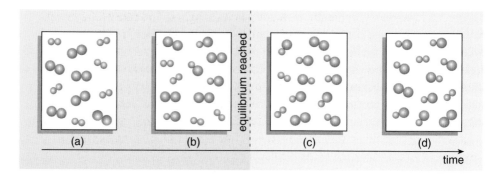

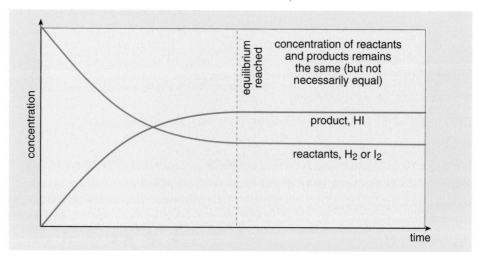

Figure 10.16   Schematic diagram at a molecular level of how the hydrogen molecules (blue, smaller spheres) and iodine molecules (red, larger spheres) react towards and at equilibrium. (a) Equal amounts of H_2 and I_2 are mixed; (b) the reaction proceeds giving HI molecules; (c) equilibrium is reached and then (d) remains constant over time.

For the reaction, at a molecular level, if the hydrogen and iodine gases are mixed in equal amounts in a sealed vessel, they start to react and form hydrogen iodide gas and eventually an equilibrium is reached. This is shown in Figure 10.16, where the two gases in box (a) mix and react to form products (b) and with time an equilibrium mixture is reached in (c) which remains constant with time in (d). For this reaction, if you were to follow the concentrations of the reactants and products to and beyond equilibrium, you would be able to plot a graph like that in Figure 10.17.

Figure 10.17   Changes in the concentration of reactants and products for the reaction in Equation 10.9, as equilibrium is reached and beyond.

Figure 10.17 shows that at the start of the reaction, the concentration of HI initially increases rapidly, but the rate of its formation slows as the H_2 and I_2 reactants are used up. As time proceeds, the increased concentration of HI begins to undergo the reverse reaction, to form reactants again. The rate of the reverse reaction increases as the concentration of HI produced by the forward reaction increases. The rate of the forward reaction is decreasing, while that of the reverse reaction is increasing. Eventually the rates of the forward and reverse reaction are equal and equilibrium is reached. The concentrations of the products and reactants are constant but not the same as each other. Notice that in the graph, the equilibrium concentration of HI is greater than that of the reactants: the product is said to be *favoured* in this particular reaction, under these conditions. However, this is not always the case; it can be the reactants that dominate when the mixture has reached equilibrium. To investigate this further and to be able to identify whether the products or reactants dominate at equilibrium, we need a way to determine the extent of a reaction. In the next section we will approach this problem using a mathematical expression.

10.7   Equilibrium: a quantitative approach

A knowledge of chemical equilibrium can provide important information about the extent of a reaction: for example, whether a product or reactant is favoured at a given temperature. A convenient way of quantitatively describing the composition of a reaction mixture at equilibrium is to use the mathematical relationship called the *equilibrium expression*. This expression is ultimately derived from the *law of mass action* originally derived by two Norwegian chemists, Peter Waage and Cato Guldberg, in 1864 after experimentation and observations of many chemical reactions. Deriving an equilibrium expression for a reaction will involve all the reacting substances; this will be done here for a simple reaction. Suppose we have reactant C which forms A and B at a given temperature; the equilibrium chemical equation can be written as:

$$C \rightleftharpoons A + B \qquad (10.10)$$

We can illustrate the relationship between the concentrations of A, B and C in the equilibrium mixture by plotting a graph of the product of molar concentrations of A and B (products) on the vertical axis versus the molar concentration of C (reactant) on the horizontal axis. The result is a straight line graph like that shown in Figure 10.18, for the equilibrium reaction in Equation 10.10. The straight line graph indicates that there is a proportionality relationship:

$$\left(\begin{array}{c}\text{equilibrium molar}\\\text{concentration}\\\text{of A}\end{array}\right) \times \left(\begin{array}{c}\text{equilibrium molar}\\\text{concentration}\\\text{of B}\end{array}\right) \propto \left(\begin{array}{c}\text{equilibrium molar}\\\text{concentration}\\\text{of C}\end{array}\right) \qquad (10.11)$$

This tells you that the product of the molar concentrations of A and B is proportional to the molar concentration of reactant C. (You met the symbol for proportionality, $\propto$, and its mathematical usage earlier in Section 4.1.2 of Book 3.)

Figure 10.18   Graph illustrating the equilibrium expression in Equation 10.11, for the reaction in Equation 10.10 at a given temperature.

Writing the equilibrium expression for a reaction mixture like that in Equation 10.11 is rather cumbersome, so a simple notation for molar concentration is used where the substance is enclosed in square brackets. Now, a more simple form of the equation can be written as:

$$[A] \times [B] \propto [C] \tag{10.12}$$

From the expression in Equation 10.12, a proportionality relationship can be turned into an equation by introducing a constant of proportionality. In this case, the constant of proportionality is known as the *equilibrium constant, K*. Introducing this into Equation 10.12, the equilibrium expression can now be written as:

$$[A] \times [B] = K[C] \tag{10.13}$$

In Equation 10.13, you have the product of the concentration of the products (A and B) being equal to the concentration of reactant (C) multiplied by K, the equilibrium constant. If you now rearrange the equation so that the concentration terms of reactants and products are all on one side, you have the final equilibrium expression with respect to the equilibrium concentrations in a mixture:

$$K = \frac{[A] \times [B]}{[C]} \tag{10.14}$$

You can now interpret the equilibrium expression in Equation 10.14 as the equilibrium constant, K, being equal to the product of the concentrations of A and B (the products) divided by the concentration of reactant C. Here, there was one reactant, C, but if there were two or three, etc. the same would apply in the equilibrium expression, and the concentrations of all the products would be multiplied together on the top of the expression and those of the reactants would be multiplied together on the bottom of the expression in Equation 10.14. So, an equilibrium expression can be written, and an equilibrium constant obtained experimentally, for any equilibrium mixture. Now consider the example of writing out an equilibrium expression for the reaction between carbon monoxide and steam to give hydrogen and carbon dioxide. This reaction, known as the 'water–gas shift' reaction, is industrially important in generating hydrogen gas. At equilibrium, the reaction can be written as:

$$H_2O(g) + CO(g) \rightleftharpoons H_2(g) + CO_2(g) \tag{10.15}$$

and the equilibrium expression for Equation 10.15 will be:

$$K = \frac{[H_2(g)] \times [CO_2(g)]}{[H_2O(g)] \times [CO(g)]} \tag{10.16}$$

The equilibrium expression (Equation 10.16) can be read as the product of the concentrations of hydrogen and carbon dioxide divided by the product of the concentrations of water and carbon monoxide.

Returning to the equation you met earlier, hydrogen and iodine gas react to form two moles of hydrogen iodide gas:

$$H_2(g) + I_2(g) \rightleftharpoons 2HI(g) \tag{10.9}$$

You can write down the equilibrium expression for this reaction as:

$$K = \frac{[HI(g)]^2}{[H_2(g)] \times [I_2(g)]} \tag{10.17}$$

Can you see the connection between the equilibrium expression and the balanced equation in Equation 10.9?

Here, the product concentration of hydrogen iodide gas, HI(g), on the top of the expression is raised to the power of 2 (it is squared), which is determined from the balanced equation where there are two moles of HI formed. In the expression, one mole of each of the reactants, H_2 and I_2, is used and therefore each is effectively raised to the power of 1 (which isn't indicated in the expression).

So, a *general expression* for K can be written that relates to the equilibrium reaction containing reactants A and B and product C and taking into account the molar amounts of reactants or products. Consider the reaction:

$$A + B \rightleftharpoons C + C \qquad (10.18)$$

Here there are two lots of the product C, so the equation for this reaction would usually be written as:

$$A + B \rightleftharpoons 2C \qquad (10.19)$$

Therefore the equilibrium expression takes the form:

$$K = \frac{[C] \times [C]}{[A] \times [B]} = \frac{[C]^2}{[A] \times [B]} \qquad (10.20)$$

It is conventional that in an equilibrium expression the concentrations of the products are put in as the numerator (on top of the fraction) and the concentrations of the reactants as the denominator (on the bottom of the fraction). The molar amounts in the balanced equation for each substance are written into the expression as the 'power' to which the concentration of that substance is raised. For example, for a reaction in which two moles of A and one mole of B give one mole of C and three moles of D, the balanced equation is:

$$2A + B \rightleftharpoons C + 3D \qquad (10.21)$$

We can thus write the corresponding equilibrium expression in which the products and reactants are all raised to their molar amounts from the balanced equation:

$$K = \frac{[C] \times [D]^3}{[A]^2 \times [B]} \qquad (10.22)$$

■ What would be the equilibrium expression for the reaction between nitrogen and oxygen giving nitrogen dioxide from the chemical equation below?

$$N_2(g) + 2O_2(g) \rightleftharpoons 2NO_2(g)$$

☐ The equilibrium expression for this reaction would be:

$$K = \frac{[NO_2(g)]^2}{[N_2(g)] \times [O_2(g)]^2}$$

10.7.1   The units for the equilibrium constant

Finally, you also need to think about the units of an equilibrium expression and hence for the equilibrium constant, K. This will depend again on the molar amounts of products and reactants in the balanced equation.

Returning again to the equation for the formation of hydrogen iodide gas in Equation 10.9:

$$H_2(g) + I_2(g) \rightleftharpoons 2HI(g) \tag{10.9}$$

The equilibrium constant is expressed in Equation 10.17 as:

$$K = \frac{[HI(g)]^2}{[H_2(g)] \times [I_2(g)]} \tag{10.17}$$

■   What would be the appropriate units for the equilibrium constant in Equation 10.17, given that the concentrations of all the gases are measured in mol dm^{-3}?

☐   You can insert the units mol dm^{-3} into Equation 10.17 and see that, in this particular reaction, the units of K cancel out:

$$\text{units of } K = \frac{(\text{mol dm}^{-3})^2}{(\text{mol dm}^{-3}) \times (\text{mol dm}^{-3})} = \frac{(\text{mol dm}^{-3})^2}{(\text{mol dm}^{-3})^2}$$

However, it should be noted that K is not always unitless; this is only the case when there are equal molar amounts on each side of the equation. If you take the equilibrium reaction between hydrogen and oxygen gas to give water vapour, you can write a balanced equation as follows:

$$2H_2(g) + O_2(g) \rightleftharpoons 2H_2O(g) \tag{10.23}$$

For Equation 10.23, the equilibrium expression is:

$$K = \frac{[H_2O(g)]^2}{[H_2(g)]^2 \times [O_2(g)]} \tag{10.24}$$

If the concentrations of the reactants and products for this reaction are measured in mol dm^{-3}, these units can be substituted into the equilibrium expression to find out the units of K:

$$\text{units of } K = \frac{(\text{mol dm}^{-3})^2}{(\text{mol dm}^{-3})^2 \times (\text{mol dm}^{-3})} = \frac{(\text{mol dm}^{-3})^2}{(\text{mol dm}^{-3})^3}$$

$$= \frac{1}{\text{mol dm}^{-3}} = \text{mol}^{-1}\,\text{dm}^3 \tag{10.25}$$

As you can see, with this particular reaction the equilibrium constant, K, does have units (mol^{-1} dm^3) as there are not equal molar amounts of reactants and products on both sides of the balanced equation.

Question 10.2

Write down the equilibrium expressions for the following reactions.

(a) $N_2(g) + 3H_2(g) \rightleftharpoons 2NH_3(g)$

(b) $2NO(g) + O_2(g) \rightleftharpoons 2NO_2(g)$

(c) $2HI(g) \rightleftharpoons H_2(g) + I_2(g)$

The value of the equilibrium constant for any reaction depends only on temperature. So, *at a given temperature* the magnitude of K is *fixed*. In other words, no matter what the initial composition of a reaction mixture at a given temperature, the value of K determined from the equilibrium concentrations of reactants and products will always be the same.

We can calculate the equilibrium constant for a reaction if we know the concentrations of the reactants and products at equilibrium, at a particular temperature. For example, at 730 K in the formation of hydrogen iodide from hydrogen and iodine (Equation 10.9), the equilibrium concentrations were found to be: $H_2(g) = 1.14 \times 10^{-2}$ mol dm^{-3}, $I_2(g) = 0.12 \times 10^{-2}$ mol dm^{-3} and $HI(g) = 2.52 \times 10^{-2}$ mol dm^{-3}.

■ What would be the equilibrium constant at this temperature?

☐ If you substitute the concentration values into the equilibrium expression (Equation 10.17), you can calculate K for the reaction at 730 K:

$$K = \frac{[HI(g)]^2}{[H_2(g)] \times [I_2(g)]} = \frac{(2.52 \times 10^{-2} \text{ mol dm}^{-3})^2}{(1.14 \times 10^{-2} \text{ mol dm}^{-3}) \times (0.12 \times 10^{-2} \text{ mol dm}^{-3})} = 46.4$$

Therefore, the equilibrium constant, K, for the reaction in Equation 10.9 at 730 K is 46.4.

Similarly, you could also calculate the equilibrium concentration of one of the reactants or products if you were told the equilibrium constant and the equilibrium concentrations of the other reactants or products, by substituting these values into the equilibrium expression, and rearranging.

■ From the equilibrium constant calculated for the reaction at 730 K,

$$H_2(g) + I_2(g) \rightleftharpoons 2HI(g) \tag{10.9}$$

what would be the equilibrium concentration of HI(g) if the equilibrium concentrations of $H_2(g) = 0.92 \times 10^{-2}$ mol dm^{-3} and $I_2(g) = 0.22 \times 10^{-2}$ mol dm^{-3}?

☐ From the equilibrium expression in Equation 10.17:

$$46.4 = \frac{[HI(g)]^2}{(0.92 \times 10^{-2} \text{ mol dm}^{-3}) \times (0.22 \times 10^{-2} \text{ mol dm}^{-3})}$$

$$[HI(g)]^2 = 46.4 \times (0.92 \times 10^{-2} \text{ mol dm}^{-3}) \times (0.22 \times 10^{-2} \text{ mol dm}^{-3})$$

$$= 9.391 \times 10^{-4} (\text{mol dm}^{-3})^2$$

131

Then:

$$[HI(g)] = \sqrt{9.391 \times 10^{-4}(\text{mol dm}^{-3})^2} = 3.06 \times 10^{-2}\text{mol dm}^{-3}$$

Therefore, the equilibrium concentration of HI(g) is 3.06×10^{-2} mol dm^{-3}.

Question 10.3

Nitrous acid dissociates in water according to the equation:

$$HNO_2(aq) \rightleftharpoons H^+(aq) + NO_2^-(aq) \qquad\qquad (10.26)$$

where $NO_2^-(aq)$ is the nitrite ion. Table 10.1 provides information about the concentrations of reactants and products of three solutions of this acid in water at 25 °C. Use this information to calculate the equilibrium constant for the dissociation reaction at 25 °C, for each solution. What do you notice about the magnitude of the equilibrium constant for each solution?

Table 10.1 Equilibrium molar concentrations in three solutions of nitrous acid in water at 25 °C.

Solution	[HNO$_2$(aq)]/mol dm^{-3}	[H$^+$(aq)]/mol dm^{-3}	[NO$_2^-$(aq)]/mol dm^{-3}
1	0.090	6.2×10^{-3}	6.2×10^{-3}
2	0.20	9.3×10^{-3}	9.3×10^{-3}
3	0.30	11.4×10^{-3}	11.4×10^{-3}

10.7.2   The magnitude of the equilibrium constant

The magnitude of the equilibrium constant can tell you if a product or a reactant is favoured in a particular equilibrium mixture, hence the direction in which a reaction will go. For the equilibrium expression in Equation 10.17, at 25 °C, $K = 794$, so from the equation it can be assumed that [HI(g)] in the equilibrium mixture is greater than the reactant concentrations, [H$_2$(g)] and [I$_2$(g)]. Thus the product is said to be favoured. In general, we can say that if K is large (> 1), the equilibrium concentration of the products is large; if $K = 1$, neither the products nor reactants dominate; and if K is small (< 1), the reactants dominate.

> If K is very large, the products are favoured; if K is very small, the reactants are favoured in an equilibrium mixture.

The equilibrium constant can also allow you to calculate the equilibrium concentrations of reactants or products, or you could calculate K if you know the equilibrium concentrations of the reactants and products at a given temperature, as you did in Question 10.3. It is worth remembering that the size of K is not related at all to the rate of reaction (the time required to reach equilibrium) which, as you have seen, is dependent on the energy barrier for the reaction (Section 10.3).

10.8   Equilibrium and response to change: Le Chatelier's principle

So far, you have learned that an important concept about chemical equilibrium is that it represents a state of dynamic balance, where reactants are continuously being converted into products, and vice versa. At equilibrium, the relative proportions of reactants and products in a reaction mixture remain fixed, provided that there is no change in any of the reaction conditions. However, if a particular reaction condition, such as pressure or temperature, is changed, then there is a change in the overall composition of the equilibrium mixture. This section focuses on predicting the changes that occur to equilibria if certain specific conditions are changed, and also relates these to the equilibrium constant. You will begin with a computer-based activity.

Activity 10.1   Chemical equilibrium: Part 1

We expect this part of the activity will take you approximately 30 minutes.

This activity is split into two parts, both requiring use of the computer-based activity *Chemical Equilibrium*. You will now do Part 1. Part 2 should be attempted once you have worked through Section 10.8.

This computer-based activity starts with an introduction to chemical equilibrium. You will then investigate how a change in pressure or temperature can affect the relative proportions of reactants and products in a reaction mixture at equilibrium.

The first part of the activity will introduce you to the idea of chemical equilibria in reactions between gases. There are three sections: Introduction; Effect of pressure; and Effect of temperature. At various points in the activity, you are asked to note down your observations.

Introduction

In the initial part of the activity you are asked to record the number of red product molecules you have counted each time you stop the reaction, both when you start with 'reactant' molecules and when you start with 'product' molecules. A suitable table to record your data is given in Table 10.2.

Table 10.2 Number of red product molecules counted once the reaction is stopped.

Count/attempt	1	2	3	4	5	6	7	8	9	10	11
red product molecules (starting with reactants)											
red product molecules (starting with products)											

Effect of pressure

For each of the reactions that you choose to investigate, you should note down whether the proportion of product(s) increased or decreased or stayed the same as you increased the pressure. For this part of the activity, it is useful to fill in

Table 10.3 for the reactions you choose to investigate in each of the three sets (A, B and C) by changing the pressure.

Table 10.3 Effect of increased pressure on proportion of product(s).

Reaction	Reaction proportion of product(s) increased/decreased/stayed the same
Set A	
$N_2(g) + 3H_2(g) \rightleftharpoons 2NH_3(g)$	
$CO(g) + 2H_2(g) \rightleftharpoons CH_3OH(g)^*$	
$2SO_2(g) + O_2(g) \rightleftharpoons 2SO_3(g)$	
Set B	
$2NH_3(g) \rightleftharpoons N_2(g) + 3H_2(g)$	
$2NO_2(g) \rightleftharpoons 2NO(g) + O_2(g)$	
$PCl_5(g) \rightleftharpoons PCl_3(g) + Cl_2(g)$	
Set C	
$H_2(g) + I_2(g) \rightleftharpoons 2HI(g)$	
$N_2(g) + O_2(g) \rightleftharpoons 2NO(g)$	
$CO(g) + H_2O(g) \rightleftharpoons CO_2(g) + H_2(g)$	

*CH_3OH is methanol.

Effect of temperature

For each reaction you investigate, note down in Table 10.4 whether the proportion of product(s) increased or decreased or stayed the same as you raised the temperature.

Table 10.4 Effect of increased temperature on proportion of product(s).

Reaction enthalpy change/kJ mol^{-1}		Reaction proportion of product(s) increased/decreased/stayed the same
Set A		
$N_2(g) + 3H_2(g) \rightleftharpoons 2NH_3(g)$	$\Delta H = -92.2$ kJ mol^{-1}	
$H_2(g) + I_2(g) \rightleftharpoons 2HI(g)$	$\Delta H = -9.4$ kJ mol^{-1}	
$2SO_2(g) + O_2(g) \rightleftharpoons 2SO_3(g)$	$\Delta H = -197.8$ kJ mol^{-1}	
$CO(g) + H_2O(g) \rightleftharpoons CO_2(g) + H_2(g)$	$\Delta H = -41.2$ kJ mol^{-1}	
Set B		
$2NH_3(g) \rightleftharpoons N_2(g) + 3H_2(g)$	$\Delta H = +92.2$ kJ mol^{-1}	
$N_2(g) + O_2(g) \rightleftharpoons 2NO(g)$	$\Delta H = +180.6$ kJ mol^{-1}	
$CO_2(g) + H_2(g) \rightleftharpoons CO(g) + H_2O(g)$	$\Delta H = +41.2$ kJ mol^{-1}	
$PCl_5(g) \rightleftharpoons PCl_3(g) + Cl_2(g)$	$\Delta H = +87.9$ kJ mol^{-1}	

When you have completed this part of the activity, look at the comments at the end of this book.

As you saw in Part 1 of Activity 10.1, it is possible to *predict qualitatively* the way in which an equilibrium mixture will respond to a change in conditions. The basis for making these predictions is summarised by **Le Chatelier's principle** (named after Henri Louis Le Chatelier, a French chemist; 1850–1936), which has the general form:

When a system in equilibrium is subject to a change in temperature, pressure or concentration, the system responds in a way that tends to minimise the effect of that change.

So what does this effectively mean in an equilibrium mixture? If you take the example of increasing the concentration of either a reactant or a product, the system would try to minimise this effect by trying to decrease the concentration of reactants or products. If you increase the pressure of an equilibrium mixture in a vessel, it will try to minimise the effect by reducing that pressure. It is important to note that the equilibrium position changes in such cases but the equilibrium constant stays the same (remember this only changes with temperature). In the following sections, you will explore further the changes to external conditions on the equilibrium position, starting with the changes in pressure for gaseous reactions, then temperature and finally concentration.

10.8.1 The effect of a change in pressure

As you have already seen, many chemical reactions, including some of considerable industrial importance, involve reactants and products that are gases. For this type of reaction, the relative proportion of reactants and products in the equilibrium mixture can depend on the pressure in the reaction vessel. You can use Le Chatelier's principle to predict how the composition of this equilibrium mixture will change if the pressure in the vessel is increased. As pressure, depends on the number of particles hitting the walls of the containing vessel, you would predict that, to reduce the pressure, the composition of the equilibrium mixture will shift in a direction that corresponds, if possible, to a reduction in the number of molecules in the gas phase. This direction can be determined from the chemical equation for the equilibrium mixture. Consider an example from the production of sulfuric acid, a major product of the chemical industry. One stage in the most common method of production involves the reaction of sulfur dioxide, SO_2, with oxygen to give sulfur trioxide, SO_3. The chemical equation for this reaction is:

$$2SO_2(g) + O_2(g) \rightleftharpoons 2SO_3(g) \tag{10.27}$$

Le Chatelier's principle can be used to predict how the proportion of sulfur trioxide present at equilibrium, i.e. the **equilibrium yield** of this substance, varies with pressure. Consider the effect of increasing the pressure, of the equilibrium mixture. To respond to this increase in pressure, the composition of the equilibrium mixture will shift in a direction that results in a *decrease* in the number of molecules in the gas phase. According to the balanced chemical equation, there are two moles of sulfur dioxide molecules and one mole of oxygen molecules, giving a total of three moles of reactant molecules. There are only two moles of product molecules. Thus an increase in pressure will favour the formation of the product, sulfur trioxide, and there will be a larger proportion of this substance in the equilibrium mixture. In other words, the equilibrium yield of sulfur trioxide will increase with increasing pressure.

As a second example, consider the production of hydrogen gas from natural gas and steam, which is used as a source of hydrogen in industrial processes. Natural gas is mostly methane, CH_4, and so the chemical reaction that takes place can be written as:

$$CH_4(g) + H_2O(g) \rightleftharpoons CO(g) + 3H_2(g) \tag{10.28}$$

■ For this balanced chemical equation, which direction corresponds to a reduction in the number of gas-phase molecules?

☐ There are two moles of reactant molecules (one of methane and one of water) and four moles of product molecules (one of carbon monoxide and three of hydrogen). The direction right to left, i.e. the reverse reaction as written, corresponds to a reduction in the number of gas-phase molecules.

An increase in pressure, therefore, will result in a decrease in the proportion of hydrogen gas in the equilibrium mixture. Thus, in the absence of any other considerations, to increase the equilibrium yield of hydrogen gas it would be necessary to operate the process at a lower pressure.

Another very important reaction that is often used as an example to describe the effects of pressure on equilibrium yield and Le Chatelier's principle is the Haber–Bosch process. This is commonly used to manufacture ammonia, NH_3, for nitrogen fertilisers in the chemical industry. The chemical equilibrium reaction is given as:

$$N_2(g) + 3H_2(g) \rightleftharpoons 2NH_3(g) \tag{10.29}$$

■ Looking at Equation 10.29, what effect on the proportion of ammonia in the equilibrium mixture will increasing the pressure have?

☐ According to Le Chatelier's principle, to respond to an increase in pressure the composition of the equilibrium mixture will tend to shift in a direction that favours a reduction in the number of gas molecules. There are two moles of product molecules compared with four moles of reactant molecules, so the increase in pressure will favour the formation of ammonia. There will be a larger proportion of ammonia in the equilibrium mixture.

Figure 10.19 illustrates the effect of an increase in pressure on an equilibrium mixture of ammonia, hydrogen and nitrogen gases: the increase in pressure causes a change in the equilibrium position, and the new equilibrium mixture contains an increased proportion of ammonia molecules. This is one important reason why industry uses high pressure, despite the costs involved, to gain the best equilibrium yield for this particular reaction.

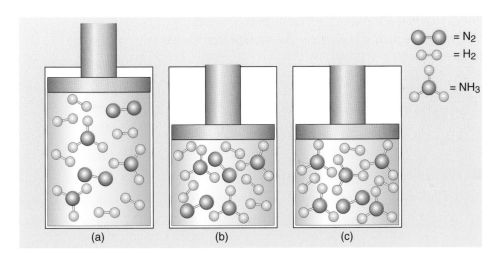

Figure 10.19 The effect of a change in pressure on an equilibrium mixture in the production of ammonia. (a) The initial equilibrium mixture. (b) The increase in pressure disturbs the equilibrium position. (c) The new equilibrium is established to minimise the pressure increase and the concentration of ammonia molecules has increased.

The flow diagram in Figure 10.20 summarises the effect of pressure changes on an equilibrium mixture involving gases only.

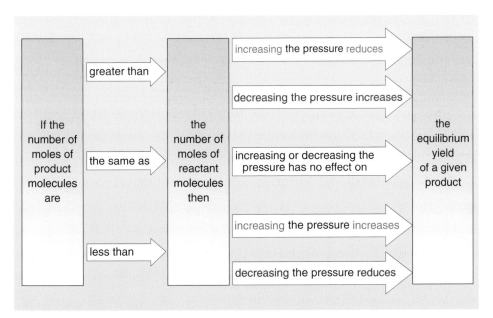

Figure 10.20 Flow diagram summarising the effect of pressure changes on an equilibrium mixture involving gases only.

10.8.2   The effect of a change in temperature

A change in temperature can also have a significant effect on the composition of an equilibrium mixture. Once again, Le Chatelier's principle can be used to predict the effect, which depends on whether the reaction is exothermic or endothermic.

■   What are the respective characteristics of an exothermic reaction and an endothermic reaction?

☐   These were discussed in Section 9.2. An exothermic reaction is one that releases energy in the form of heat to its surroundings. An endothermic reaction is one that absorbs energy in the form of heat from its surroundings.

The thermochemical nature of the forward and reverse directions of a reaction that proceeds to equilibrium can be considered separately. Thus, if the reaction is exothermic in the forward direction, then it will be endothermic in the reverse direction, and vice versa.

If the temperature of a reaction mixture at equilibrium is raised, then Le Chatelier's principle predicts that the equilibrium mixture will change its composition so as to favour the direction of reaction that is endothermic. This is because, in this direction, energy in the form of heat is absorbed, and this tends to minimise the effect of raising the temperature. Similarly, if the temperature of a reaction mixture at equilibrium is lowered, then the equilibrium mixture will change its composition so as to favour the direction of reaction that is exothermic.

■ Why is this?

☐ An exothermic reaction releases energy in the form of heat, and this will tend to minimise the effect of lowering the temperature.

We will now consider how some of the reactions we looked at in the last section respond to changes in temperature.

The formation of hydrogen from methane and steam is represented by the thermochemical equation:

$$CH_4(g) + H_2O(g) \rightleftharpoons CO(g) + 3H_2(g) \quad \Delta H = +206 \text{ kJ mol}^{-1} \quad (10.30)$$

Note that the enthalpy change, ΔH, refers *only* to the forward direction of the reaction. This statement applies to *all* of the thermochemical equations considered in this book. The enthalpy change for the reaction in Equation 10.30 is positive; therefore the reaction is endothermic. So an increase in temperature will result in a higher equilibrium yield of hydrogen gas.

The thermochemical equation for the formation of sulfur trioxide is:

$$2SO_2(g) + O_2(g) \rightleftharpoons 2SO_3(g) \quad \Delta H = -198 \text{ kJ mol}^{-1} \quad (10.31)$$

■ For the production of sulfur trioxide, would operating the reaction at a higher temperature increase the equilibrium yield of this product?

☐ The forward reaction is exothermic. Thus, a rise in temperature will *not* favour an increase in the equilibrium yield of sulfur trioxide.

Operating the reaction in Equation 10.31 at a higher temperature will result in the composition of the equilibrium mixture changing so that the relative proportion of the reactants is increased. That is, the reverse direction of the reaction, which is endothermic, will be favoured.

Question 10.4

At room temperature, the thermochemical equation for the reaction between nitrogen and oxygen to form nitrogen monoxide is:

$$N_2(g) + O_2(g) \rightleftharpoons 2NO(g) \quad \Delta H = +181 \text{ kJ mol}^{-1} \quad (10.32)$$

Will the equilibrium yield of nitrogen monoxide at 500 °C be greater or less than that at room temperature?

Question 10.5

The equilibrium reaction between nitrogen dioxide (NO_2), a brown gas, and dinitrogen tetroxide (N_2O_4), a colourless gas, has the following thermochemical equation:

$$2NO_2(g) \rightleftharpoons N_2O_4(g) \quad \Delta H = -57 \text{ kJ mol}^{-1} \tag{10.33}$$

Is the reaction exothermic or endothermic? In a sealed vessel, what would you expect to happen to the intensity of the brown colour for the gas mixture as the temperature is reduced?

A flow diagram that summarises the effect of temperature on an equilibrium mixture of gases is shown in Figure 10.21.

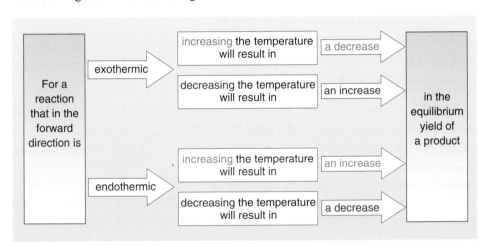

Figure 10.21   Flow diagram summarising the effect of temperature changes on an equilibrium mixture involving gases only.

10.8.3   The effect of changes in concentration

Changing the concentration of (or removing) a reactant or product will shift the equilibrium position and so, again using Le Chatelier's principle, the equilibrium position will move to oppose that change. Consider the reaction between hydrogen and iodine gas:

$$H_2(g) + I_2(g) \rightleftharpoons 2HI(g) \tag{10.9}$$

If you were to lower the concentration of H_2 by removing some of it, the equilibrium will move to the left (the reverse reaction) to increase the concentration of H_2 again and re-establish the equilibrium. Similarly, if you were to remove the HI product, the equilibrium position would move to the right (the forward reaction) to replenish the products.

Consider another example: the equilibrium reaction between the two gases nitrogen dioxide (NO_2) and dinitrogen tetroxide (N_2O_4), which you met in Question 10.5.

$$2NO_2(g) \rightleftharpoons N_2O_4(g) \tag{10.34}$$

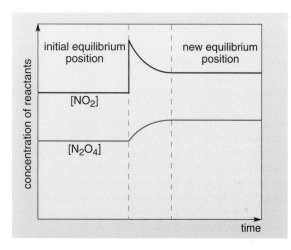

Figure 10.22   The change in equilibrium position when a reactant concentration is increased for the reaction in Equation 10.34.

You can see graphically in Figure 10.22 how the position of equilibrium changes in an equilibrium mixture, when more of the gas NO_2 is added.

It is clear from Figure 10.22 that the increase in the concentration of NO_2 produces a disruption of the initial equilibrium concentrations of the reactant and product. The equilibrium readjusts to produce more product, N_2O_4, which in turn reduces the increase in concentration of NO_2, and a new equilibrium position is obtained.

It should be noted that, if the reaction has a catalyst present, this will not affect the position of equilibrium or the concentrations of reactants and products in the mixture. As you have seen in Section 10.4, a catalyst does not appear in the general reaction equation and is not consumed in the reaction either. Therefore, the addition of a catalyst to an equilibrium reaction will only speed up the rate of reaction so that equilibrium is attained more rapidly.

Activity 10.1   Chemical equilibrium: Part 2

We expect this part of the activity will take you approximately 30 minutes.

In the second part of this activity, you will investigate how changes in concentration of reactants or products will affect chemical equilibrium.

Part of this activity involves plotting a graph using the computer package.

The reactions in the final section of this activity involve ions in solution. (In some of the reaction equations here, some ions that do not react have been left out. For example, if in a solution of sodium chloride, the chloride ions take part in a reaction but the sodium ions do not, then the sodium ions can be left out of the equation. The sodium ions in such a case are called 'spectator' ions.)

Make notes about the changes in the equilibrium concentrations of the other ions when you increase the concentration of either a product or reactant.

Record the equilibrium constant, K, in Table 10.5.

Table 10.5 Value of the equilibrium constant, K, from the graph of product concentrations multiplied together against reactant concentrations multiplied together.

Reaction	K (equilibrium constant)
$BrO_3^-(aq) + Cl^-(aq) \rightleftharpoons ClO_3^-(aq) + Br^-(aq)$	
$HIO_3(aq) \rightleftharpoons H^+(aq) + IO_3^-(aq)$	
$H^+(aq) + SO_4^{2-}(aq) \rightleftharpoons HSO_4^-(aq)$	
$H_3PO_3(aq) \rightleftharpoons H_2PO_3^-(aq) + H^+(aq)$	
$H^+(aq) + NO_2^-(aq) \rightleftharpoons HNO_2(aq)$	

Now look at the comments on this activity at the end of this book.

Le Chatelier's principle is useful in determining the ideal conditions for the best yield of products in industrial processes. This may be a compromise between temperature, pressure and other factors, to get the best product yield while still considering the manufacturing economics as a whole.

Question 10.6

The production of hydrogen cyanide from methane and ammonia is represented by the following thermochemical equation:

$$CH_4(g) + NH_3(g) \rightleftharpoons HCN(g) + 3H_2(g) \quad \Delta H = +256 \text{ kJ mol}^{-1} \quad (10.35)$$

(a) Sketch a diagram showing how the internal energy changes as the reaction progresses.

(b) At normal temperatures and pressures, the equilibrium yield of hydrogen cyanide is too low for the reaction to be useful. Would any of the following improve the equilibrium yield: (i) raising the temperature; (ii) increasing the pressure in the reaction vessel; (iii) using a catalyst?

Question 10.7

In the catalytic converters in modern car exhaust systems, the exhaust gases carbon monoxide and nitrogen monoxide react to produce nitrogen and carbon dioxide. The thermochemical equation for this reaction is:

$$2CO(g) + 2NO(g) \rightleftharpoons N_2(g) + 2CO_2(g) \quad \Delta H = -747 \text{ kJ mol}^{-1} \quad (10.36)$$

If the exhaust gases escape without passing over the catalytic converter, they react with oxygen in the atmosphere to form carbon dioxide and nitrogen dioxide. The thermochemical equations for these reactions are:

$$2CO(g) + O_2(g) \rightleftharpoons 2CO_2(g) \quad \Delta H = -566 \text{ kJ mol}^{-1} \quad (10.37)$$

$$2NO(g) + O_2(g) \rightleftharpoons 2NO_2(g) \quad \Delta H = -114 \text{ kJ mol}^{-1} \quad (10.38)$$

(a) How will raising the temperature of the exhaust gases affect the equilibrium yield of nitrogen in reaction 10.36?

(b) How will raising the temperature and the presence of a catalyst affect the rate of reaction 10.36?

(c) How does the catalyst minimise the formation of nitrogen dioxide?

10.9   Summary of Chapter 10

The rate of a reaction can be defined as the rate at which the concentration of a product increases, or the rate at which the concentration of a reactant decreases.

Because molecules must come into contact to react, reactions in solution usually go faster when the concentrations of the reactants are greater, and gaseous reactions usually go faster when the pressure is greater.

For all chemical reactions there is an energy barrier. In order for a reaction to occur, reactant molecules must encounter each other with sufficient energy to overcome the energy barrier.

The rate of reaction increases when the temperature increases, because a greater proportion of reactants encounter each other with sufficient energy to overcome the energy barrier.

Catalysts increase the rate of a reaction by providing an alternative path with a lower energy barrier. They are not used up during a reaction and do not affect the composition of the equilibrium mixture.

Chemical equilibrium represents a state of dynamic balance.

The equilibrium relationship for a reaction involves the equilibrium constant K and the equilibrium molar concentrations of the reactants and products. For the simple reaction of:

$$C \rightleftharpoons A + B$$

the equilibrium constant is:

$$K = \frac{[A] \times [B]}{[C]}$$

The magnitude of the equilibrium constant for a given reaction is related to how far the reaction will proceed before equilibrium is reached. If the magnitude is large, the equilibrium position will strongly favour the formation of products; if it is small, then reactants will be favoured.

The form of the equilibrium expression for a given solution reaction can be used to predict what will happen when the concentration of a particular substance in the equilibrium mixture is changed at constant temperature. This approach emphasises that it is the fixed value of the equilibrium constant that determines the changes that occur in the overall composition of the equilibrium mixture.

The response of an equilibrium mixture to a change in conditions can be predicted using Le Chatelier's principle. This states that when a system in equilibrium is subject to an external constraint, the system responds in a way that tends to oppose the effect of the constraint.

For any chemical reaction at a given temperature, the equilibrium constant has a specific fixed numerical value. For an increase in temperature, the magnitude of the equilibrium constant decreases for a reaction that is exothermic in the forward direction and increases for a reaction that is endothermic in the forward direction.

The nature of the response of an equilibrium mixture to a change in temperature depends on whether the reaction is exothermic or endothermic. Figure 10.21 summarises the behaviour.

For a solution reaction at constant temperature, changing the concentration of a particular substance in the equilibrium mixture results in the concentrations of other substances in the mixture also changing. Le Chatelier's principle can be used to determine whether the change in the composition of the equilibrium mixture corresponds to moving the reaction to the left or to the right.

The proportion of a product in an equilibrium mixture can be referred to as the equilibrium yield of that substance.

You have once again practised your mathematical skills in a chemical context and drawn inferences from careful observation.

Chapter 11
Acids, bases and equilibrium

Water plays a central role in chemistry – it is of fundamental importance as a solvent. A particular aspect of this role is that when certain substances dissolve in water they dissociate to give hydrogen ions, H^+, and so reveal their acidic properties; in other words, water has an ability to reveal the acidic behaviour of certain chemical compounds. For example, the three common acids that you met in Chapter 8 were hydrochloric acid, nitric acid and sulfuric acid. They dissolve in water, and then dissociate as follows:

$$HCl(aq) = H^+(aq) + Cl^-(aq) \qquad (11.1)$$

$$HNO_3(aq) = H^+(aq) + NO_3^-(aq) \qquad (11.2)$$

$$H_2SO_4(aq) = 2H^+(aq) + SO_4^{2-}(aq) \qquad (11.3)$$

■ Make a list of the points you remember about acids from Chapter 8.

☐ In Section 8.2, you learned that an acid does the following: dissolves in water to give H^+ ions; reacts with metals, such as magnesium and zinc, with the liberation of hydrogen; and is neutralised by basic hydroxides to form salts. (During neutralisation, the hydrogen atoms of the acid and the hydroxide groups of the basic hydroxide combine to form water.)

You should recall that, during neutralisation, a hydrogen ion (H^+) and a hydroxide ion (OH^-) react to give a molecule of water.

$$H^+(aq) + OH^-(aq) = H_2O(l) \qquad (11.4)$$

In a general reaction with an acid and a base, such as nitric acid (HNO_3) and potassium hydroxide (KOH), the overall neutralisation reaction takes the form:

acid + base = salt + water

which, for this reaction, you would write:

$$HNO_3(aq) + KOH(aq) = KNO_3(aq) + H_2O(l) \qquad (11.5)$$

The salt in this case is potassium nitrate, KNO_3. Neutralisation reactions always result in the formation of salts in which the hydrogen ion of the acid is replaced by a metal ion. As a further example, you can look at the neutralisation of nitric acid, HNO_3, with calcium hydroxide, $Ca(OH)_2$. Here, to form water, the two hydroxide groups of $Ca(OH)_2$ must combine with *two* hydrogen ions. Since each HNO_3 contains only one hydrogen ion, each $Ca(OH)_2$ must react with *two* HNO_3:

$$Ca(OH)_2(aq) + 2HNO_3(aq) = Ca(NO_3)_2(aq) + 2H_2O(l) \qquad (11.6)$$

■ What salt is formed in this reaction?

☐ Calcium nitrate, $Ca(NO_3)_2$, in which the two hydrogen ions of two HNO_3 units have been replaced by a calcium ion.

Like $Ca(OH)_2$, the formula of calcium nitrate contains brackets. One $Ca(NO_3)_2$ unit contains one calcium, two nitrogen and six oxygen atoms. In these neutralisation reactions, salts arise from a combination of the metal ions of basic hydroxides with the anionic group of the acid. Figure 11.1 shows some of the many different salts that can be made in this way. But in all such neutralisation reactions, hydrogen ions from the acid combine with hydroxide ions from the basic hydroxide to form water.

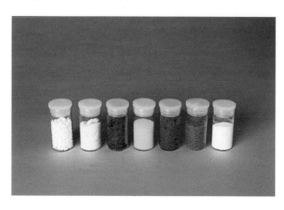

Figure 11.1   Some salts formed by combining metal atoms with groups allied to hydrogen in acids. From the left: calcium dichloride, $CaCl_2$; manganese dichloride, $MnCl_2$; cobalt sulfate, $CoSO_4$; potassium chromate, K_2CrO_4; nickel dinitrate, $Ni(NO_3)_2$; copper sulfate, $CuSO_4$; magnesium sulfate, $MgSO_4$. The salts $MnCl_2$, $CoSO_4$, $Ni(NO_3)_2$ and $CuSO_4$ retain, in addition to the quoted formulas, water molecules from the aqueous solutions in which they were made.

Question 11.1

For the neutralisation reaction between magnesium hydroxide ($Mg(OH)_2$) and sulfuric acid (H_2SO_4) in aqueous solution, write down:

(a) a balanced equation indicating all the ions in solution

(b) the general balanced equation for the reaction.

As well as the acids mentioned above in Equations 11.1–11.3, you may have come across other acids, such as acetic acid, which is a component of vinegar, and citric acid, which is found in lemons. Such acids are mild enough to be used in food, whereas the sulfuric acid used in car batteries most certainly cannot be drunk, and has to be handled with care as it can burn skin and damage clothing. As you will see, the difference between these solutions is mainly due to differences in their hydrogen ion concentrations. You will now look at how the H^+ concentration differs according to the strength of the acid and be introduced to a more quantitative view of acids and bases by examining the part that equilibrium plays in these solutions.

11.1   Hydrogen ion concentration

Acids and bases are easily recognised by the effect that they have on the colour of some natural dyes known as indicators. The colours of these dyes indicate the concentration of the ions $H^+(aq)$ or $OH^-(aq)$ in solution. One such dye is the colouring material in red cabbage and a more common indicator in the chemistry laboratory is known as 'universal indicator', which is comprised of a mixture of dyes. The colours of these dyes (red cabbage and universal indicator) are shown in Figure 11.2, for a range of $H^+(aq)$ ion concentrations. For example, in the cells marked as pH 1 in the figure for both indicators, the $H^+(aq)$ ion concentration is 1.0×10^{-1} mol dm^{-3}, whereas in the cells marked as pH 14, the $H^+(aq)$ ion concentration is 1.0×10^{-14} mol dm^{-3}. Thus, in cell 1, the $H^+(aq)$ ion concentration is 10^{13} times greater than it is in cell 14. The relationship between pH and hydrogen ion concentration is illustrated in Figure 11.3, and is commonly known as the **pH scale**.

In Figure 11.3, the $H^+(aq)$ and $OH^-(aq)$ ion concentrations are represented by the vertical bars and the corresponding pH values for these concentrations are given along the top horizontal axis. pH is a convenient method used to describe the hydrogen ion concentration of a solution, which avoids the need to use very small numbers that include scientific notation. For example, when the hydrogen ion concentration is written as 1.0×10^{-n} mol dm^{-3}, the pH value is equal to n

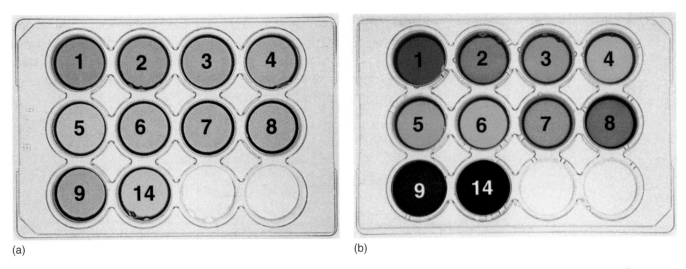

(a)

(b)

Figure 11.2 (a) Colours of red cabbage juice and (b) the colour range of universal indicator in solutions of different hydrogen ion concentrations. Numbers represent the pH values of the solutions in the cells.

(the power to which the ten is raised, with the sign changed). Thus, the higher the concentration of hydrogen ions in a solution, the lower the pH value.

■ A solution is found to have a $H^+(aq)$ ion concentration of 1.0×10^{-4} mol dm^{-3}. What is the pH of the solution?

□ The pH is 4; that is, the power to which 10 was raised, with the sign changed.

In Section 11.4 we will discuss a quantitative method of calculating the pH of a variety of acids and bases when the hydrogen ion concentration is not given in

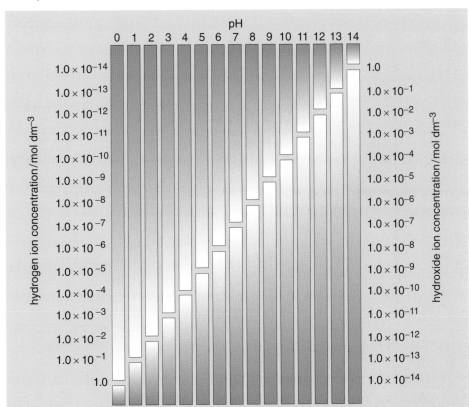

Figure 11.3 The pH scale. The lengths of the bars at the top represent the hydrogen ion concentration, read from the scale on the left. The lengths of the bars at the bottom represent the hydroxide ion concentration, read from the scale on the right. We will discuss the relation between the concentrations of H^+ and OH^- in Section 11.3.

the straightforward scientific notation mentioned above. In the following activity, you will start by using an indicator to investigate the acidic or basic nature of some common household materials and thus estimate their pH values.

Activity 11.1   Measuring the hydrogen ion concentration of household solutions

We expect this activity will take you approximately 60 minutes.

In this activity, you will measure the hydrogen ion concentrations of different household solutions.

Important safety precautions

Take note of the following safety precautions, which apply to all practical activities:

- Keep children and animals away while you are working.
- Clear your working area of clutter. Put all food away. Ensure there is nothing to trip on underfoot.
- Always wash your hands thoroughly after a practical activity.
- Any household items used should be thoroughly cleaned before returning them to domestic use.

In addition, you should note the following precautions specific to this activity:

- Wear suitable gloves and take care when handling household chemicals.
- Always remember to read any instructions on the container before using the chemicals.
- Washing soda and other household cleaning fluids may be harmful if swallowed and may irritate eyes on contact.

Aims

In this activity you will apply your skill in designing experiments (developed in Book 1, Activity 2.1, and in Book 3, Activity 6.1) to a new situation. Your task is to measure the hydrogen ion concentrations of a variety of household solutions and thus to find out how these values relate to your intuitive ideas of which solutions are more acidic and which are less acidic.

Introduction

An acid yields hydrogen ions when it dissolves in water; this suggests that the more acidic a solution is, the greater the concentration of hydrogen ions in it. To measure the hydrogen ion concentration in this activity you will use the indicator papers from your Practical Kit. These paper strips contain a mixture of dyes and they turn a range of different colours depending on the hydrogen ion concentration of the solution into which they are dipped. (You may have used papers of this type – which are sold in garden centres – to test the acidity or alkalinity of your garden soil.) If you look at the book of indicator papers, you will see that the inside covers comprise a key that relates the colour of the paper to the 'pH'. The pH scale indicates the hydrogen ion concentration of a solution. The relationship between pH and hydrogen ion concentration is given in Table 11.1. Note that the concentrations decrease from 1×10^{-1} mol dm^{-3} (0.1 mol dm^{-3}) to 1×10^{-11} mol dm^{-3}. We will explore pH further in Section 11.4.

Table 11.1 Obtaining the hydrogen ion concentration from the key on the indicator papers.

pH	Approximate concentration of hydrogen ions/ mol dm^{-3}
1	1×10^{-1}
2	1×10^{-2}
3	1×10^{-3}
4	1×10^{-4}
5	1×10^{-5}
6	1×10^{-6}
7	1×10^{-7}
8	1×10^{-8}
9	1×10^{-9}
10	1×10^{-10}
11	1×10^{-11}

Equipment required

Kit items

indicator papers

Non-Kit items

small containers to hold test solutions (clean yoghurt pots or plastic lids are ideal)

teaspoons

lemon juice (or other fruit juice)

vinegar

washing soda

baking powder

bicarbonate of soda

tap water

sparkling mineral water

ordinary household cleaning fluids (floor cleaner liquid, ordinary household bleach)

washing-up liquid or dishwasher powder

personal washing solutions (shampoo, soap, etc.)

Task 1 Thinking about design

Think about how you will tackle this activity, as defined in the aims. Note down things you will need to think about, your proposed method and how you will record your results. In particular, think about the following issues and write down some initial ideas before starting the experiment.

- What substances shall I use?
- What equipment shall I use?
- How will I do the tests?
- How will I record the results?

Task 2 Practical procedure: obtaining and recording the results

1   Collect together all the liquids and solids to be tested – you should aim to test at least eight.

2   For solids, such as washing soda and bicarbonate of soda, you will first need to make a saturated solution – one that contains undissolved solid – with tap water. To do this, put a teaspoonful of the solid in a small container and add several teaspoonfuls of tap water, such that most, but not all, of the solid dissolves. Make sure you label these samples clearly and correctly so that they do not get mixed up.

3   Cut the indicator papers in half lengthways, in order to double the number of papers available.

4   In turn, test each liquid or solution as follows.

- Pour a small amount of liquid into a small container; for many liquids, the top of its container is ideal.

- *Using a new, clean indicator paper strip for each solution tested*, dip the paper into the solution so that between 1 and 2 cm is immersed. Take the paper out of the solution and carefully shake off any drips.

- Compare the colour of the indicator paper with the colour key in the indicator paper booklet and record in Table 11.2 the pH value corresponding to the colour that matches best. You may find it difficult to decide between two colours, in which case you should write down a range. You should write a comment each time to say how sure you are of the value you have recorded.

- Then use Table 11.1 to convert this pH value into a hydrogen ion concentration and write it down in Table 11.2. You do not have to complete all rows in the table, but try to test as many different substances as you can; some blank rows have been included for additional substances you might have available.

- For reference during the investigation, you may find it interesting to place the coloured indicator strips on a sheet of white paper with the name of the liquid tested alongside.

- Pour the tested liquid down the sink and wash the container used thoroughly.

Table 11.2 Results of measuring the hydrogen ion concentration of household solutions.

Solution	pH	Approximate concentration of hydrogen ions/mol dm^{-3}	Comments
tap water			
freshly boiled tap water			
sparkling mineral water			
lemon juice			
vinegar			
bicarbonate of soda			
washing soda			
ordinary household bleach			
washing-up liquid			
dishwasher powder			
hair shampoo			
floor cleaner liquid			

5   Now investigate the effect of diluting some of the solutions. Choose
three solutions: one with a lowish hydrogen ion concentration, about
1×10^{-11} mol dm^{-3}; one with a highish hydrogen ion concentration, about
1×10^{-3} mol dm^{-3}; and one with an intermediate hydrogen ion concentration,
about 1×10^{-7} mol dm^{-3}. Dilute these solutions as follows, using a clean dry
container for each diluted solution.

- Put one teaspoonful of the substance (or saturated solution, taking
  care not to include any undissolved solid) in a container, and add
  9 teaspoonfuls of tap water. The substance has thus been diluted to
  one-tenth of its original concentration.

- Put one teaspoonful of the solution you have just diluted by a factor of 10
  in another container, and add 9 teaspoonfuls of tap water. The substance
  has thus been diluted to one-hundredth of its original concentration.
  (Alternatively, you can use larger volumes and do the dilutions in a
  measuring jug.)

- Make sure you label the samples clearly and correctly so that they do not
  get mixed up.

- Use the indicator paper strips as before to measure the hydrogen ion
  concentrations and record your results in Table 11.3.

Table 11.3 Results of measuring the effect of dilution on hydrogen ion
concentration.

Solution	Undiluted sample		Diluted 10-fold		Diluted 100-fold	
	pH	Hydrogen ion concentration /mol dm^{-3}	pH	Hydrogen ion concentration /mol dm^{-3}	pH	Hydrogen ion concentration /mol dm^{-3}

Now look at the comments on Tasks 1 and 2 (at the end of this book) before
starting Task 3.

Task 3 Analysis of results: Conclusions

From Task 2, what can you conclude about:

(a) the relationship between the hydrogen ion concentration and your
preconceptions of which are the most acidic substances?

(b) the hydrogen ion concentration of personal washing solutions compared with
household cleaning fluids?

(c) the effect on the hydrogen ion concentration of diluting a solution by a factor
of 10 and 100?

Task 4 Review: Thinking critically about the method

When you have completed the investigation, reflect on it and note down what
you did well, and where you could make some improvements.

Now look at the comments on Tasks 3 and 4 at the end of this book.

In Activity 11.1, you should have seen how the hydrogen ion concentration can be related to the acidity of a solution.

■ What is the hydrogen ion concentration, in mol dm^{-3}, if 20.0 g of hydrogen chloride is dissolved in water to give 1.00 dm^3 of solution?

□ The formula unit of hydrogen chloride is HCl. The molar mass of hydrogen chloride is thus $(1.01 + 35.5)$ g mol^{-1}, or 36.5 g mol^{-1}.

20.0 g of hydrogen chloride is $\dfrac{20.0 \text{ g}}{36.5 \text{ g mol}^{-1}} = 0.548$ mol.

This amount is contained in 1.00 dm^3 of solution, so the concentration of hydrogen chloride is 0.548 mol dm^{-3}. According to Equation 11.1, hydrogen chloride dissolves in water to give one hydrogen ion and one chloride ion for every formula unit of dissolved hydrogen chloride, and so the hydrogen ion concentration is 0.548 mol dm^{-3}.

Question 11.2

What is the hydrogen ion concentration, in mol dm^{-3}, when 10.0 g of sulfuric acid is dissolved in water to give 1.00 dm^3 of solution?

As you have seen, when hydrogen chloride dissolves in water, effectively all the HCl molecules dissociate to give H$^+$(aq) and Cl$^-$(aq) ions. This acid is said to be nearly 100% dissociated. However, this is not always the case, and the amount of dissociation of an acid indicates whether that acid is strong or weak.

For example, vinegar contains acetic acid. (Its chemical name is ethanoic acid but its common name 'acetic acid' will be used here.) You will learn more about the structure of this acid in Section 14.1.3, but for now things will be kept simple and a molecule of acetic acid will be referred to as HAc, where the H refers to the hydrogen that forms H$^+$(aq) when the acid dissolves in water, and Ac is shorthand for acetate – the rest of the molecule (note that Ac is *not* the single element actinium in this case). Thus, acetic acid dissociates in water to give hydrogen ions and acetate ions, Ac$^-$(aq):

$$HAc(aq) = H^+(aq) + Ac^-(aq) \tag{11.7}$$

If you were to test the conductivity of vinegar and hydrochloric acid, using the apparatus in Figure 11.4, you would find that the light would not come on in the case of the vinegar solution but the light would illuminate in the hydrogen chloride solution. What does this say about the concentration of the ions in this solution? Clearly, vinegar is not a good electrical conductor. So the concentration of the ions in vinegar must be very low compared with that of the hydrochloric acid.

This conclusion is consistent with the measurement you may have made of the hydrogen ion concentration in vinegar in Activity 11.1. You should have found a value in the range from 1×10^{-2} to 1×10^{-3} mol dm^{-3}. This value is *considerably less* than might have been expected, because vinegar has a composition that is roughly equivalent to dissolving two moles of acetic acid in sufficient water to make up 1 dm^3 of solution. If this acetic acid dissociated completely, the hydrogen ion concentration would be about 2 mol dm^{-3}.

When hydrogen chloride dissolves in water, effectively all the HCl molecules dissociate to give H$^+$(aq) and Cl$^-$(aq) ions (Equation 11.1). However, when

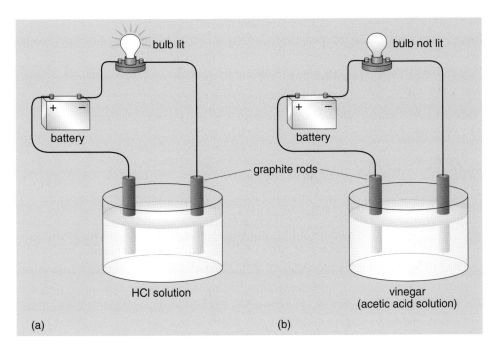

Figure 11.4 An electrical circuit between the two terminals of a battery and graphite rods, including a light bulb (a) with a solution of hydrochloric acid where the bulb is lit, showing a completed electrical circuit, and (b) with a solution of vinegar, where the bulb does not light up, indicating the electrical circuit is incomplete.

acetic acid dissolves in water only a *small fraction* of the acetic acid molecules dissociate to give hydrogen ions and acetate ions. This is shown in Figure 11.5; here the dissociation of the ions in solutions of acetic acid and hydrochloric acid are shown at a molecular level. For example, if 1.000 mol of acetic acid is dissolved in sufficient water to give 1 dm^3 of solution, you end up with 0.996 mol of acetic acid molecules and only 0.004 mol of H$^+$(aq) and 0.004 mol of Ac$^-$(aq) in this volume. *The solute consists mainly of undissociated acetic acid molecules.*

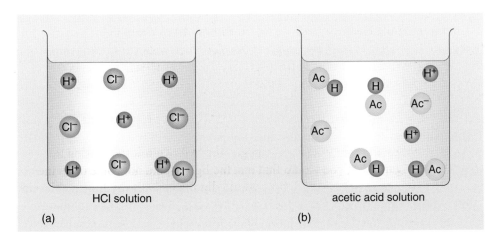

Figure 11.5 (a) Hydrochloric (HCl) acid in solution, where all the acid is dissociated into ions; (b) acetic acid (HAc) in solution, where only a very small proportion of the acid has dissociated into ions.

The dissociation of acetic acid in water is another example of a reaction that only goes so far and then no further; it reaches chemical equilibrium as you have seen in Chapter 10. The equilibrium state is dynamic; acetic acid molecules are continuously breaking down into hydrogen ions and acetate ions and this is balanced by the reverse reaction – hydrogen ions and acetate ions recombining to give acetic acid molecules. To highlight the equilibrium, it is best written as:

$$\text{HAc(aq)} \rightleftharpoons \text{H}^+\text{(aq)} + \text{Ac}^-\text{(aq)} \tag{11.7a}$$

where the symbol $\rightleftharpoons$ indicates that the reaction takes place in both directions; you met this symbol in Chapter 10. Acids, such as hydrogen chloride, which dissolve in water and effectively dissociate completely to give hydrogen ions, $H^+(aq)$, and the corresponding negatively charged ions are known as **strong acids**. Acids, such as acetic acid, that dissolve in water and are only *partially* dissociated are called **weak acids**. Table 11.4 gives examples of common strong and weak acids.

Table 11.4 Some common strong and weak acids; the formal chemical names are given in brackets.

Common strong acids		Common weak acids	
Name	Formula	Name	Formula
sulfuric acid	H_2SO_4	formic (methanoic) acid	HCOOH
nitric acid	HNO_3	acetic (ethanoic) acid	CH_3COOH
hydrochloric acid	HCl	hydrofluoric acid	HF
perchloric acid	$HClO_4$	prussic acid (hydrocyanic) acid	HCN

It should also be noted that likewise there are strong and weak bases that follow the same rules of dissociation. For example, sodium hydroxide dissociates completely in water to give a strong base, whereas ammonia is a weak base. Although ammonia, NH_3, does not contain any hydroxide ions, it reacts with water to give ammonium ions, NH_4^+, and hydroxide ions (Equation 11.8). Once again, this reaction is reversible and, as with acetic acid, only a very small proportion of ions are produced; in fact, around 99% of the ammonia is still present in the aqueous solution.

$$NH_3(aq) + H_2O(l) \rightleftharpoons NH_4^+(aq) + OH^-(aq) \tag{11.8}$$

In Table 11.5, a list of common strong and weak bases is given.

Table 11.5 Some common strong and weak bases.

Common strong bases		Common weak bases	
Name	Formula	Name	Formula
sodium hydroxide	NaOH	ammonia	NH_3
potassium hydroxide	KOH	ammonium hydroxide	NH_4OH
magnesium hydroxide	$Mg(OH)_2$	pyridine	C_5H_5N

It is important to distinguish between the *strength* of an acid and the *concentration* of an acid. A solution is said to be concentrated if the concentration of the solute in the solution is high. For example, a 12 mol dm^{-3} solution of HCl is a very concentrated solution of a strong acid (100% dissociated); however, you can make a **dilute** solution of 0.1 mol dm^{-3} of HCl from the concentrated solution, so in this case you have a dilute solution of a strong acid. Conversely, you can have a concentrated solution of a weak acid (undissociated) such as acetic acid at 15 mol dm^{-3}, which again you could dilute to give a dilute solution of a weak acid. The concept of strength, however, simply refers to the extent to which an acid is dissociated in solution; strong acids lie at one end of the scale because they are completely dissociated. Acids that do not satisfy this criterion are designated as weak. So, when talking about the concentration of acid solutions, it is a good idea to refer to 'dilute' or 'concentrated' solutions, rather than 'weak' or 'strong' solutions.

You have now investigated the difference between the strength of an acid or a base, in terms of the amount of ion dissociation when in solution. In the next section, you will take this a step further by obtaining a quantitative description of the strength of an acid by returning to the concepts you have learned in Chapter 10 regarding equilibrium constants.

11.2   The equilibrium constant for acid dissociation

As you saw in the previous section, acetic acid, HAc, in solution consists mainly of undissociated HAc molecules and the equilibrium expression is written as in Equation 11.7a:

$$HAc(aq) \rightleftharpoons H^+(aq) + Ac^-(aq) \tag{11.7a}$$

■ If you increased the concentration of Ac^- ions (by dissolving solid sodium acetate in the solution), what would happen to the position of equilibrium?

☐ The position of equilibrium would shift towards increasing the concentration of HAc, to counteract the effect of adding more Ac^- ions (Le Chatelier's principle).

The explanation for the above question is not quantitative, but is an example of an equilibrium position changing in response to an external influence, i.e. an increase in concentration of the Ac^- ion. However, the dissociation of an acid can be discussed in a quantitative manner which can lead to a determination of the actual amount of dissociation that occurs for any acid in solution.

The fact that HAc is a weak acid means that its dissociation into H^+ and Ac^- ions is small and so the equilibrium lies well over to the left-hand side of the equation. Like any equilibrium reaction, the equation can be expressed in terms of an equilibrium constant. This will give a useful numerical relationship between the concentrations of the HAc molecules and dissociated ions in solution. As before, the symbols for the species are enclosed in square brackets to represent the concentration. Hence the equilibrium constant, K, for the dissociation of acetic acid can be written as:

$$K = \frac{[H^+(aq)] \times [Ac^-(aq)]}{[HAc(aq)]} \tag{11.9}$$

Here, the equilibrium constant, K, is the multiplication of the concentration of the H^+ and Ac^- ions on the right-hand side, divided by the concentration of the HAc molecules on the left-hand side of Equation 11.7a. The equilibrium equation above will help you understand the effect that increasing the concentration of Ac^- ions in solution will have. As $[Ac^-(aq)]$ is increased, the value of the numerator (top of the fraction in Equation 11.9) will increase, and so K will effectively rise and so the system is not at equilibrium. However, you know that at a fixed temperature, K is constant for the equilibrium and the system must return to its equilibrium value. This is done by the equilibrium position shifting to produce more HAc. As the concentration of HAc increases, this increases the denominator (bottom of the fraction in Equation 11.9) and the two concentrations in the numerator will decrease to make more HAc. So, these changes lower the value of K and it is returned to its original equilibrium value.

So, the equilibrium constant expression can provide quantitative information about an acid dissociation. If you know the equilibrium concentrations of all or some of the species, you can calculate the equilibrium constant for that acid or the concentrations of an unknown species at equilibrium. For example, at 25 °C, the equilibrium constant for acetic acid $K = 1.8 \times 10^{-5}$ mol dm^{-3}, and if the equilibrium concentration of HAc is 1 mol dm^{-3}, you can calculate the equilibrium concentrations of H$^+$ and Ac$^-$ ions in the solution.

For the equilibrium constant expression, inserting values for K and [HAc(aq)], you can write:

$$1.8 \times 10^{-5} \text{ mol dm}^{-3} = \frac{[H^+(aq)] \times [Ac^-(aq)]}{1 \text{ mol dm}^{-3}} \qquad (11.10)$$

Recall that for every acetic acid molecule that dissociates in water, one H$^+$(aq) ion and one Ac$^-$(aq) ion enter into solution (Equation 11.7a). This means that the numbers of these two kinds of ion, and hence their concentrations, must be equal; so at equilibrium [H$^+$(aq)] = [Ac$^-$(aq)], and y will be used to represent this common concentration for [H$^+$(aq)] and [Ac$^-$(aq)]. You are now in a position to calculate the concentration of acetate ions in the equilibrium mixture. To do this, you substitute both [Ac$^-$(aq)] and [H$^+$(aq)] in Equation 11.10, with y:

$$1.8 \times 10^{-5} \text{mol dm}^{-3} = \frac{y \times y}{1 \text{ mol dm}^{-3}} = \frac{y^2}{1 \text{ mol dm}^{-3}}$$

Rearranging:

$$y^2 = 1.8 \times 10^{-5} \text{ mol}^2 \text{ dm}^{-6}$$

Taking the square root:

$$y = \sqrt{1.8 \times 10^{-5} \text{ mol}^2 \text{ dm}^{-6}} = 4.2 \times 10^{-3} \text{ mol dm}^{-3}$$

Thus, the concentrations of H$^+$(aq) and Ac$^-$(aq) are equal at 0.0042 mol dm^{-3}.

■   Is the calculation consistent with the view that acetic acid is a weak acid at 25 °C?

☐   Yes, a weak acid is defined as an acid that partially dissociates in water and here the equilibrium concentration of H$^+$ and Ac$^-$ ions of 0.0042 mol dm^{-3} in solution is much lower than the concentration of HAc of 1 mol dm^{-3}.

This has demonstrated that the dissociation of acetic acid is small by calculating the concentrations of the H$^+$ and Ac$^-$ ions present in the final equilibrium solution mixture. In fact, you can also predict if an acid will be a strong or weak acid by looking at the magnitude of K. If you take a general acid (HX) as an example, the acid dissociates in solution to give H$^+$(aq) and X$^-$(aq); the aqueous solution exists as an equilibrium which can be written in the general form:

$$HX(aq) \rightleftharpoons H^+(aq) + X^-(aq) \qquad (11.11)$$

The general form of the equilibrium constant for this acid dissociation can be written as:

$$K_a = \frac{[H^+(aq)] \times [X^-(aq)]}{[HX(aq)]} \qquad (11.12)$$

This time a subscript 'a' has been added to K to indicate this is an equilibrium constant for a particular kind of reaction: the dissociation of an acid. The equilibrium constant, K_a, is called the acid dissociation constant. From the magnitude of K_a you can determine whether an acid is strong or weak. For example, in your earlier calculation with acetic acid, you saw that at 25 °C, $K_a = 1.8 \times 10^{-5}$ mol dm^{-3}, which is small and indicates that acetic acid is a weak acid and that little dissociation occurs in solution. However, K_a values of strong acids, such as HCl, are very large and tend to infinity as complete dissociation occurs. Table 11.6 shows some K_a values for several acids, but note that hydrochloric and nitric acid are simply labelled 'strong acid' as K_a is so large in these cases.

Table 11.6 Values of K_a for acids at 25 °C.

Acid	Dissociation equilibrium	K_a/mol dm^{-3}
hydrochloric	$HCl(aq) \rightleftharpoons H^+(aq) + Cl^-(aq)$	strong acid, >1
nitric	$HNO_3(aq) \rightleftharpoons H^+(aq) + NO_3^-(aq)$	strong acid, >1
iodic	$HIO_3(aq) \rightleftharpoons H^+(aq) + IO_3^-(aq)$	1.7×10^{-1}
acetic	$HAc(aq) \rightleftharpoons H^+(aq) + Ac^-(aq)$	1.8×10^{-5}
hypochlorous	$HClO(aq) \rightleftharpoons H^+(aq) + ClO^-(aq)$	2.9×10^{-8}

In general, it can be assumed that strong acids have K_a values >1 and have almost complete dissociation into ions in solutions; weak acids have K_a values <1 and the ions are not completely dissociated in solution.

Strong acid: $K_a > 1$

Weak acid: $K_a < 1$

Question 11.3

Iodic acid dissociates in water according to the equation:

$$HIO_3(aq) \rightleftharpoons H^+(aq) + IO_3^-(aq) \tag{11.13}$$

Table 11.7 provides information about the concentrations of $HIO_3(aq)$, $H^+(aq)$ and $IO_3^-(aq)$ for a particular equilibrium mixture as the temperature is raised from 25 °C to 45 °C.

(a) At each temperature, calculate the value of the equilibrium constant, K_a.

(b) Is the dissociation of iodic acid in water exothermic or endothermic in the forward direction?

Table 11.7 Equilibrium molar concentrations in a particular equilibrium mixture of iodic acid in water at 25 and 45 °C.

Temperature/ °C	[HIO_3(aq)]/ mol dm^{-3}	[H^+(aq)]/ mol dm^{-3}	[IO_3^-(aq)]/ mol dm^{-3}
25	0.029	0.071	0.071
45	0.034	0.066	0.066

11.3   The equilibrium dissociation of water

So far, you have considered the dissociation of acids in water and how to determine whether they are strong or weak acids with respect to their K_a values. However, in these examples it has been assumed that the $H^+(aq)$ has originated from the acid contribution and its dissociation in water as a solvent. This is not exactly correct, as there will be a small contribution to the $H^+(aq)$ concentration from the water itself. In Section 11.2, the contribution of hydrogen ions from the water was omitted as it is negligible in comparison with the amount contributed by the acid. In solutions of low acidity, though, you cannot dismiss the contribution of the hydrogen ion concentration from the water. This is indeed an important aspect when considering natural water in rain, seas, rivers and lakes, which circulate through plants and animals on our planet in the water cycle. Here very small changes in the hydrogen ion concentration of a solution can have a great and possibly lethal effect on both living things and the environment. For example, the effects of acid rain on trees and historic buildings can be devastating, as shown in Figure 11.6. Many examples of eroded stonework have been seen in cities, and whole forests have been destroyed due to the effects of increased acidity of rain from the release of sulfur and nitrogen oxides into the atmosphere from anthropogenic sources (e.g. coal-fired power stations).

(a)

(b)

Figure 11.6   Acid rain damage (a) to a forest and (b) to a cathedral's stonework.

There is a tiny concentration of H^+ and OH^- ions in pure water; in fact, in $1\ dm^{-3}$ there is 1×10^{-7} mol of both H^+ ions and OH^- ions. The molecules and ions in pure water that will be present are H_2O, H^+ and OH^-. You can now relate this to an equilibrium expression, as the dissociation of water molecules is small but still dynamic. The equilibrium relationship for the dissociation of water molecules can be written as:

$$H_2O(l) \rightleftharpoons H^+(aq) + OH^-(aq) \tag{11.14}$$

Thus, pure water is a medium that is mainly water molecules, $H_2O(l)$, with tiny amounts of $H^+(aq)$ and $OH^-(aq)$ ions also present. The equilibrium position lies well over to the left in Equation 11.14. As you can see, the equilibrium for water given in Equation 11.14 is similar to that for the dissociation of a weak acid. Thus, the equilibrium relationship involving an equilibrium constant can be written as:

$$K = \frac{[H^+(aq)] \times [OH^-(aq)]}{[H_2O(l)]} \qquad (11.15)$$

■ Would you expect the magnitude of the equilibrium constant for pure water at room temperature to be large or small?

☐ Since the equilibrium position lies well over to the left in Equation 11.14, the magnitude of K will be very small.

In Equation 11.15, the terms $[H^+(aq)]$ and $[OH^-(aq)]$ represent equilibrium molar ion concentrations. The term $[H_2O(l)]$ is also an equilibrium concentration, but of water itself! Literally, it is the number of moles of water molecules in 1.00 dm^{-3} of pure water. If the minute amount of water that breaks down into ions is ignored, then at a given temperature $[H_2O(l)]$ must represent a fixed concentration: you cannot increase or decrease the amount of pure water in a fixed volume.

By convention, it is usual to rearrange the equilibrium relationship in Equation 11.15 by taking the fixed term $[H_2O(l)]$ over to the left-hand side, i.e.:

$$K[H_2O(l)] = [H^+(aq)] \times [OH^-(aq)] \qquad (11.16)$$

The combination $K[H_2O(l)]$ is then itself a constant at a fixed temperature. It is given both a special name, the **ion product of water**, and a special symbol, $\boldsymbol{K_w}$. So, finally, we have:

$$K_w = [H^+(aq)] \times [OH^-(aq)] \qquad (11.17)$$

The experimental value of the ion product of water at 25 °C is 1.0×10^{-14} mol^2 dm^{-6}. It is useful to consider the implications of this value, both for pure water and for solutions of acids and bases. The size of $\boldsymbol{K_w}$ does limit the concentrations of hydrogen and hydroxide ions that can coexist in pure water. Each water molecule that dissociates gives one hydrogen ion and one hydroxide ion. Thus the numbers, and hence the concentrations, of these ions at equilibrium will be the same, i.e. $[H^+(aq)] = [OH^-(aq)]$. To find the equilibrium concentration of hydrogen ions, the term $[OH^-(aq)]$ in Equation 11.17 is replaced by $[H^+(aq)]$, so that

$$K_w = [H^+(aq)] \times [H^+(aq)]$$

or

$$1.0 \times 10^{-14} \text{ mol}^2 \text{ dm}^{-6} = [H^+(aq)] \times [H^+(aq)]$$

The equilibrium hydrogen ion concentration is found by taking the square root of both sides of this equation:

$$[H^+(aq)] = \sqrt{1.0 \times 10^{-14} \text{ mol}^2 \text{ dm}^{-6}}$$

So, $[H^+(aq)] = 1.0 \times 10^{-7}$ mol dm^{-3}

So, from the use of K_w, you can see that the hydrogen and hydroxide ion concentrations in pure water at 25 °C are equal: $[H^+(aq)] = [OH^-(aq)] = 1.0 \times 10^{-7}$ mol dm^{-3}. These concentrations are very low, but they cannot be dismissed lightly, as you will see.

Water can be viewed as possessing both acidic and basic hydroxide properties because, when it dissociates, both hydrogen ions and hydroxide ions are produced. However, these two types of ion are always produced in equal numbers. Thus the acidic nature of water is always balanced by its basic nature. It is said to be *neutral*.

In a wider context, the idea of neutrality can be applied to any aqueous solution in which the hydrogen and hydroxide ion concentrations are equal. To be more specific, at 25 °C a **neutral solution** is defined as one in which the hydrogen ion concentration is 1.0×10^{-7} mol dm^{-3}.

It is worth re-emphasising that the ion product of water at 25 °C has a *fixed* magnitude. In practice, this means that there is a limitation on the concentrations of hydrogen and hydroxide ions that can coexist in *any* solution for which water is the solvent at 25 °C. Whatever the individual concentrations of hydrogen ions and hydroxide ions, they must satisfy the relationship in Equation 11.17; i.e., when multiplied together they must give a result equal to K_w.

Suppose you prepare a solution of hydrochloric acid at 25 °C by dissolving 0.10 mol of hydrogen chloride in sufficient water to make one dm^3 of solution. Since hydrochloric acid is a strong acid, it will effectively dissociate completely into ions. The concentration of hydrogen ions that has been 'added' to the water is equivalent therefore to 0.10 mol dm^{-3}. This concentration far outweighs the concentration of hydrogen ions already present due to the dissociation of water itself. It is therefore perfectly valid to ignore any contribution of the latter and to take the hydrogen ion concentration in the solution to be 0.10 mol dm^{-3}. It is only ever necessary to consider a contribution from the dissociation of water itself when an 'added' hydrogen ion concentration is close to or less than the neutral value of 1.0×10^{-7} mol dm^{-3}. This is of more theoretical than practical interest and will not be considered further here.

■   What is the concentration of hydroxide ions in the solution of 0.10 mol dm^{-3} hydrochloric acid at 25 °C?

☐   You know that at 25 °C, and using Equation 11.17:

$$1.0 \times 10^{-14} \text{ mol}^2 \text{ dm}^{-6} = [\text{H}^+(\text{aq})] \times [\text{OH}^-(\text{aq})]$$

so you can rearrange this equation to find [OH$^-$(aq)]:

$$[\text{OH}^-(\text{aq})] = \frac{1.0 \times 10^{-14} \text{ mol}^2 \text{ dm}^{-6}}{[\text{H}^+(\text{aq})]}$$

Since the solution in question has [H$^+$(aq)] = 0.10 mol dm^{-3}, then:

$$[\text{OH}^-(\text{aq})] = \frac{1.0 \times 10^{-14} \text{ mol}^2 \text{ dm}^{-6}}{0.10 \text{ mol dm}^{-3}}$$

$$= 1.0 \times 10^{-13} \text{ mol dm}^{-3}$$

Thus, in an acidic solution of 0.10 mol dm^{-3} there is a very low, but none the less finite, concentration of hydroxide ions.

■ What is the concentration of hydrogen ions in a solution of the base sodium hydroxide in water in which the hydroxide ion concentration, [OH⁻(aq)], is 0.10 mol dm⁻³ at 25 °C?

□ There are direct parallels here with the calculation for hydrochloric acid. In this case, you have:

$$[H^+(aq)] = \frac{1.0 \times 10^{-14} \text{ mol}^2 \text{ dm}^{-6}}{[OH^-(aq)]}$$

Since $[OH^-(aq)] = 0.10$ mol dm⁻³, it follows that in this case $[H^+(aq)] = 1.0 \times 10^{-13}$ mol dm⁻³.

So, in a basic solution of 0.10 mol dm⁻³ there is a very small, but none the less finite, concentration of hydrogen ions.

Overall, a picture of solutions of acids and bases begins to emerge in which there is a type of 'see-saw effect'. If the hydrogen ion concentration is high, the hydroxide ion concentration will be correspondingly low, and vice versa. This behaviour is due to the form of the relationship in Equation 11.17.

■ If a solution has a hydrogen ion concentration greater than 1.0×10^{-7} mol dm⁻³, will the hydroxide ion concentration be greater or less than 1.0×10^{-7} mol dm⁻³?

□ It will be less than 1.0×10^{-7} mol dm⁻³, as predicted by the relationship in Equation 11.17.

Thus the concentration of hydrogen ions exceeds the concentration of hydroxide ions, and the solution can be justifiably called acidic. The more the hydrogen ion concentration exceeds the neutral value of 1.0×10^{-7} mol dm⁻³, the more acidic is the solution.

> An acidic solution can be defined as one in which the hydrogen ion concentration is greater than 1.0×10^{-7} mol dm⁻³ at 25 °C.

Strictly, this definition applies only at 25 °C because the value of the ion product for water, K_w, varies with temperature. For instance, at 37 °C (human body temperature) $K_w = 2.5 \times 10^{-14}$ mol² dm⁻⁶, so that in a neutral solution at this temperature $[H^+(aq)] = 1.6 \times 10^{-7}$ mol dm⁻³.

In a solution at 25 °C in which the hydroxide ion concentration is greater than 1.0×10^{-7} mol dm⁻³, the hydrogen ion concentration will be correspondingly less than this value. In this case, the solution can justifiably be called basic. A basic solution could thus be defined as one in which the hydroxide ion concentration is greater than 1.0×10^{-7} mol dm⁻³ at 25 °C. However, it is more useful to phrase the definition in terms of the hydrogen ion concentration.

> A basic solution can be defined as one in which the hydrogen ion concentration is less than 1.0×10^{-7} mol dm⁻³ at 25 °C.

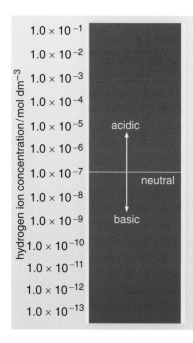

Figure 11.7 The hydrogen ion concentration defines whether a solution is acidic, neutral or basic.

Given a hydrogen ion concentration for a solution at 25 °C, you are now in a position to state whether the solution is acidic, neutral or basic. The basis for such a decision is summarised in Figure 11.7.

Question 11.4

State, giving your reasons, whether the following aqueous solutions are acidic, neutral or basic at 25 °C.

(a) NaOH of concentration 1.0×10^{-2} mol dm^{-3}

(b) HCl of concentration 1.0×10^{-5} mol dm^{-3}

(c) NaCl of concentration 1.0×10^{3} mol dm^{-3}

(d) HAc (acetic acid) of concentration 1.0 mol dm^{-3}.

Question 11.5

(a) What happens to the hydrogen ion concentration when 1.00 dm^3 of a 1.0 mol dm^{-3} solution of hydrochloric acid is fully mixed with 1.00 dm^3 of a 1.0 mol dm^{-3} solution of sodium hydroxide?

(b) What happens to the hydrogen ion concentration when 2.00 dm^3 of a 1.0 mol dm^{-3} solution of hydrochloric acid are fully mixed with 1.00 dm^3 of a 1.0 mol dm^{-3} solution of sodium hydroxide?

11.4   Measuring acidity: the pH scale; a quantitative method

In the last section, you learned how strong and weak acids can be distinguished. Equilibrium plays a large part in determining the strength of an acid and that sometimes the contribution of water as an acidic or basic solution cannot be ignored. In this section, you will see how the strength of an acid is described in terms of the pH scale, which is a universal scale for describing acidity and basicity. As you saw in Table 11.1 and Figure 11.3, the hydrogen ion concentration ranges are given as a pH value: the higher the hydrogen ion concentration in a solution, the lower its pH value and hence the stronger the acid.

The pH scale was introduced in 1909 by the Danish biochemist Søren Sørensen, who at the time was director of chemistry at the Carlsberg Laboratory. The pH scale simplified the huge ranges of values of acidic to basic solutions as a number from 0 to 14 instead of using the range of numbers in Figure 11.7 and Table 11.1. You can see that there is a huge drop of a millionfold between a hydrogen ion concentration of 1×10^{-1} to 1×10^{-7} in Figure 11.7. However, the power of 10 index drops from −1 to −7. So the pH scale in Figure 11.3 provides a more manageable measure of hydrogen ion concentrations, as they cover many orders of magnitude. This index of 10 is called the logarithm to the base ten scale or the common logarithm and is written as 'log$_{10}$' or simply 'log'. In Section 11.1, you saw that if the concentration of hydrogen ions is 1×10^{-n} mol dm^{-3}, the pH will be n. This is a simple way of describing the pH of a solution and the logarithmic scale (Box 11.1). However, you may want to find the pH of a solution that is not a simple whole-number power of 10. Since the pH scale is in fact a logarithmic scale of the hydrogen ion concentration, the logarithm of the hydrogen ion concentration can be used to calculate any pH value. As a mathematical operation, you can simply take the logarithm of any number using a scientific calculator, as it will have a special key, labelled 'log', to calculate the value.

■ Use your calculator to find the logarithm of each of the following numbers: 10, 40, 100, 400, 1000 and 0.1.

☐ The answers should be: log 10 = 1, log 40 = 1.6, log 100 = 2, log 400 = 2.6, log 1000 = 3 and log 0.1 = −1.

Box 11.1 Logarithms

Invented in 1614 by the Scottish mathematician John Napier, logarithms had the express purpose of simplifying mathematical calculations involving multiplication and divisions. Logarithms have been in regular use for these purposes since the second half of the 17th century. Of course, today the use of electronic calculators and computers enables us to perform long multiplication and division with ease but, despite this, the use of logarithms is still an invaluable aid to arithmetic, and there are many applications in which logarithms are still widely used. One of these applications is in chemistry, with the pH scale. The basics of logarithms and their application to the pH scale are detailed below.

Logarithms to the base 10

Henry Briggs, an English professor of geometry, visited John Napier in 1615 and with his blessing developed what is now known as logarithms to the base 10, or 'common logarithms'. You know that, using power laws:

$$10^6 = 1\,000\,000$$

$$10^3 = 1000$$

$$10^0 = 1$$

$$10^{-1} = \frac{1}{10} = 0.1$$

$$10^{-5} = \frac{1}{10^5} = 0.000\,01$$

Here, 10 is known as the base number. The process of obtaining a logarithm to the base 10 (usually described as 'taking the log to base 10') is the opposite of raising the base 10 to a power. So, from the examples above, the logarithm to base 10 of the number on the right-hand side of the equation is the power to which the 10 on the left-hand side is raised. The logarithm to base 10 is usually abbreviated to $\log_{10}$ but you will also come across other abbreviations such as 'lg' or 'log' which do not have the 10 as a subscript.

So, from the examples above:

$$10^3 = 1000 \qquad \text{so} \qquad \log_{10} 1000 = 3$$

10 raised to the power 3 equals 1000, so the logarithm to base 10 of 1000 equals 3.

$$10^0 = 1 \qquad \text{so} \qquad \log_{10} 1 = 0$$

10 raised to the power 0 equals 1, so the logarithm to base 10 of 1 equals 0.

$$10^{-1} = 0.1 \qquad \text{so} \qquad \log_{10} 0.1 = -1$$

10 raised to the power −1 equals 0.1, so the logarithm to base 10 of 0.1 equals −1.

In general terms, the following relationship can be applied:

The logarithm to base 10 of p is the power to which 10 must be raised in order to equal p; in symbols:

$$\text{if } p = 10^n \qquad \text{then} \qquad \log_{10} p = n$$

The pH scale and logarithms

pH is an abbreviation for 'potential hydrogen' and the scale is based on the concentration of hydrogen ions in solution. Concentration is measured in mol dm^{-3}, and the concentration of hydrogen ions in pure water at 25 °C, for example, is 1×10^{-7} mol dm^{-3} while that of household bleach is around 1×10^{-12} mol dm^{-3} and lemon juice is about 8×10^{-3} mol dm^{-3}. These values are wide ranging and are small, which can make them difficult to deal with. The use of the pH scale allows us to deal with such numbers. The definition of pH is written as follows:

$$\text{pH} = -\log_{10}\left(\frac{\text{hydrogen ion concentration in mol dm}^{-3}}{\text{mol dm}^{-3}}\right)$$

Since the hydrogen ion concentration is measured in mol dm^{-3} and since you divide by mol dm^{-3} before taking the logarithm, you are obtaining the logarithm of a dimensionless number. From the definition of pH, for pure water:

$$\text{pH} = -\log_{10}\left(\frac{1 \times 10^{-7} \text{ mol dm}^{-3}}{\text{mol dm}^{-3}}\right) = -\log_{10}(10^{-7}) = -(-7) = 7$$

For household bleach:

$$\text{pH} = -\log_{10}\left(\frac{1 \times 10^{-12} \text{ mol dm}^{-3}}{\text{mol dm}^{-3}}\right) = -\log_{10}(10^{-12}) = -(-12) = 12$$

For lemon juice:

$$\text{pH} = -\log_{10}\left(\frac{8 \times 10^{-3} \text{ mol dm}^{-3}}{\text{mol dm}^{-3}}\right) = -\log_{10}(8 \times 10^{-3}) = -(-2.1) = 2.1$$

The pH values are now on a much more manageable scale: the entire range of hydrogen ion concentration of 1.0 mol dm^{-3} to 1×10^{-14} mol dm^{-3} is represented by pH values between 0 and 14. A pH of 7 for pure water is said to be a neutral solution, with the lower numbers representing increasing acidity and the higher numbers increasing basicity.

You should have noticed that the logarithm of 0.1 is a negative number. Indeed, if you look at the concentrations of hydrogen ions in Figure 11.7, all these numbers will give a negative logarithm. This means that effectively the pH values of most solutions would be negative, but pH is always quoted as a positive number between 0 and 14. The widely used scale of pH is therefore defined as the *negative* of the logarithm of the hydrogen ion concentration, $[H^+(aq)]$, in mol dm^{-3}. This relationship can be written simply as:

$$pH = -\log\left(\frac{[H^+(aq)]}{mol\ dm^{-3}}\right) \qquad (11.18)$$

Using the relationship in Equation 11.18, the pH of any solution can be calculated if the corresponding hydrogen ion concentration is given.

■ In human blood, $[H^+(aq)] = 4.0 \times 10^{-8}$ mol dm^{-3}. What is the pH of human blood?

☐ From Equation 11.18, you simply substitute the concentration of $H^+(aq)$ ions and use a calculator to calculate the pH value:

$$pH = -\log\left(\frac{4.0 \times 10^{-8}\ mol\ dm^{-3}}{mol\ dm^{-3}}\right) = 7.4$$

So for human blood the pH = 7.4, which is slightly basic. Note that pH is a dimensionless quantity (it has no units) as the 'mol dm^{-3}' cancel out in the equation.

As mentioned above, the $H^+(aq)$ ion concentration of a solution can also be calculated if the pH is already known. You do this by calculating the antilogarithm of the negative pH value, which is in fact 10^{-pH}. Again you can do this quite simply on your calculator. The general equation will now be:

$$[H^+(aq)] = 10^{-pH}\ mol\ dm^{-3} \qquad (11.19)$$

■ The pH of gastric juice is about 1.7 at 37 °C. What is the hydrogen ion concentration of stomach fluids at 37 °C?

☐ From Equation 11.19, you can calculate the hydrogen ion concentration by raising 10 to the power of (−pH). So you can write:

$$[H^+(aq)] = 10^{-1.7}\ mol\ dm^{-3}$$

So, the concentration of $H^+(aq)$ ions in stomach fluids is 0.02 mol dm^{-3}.

Increasingly, the term pH is creeping into everyday language (Figure 11.8). For instance, it is used in connection with commercial personal care products such as bath foam or face wash that claim to have a pH the same as your skin (the value given is about the same as the pH of rainwater). Other similar products claim that they are mild or pure because they have neutral pH, i.e. 7.

Figure 11.8   A bottle of bath foam; note the pH value of 5.5.

To give you some further ideas of the pH values of solutions you may come across, Table 11.8 gives some pH values for some common solutions of chemicals, both natural and those found in your household. Some of these you investigated for yourself in Activity 11.1.

Table 11.8 pH values of some common solutions.

Solution	pH
hydrochloric acid (0.1 mol dm^{-3})	1.0
human gastric juice	1.0–2.5
lemon juice	about 2.1
acetic acid (0.1 mol dm^{-3})*	2.9
orange juice	about 3.0
tomato juice	about 4.1
urine	6.0
unpolluted rainwater	5.2–6.5
human saliva	6.8
milk	about 6.9
pure water (25 °C)	7.0
human blood	7.4
seawater	7.9–8.3
ammonia (0.1 mol dm^{-3})†	11.1
sodium hydroxide (0.1 mol dm^{-3})	13.0

*Approximately the concentration of household vinegar.
†Approximately the concentration of household ammonia solutions.

Question 11.6

(a) What is the pH of (i) a 0.01 mol dm^{-3} solution of nitric acid and (ii) a 0.05 mol dm^{-3} solution of sulfuric acid?

(b) What is the hydrogen ion concentration of a solution of nitric acid with a pH of 2.5?

Question 11.7

A sample of seawater is found to have a pH of 7.9 at 25 °C. What is the concentration of hydroxide ions, [OH$^-$(aq)], in the sample?

Question 11.8

0.001 mol of nitric acid is dissolved in 10 dm^3 of water at 25 °C. Calculate the hydrogen ion concentration, [H$^+$(aq)], the pH and the hydroxide ion concentration of the resulting solution.

11.5   Summary of Chapter 11

Acids yield hydrogen ions when they dissolve in water. Acidity depends on the hydrogen ion concentration. When strong acids dissolve, they dissociate completely to give hydrogen ions and their corresponding negatively charged ions. Weak acids only partially dissociate in water.

Pure water dissociates to give very small concentrations of hydrogen ions, $H^+(aq)$, and hydroxide ions, $OH^-(aq)$. The equilibrium position for the dissociation reaction:

$$H_2O(l) \rightleftharpoons H^+(aq) + OH^-(aq)$$

lies well over to the left.

The ion product of water is defined by the relationship:

$$K_w = [H^+(aq)] \times [OH^-(aq)].$$

At 25 °C the experimental value of K_w is 1.0×10^{-14} mol^2 dm^{-6}.

The ion product of water controls the concentrations of hydrogen and hydroxide ions that can coexist in any solution at a given temperature.

In pure water, or any neutral solution, at 25 °C:

$$[H^+(aq)] = [OH^-(aq)] = 1.0 \times 10^{-7} \text{ mol dm}^{-3}$$

An acidic solution is one in which the hydrogen ion concentration is greater than 1.0×10^{-7} mol dm^{-3} at 25 °C. A basic solution is one in which the hydrogen ion concentration is less than 1.0×10^{-7} mol dm^{-3} at 25 °C.

One way of expressing the pH scale is to write a hydrogen ion concentration as 1.0×10^{-n} mol dm^{-3}. The pH is then equal to n. Conversely, if the pH of a solution is equal to n, the corresponding hydrogen ion concentration is 1.0×10^{-n} mol dm^{-3}.

At 25 °C a neutral solution has a pH of 7, an acidic solution has a pH less than 7 and a basic solution has a pH greater than 7.

The pH of any solution of aqueous hydrogen ions can be calculated by the following general relationship:

$$pH = -\log\left(\frac{[H^+(aq)]}{\text{mol dm}^{-3}}\right)$$

and the hydrogen ion concentration of any solution can be calculated from its pH using the relationship:

$$[H^+(aq)] = 10^{-pH} \text{ mol dm}^{-3}$$

You have designed and carried out an experiment, and practised your mathematical skills in a chemical context.

Chapter 12
Introducing carbon compounds: crude oil

In earlier chapters of this book we have explored some of the most important aspects of chemistry in general but, for the remainder of the book, the focus will be on the compounds of one element: carbon. It may seem strange to focus on one element in this way, but you might recall from your work on the carbon cycle in Book 1 that this element plays a key role in all living organisms on this planet. There is an exceptionally large number of carbon compounds, many of which are essential to life.

In Chapters 12 and 13, you will examine the chemistry of the carbon compounds found in **crude oil**. These carbon compounds are widely used as fuels but, as you will see, they are also the source of the building blocks used to make many of the materials fundamental to modern life – materials as varied as plastics, detergents, food flavourings and drugs. In later chapters, you will begin to look at some of the more complex carbon compounds found in living things. You will return to these compounds in Book 5, where you will explore in more detail their biological role.

12.1 Processing crude oil: fractional distillation

You might recall that crude oil is formed from organic matter in ancient ocean sediments (Book 1, Chapter 7). Over millions of years, these ancient sediments were lithified (turned to rock). Under certain conditions, the biological material in the sediments (the soft bodies of plankton, faeces, etc.) underwent a chemical transformation to produce oil.

Crude oil is a mixture of thousands of different substances, most of which contain only carbon and hydrogen. The mixture itself is not very useful and, in order to convert it into more useful materials, it is necessary to separate the mixture into a number of components, known as fractions. The process used to separate the mixture is **distillation**.

When a substance is heated at a particular pressure, it boils at a specific temperature – the boiling temperature (Section 4.7). If the gas produced is then cooled, it condenses to give the pure liquid. This condensation process can be observed if a cold ladle is placed in the steam above a kettle – water droplets appear as the steam condenses on the ladle (Figure 12.1). This is a simple example of distillation, a centuries-old technique used to purify

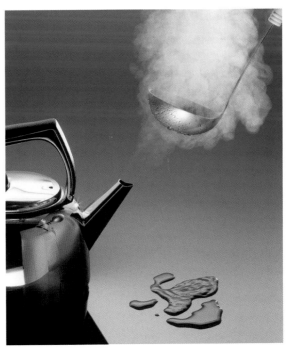

Figure 12.1 Condensation of water vapour from steam. The hot water vapour condenses to form water when it makes contact with the cold ladle.

liquids. The designs of distillation apparatus vary a great deal, but all involve a source of heat to boil the liquid, and a mechanism to cool the vapour. Figure 12.2 is a sketch of a design reputedly used by ancient Greek sailors to generate drinking water from seawater – a process known as desalination.

Figure 12.2 Desalination by distillation. Seawater is heated in a boiling chamber and, as the temperature rises, an increasing proportion of the water molecules escape into the vapour phase, leaving behind the salt and other impurities. The water vapour (steam) rises and is cooled in the condensing dome; this cooling converts the water vapour back to a liquid. The condensed liquid water runs down the sides of the condensing dome and is collected in a clean vessel. This is one way of producing drinkable water from seawater.

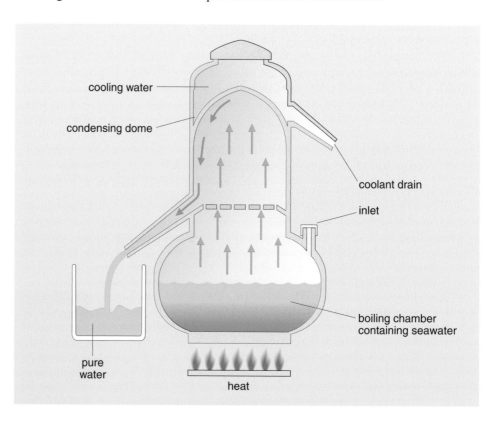

The purification of seawater by distillation is relatively simple. Seawater is about 96% water (by mass); the rest is mostly common salt (sodium chloride, NaCl). When heated, the pure water escapes as vapour, leaving the impurities behind. By contrast, crude oil (Figure 12.3) is a mixture containing so many compounds that it boils over a continuous range of temperatures. At the lower temperatures, compounds with a lower boiling temperature vaporise. As the temperature increases, substances with progressively higher boiling temperatures vaporise. Thus, if the crude oil is heated up slowly, the liquid that condenses at the beginning of the distillation will be rich in compounds with low boiling temperatures, whereas the liquid that condenses later will be rich in compounds with high boiling temperatures. By collecting different samples at different times during the distillation, the crude oil can be separated into samples that have different ranges of boiling temperatures. Each sample is known as a fraction and the complete set of fractions from crude oil is shown in Figure 12.4. However, these fractions are not pure compounds; they are still mixtures of many compounds.

Figure 12.3 Crude oil is a thick, sticky liquid with the pouring consistency of honey.

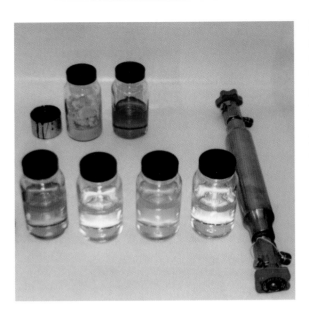

Figure 12.4 The fractions obtained by distillation of crude oil. At room temperature, they range from solids (top left) through various liquids to gases which have to be stored in pressurised containers (bottom right).

Typical uses of the fractions obtained by industrial distillation are listed in Table 12.1, in ascending order of boiling temperature.

Table 12.1 Fractions from industrial distillation of crude oil.

Fraction	Boiling temperature/°C	Typical percentage by mass of crude oil	Uses
gases	below 15	2	Fuels for burners and electricity generators in refineries; propane and butane are widely used for heating and cooking in rural communities and for camping stoves, etc.
gasoline	15–149	14	Motor car fuel – petrol
kerosene	149–232	12	Domestic 'paraffin' and the main constituent of jet fuel
diesel	232–371	21	Fuel for commercial and domestic vehicles with diesel engines and for domestic central heating systems
lubricating oils	371–525	19	Lubricants for machinery, such as cars, steam turbine generators and bicycles
waxes	371–525	2	Candles, impregnating food packaging and electrical insulation
bitumen	above 525	30	Road surfacing and as a waterproofing agent, particularly in the building industry

■ The compounds in crude oil are covalent, meaning that they exist as separate molecules made up of atoms held together by covalent bonds. Assuming that the main intermolecular forces between the molecules in crude oil are van der Waals forces, what can you say about the average size of the molecules in the various fractions listed in Table 12.1?

☐ In Section 4.3 you saw that van der Waals forces between molecules increase with increasing molecular size, and this leads to higher boiling temperatures. This suggests that the higher boiling fractions of crude oil contain larger molecules than the lower boiling fractions.

12.2   Hydrocarbons

Most of the thousands of compounds in crude oil consist of covalent molecules made from only carbon and hydrogen atoms. These compounds are collectively known as **hydrocarbons**. How can there be such a rich diversity of compounds made from such simple building blocks?

12.2.1   Linear-chain hydrocarbons

One property of carbon that gives it such a rich chemistry is its ability to form chains of atoms of almost any length, to which other atoms can be attached. You will look at some of these carbon compounds in more detail, but first you need to revisit and extend the chemistry in Sections 3.3 and 5.5. There you learned that carbon invariably forms covalent bonds by sharing electrons with other atoms rather than by forming ions, and that a covalent bond involves a pair of electrons.

The simplest hydrocarbon is methane. Each molecule of methane consists of one carbon atom linked to four hydrogen atoms by covalent bonds. There are a number of ways in which the structure can be represented, as shown in Figure 12.5. First, there is the molecular formula, CH_4 (Figure 12.5a), which tells us only the numbers of each type of atom in the molecule, not how the atoms are attached to each other. Second, there is the Lewis structure (Figure 12.5b) we first met in Section 5.5. Third, as you saw in Section 5.5, there is the structural formula (Figure 12.5c), in which each shared electron pair, i.e. each covalent bond, is denoted by a line. The structural formula is tremendously useful, but it only indicates the way in which the atoms are connected together; it is important to emphasise that it says nothing about the three-dimensional shape of the molecule.

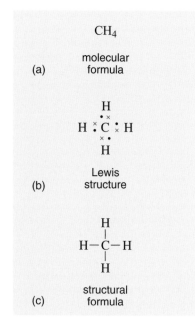

Figure 12.5   Three ways of representing methane.

Carbon always forms four bonds. So any structural formula that shows a carbon atom with more or less than four bonds is almost certainly wrong. Put another way, in a structural formula a carbon atom, C, always has four lines (bonds) associated with it. You might recall from Section 5.4 that the number of bonds that an atom can form is often referred to as its valency. Carbon therefore has a valency of four. Hydrogen, whose atoms can form only one bond, has a valency of one.

Butane is another hydrocarbon; its molecular formula is C_4H_{10}. You will spend some time exploring how you might draw its structural formula. Drawing structural formulas is an important skill and, as this is your first example, you will be taken through it fairly slowly.

Butane is a **linear-chain hydrocarbon**; its molecules consist of a chain of four carbons joined by single bonds, as shown in Figure 12.6a. Each carbon atom needs four bonds, so you can draw in the remaining bonds from each carbon, as shown in Figure 12.6b. Each hydrogen atom will be attached to the carbon by one bond, so you end up with the structure in Figure 12.6c. Note that there are ten hydrogen atoms attached to the carbons, in agreement with the molecular formula. Note also that the chain is created by joining together only carbon atoms; because hydrogen has a valency of one, it can never be joined to two other atoms by covalent bonds. In other words, in a structural formula, a hydrogen atom, H, always has only one line (bond) associated with it.

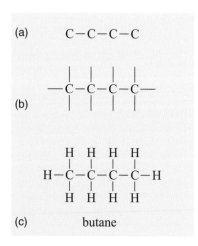

Figure 12.6   Three stages in drawing the structural formula of butane, C_4H_{10}.

It is important that you are able to draw structural formulas in this way, so you should attempt the following questions before proceeding.

Question 12.1

The molecules ethane, C_2H_6, and pentane, C_5H_{12}, contain linear chains of two and five carbon atoms, respectively. Draw the structural formula for each molecule.

Question 12.2

Propane consists of a chain of three carbon atoms attached to each other by covalent bonds. It has sufficient hydrogen atoms to satisfy the valency of each carbon. Draw out the structural formula of propane. What is its molecular formula?

Clearly, with long chains of carbon atoms, the structural formulas will soon get very cumbersome. Things can be simplified a little by using an **abbreviated structural formula**. Here only the bonds between the carbon atoms are drawn and not the bonds to the hydrogen atoms. The number of hydrogen atoms on each carbon (which are needed to satisfy the valency of 4) is shown by the hydrogen symbol, H, with a subscript. For example, butane (Figure 12.6c) is represented as $CH_3-CH_2-CH_2-CH_3$. Note that the bonds shown in the abbreviated structural formula are the carbon-to-carbon bonds; they do not link the hydrogen atoms to the carbons.

Methane, ethane, propane, butane and pentane are called linear-chain hydrocarbons, because each carbon atom is bonded to a maximum of two other carbon atoms, giving the appearance of a linear chain of carbon atoms when the structural formula is written down. Crude oil contains many different linear-chain hydrocarbons: every one from methane to $C_{78}H_{158}$ has been found in crude oil.

Throughout the rest of this book, you will meet many new compounds. These will be referred to either by a name or by a structure numbered in bold type. The names of carbon compounds can get quite complex, and in Section 12.2.3 you will be given an indication of where some names come from. However, in this course you do not need to learn or even understand the names of the compounds. If you are worried by the names, just think of them as labels. Similarly, it is not necessary for you to remember particular structures; when a structure is needed you will always be given it.

Activity 12.1   Identifying patterns in structural formulas

We expect this activity will take you approximately 15 minutes.

In this activity, you will examine a number of linear-chain hydrocarbons and the ways in which they can be represented. The activity will help you begin to make sense of their names and structures, which are given in Table 12.2.

(a) Look at the first column of Table 12.2; what do all the names have in common?

(b) As you progress from the top to the bottom of the second column, how does the molecular formula change? In particular, what is the difference between adjacent pairs? Repeat this analysis for the structural formulas and abbreviated structural formulas in the third and fourth columns.

(c) What is the trend in the boiling temperature, and what is the explanation for this trend?

(d) Predict the molecular formula, structural formula, abbreviated structural formula and boiling temperature of the next member after octane.

Table 12.2 Names, formulas and boiling temperatures (b.t.) of the first eight linear-chain hydrocarbons.

Name	Molecular formula	Structural formula	Abbreviated structural formula	b.t./°C
methane	CH_4	H | H−C−H | H	CH_4	−164
ethane	C_2H_6	H H | | H−C−C−H | | H H	CH_3-CH_3	−89
propane	C_3H_8	H H H | | | H−C−C−C−H | | | H H H	$CH_3-CH_2-CH_3$	−42
butane	C_4H_{10}	H H H H | | | | H−C−C−C−C−H | | | | H H H H	$CH_3-CH_2-CH_2-CH_3$	0
pentane	C_5H_{12}	H H H H H | | | | | H−C−C−C−C−C−H | | | | | H H H H H	$CH_3-CH_2-CH_2-CH_2-CH_3$	36
hexane	C_6H_{14}	H H H H H H | | | | | | H−C−C−C−C−C−C−H | | | | | | H H H H H H	$CH_3-CH_2-CH_2-CH_2-CH_2-CH_3$	69
heptane	C_7H_{16}	H H H H H H H | | | | | | | H−C−C−C−C−C−C−C−H | | | | | | | H H H H H H H	$CH_3-CH_2-CH_2-CH_2-CH_2-CH_2-CH_3$	98
octane	C_8H_{18}	H H H H H H H H | | | | | | | | H−C−C−C−C−C−C−C−C−H | | | | | | | | H H H H H H H H	$CH_3-CH_2-CH_2-CH_2-CH_2-CH_2-CH_2-CH_3$	126

Now look at the comments on this activity at the end of this book.

12.2.2   Branched-chain hydrocarbons

Another type of hydrocarbon found in crude oil is the **branched-chain hydrocarbon**. Compounds in this category consist of molecules with a branched chain of carbon; i.e. you cannot represent the connected carbon atoms as a linear chain, because at some point or other there is a 'fork' in the chain. The simplest branched-chain hydrocarbons have a single carbon atom attached to one side of a linear chain, and some are listed in Table 12.3.

Note that the one carbon atom branch can be represented in various ways:

$$CH_3 \quad | \quad -CH_3 \quad H_3C- \quad CH_3-$$
$$| \quad CH_3$$

All these forms mean the same thing, and refer to a part of a molecule containing one carbon atom with three hydrogen atoms attached. CH_3- is known as a methyl group because it is like methane, but has one bond to another carbon instead of a fourth hydrogen.

As you progress through this section, you will sometimes see groups such as CH_3 or CH_2, which do not seem to be attached to other atoms. It is very important to remember that these are not separate molecules, but represent individual parts of a molecule. It is always assumed that in a molecule they are attached to other atoms. For example, in $CH_3-CH_2-CH_3$, you can identify one CH_2 and two CH_3 groups.

Table 12.3 Names, formulas and boiling temperatures (b.t.) of some branched-chain hydrocarbons in crude oil.

Name	Molecular formula	Structural formula	Abbreviated structural formula	b.t./°C
2-methylpropane	C_4H_{10}	$\begin{array}{c} H \; H \; H \\ | \; | \; | \\ H-C-C-C-H \\ | \; | \; | \\ H \; | \; H \\ H-C-H \\ | \\ H \end{array}$	$CH_3-CH-CH_3$ $\quad\quad |$ $\quad\quad CH_3$	−12
2-methylbutane	C_5H_{12}	$\begin{array}{c} H \; H \; H \; H \\ | \; | \; | \; | \\ H-C-C-C-C-H \\ | \; | \; | \; | \\ H \; | \; H \; H \\ H-C-H \\ | \\ H \end{array}$	$CH_3-CH-CH_2-CH_3$ $\quad\quad |$ $\quad\quad CH_3$	28
2-methylpentane	C_6H_{14}	$\begin{array}{c} H \; H \; H \; H \; H \\ | \; | \; | \; | \; | \\ H-C-C-C-C-C-H \\ | \; | \; | \; | \; | \\ H \; | \; H \; H \; H \\ H-C-H \\ | \\ H \end{array}$	$CH_3-CH-CH_2-CH_2-CH_3$ $\quad\quad |$ $\quad\quad CH_3$	60

You may notice from Table 12.3 that the molecular formula of 2-methylpropane, C_4H_{10}, is the same as that of butane (Figure 12.6). However, their boiling temperatures are different (butane boils at 0 °C). Different compounds that have the same molecular formula are called **isomers**. They are described as **isomeric**. The chemical individuality of the isomers results from the same atoms being joined together in different ways to give differently shaped molecules. In this case, butane involves a chain of four carbon atoms, whereas 2-methylpropane has a chain of three carbon atoms and a branch of one carbon atom – a methyl group.

The ability to form different structures from the same constituent parts can be simply demonstrated using a child's building blocks (Figure 12.7). In this case, the blocks have been labelled with C, CH, CH_2 and CH_3 groups to construct three-dimensional, abbreviated structural formulas of the isomers which have the molecular formula C_5H_{12} – the compounds illustrated in Figure 12.8.

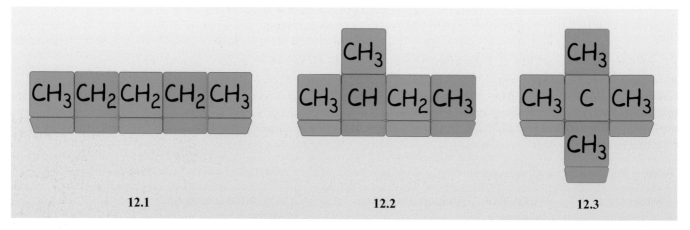

Figure 12.7   Using children's building blocks to make models of compounds. The blocks illustrate the abbreviated structural formulas of compounds **12.1**, **12.2** and **12.3**. (See Figure 12.8.)

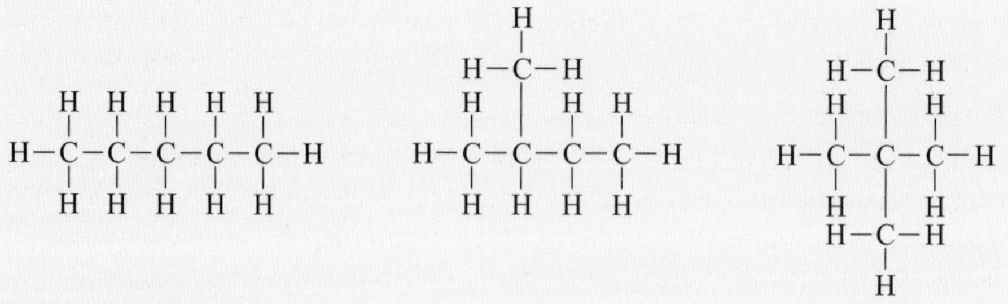

Figure 12.8 Structural formulas of compounds **12.1**, **12.2** and **12.3**.

Building blocks can be arranged in any way you like but, in order to arrange carbon and hydrogen atoms, it is important to remember that each carbon needs to have four bonds attached and each hydrogen one bond attached. Applying this simple rule means that there are three ways in which you can arrange five carbon atoms and 12 hydrogen atoms, as shown in structures **12.1**, **12.2** and **12.3**. These isomers all have the same molecular formula, C_5H_{12}, but different boiling temperatures: 36, 28 and 10 °C, respectively.

■ What are the molecular formulas of structures **12.4**, **12.5** and **12.6**?

12.4   **12.5**   **12.6**

☐ All three structures have five carbon atoms and 12 hydrogen atoms, so they all have the molecular formula C_5H_{12}.

At first sight, you may think that structures **12.4**, **12.5** and **12.6** represent different compounds. After all, the structural formulas certainly look very different. In fact, they are all the same linear-chain hydrocarbon. Remember that the structural formula says nothing about the shape of the molecule; it only shows the order in which the constituent atoms are bonded together. If you compare the structures, you will see that each has a chain of five carbon atoms with three hydrogen atoms attached to each of the carbon atoms at the ends, and two hydrogen atoms attached to each of the three carbon atoms in the middle. They have simply been drawn differently.

■ Structures **12.4**, **12.5** and **12.6** are different representations of one of structures **12.1**, **12.2** and **12.3**. Identify which one.

☐ Structure **12.1**. It has the molecular formula C_5H_{12} and has a chain of five carbon atoms with three hydrogen atoms attached to each of the carbon atoms at the ends and two hydrogen atoms attached to each of the three carbon atoms in the middle.

Structures **12.4**, **12.5** and **12.6** are folded representations of **12.1** and if you were to pull them out, as you would a folded piece of string, you would get the linear form, **12.1**.

Structures such as **12.4**, **12.5** and **12.6** look like different molecules at first, because, when you draw a structural formula on a page, you represent the molecule in two dimensions. However, atoms and molecules exist in a three-dimensional world. Two-dimensional representations of structural formulas do not show the shape, and so you need a three-dimensional representation. There are several types of such representation. Two of the most important are space-filling representations (Figure 12.9a) and ball-and-stick representations (Figure 12.9b). You met these in Section 3.3 and they are both used in the computer-based activities associated with this book.

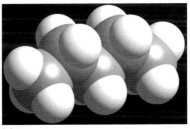
(a)

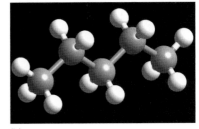
(b)

Figure 12.9   (a) Space-filling representation and (b) ball-and-stick representation of pentane, the linear-chain form of C_5H_{12}. Carbon atoms are shown in grey, hydrogen atoms in white.

12.2.3   The names of carbon compounds

You may have noticed that many of the compounds discussed so far have very similar names. The names all end in -ane, many have the word methyl in them, and some contain numbers. These are all examples of the modern system for naming organic compounds. In fact, there are two ways of naming compounds. The first is an older system that sometimes reflects the first source of the compound; for example, citric acid was originally obtained from citrus fruits. Under the older system, chemists who first discovered a new compound could choose a name. Sometimes the origin of a name can be quite obscure. There are debates as to why the German chemist Johann von Baeyer named the drug he synthesised in 1863, barbituric acid. Does the name derive from the German for beard, reflecting the shape of the molecule? Did it reflect von Baeyer's religious beliefs – and the fact that it was allegedly isolated on St Barbara's Day? Or was it that he was particularly fond of a young woman called Barbara? We may never know.

Given the millions of carbon compounds known today, a more organised way of naming compounds is needed. Modern systematic nomenclature is based on a universally agreed system. Any experienced chemist reading the systematic name should be able to work out its structural formula. For example, the compounds in Table 12.3 are all called 2-methyl something. This means that the second carbon of the main hydrocarbon chain (in this case propane, butane or pentane) has a methyl group attached to it. However, the names can get very complex. For example, citric acid, a relatively simple compound, has the systematic name 2-hydroxy-1,2,3-propanetricarboxylic acid! One method is neat, but doesn't tell you much about its structure, whereas the other is precise but very unwieldy. Either way you are not expected to learn the names. In general, systematic naming will be used here, except when the older name is in general use, in which case the systematic name will be given in brackets.

Please remember that you are not expected to learn the names of any organic compounds, or to know in detail how the systematic names are derived.

Activity 12.2   The shapes of molecules

We expect this activity will take you approximately 60 minutes.

In this activity you will study the first section of the *Organic Molecules* computer-based package, which is called *Shapes of Molecules*. The activity allows you to practise drawing structural formulas in two dimensions. It also allows you to visualise some of the molecules discussed here in three dimensions, and learn about the way the atoms can move in relation to one another within a molecule.

There are no comments on this activity.

12.2.4   What else is in crude oil?

In science, one of the ways of making sense of many different things is to classify them – organise them into groups that have similar features.

■ Where else in the course has classification been important?

□ Some examples are:

- bodies in the Solar System (other than the Sun) are classified as planets, satellites, asteroids and comets (Book 2, Chapter 11)

- the classification of materials as electrical conductors, insulators and semiconductors (Book 3, Section 7.2)
- elements in the Periodic Table are arranged into various groups which show similar properties (Section 5.3).

You might have thought of other examples.

Figure 12.10 shows one way of classifying most of the thousands of compounds in crude oil.

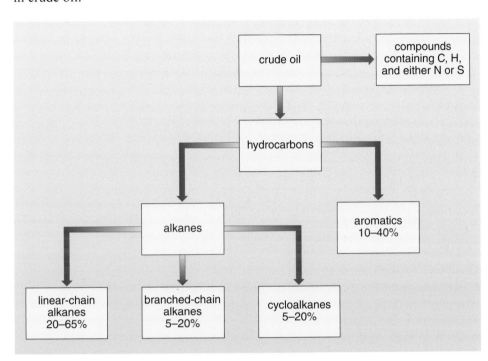

Figure 12.10   A classification of the compounds in crude oil. Oil from different sources has different compositions, so the percentages are shown here as ranges.

The compounds in crude oil are almost all hydrocarbons. In crude oil, these can be divided into two groups: **alkanes** and **aromatics**. (There are various other types of hydrocarbons that are not found in crude oil.)

Alkanes contain only carbon–carbon single bonds and carbon–hydrogen bonds. Alkanes form a class of compounds. In this context, a class of compounds contains compounds with similar chemical structures and similar elemental compositions. So far, you have learned that crude oil contains the subclasses of linear-chain hydrocarbons and branched-chain hydrocarbons, or more precisely linear-chain alkanes and branched-chain alkanes. Another subclass of alkanes in crude oil is the cycloalkanes. As the name implies, cycloalkanes are alkanes whose structures involve carbon atoms joined in a ring (cycle) by single bonds, for example cyclohexane (**12.7**) and cyclopentane (**12.8**), so each carbon is bonded to two other carbons and to two hydrogen atoms.

12.7	12.8	

Question 12.3

Classify the structures **12.9**, **12.10**, **12.11** and **12.12** as a linear-chain alkane, a branched-chain alkane, a cycloalkane or a compound that is not an alkane.

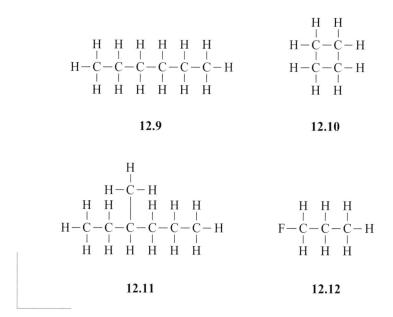

12.9

12.10

12.11

12.12

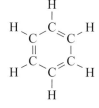

12.13

The other class of hydrocarbons present in crude oil is the aromatics. These are compounds that have a characteristic group in which six carbon atoms are joined in a ring. It is difficult to represent accurately the bonding in this ring, but it is usually drawn as a ring of six carbon atoms with alternating double and single bonds. You may recall that when two atoms are joined by two covalent bonds (i.e. there are two shared pairs of electrons) the result is called a double bond (Section 5.5). The simplest aromatic compound is benzene (**12.13**).

■ Are the valencies of all the atoms satisfied in benzene?

☐ Yes, each of the hydrogen atoms is attached by one bond and each of the carbon atoms has four bonds – two single bonds and one double bond.

■ Why isn't benzene an alkane?

☐ Alkanes are compounds that contain only carbon and hydrogen, with the carbons joined by single bonds. In benzene, some of the carbons are joined by double bonds.

As Figure 12.10 shows, crude oils also contain small amounts of compounds that are not hydrocarbons, because they contain sulfur and/or nitrogen as well as carbon and hydrogen. They too can be divided into subclasses, some of which you will meet later.

Question 12.4

Identify the classes, and subclasses where appropriate, of the compounds **12.14**, **12.15**, **12.16** and **12.17**.

12.14

12.15

12.16

12.17

Question 12.5

Which one of the alkanes **12.18, 12.19** or **12.20** does not have a correct structural formula in which all the valencies are satisfied?

12.18   **12.19**   **12.20**

Question 12.6

Without looking back, draw out the structural formulas and the abbreviated structural formulas for:

(a) the linear-chain alkane C_8H_{18}

(b) the cycloalkane C_4H_8, which contains a ring of four carbon atoms

(c) the branched-chain alkane C_4H_{10}

(d) the cycloalkane C_5H_{10}, which contains a ring of four carbon atoms.

12.3   Crude oil as a source of fuel

In this section, you will re-examine how crude oil is used as a source of fuel. To illustrate this, the focus will be on petrol (or, as it is known in the USA, gasoline), the most familiar of the fuel fractions. The gasoline fraction from the distillation of crude oil consists mainly of linear-chain alkanes containing between six and ten carbon atoms. The combustion of octane, C_8H_{18}, is typical of the combustion reaction of petrol:

$$2C_8H_{18}(g) + 25O_2(g) = 16CO_2(g) + 18H_2O(g) \qquad (12.1)$$

■ At 20 °C octane has a density of 0.702 kg dm^{-3}; that is to say, 1 dm^3 has a mass of 0.702 kg. Using data from Table 9.4, calculate how much energy is released when 1.00 dm^3 of octane is burned.

□ From Table 9.4, the energy released from a kilogram of octane is 4.50×10^4 kJ. Because one dm^3 of octane has a mass of about 0.702 kg, the energy released when 1.00 dm^3 is burned is:

4.50×10^4 kJ kg$^{-1} \times 0.702$ kg $= 3.16 \times 10^4$ kJ

The gasoline fraction from crude oil is rather poor as a fuel for the modern internal combustion engine. It tends to burn in an uneven way, with occasional small explosions interrupting the smooth running of the engine. This causes a 'knocking' sound. Different subclasses of alkanes vary in the amount of knocking they cause: linear-chain alkanes cause more knocking than the other subclasses.

The extent of the knocking caused by a fuel is expressed as its **octane number**. The values are equivalent to the percentage (by volume) of iso-octane (2,2,4-trimethylpentane) (**12.21**) in a mixture of iso-octane and heptane (**12.22**) that has the same extent of knocking as the fuel. So, for example, because cyclohexane causes the same amount of knocking as a mixture of 83% iso-octane and 17% heptane, its octane number is 83. Pure iso-octane has an octane number of 100; the percentage of iso-octane is 100%. Some sample values are listed in Table 12.4. Note that some substances have an octane number of greater than 100, which means that they burn more efficiently than pure iso-octane.

12.21 iso-octane   **12.22** heptane

Table 12.4 Some typical octane numbers.

Compound	Octane number	Subclass
heptane	0	linear-chain alkane
hexane	25	linear-chain alkane
2-methylhexane	42	branched-chain alkane
cyclohexane	83	cycloalkane
2,2-dimethylpentane	93	branched-chain alkane
iso-octane	100	branched-chain alkane
benzene	106	aromatic
toluene	121	aromatic

The different grades of the petrol put into cars have slightly different compositions, and thus different octane numbers. The latter are shown on the pumps at filling stations – 95 for 'premium' grades and 97 or more for 'super' grades. The higher the octane number, the better the fuel performs.

In the past, one way of improving the octane number was to add tetraethyl-lead, which acts as an anti-knock agent. Adding 0.61 g of tetraethyl-lead to 1 dm^3 of a fuel can improve the octane number by between 5 and 10. Concern about the hazard to health from lead in the atmosphere has meant that the use of 'leaded' petrol has been phased out in most countries. However, unleaded fuels cause other problems: in order to achieve an acceptable octane number, high proportions of aromatic compounds are often added to a fuel, and many of these are relatively toxic.

Compounds that are suitable for motor fuel make up only 20% by mass of crude oil. The fractions containing bigger molecules, such as the lubricating oils, are too viscous, and have too high a boiling temperature, so they do not burn efficiently in an internal combustion engine. However, the compounds in the other fractions can be converted into compounds that are more suitable for motor fuel. In most refineries, the crude oil is first distilled to give a range of fractions, and then each fraction undergoes a different treatment. For example, if the high-boiling fractions are heated in the presence of a catalyst, the larger molecules 'crack' into smaller hydrocarbons.

■ Suppose the molecule $C_{16}H_{34}$ is cracked into two smaller molecules, C_8H_{18}:

$$C_{16}H_{34}(g) + ? = 2C_8H_{18}(g) \tag{12.2}$$

What is needed to balance the equation?

□ Both sides have 16 carbon atoms but, whereas the right-hand side has 36 hydrogen atoms (2×18), the left-hand side has only 34. Thus, hydrogen, H_2, is needed on the left-hand side to balance the equation:

$$C_{16}H_{34}(g) + H_2(g) = 2C_8H_{18}(g) \tag{12.3}$$

When any hydrocarbon is broken down into smaller fragments, hydrogen needs to be supplied if linear-chain or branched-chain alkanes are to be obtained. This process is called **hydrocracking**, in which the atoms are rearranged to give a mixture of mainly branched-chain alkanes. (The 'hydro' in hydrocracking simply refers to the presence of hydrogen gas during the process.) This produces a more suitable motor fuel, not only because the molecules are shorter, but also because, as Table 12.4 shows, branched hydrocarbons tend to have higher octane numbers than linear ones.

Modern hydrocracking processes use catalysts, known as zeolites, which contain aluminium, silicon and oxygen, at temperatures around 500 °C.

■ Why is a catalyst used?

☐ A catalyst is used to speed up a reaction. It provides the reaction with an alternative reaction pathway involving a lower energy barrier. It does not alter the position of the equilibrium. In the absence of a catalyst, higher temperatures and pressures would be necessary (Section 10.4).

Even with a catalyst, pressures of up to 200 atmospheres are still necessary to obtain acceptable yields. The high temperatures and pressures reflect the fact that the process involves breaking strong covalent bonds. The high pressures mean that the reaction vessels need to be very strong – their walls are often 15–20 cm thick and their design and construction pose many difficult engineering problems. Hydrocracking is a continuous process, in that reactants go in one end, react together, and the products are then separated and isolated at the other end.

Another process that is important in the production of petrol is **catalytic reforming**. This involves converting linear-chain alkanes into aromatic compounds, cycloalkanes and branched-chain alkanes.

■ What is the advantage, for the production of petrol, of forming such compounds?

☐ Table 12.4 shows that aromatic compounds, cycloalkanes and branched-chain alkanes have higher octane numbers than linear-chain alkanes.

A typical process is the conversion of heptane into toluene (methylbenzene):

$$\begin{array}{c} \underset{|}{\overset{|}{H}} \\ H-C-C-C-C-C-C-C-H \end{array} \longrightarrow \text{(toluene structure)} + 4H_2 \qquad (12.4)$$

Note that one of the products is hydrogen, which can be collected and used in hydrocracking. Again a catalyst is used to speed up the process.

Processes such as hydrocracking and catalytic reforming are used to treat the various fractions obtained by distillation of crude oil so that, when the products are mixed together, a high performance petrol with a high octane number is produced, which meets the demands of the modern car.

You may have noticed that Equation 12.4 has an arrow rather than an equals sign, and that the state symbols (s), (g), (l) and (aq) have been omitted. When the full details of a reaction are not included, or when the equation is unbalanced, it is appropriate to use an arrow rather than an equals sign. Carbon chemists tend to concentrate on the changes taking place to the carbon framework – other details are often seen as less relevant. For that reason, arrows are used in most equations in carbon chemistry.

Question 12.7

Another process used in refineries is known as **isomerisation**. It converts pentane and hexane, which are linear-chain alkanes, into compounds with higher octane numbers. Write out one typical reaction for hexane (structure **12.23**) – the name of the process gives you the clue.

12.23

12.4   Summary of Section 12

Crude oil is a mixture of hydrocarbons, consisting mainly of alkanes and aromatic compounds, together with small amounts of compounds containing sulfur and nitrogen. The alkanes can be classified as linear-chain, branched-chain and cycloalkanes.

Crude oil contains so many different hydrocarbons that individual compounds cannot be easily isolated. However, it can be separated into different fractions on the basis of their boiling temperatures. Each fraction has different uses.

Carbon readily forms bonds to other carbon atoms, and large numbers of compounds can be formed containing chains or rings of carbon atoms. Such molecules can be represented using structural formulas and abbreviated structural formulas.

Different compounds that have the same molecular formula are known as isomers.

The atoms within organic molecules are arranged in very specific three-dimensional shapes. Within the molecules, atoms can often move relative to one another without breaking covalent bonds.

The octane number of a fuel reflects how much knocking it causes. The higher the octane number, the better the fuel performs. Mixtures containing high proportions of branched-chain alkanes and aromatics tend to have higher octane numbers.

The gasoline fraction of crude oil is supplemented by the manufacture of branched-chain alkanes from larger molecules using the process of hydrocracking. A related process – catalytic reforming – involves the formation of aromatic compounds that can also be used to increase the octane number.

In this chapter you have begun to develop the skill of drawing and recognising structural formulas.

Chapter 13
Further uses for crude oil

Chapter 12 described crude oil and some of its uses as a fuel, but is this the only reason why crude oil is so important – to burn? Figure 13.1 shows that if you measure the volumes of the different fractions derived from a barrel of crude oil, the bulk of them are indeed used as fuels of one sort or another. However, this might give a distorted impression of the part that derivatives of crude oil play in the modern world.

In general, 2 to 7% of crude oil is converted into **petrochemicals** – materials that end up as plastics, pesticides, drugs, adhesives, paints, solvents, and so on.

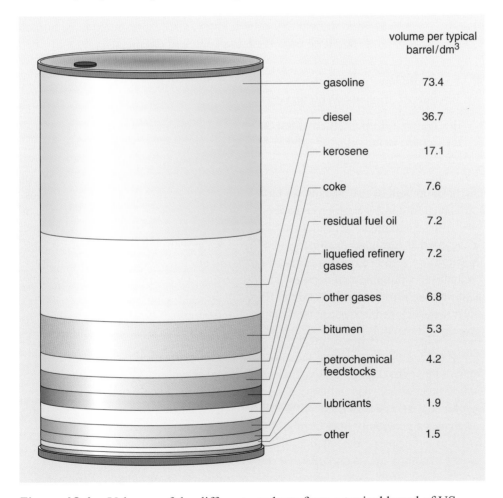

	volume per typical barrel/dm^3
gasoline	73.4
diesel	36.7
kerosene	17.1
coke	7.6
residual fuel oil	7.2
liquefied refinery gases	7.2
other gases	6.8
bitumen	5.3
petrochemical feedstocks	4.2
lubricants	1.9
other	1.5

Figure 13.1   Volumes of the different products from a typical barrel of US crude oil. Volumes of crude oil are traditionally measured in barrels (each barrel contains roughly 159 dm^3). Many of these products and their uses are listed in Table 12.1. Coke is a solid residue left after the cracking process, with properties similar to charcoal, or is derived from coal. Residual fuel oil comprises heavy oils used as fuels in industry, marine transportation and for electric power generation. Liquefied refinery gases are propane and butane, used as fuels. Figures are based on average yields for US refineries in 2000.

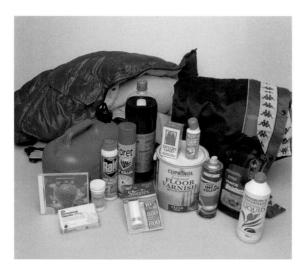

Figure 13.2 A selection of objects derived from petrochemicals.

Despite this apparently small proportion, these materials play an extremely important role in modern life. It would be difficult to imagine a world without them – think of clothing made from artificial fibre; food packaging, food flavourings and preservatives; computers and other electrical devices; coloured inks and dyes; lipstick, toothpaste and painkillers (Figure 13.2). They are all made wholly or in part from petrochemicals.

There is always controversy about the use of coal and crude oil derivatives as fuels rather than for what the petrochemical industry refers to as their 'more noble use' as raw materials (feedstocks) for the manufacturing and petrochemical industries. This is by no means a recent concern; as early as 1872, Mendeléev (the Russian chemist who devised the Periodic Table, which you saw in Figure 5.3) is said to have reported to his government that oil was too valuable a resource to be burned and should be preserved as a source of chemicals.

■ You might have noticed that in Figure 13.1 the 159 dm^3 of crude oil produced 169 dm^3 of products. Why do you think this 'processing gain' arises?

☐ In Chapter 12, you looked at the cracking of heavy oil fractions to produce the lighter, more valuable grades. These are less dense and will therefore have a greater volume.

The development of petrochemicals has revolutionised our lives. All these changes, and many more, have been brought about through the discovery and exploitation of the chemical and physical properties of carbon compounds. Carbon chemistry can be regarded as 'designer chemistry' in a literal sense. Petrochemicals have not just appeared as a result of the discovery of crude oil, but have required the ingenuity of chemists to build new molecules. The properties of a compound are related to its molecular structure, and, as you will see, by designing particular features into molecules, their properties can be dictated. For example, it is possible to make a drug that acts on only one part of the body, or a plastic that is as strong as steel.

However, as well as improving the quality of life for many millions of people, some of these developments have had adverse consequences. Some medicines, such as thalidomide, had unforeseen side effects (this drug is discussed briefly in Section 16.2.3). The use of chlorofluorcarbons (CFCs) as refrigerants and propellants has created a potentially long-term problem by damaging the ozone layer around the Earth. Some pesticides, such as dichlorodiphenyltrichloroethane (DDT), while helping to control the mosquitoes that carry malaria, have also had a detrimental impact on wildlife. Nevertheless, for better or for worse, in most parts of the world our lives rely heavily on the chemistry of industrially produced carbon compounds.

Naturally occurring carbon compounds are also very important because the existence of life is based on carbon chemistry. As you will see in Book 5, all living things on this planet rely on the reactions and products of an incredible variety of complex carbon compounds. It was because carbon compounds were produced from living organisms that this branch of chemistry became known as **organic chemistry**, a name it retains today, even though many of the new compounds have nothing to do with living organisms. The branch of chemistry associated with compounds that do not contain carbon is known as **inorganic chemistry**. Even though organic chemistry is based on only a few elements of the Periodic Table, over 90% of all known chemical compounds are organic compounds! This is due to the unique ability of carbon to form bonds with other carbon atoms to give chains and rings of almost any length and shape.

Earlier, building molecules was compared to making structures with a child's building blocks (Figure 12.7). When building a model using a child's building blocks, the basic pieces can be joined together to form a variety of structures. In the same way, organic molecules are constructed using building blocks made up of one or more atoms that can be joined together using chemical reactions. You will now investigate how crude oil supplies the building blocks to create products such as drugs, detergents, plastics, paints and vitamins. You will also examine the relatively small number of reactions that allow these building blocks to be joined together.

13.1 Important chemical feedstocks

Crude oil is mainly made up of alkanes but, unfortunately, such compounds are not particularly adaptable starting materials for the chemical industry. This is because, apart from combustion, alkanes react only under extreme conditions. When they do react, they tend to generate mixtures of products which are difficult to separate. Instead, the compounds in crude oil need to be converted into more reactive compounds.

You should recall (from Section 12.3) that when alkanes are heated strongly with hydrogen gas, smaller, more useful compounds are produced. This process is called hydrocracking. When the same process is carried out without hydrogen gas, it is called simply **cracking**. A typical transformation for cracking is:

$$CH_3-CH_2-CH_2-CH_2-CH_2-CH_2-CH_2-CH_2-CH_3$$

$$\downarrow \qquad\qquad (13.1)$$

$$H_2 \;+\; CH_2{=}CH_2 \;+\; CH_3-CH{=}CH_2 \;+\; CH_3-CH_2-CH{=}CH_2$$

Most of the compounds produced by cracking contain the unit C=C, because without added hydrogen gas there are not enough hydrogen atoms available to satisfy carbon's need to form four covalent bonds. The two carbon atoms in the unit are linked by a double bond. The simplest compound containing this unit has the abbreviated structural formula $CH_2{=}CH_2$, and is called ethene (structure **13.1**).

13.1

■ How many electrons are shared by the two carbon atoms?

□ There are two covalent bonds between the carbon atoms, each containing a shared pair of electrons. Thus there are four shared electrons overall. You met double bonds in Section 5.5.

Recall that alkanes do not contain double bonds; each carbon atom is attached to four other atoms by single covalent bonds. Organic compounds containing only single bonds are called **saturated compounds**. Compounds that contain one or more C=C double bonds are called **unsaturated compounds**. You may have met the term 'polyunsaturates' or 'polyunsaturated' in connection with the oils and fats found in food; this merely means that the molecules that make up the oil or fat contain more than one C=C double bond. You will return to the chemistry of food molecules in Chapter 15.

The hydrocarbons that contain one or more C=C units are also classified as **alkenes** and some examples are given in Table 13.1. Note the subtle and easily missed difference of one letter between alk<u>a</u>nes, saturated hydrocarbons, and alk<u>e</u>nes, unsaturated hydrocarbons.

Table 13.1 Some typical alkenes.

Name	Molecular structure
ethene	CH_2=CH_2
propene	CH_3–CH=CH_2
but-1-ene	CH_3–CH_2–CH=CH_2
but-2-ene	CH_3–CH=CH–CH_3
buta-1,3-diene	CH_2=CH–CH=CH_2
2-methylpropene	CH_2=$C \begin{smallmatrix} CH_3 \\ \\ CH_3 \end{smallmatrix}$

The simple alkenes are generally made by cracking under the influence of a catalyst – **catalytic cracking**. One of the higher-boiling fractions of crude oil is heated to about 350 °C and then passed over a zeolite catalyst. By adjusting temperature, pressure and contact time with the catalyst, the nature of the reaction products can be controlled quite precisely. Although the starting mixture contains thousands of different compounds, the molecules 'crack' to give a mixture of the same five or six alkenes. The products from a typical catalytic cracker are the alkenes in Table 13.1.

Activity 13.1   Summarising chemical processes

We expect this activity will take you approximately 20 minutes.

This activity develops your skill at summarising chemical processes.
In Chapters 12 and 13 you have met four types of industrial reaction:

(i)   hydrocracking

(ii) catalytic cracking

(iii) catalytic reforming

(iv) isomerisation (introduced in Question 12.7).

Summarise the key points of each of the four processes and identify similarities and differences between them. Use equations where possible.

Now look at the comments on this activity at the end of this book.

13.2   Reactions of alkenes

Each of the alkenes formed by catalytic cracking finds extensive use as a raw material in laboratory and industrial chemistry. They are good building blocks because they are small molecules and are reactive. The alkene double bond provides an excellent site for chemical transformation, because the carbon–carbon double bond reacts readily and in a controllable fashion. For reasons not explored here, one of the two covalent bonds in the C=C unit is much weaker, and the reactions of alkenes all tend to involve breaking this weaker bond.

In particular, alkenes can undergo what are known as **addition reactions**, as shown below:

$$X-Y \ + \ CH_2{=}CH_2 \ \longrightarrow \ X-CH_2-CH_2-Y \tag{13.2}$$

It is important to note that a number of covalent bonds have been broken in this reaction, and several more have been formed. The covalent bond joining the hypothetical atoms or groups X and Y has been broken, as has one of the bonds in the double bond between the carbons. In producing the product, new covalent bonds have been formed attaching X and Y to carbon atoms.

Overall, the hypothetical molecule X—Y, where both X and Y are atoms or groups of atoms, is incorporated in (added to) the alkene. X and Y are said to have been *added across* the double bond. Hence the reaction is described as an addition reaction. Addition reactions are one of the five key types of reaction that are described in this book, and listed in Table 14.3 at the end of Chapter 14.

Typical addition reactions of ethene are:

$$H_2 \ + \ CH_2{=}CH_2 \ \longrightarrow \ H-CH_2-CH_2-H \tag{13.3}$$

This product can also be written as $CH_3{-}CH_3$.

$$Br_2 \ + \ CH_2{=}CH_2 \ \longrightarrow \ Br-CH_2-CH_2-Br \tag{13.4}$$

This product can also be written as $BrCH_2{-}CH_2Br$.

$$H_2O \ + \ CH_2{=}CH_2 \ \longrightarrow \ H-CH_2-CH_2-OH \tag{13.5}$$

This product can also be written as $CH_3{-}CH_2{-}OH$.

All these cases involve the addition of extra atoms or groups to the reactant to form new single bonds.

■ Identify X and Y in Equations 13.3 to 13.5.

☐ In Equation 13.3, hydrogen is added across the double bond. Hydrogen can be written as H—H, so both X and Y are H. In Equation 13.4, bromine is added across the double bond. Bromine can be written as Br—Br, so both X and Y are Br. In Equation 13.5, water, H_2O, is added across the double bond. Water can be written as H—OH, so X is H and Y is OH.

Other alkenes in Table 13.1 react with bromine in a similar fashion:

$$CH_3-CH{=}CH_2 \ + \ Br_2 \ \longrightarrow \ CH_3-\overset{\displaystyle Br}{\underset{\displaystyle |}{C}}H-\overset{\displaystyle Br}{\underset{\displaystyle |}{C}}H_2 \tag{13.6}$$

This product can also be written as $CH_3—CHBr—CH_2Br$.

$$CH_3—CH=CH—CH_3 \ + \ Br_2 \ \longrightarrow \ CH_3—\overset{\overset{\displaystyle Br}{|}}{CH}—\overset{\overset{\displaystyle Br}{|}}{CH}—CH_3 \qquad (13.7)$$

This product can also be written as $CH_3—CHBr—CHBr—CH_3$.

So, by converting crude oil into a mixture of just a few alkenes, a suitable feedstock is produced that readily undergoes conversion into other compounds. As you will see, these compounds can themselves undergo further transformations, leading to a wide range of petrochemical products.

■   Draw the reaction between but-1-ene, $CH_3—CH_2—CH=CH_2$, and hydrogen, H_2.

☐ $$CH_3—CH_2—CH=CH_2 \ + \ H_2 \ \longrightarrow \ CH_3—CH_2—\overset{\overset{\displaystyle H}{|}}{CH}—\overset{\overset{\displaystyle H}{|}}{CH_2} \qquad (13.8)$$

In answering this question you have used a strategy that is probably the most important in organic chemistry – the **functional group** approach. You have reasoned that the saturated, alkane part of the molecule, $CH_3—CH_2$, is unreactive, and hydrogen reacts only with the double bond in a reaction similar to Equation 13.3. This reasoning follows the pattern of reactivity demonstrated in the addition of bromine to different alkenes (Equations 13.4, 13.6 and 13.7). In these cases the functional group – the reactive part of the organic molecule is the double bond. The remainder of the molecule does not take part in the reaction. The strategy of identifying the reactive part of the molecule and ignoring the rest is the functional group approach – the topic of Chapter 14.

Question 13.1

Complete the following addition reactions.

(a) $CH_3—CH=CH_2 \quad + \quad H_2 \quad \longrightarrow \quad ?$

(b) $CH_3—CH_2—CH=CH_2 \quad + \quad H_2 \quad \longrightarrow \quad ?$

(c) $CH_3—CH=CH—CH_3 \quad + \quad H_2O \quad \longrightarrow \quad ?$

13.3   Polymers

An important group of products derived from crude oil is plastics. The word 'plastics' is a rather colloquial term. A better term, which includes all the materials called plastics, and many others, is **polymers**. As you will see shortly, a polymer is made up of molecules comprising very long chains of atoms.

To say that polymers are important in our modern world is a gross understatement. All life depends, and indeed always has depended, on polymers of one sort or another. Our bodies contain many polymers, such as proteins, polysaccharides, DNA and RNA, which you will meet in Book 5. Many of the natural materials that we use are polymers, such as wood, rubber, cotton, wool, linen and silk. These materials were used for many centuries without any knowledge of their molecular structures. However, as our understanding of their structures has developed, we have been able to construct our own polymers.

You have seen in Chapter 1 that many modern materials are synthetic polymers, and it could be argued that their production has revolutionised our society. Synthetic polymers are used in clothing (such as nylon or Goretex™), packaging, insulation, non-stick pans and paints, to name but a few random items. Polymers are relatively cheap and can be manufactured to a wide variety of very different specifications. It is possible to produce a very hard, rigid polymer to form aeroplane wings, and a soft, pliable polymer for use in rubber gloves. It is possible to produce polymers that are stable at high temperatures, polymers that conduct electricity, polymers that are stronger than steel and polymers that are strong adhesives. In fact, a polymer can now be manufactured to fit almost any specification. Unfortunately, one property of many synthetic polymers is that they can take many decades to break down in the environment, and plastic packaging currently forms a huge part of the landfill waste generated in western countries (Figure 13.3).

In the first part of this book, you explored some of the properties of the materials that have been important in previous historical periods – the Bronze Age and the Iron Age. If our age were to be named after the dominant materials, it might justifiably be called the 'Polymer Age'.

Figure 13.3 Polymers can take many decades to break down, and form a substantial part of the waste generated by modern society. This photograph shows a variety of polymer-based materials in a landfill site.

13.3.1   What is a polymer?

A polymer is made up of molecules comprising very long chains of atoms. For example, polythene is a saturated hydrocarbon and its molecules are linear chains of many carbon atoms, with hydrogen atoms attached; often there are thousands of carbon atoms (Figure 13.4). One way of representing such large structures is by the formula $CH_3-(CH_2)_n-CH_3$, where n stands for a very large number, about 11 000–21 000. This section will concentrate on polymers where the extended chain is made exclusively of carbon atoms, but you should be aware that other types of atoms like oxygen and nitrogen can also form part of the chain (in nylon for example).

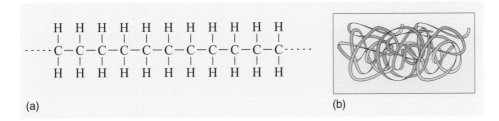

(a)   (b)

Figure 13.4   (a) A single strand of polythene showing the carbon atoms linked by covalent bonds. This figure shows a tiny proportion of the many thousands of carbon atoms in each chain. (b) Multiple strands of a polymer intertwined.

Even though the polymer molecule is a chain of atoms, it does not usually exist in a linear form. As you saw in Activity 12.2, rotation about single bonds is easy, so the molecule readily coils up, as shown in Figure 13.4b. Now imagine what the polymer must be like with millions and millions of these molecules all physically entangled to produce something like a mass of cooked spaghetti.

Some of the most important polymers are manufactured directly from the alkenes produced by the cracking process described in Section 13.1. You may recall that compounds with double bonds, such as ethene, can take part in addition reactions to form two new single bonds to other atoms or groups of atoms.

In 1933, scientists at Imperial Chemical Industries (ICI) in London found that when ethene was heated under high pressure a hard waxy solid was formed, which appeared to contain only carbon and hydrogen atoms in the ratio 1 : 2. They concluded that instead of adding to a *different* type of molecule, the ethene molecules had linked *to one another*:

$$CH_2{=}CH_2 \; + \; CH_2{=}CH_2 \; + \; CH_2{=}CH_2 \; + \; CH_2{=}CH_2 \; + \; CH_2{=}CH_2$$

$$\downarrow \hspace{6cm} (13.9)$$

$$\cdots\cdots CH_2{-}CH_2{-}CH_2{-}CH_2{-}CH_2{-}CH_2{-}CH_2{-}CH_2{-}CH_2{-}CH_2 \cdots\cdots$$

In this process, one of the bonds in the carbon–carbon double bond of each of the ethene molecules (shown in red above) is broken, and each carbon forms a new bond (also shown in red) to another ethene molecule. This polymer of ethene is *polyethene*, commonly known as polythene.

The details of this process are specific to the preparation of polymers from alkenes, but all polymers are formed by linking together many hundreds or thousands of simple molecules, referred to as **monomers**. The process is known as **polymerisation**.

A large number of different polymers are produced by polymerisation using alkenes of the type $CH_2{=}CH{-}X$, where X can be one of a range of atoms or groups, as shown in Table 13.2.

Table 13.2 Some polymers derived from alkenes.

Alkene name*	Abbreviated structural formula of alkene monomer	Polymer name	Uses
vinyl chloride (chloroethene)	$CH_2{=}CH{-}Cl$	poly(vinyl chloride) or PVC	pipes and tubing, floor coverings, wire insulation, window frames, bottles
propylene (propene)	$CH_2{=}CH{-}CH_3$	polypropylene	rope, carpet fibre, car parts, packaging
styrene (phenylethene)	$CH_2{=}CH$ ⬡	polystyrene	packaging, insulation, bottles, toys

*The common name in the polymer industry is given first, with the systematic name in brackets.

The general equation for this type of polymerisation is:

$$CH_2{=}CH{-}X \quad + \quad CH_2{=}CH{-}X \quad + \quad CH_2{=}CH{-}X \quad + \quad CH_2{=}CH{-}X$$

$$\downarrow \qquad\qquad\qquad\qquad (13.10)$$

$$\cdots\cdots CH_2{-}\overset{\displaystyle X}{\underset{|}{C}}H{-}CH_2{-}\overset{\displaystyle X}{\underset{|}{C}}H{-}CH_2{-}\overset{\displaystyle X}{\underset{|}{C}}H{-}CH_2{-}\overset{\displaystyle X}{\underset{|}{C}}H\cdots\cdots$$

By choosing an alkene with a particular group X, the properties of the polymer that is formed can be closely defined.

The explosion in the use of polymers has depended on a ready supply of monomers.

■ Where do monomers such as ethene and propene come from?

☐ These compounds are products of the oil industry. They are obtained by cracking fractions of crude oil.

Question 13.2

Identify the alkenes (monomers) that were used to form each of the following polymers.

(a) $\cdots\cdots CH_2{-}\overset{\displaystyle Cl}{\underset{|}{C}}H{-}CH_2{-}\overset{\displaystyle Cl}{\underset{|}{C}}H{-}CH_2{-}\overset{\displaystyle Cl}{\underset{|}{C}}H{-}CH_2{-}\overset{\displaystyle Cl}{\underset{|}{C}}H\cdots\cdots$

(b) $\cdots\cdots CH_2{-}\overset{\displaystyle CH_3}{\underset{|}{C}}H{-}CH_2{-}\overset{\displaystyle CH_3}{\underset{|}{C}}H{-}CH_2{-}\overset{\displaystyle CH_3}{\underset{|}{C}}H{-}CH_2{-}\overset{\displaystyle CH_3}{\underset{|}{C}}H\cdots\cdots$

Question 13.3

One important monomer is tetrafluoroethene, $CF_2{=}CF_2$, which gives the polymer known variously as PTFE (polytetrafluoroethene), or Teflon, which is used to coat non-stick cooking pans. Draw the polymer chain.

13.4 Summary of Chapter 13

The complex mixture of alkanes in crude oil can be converted into five or six alkenes (compounds that contain carbon–carbon double bonds) by catalytic cracking.

The alkenes obtained from crude oil are small molecules that are reactive and undergo addition reactions, enabling them to be converted into other useful compounds.

One important class of materials derived from alkenes is the synthetic polymers.

Polymers are long-chain molecules made from smaller molecules known as monomers. The process is called polymerisation.

Chapter 14
Functional groups and their reactions

14.1 The functional group approach

This discussion of functional groups will start with a computer-based overview. The remainder of this chapter reinforces and elaborates on the material in Activity 14.1, so unless you are already very familiar with organic chemistry, it is important that you complete the activity before reading this chapter.

Activity 14.1 An introduction to functional groups

We expect this activity will take you approximately 45 minutes.

In this activity, you will study the second section of the *Organic Molecules* computer-based package, which is called *Introduction to functional groups*. This will introduce you to a number of different functional groups, and give you practice in identifying them and the reactions that they undergo.

There are no further comments on this activity.

Activity 14.1 demonstrates that the functional group approach helps in making sense of the mass of data available on the 13 million or so known organic compounds. It enables us to examine the structure of a molecule and to predict and understand its chemical reactivity and its physical properties. Essentially, the assumption is made that only certain parts of a molecule contribute to its reactivity. This is an oversimplification because reactivity is determined by the structure of the whole molecule but, as a first approximation it works surprisingly well. Organic molecules can be regarded as having two distinct parts: the functional group or groups, and the rest of the molecule. The reason for this is that when organic compounds react, *only the functional group undergoes chemical change*. The functional groups are relatively easy to spot because they usually involve atoms other than carbon and hydrogen, such as oxygen and nitrogen; alkenes are one of the few exceptions. Remember, the molecules are not physically broken up into functional groups and the rest of the molecule; this is simply an imaginary distinction that helps us to make sense of their reactivity.

Functional groups are also used as a means of classifying organic compounds. All the compounds in Table 13.1 are alkenes because they all contain a carbon–carbon double-bond functional group, which can undergo addition reactions. From now on, functional groups will usually be highlighted with a tinted background. Thus the first two of the alkenes in Table 13.1 can be represented as structures **14.1** and **14.2**.

The classes of organic compounds and their characteristic functional groups that you will meet most frequently in this course are listed at the end of this chapter, in Table 14.3.

When drawing structural formulas of organic compounds, it is essential to ensure that the number of bonds to each type of atom reflects the *valencies* of the atoms. You might recall from Sections 5.4 and 12.2 that the valency of an atom is the number of covalent bonds that it must form in order to be part of a stable molecule. The functional groups you will meet contain the elements carbon, hydrogen, nitrogen, oxygen and the halogens, and their valencies are given in Table 14.1.

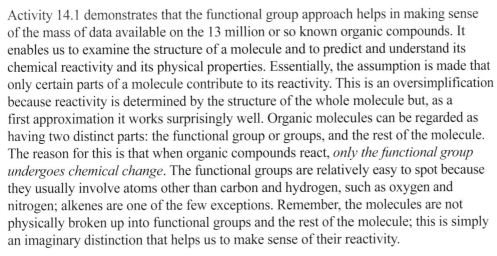

14.1 ethene

14.2 propene

Table 14.1 The most common valencies of some elements found in functional groups.

Element	Valency
hydrogen	1
carbon	4
nitrogen	3
oxygen	2
fluorine	1
chlorine	1
bromine	1
iodine	1

You will now look at some of these functional groups in more detail to illustrate the strength of the functional group approach. The remaining sections of this chapter revise and elaborate on material that was covered in Activity 14.1.

14.1.1 Haloalkanes

The **haloalkanes** are a class of compounds that contain one or more halogen atoms as well as carbon and hydrogen atoms. They contain one or more of the functional groups $-F$, $-Cl$, $-Br$ and $-I$.

■ Draw the structural and molecular formulas of fluoromethane, which contains one fluorine atom, one carbon atom and sufficient hydrogen atoms to satisfy the valency of the carbon atom.

□ Fluorine has a valency of one. This means that fluorine forms only one covalent bond, so three hydrogen atoms are needed to satisfy the valency of carbon. The molecular formula of fluoromethane is CH_3F, and its structural formula is shown in structure **14.3**.

$$
\begin{array}{c}
H \\
| \\
H-C-\boxed{F} \\
| \\
H
\end{array}
$$

14.3

You might have written the molecular formula as H_3CF, FH_3C or H_3FC, which are all reasonable answers, but chemists have a convention that the molecular formula of an organic compound is always written with the symbol for the carbon atoms first, then the symbol for the hydrogen atoms, followed by the symbols for any other elements, in alphabetical order.

All the halogens have a valency of one, which enables us to predict the formulas of the compounds they form with carbon.

■ Write down the molecular formulas of all the compounds that contain one carbon atom and as many chlorine atoms, or hydrogen atoms, or mixtures of the two, as are required for the valency of carbon to be satisfied.

□ Hydrogen and chlorine both have a valency of one, so you can attach four of these atoms in any combination to the carbon atom. There are five such compounds: CH_4, CH_3Cl, CH_2Cl_2, $CHCl_3$ and CCl_4. (Note that these formulas are written to conform to the convention described above.)

$$
\begin{array}{c}
Cl \\
| \\
F-C-Cl \\
| \\
Cl
\end{array}
\qquad
\begin{array}{c}
Cl \\
| \\
F-C-F \\
| \\
Cl
\end{array}
$$

14.4   **14.5**

CCl_4 is known as tetrachloromethane (carbon tetrachloride). It was formerly used as a solvent for removing stains in proprietary dry-cleaning products such as 'Dabitoff'. $CHCl_3$, trichloromethane, is also known as chloroform. It is used as a solvent and in the 19th century was used as an anaesthetic (Figure 14.1). More recently, haloalkanes containing chlorine and fluorine, known as freons or CFCs (structures **14.4** and **14.5**), were used in refrigerators and aerosols and as blowing agents for the production of foam plastics. However, their use is being phased out because there is clear evidence that their presence in the atmosphere leads to a depletion of the ozone in the stratosphere.

Figure 14.1 A trichloromethane inhaler, as used in the 1850s. Trichloromethane (or chloroform) was widely used as an anaesthetic during childbirth. In early 19th century Britain, there was widespread opposition to the use of any anaesthesia during childbirth, as pain was widely perceived to be morally and biologically important. This opposition was largely overcome when, in 1853, Queen Victoria used chloroform to assist in the birth of her seventh child.

14.1.2   Alcohols

Some examples of **alcohols** are shown in Figure 14.2; they all contain the **hydroxyl** (OH) functional group.

Figure 14.2   Common substances containing alcohols.

alcohol and abbreviated formula	uses
CH_3-OH methanol	Sometimes known as wood alcohol, obtained by the destructive distillation of wood. Used as a solvent in industry, it forms part of the mixture known as methylated spirit.
CH_3-CH_2-OH ethanol	The alcohol in alcoholic drinks, also part of methylated spirit.
$\overset{\displaystyle OH}{\underset{\displaystyle}{CH_3-CH-CH_2-CH_2-CH_2-CH_2-CH_3}}$ heptan-2-ol	Found in oil of cloves.
$HO-CH_2-CH_2-OH$ ethylene gycol (ethane-1,2-diol)	Used in antifreeze.
$CH_3-\overset{CH_3}{C}=CH-CH_2-CH_2-\overset{CH_3}{C}=CH-CH_2-OH$ geraniol	Main constituent of oil of rose, also found in other essential oils.
The alcohol functional group can be written as $-OH$ or $HO-$	

■ What are the molecular formula and structural formula of the simplest alcohol, methanol, which contains only one carbon atom?

☐ They are:

$$CH_4O \qquad \begin{array}{c} H \\ | \\ H-C-O-H \\ | \\ H \end{array}$$

molecular formula   structural formula

The molecular formula of methanol is often written as CH_3OH, emphasising the OH functional group.

14.1.3   Carboxylic acids

Some typical examples of **carboxylic acids** are shown in Figure 14.3; they all contain the carboxylic acid functional group:

$$-C \overset{\displaystyle O}{\underset{\displaystyle O-H}{\big\|}}$$

Note that one oxygen atom is bonded to the carbon via a single bond whereas the other is bonded to the carbon by a double bond. For shorthand, this group is often written as COOH, and this practice will be adopted in this book where appropriate.

Figure 14.3   Common substances containing carboxylic acids.

carboxylic acid and abbreviated formula	uses
$CH_3-C\overset{O}{\underset{O-H}{\big\|}}$ acetic acid (ethanoic acid)	Main constituent of vinegar.
$CH_3-CH_2-CH_2-C\overset{O}{\underset{O-H}{\big\|}}$ butanoic acid	Gives rise to the smell of rancid butter.
$CH_3-CH_2-CH_2-CH_2-CH_2-C\overset{O}{\underset{O-H}{\big\|}}$ hexanoic acid	Gives rise to the smell of goats.
$\overset{O}{\underset{H-O}{\big\|}}C-C\overset{O}{\underset{O-H}{\big\|}}$ oxalic acid	Found in rhubarb leaves, poisonous to humans.
The carboxylic acid group can be written as $\quad -C\overset{O}{\underset{O-H}{\big\|}}\quad$ or $\quad \overset{O}{\underset{H-O}{\big\|}}C-$	

14.1.4 Esters

Esters are widespread in nature. They are often pleasant-smelling liquids that contribute to the fragrance and flavour of many plants and drinks. Some typical examples are shown in Figure 14.4; they all contain the ester functional group:

$$\begin{array}{c} \quad\quad O \\ \quad\quad \| \\ -C \\ \quad \diagdown \quad | \\ \quad\quad O-C- \\ \quad\quad\quad\quad | \end{array}$$

Note that the difference between esters and carboxylic acids is that in an ester one of the oxygen atoms links two carbon atoms, $C-O-C$, whereas in a carboxylic acid it is attached to a hydrogen atom, $C-O-H$.

Figure 14.4 Common substances containing esters.

ester and abbreviated formula	uses
$$CH_3-C\begin{array}{c}\nearrow O\\ \diagdown O-CH_2-CH_3\end{array}$$ ethyl acetate (ethyl ethanoate)	Used as a solvent and in nail varnish remover. Smells of pear drops.
$$CH_3-CH_2-CH_2-C\begin{array}{c}\nearrow O\\ \diagdown O-CH_3\end{array}$$ methyl butanoate	Found in pineapples.
$$CH_3-C\begin{array}{c}\nearrow O\\ \diagdown O-CH_2-CH_2-CH-CH_3\\ \;|\\ \;CH_3\end{array}$$ isopentyl acetate	Constituent of banana oil, used as a flavouring.
methyl salicylate (oil of wintergreen)	A constituent of deep heating liniments. Used in small amounts as a flavouring. (Note that, conventionally, benzene rings are drawn without the element symbols C and H, as in the structural formula for methyl salicylate.)
The carboxylic acid group can be written as $$\begin{array}{c}O\\ \|\\ -C\\ \diagdown\\ O-C-\\ |\end{array} \quad or \quad \begin{array}{c}O\\ \|\\ C-\\ \diagup\\ -C-O\\ |\end{array}$$	

So far, when a functional group has been introduced, the structural formulas have usually been written in a particular order. For example, ethanol has been represented as CH_3-CH_2-OH. As you saw in Activity 14.1, molecules can be viewed from any angle, so it could just as correctly be written as $HO—CH_2—CH_3$. Similarly, acetic acid could be written as:

$$CH_3 - \overset{\displaystyle O}{\underset{\displaystyle O-H}{C}} \quad \text{or} \quad \overset{\displaystyle O}{\underset{\displaystyle H-O}{C}} - CH_3$$

For the rest of this book such structures will be written either way round, according to which makes it easier to see what happens in a reaction.

You have now looked at molecules containing five functional groups: alkenes, haloalkanes, alcohols, carboxylic acids and esters. In some instances, there are alternative ways of representing them, so do make sure you can recognise these functional groups however they happen to be drawn. The information is summarised in Table 14.3, at the end of this chapter.

Activity 14.2   Analysing the structure of organic compounds

We expect this activity will take you approximately 15 minutes.

This activity helps you to develop a strategy for analysing the structure of organic compounds.

Glyceryl monostearate, structure **14.6**, is a widely used food additive sometimes referred to as E471. It is an emulsifier, which means that it is used to help stabilise mixtures of oil and water, slowing the processes by which they separate. It is found in products such as margarine. In this activity, you use this molecule to work out a strategy for analysing the structure of organic molecules.

14.6

Task 1

Look at structure **14.6** and try to identify any functional groups, carbon chains or carbon rings that are present. Make a note of the features that you have identified, perhaps by labelling the structure in pencil.

Task 2

Now think about how you tackled the identification of these parts of the molecule. Note down a list of steps that you took. These steps will comprise the basis of a strategy for analysing organic structures. Then compare your strategy with a strategy devised by a tutor in the comments section.

Look at the comments on Tasks 1 and 2 at the end of this book before moving on to Task 3.

Task 3

In Task 2 you developed a strategy for analysing organic structures. Try out this strategy, or the tutor's strategy in the comments section, with linoleic acid, structure **14.7**, a polyunsaturated fatty acid that is essential for your health.

$$H-\overset{\overset{\displaystyle H}{|}}{\underset{\underset{\displaystyle H}{|}}{C}}-\overset{\overset{\displaystyle H}{|}}{\underset{\underset{\displaystyle H}{|}}{C}}-\overset{\overset{\displaystyle H}{|}}{\underset{\underset{\displaystyle H}{|}}{C}}-\overset{\overset{\displaystyle H}{|}}{\underset{\underset{\displaystyle H}{|}}{C}}-\overset{\overset{\displaystyle H}{|}}{\underset{\underset{\displaystyle H}{|}}{C}}-CH=CH-\overset{\overset{\displaystyle H}{|}}{\underset{\underset{\displaystyle H}{|}}{C}}-CH=CH-\overset{\overset{\displaystyle H}{|}}{\underset{\underset{\displaystyle H}{|}}{C}}-\overset{\overset{\displaystyle H}{|}}{\underset{\underset{\displaystyle H}{|}}{C}}-\overset{\overset{\displaystyle H}{|}}{\underset{\underset{\displaystyle H}{|}}{C}}-\overset{\overset{\displaystyle H}{|}}{\underset{\underset{\displaystyle H}{|}}{C}}-\overset{\overset{\displaystyle H}{|}}{\underset{\underset{\displaystyle H}{|}}{C}}-\overset{\overset{\displaystyle H}{|}}{\underset{\underset{\displaystyle H}{|}}{C}}-\overset{\overset{\displaystyle H}{|}}{\underset{\underset{\displaystyle H}{|}}{C}}-C\overset{O}{\underset{O-H}{}}$$

14.7

Look at the comments on Task 3 at the end of this book before moving on to Task 4.

Task 4

Now use your strategy to decide whether structure **14.8** is also linoleic acid.

14.8

Now look at the comments on Task 4 at the end of this book.

Question 14.1

Identify the functional groups in the following compounds.

(a) $HO-CH_2-CH_2-CH_2-CH_2-CH_2-COOH$

(b)

14.2 Characteristic reactions of functional groups

Now you have met some functional groups, it is time to move on to examine some of the reactions that they undergo. You will look at some other functional groups later in the book. Remember, one of the reasons for using the functional group approach is that all compounds containing a particular functional group will tend to react in similar ways. In general, only the functional group will take part in the reaction; the hydrocarbon parts usually act as spectators – in other words, they remain unchanged.

14.2.1 Condensation reactions

Figure 14.2 shows that methanol and ethanol contain the hydroxyl functional group, as does 2-methylbutanol (structure **14.9**) – they are alcohols. Although they look different, they undergo the same pattern of reactions. In other words, chemical compounds that react with methanol also react with ethanol and

$$\overset{\overset{\displaystyle CH_3}{|}}{HO-CH_2-CH-CH_2-CH_3}$$

14.9

2-methylbutanol, and chemicals that don't react with methanol don't react with ethanol or 2-methylbutanol. It is the alcohol functional group, —OH, not the saturated hydrocarbon part of the molecule, that controls the reactivity.

One of the reactions that methanol undergoes is with acetic acid to give an ester:

$$CH_3-C\underset{OH}{\overset{O}{\Vert}} + H-O-CH_3 \longrightarrow CH_3-C\underset{O-CH_3}{\overset{O}{\Vert}} + H_2O \qquad (14.1)$$

Colour has been used to show where the atoms in the acetic acid and the methanol end up in the ester. The box contains the hydrogen and oxygen atoms that will form water. Methanol has been written as H—O—CH$_3$ rather than the more familiar CH$_3$–OH, to make it easier for you to see which parts end up where in the ester and the water. As this is the reaction of an —OH group, ethanol undergoes the same reaction (Equation 14.2), as does 2-methylbutanol (Equation 14.3).

$$CH_3-C\underset{OH}{\overset{O}{\Vert}} + H-O-CH_2-CH_3 \longrightarrow CH_3-C\underset{O-CH_2-CH_3}{\overset{O}{\Vert}} + H_2O \quad (14.2)$$

$$CH_3-C\underset{OH}{\overset{O}{\Vert}} + H-O-CH_2-\overset{CH_3}{\underset{|}{CH}}-CH_2-CH_3 \longrightarrow$$

$$(14.3)$$

$$CH_3-C\underset{O-CH_2-\underset{|}{\overset{CH_3}{CH}}-CH_2-CH_3}{\overset{O}{\Vert}} + H_2O$$

In each case, the product is an ester because each compound contains the group:

$$-C\underset{O-C-}{\overset{O}{\Vert}}$$

As you saw in Activity 14.1, this reaction is one of a group known as **condensation reactions**. Such reactions involve the joining together of two or more molecules to form a larger molecule, together with a small molecule such as water, H$_2$O, hydrogen chloride, HCl, or ammonia, NH$_3$. In this case, if an alcohol and acetic acid are heated together in the presence of a catalyst, an ester and *water* are formed. For this reaction, the catalyst is a strong acid. The reaction happens very slowly without the catalyst but, in the presence of strong acid, the reaction can occur within a few minutes.

The reaction of acetic acid with any alcohol can be described by using the symbol **R** to represent the saturated hydrocarbon part of the alcohol molecule:

$$CH_3-C\underset{OH}{\overset{O}{\Vert}} + H-O-R \longrightarrow CH_3-C\underset{O-R}{\overset{O}{\Vert}} + H_2O \qquad (14.4)$$

Thus Equation 14.4 is the same as Equation 14.1, where R—OH is CH_3—OH; i.e. R is a CH_3 group.

■ Identify the R group in Equations 14.2 and 14.3.

☐ By analogy with Equation 14.4; in Equation 14.2, R is CH_3—CH_2—, and in Equation 14.3, R is:

$$\underset{}{-CH_2-\overset{\displaystyle CH_3}{\overset{|}{CH}}-CH_2-CH_3}$$

Equation 14.4 shows the reaction between any alcohol and acetic acid. In fact, any carboxylic acid could be used here in place of acetic acid. For example, benzoic acid (**14.10**) is a carboxylic acid used as a preservative in foods. Conventionally, the ring in this acid is drawn without the element symbols (**14.11**).

14.10   **14.11**

Methanol reacts with benzoic acid to form the ester methyl benzoate:

$$+ \quad H-O-CH_3 \quad \longrightarrow \quad \cdots \quad + \quad H_2O \qquad (14.5)$$

Equation 14.4 can be rewritten in an even more general form:

$$R^1-C\underset{OH}{\overset{O}{\diagup}} \quad + \quad H-O-R^2 \quad \longrightarrow \quad R^1-C\underset{O-R^2}{\overset{O}{\diagup}} \quad + \quad H_2O \qquad (14.6)$$

Here the symbol R^1 is used to represent the hydrocarbon group in the carboxylic acid and R^2 to represent the hydrocarbon group in the alcohol. Condensation is one of the key reactions given in the summary at the end of this chapter. You will meet such reactions again.

■ Note that a superscript is used to distinguish one R group from another. Why would a subscript, e.g. R_2, not be appropriate?

☐ Subscripts are used in formulas to show how many of the relevant atoms or groups of atoms are present in the molecule. R_2 implies there are two R groups.

The strength of the functional group approach is that, once you have identified a functional group in a compound, all you have to do is to list the reactions and properties of that functional group to be able to predict how the compound will react.

■ What key property do you think carboxylic acids demonstrate?

□ The name implies they are acids and, as you saw in Chapter 11, acids dissociate in water to give hydrogen ions.

This dissociation is:

$$CH_3-C{\overset{O}{\underset{O-H}{}}} \rightleftharpoons CH_3-C{\overset{O}{\underset{O^-}{}}} + H^+ \tag{14.7}$$

Note that since the hydrocarbon part of acetic acid is regarded as inert, the hydrogen ion can't come from the methyl group, CH_3-, so it must come from the functional group, $-COOH$, where there is only one hydrogen present. Notice also that after dissociation, there must be a negative charge on the oxygen to balance the positive charge on the hydrogen ion. The negatively charged product is known as a carboxylate ion. Equation 14.7 is the full form of the simplified equation given in Section 11.1 for the dissociation of acetic acid:

$$HAc(aq) \rightleftharpoons H^+(aq) + Ac^-(aq) \tag{11.7a}$$

■ Write out the generalised form of the dissociation in Equation 14.7 using the acid $R-COOH$.

□

$$R-C{\overset{O}{\underset{O-H}{}}} \rightleftharpoons R-C{\overset{O}{\underset{O^-}{}}} + H^+ \tag{14.8}$$

■ Write out the equation for the reaction of a carboxylic acid $R-COOH$ with sodium hydroxide.

□ Sodium hydroxide is a base that reacts with acids to give a salt and water. Thus a carboxylic acid reacts with sodium hydroxide to give water and a carboxylate salt:

$$R-C{\overset{O}{\underset{O-H}{}}} + NaOH \rightleftharpoons R-C{\overset{O}{\underset{O^-}{}}} + Na^+ + H_2O \tag{14.9}$$

For example, when R is CH_3, the salt is sodium acetate.

14.2.2   Oxidation and reduction

Oxidation and reduction are two key reactions in chemistry. You explored the oxidation and reduction of metals and their compounds in Chapter 8. For example, the all too familiar formation of rust is a reaction of iron with oxygen to give iron oxide:

$$4Fe(s) + 3O_2(g) + 2nH_2O(l) = 2Fe_2O_3.nH_2O(s) \tag{14.10}$$

Because oxygen is added to the iron, the iron is said to be oxidised. However, you might recall that oxidation is often more precisely defined as the loss of electrons, and you can rewrite Equation 14.10 to show only the ions involved:

$$4Fe(s) + 3O_2(g) = 4Fe^{3+}(s) + 6O^{2-}(s) \qquad (14.10a)$$

The iron atoms have lost electrons to form Fe^{3+} ions. You might recall that reduction is defined as the addition of hydrogen atoms, or the gain of electrons.

■   Which substance has been reduced in this reaction?

☐   Oxygen has gained electrons to form O^{2-} ions; therefore, the oxygen has been reduced.

Organic chemists are generally content to view oxidation and reduction in terms of the addition or removal of hydrogen or oxygen. Electrons are being exchanged, in the same way that you observed with metals in Section 8.5.2, but organic chemists rarely bother themselves with that level of detail!

Oxidation reactions are very common; you might have met another example if you have ever left a bottle of wine open to the air for too long – the alcohol (ethanol) is converted into vinegar (acetic acid), as shown in Equation 14.11. It is an oxidation because the proportion of oxygen in the compound is increased.

$$CH_3-CH_2-OH + O_2 \longrightarrow CH_3-COOH + H_2O \qquad (14.11)$$

This oxidation can be deliberately brought about in the laboratory using an aqueous solution of potassium dichromate, $K_2Cr_2O_7$, in the presence of a strong acid, HCl, as shown in Equation 14.12:

$$CH_3-CH_2-OH + K_2Cr_2O_7 \longrightarrow CH_3-COOH \qquad (14.12)$$

■   You will probably notice that this equation is not balanced. Does this mean that the equation is incorrect?

☐   No. It is accepted that an arrow can be used when the equation is unbalanced; an equals sign would imply a balanced chemical equation.

This is another example of organic chemists writing unbalanced equations, because they are only interested in the transformation of the organic reactant into the product. The inorganic compound that brings about the oxidation is known as the *reagent* and its fate is of no interest. Another way of writing the equation is:

$$CH_3-CH_2-OH \xrightarrow[\text{HCl}]{K_2Cr_2O_7} CH_3-COOH \qquad (14.12a)$$

Here the reagents ($K_2Cr_2O_7$ and HCl) are written along the arrow. A generalised reaction scheme for the oxidation is shown in Equation 14.13, using R to represent a hydrocarbon group. Note that, in this case, the general formula for the alcohol is written as $R-CH_2-OH$ *not* $R-OH$; this is because the carbon atom attached to the oxygen is intimately involved in the reaction. (Don't worry too much about this – it is the only time it is needed in this book.)

$$R-CH_2-\boxed{OH} \xrightarrow[\text{HCl}]{K_2Cr_2O_7} R-\boxed{COOH} \qquad (14.13)$$

■ Predict the product of the following oxidation.

$$CH_3-CH_2-CH_2-CH_2-\boxed{OH} \quad \xrightarrow[\text{HCl}]{K_2Cr_2O_7} \quad ?$$

☐ By analogy with Equation 14.13, R is $CH_3-CH_2-CH_2-$, hence the reaction is:

$$CH_3-CH_2-CH_2-CH_2-\boxed{OH} \quad \xrightarrow[\text{HCl}]{K_2Cr_2O_7} \quad CH_3-CH_2-CH_2-\boxed{COOH} \quad (14.14)$$

■ What has happened to the proportion of hydrogen atoms in the molecule during this reaction?

☐ The proportion of hydrogen atoms in the molecule has decreased, from ten per molecule to eight per molecule.

This is another way of identifying an oxidation reaction – the loss of hydrogen from a compound.

Reduction is the opposite of oxidation. For example, carboxylic acids can be reduced to give alcohols, using hydrogen and a catalyst:

$$CH_3-\boxed{COOH} \quad \xrightarrow{H_2/\text{catalyst}} \quad CH_3-CH_2-\boxed{OH} \quad (14.15)$$

In this reduction, the proportion of hydrogen atoms in the molecule is increased and the proportion of oxygen atoms is decreased.

The various ways of describing oxidation and reduction are summarised in Table 14.2.

Table 14.2 Ways of defining oxidation and reduction.

Oxidation	Reduction
the proportion of oxygen in the compound increases	the proportion of oxygen in the compound decreases
the proportion of hydrogen in the compound decreases	the proportion of hydrogen in the compound increases
loss of electrons	gain of electrons

Question 14.2

Equation 14.15 shows the reduction of acetic acid to ethanol. Write out a generalised scheme for the reduction of any carboxylic acid R−COOH to an alcohol. Predict the organic product of the reduction of benzoic acid (structure **14.11**).

Activity 14.3 Predicting the products of organic reactions

We expect this activity will take you approximately 30 minutes.

In this activity, you will develop a strategy for predicting the products of reactions of organic molecules that contain various functional groups. You may find it useful to refer to Table 14.3 at the end of this chapter.

Task 1

Predict the products of the following reaction.

$$CH_3 - CH - CH_2 - OH \quad \xrightarrow[\text{HCl}]{K_2Cr_2O_7} \quad ?$$
$$\qquad\qquad |$$
$$\qquad\quad CH_3$$

Task 2

Now think about how you arrived at your prediction. Make a note of the steps that you took, and then compare them with the method used by a member of the course team (described in the comments).

Look at the comments on Tasks 1 and 2 at the end of this book before attempting Task 3.

Task 3

Now use your strategy to predict the products of the following reaction.

$$CH_3 - CH_2 - CH = CH - CH_2 - CH_3 \quad + \quad Br_2 \quad \longrightarrow \quad ?$$

Did your strategy work? If you had to revise your strategy, note any changes you made and why you made them.

Look at the comments on Task 3 at the end of this book before attempting Task 4.

Task 4

Use your strategy to predict the products of the following reaction.

$$\qquad\qquad\qquad\qquad CH_3$$
$$\qquad\qquad\qquad\qquad |$$
$$CH_3 - CH_2 - COOH \quad + \quad H - C - OH \quad \longrightarrow \quad ?$$
$$\qquad\qquad\qquad\qquad |$$
$$\qquad\qquad\qquad\qquad CH_3$$

Now look at the comments on Task 4 at the end of this book.

Question 14.3

Predict the products of the following reactions.

(a) $CH_3 - CH_2 - CH_2 - OH \quad \xrightarrow[\text{HCl}]{K_2Cr_2O_7} \quad ?$

(b) $CH_3 - CH_2 - COOH \quad + \quad CH_3 - CH_2 - CH_2 - CH_2 - OH \quad \longrightarrow \quad ?$

(c) $CH_3 - CH = CH - CH_3 \quad + \quad H_2O \quad \longrightarrow \quad ?$

Question 14.4

Predict the products of the following reactions of leaf alcohol, which is found in the leaves of some scented plants.

(a) $CH_3-CH_2-CH=CH-CH_2-CH_2-OH$ + CH_3-COOH $\longrightarrow$?

(b) $CH_3-CH_2-CH=CH-CH_2-CH_2-OH$ + Br_2 $\longrightarrow$?

Question 14.5

In the following reactions, is the reactant oxidised or reduced?

(a) $CH_3-\underset{\underset{CH_3}{|}}{CH}-CH_2-OH$ $\longrightarrow$ $CH_3-\underset{\underset{CH_3}{|}}{CH}-COOH$

(b) $CH_3-CH=CH_2$ $\longrightarrow$ $CH_3-CH_2-CH_3$

14.3   Crude oil: final thoughts

As discussed in Section 13.1, crude oil contains a mixture of alkanes, which can be converted into a small number of alkenes. You may be surprised to learn that all the functional groups discussed so far, and many others, can be produced directly or indirectly from these alkenes (Figure 14.5).

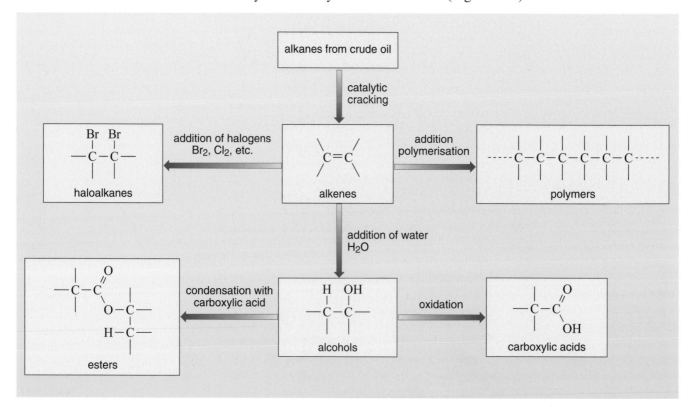

Figure 14.5   From crude oil to functional groups. Using only the reactions described so far, it is possible to create compounds containing all the functional groups in Chapter 14.

These transformations typify the building block approach, because they start with small molecules that can be converted and joined together using predictable, controllable reactions at functional groups. They form the basis of the multibillion dollar petrochemical industry, responsible for the production of the many modern materials mentioned in Section 13.1. The petrochemical industry takes simple hydrocarbons and, through an intricate series of chemical reactions, adds functional groups. It is perhaps ironic that this is the reverse of the geological process by which crude oil was formed, which involved the conversion of complex biological organic molecules, over many thousands of years, into simple hydrocarbons.

Modern society is hugely dependent on crude oil – as a source of both energy and petrochemicals. But there is a problem: at some point the oil is going to run out. Before the oil is exhausted, there will be a point at which the global production of crude oil reaches a peak and starts to decline (Figure 14.6). Some oil analysts predict that this will precipitate rocketing energy and petrochemical prices, and cause global economic crisis. Unfortunately, there is no agreement as to when the peak will occur. The Association for the Study of Peak Oil is an organisation of geologists, many of whom formerly worked in the oil industry, who believe that 'peak oil' may have been reached already (Figure 14.6). The majority of analysts are more optimistic, arguing that oil production will peak in the middle or even at the end of the 21st century. Here is a vital argument where politics, economics and science interact. It involves making scientific judgments – about how much oil is likely to be left in the ground, given our understanding of the world's geology. It involves making technological and economic judgments – how quickly will the extractive technologies develop, and how high does the price have to get to make extraction of the more difficult sources worthwhile? Many would argue that whether the oil runs out sooner or later, we still urgently need to develop alternative sources of energy, not least because we can't afford to keep burning fossil fuels and releasing carbon dioxide into the environment. Alongside the need for alternative energy sources is the need for an alternative to petrochemicals.

These problems are revisited in the final chapter but, before that, you are going to explore the chemistry of some of the complex organic compounds found in food.

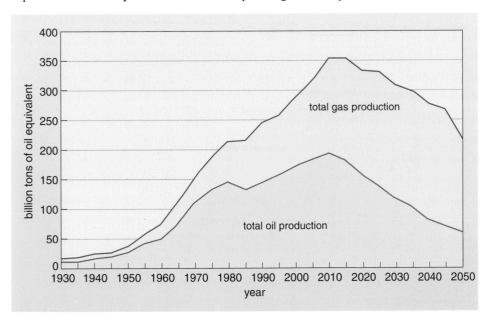

Figure 14.6 Have we reached peak oil? A controversial graph produced by the Association for the Study of Peak Oil. The upper line shows total oil and gas production. The blue area shows total gas production and the red area shows total oil production. The graph suggests that the global peak oil production occurs at around 2010, while that for natural gas will occur between 2020 and 2050.

14.4   Summary of Chapter 14

Organic molecules can be classified using the functional group approach. This approach involves the imaginary division of the molecule into parts: the reactive functional group(s) and the unreactive saturated hydrocarbon fragment(s). Only the functional group undergoes reactions, and knowledge of these reactions can be used to predict the properties of an organic compound.

The functional groups used most frequently in this book, and their key reactions, are listed in Table 14.3.

A compound is oxidised if the proportion of oxygen in it is increased or the proportion of hydrogen in it is decreased.

A compound is reduced if the proportion of oxygen in it is decreased or the proportion of hydrogen in it is increased.

The chapter has also given you the opportunity to develop your problem-solving skills, particularly in developing strategies to recognise functional groups in molecules and to predict the products of chemical reactions.

Table 14.3 Key functional groups and types of reactions. In order to bring all the relevant information together, this table includes three functional groups and one type of reaction not covered thus far. These are marked with an asterisk (*), and will be discussed in Chapter 15.

Class of compound	Name of functional group (if different from name of compound)	Molecular structure	Alternative forms of molecular structure
acetal*		$\begin{array}{c} OH \\ | \\ R-C-O-R \\ | \\ H \end{array}$	$\begin{array}{c} OH \\ | \\ R-O-C-R \\ | \\ H \end{array}$
alcohol	hydroxyl group	$R-OH$	$HO-R$
alkene	double bond	$\begin{array}{c} R^1 \quad\quad R^2 \\ \diagdown\;\;\diagup \\ C=C \\ \diagup\;\;\diagdown \\ R^4 \quad\quad R^3 \end{array}$	$R^1-CH=CH-R^2$
amine*	amino group (NH_2 only)	$R-NH_2$	H_2N-R
		$\begin{array}{c} R^1-N-H \\ | \\ R^2 \end{array}$	$\begin{array}{c} R^1-N-R^3 \\ | \\ R^2 \end{array}$

Table 14.3   *continued*

Class of compound	Name of functional group (if different from name of compound)	Molecular structure	Alternative forms of molecular structure
amide*		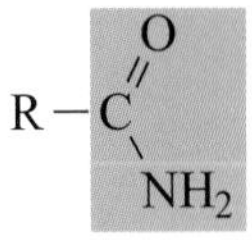 $R-\overset{\displaystyle O}{\underset{\displaystyle NH_2}{C}}$	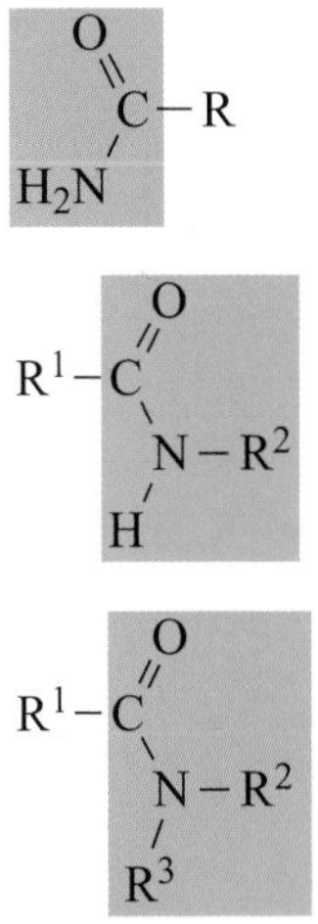 $\underset{\displaystyle H_2N}{\overset{\displaystyle O}{C}}-R$ $R^1-\overset{\displaystyle O}{\underset{\displaystyle H}{C}}\!\!\diagdown\!\!N-R^2$ $R^1-\overset{\displaystyle O}{\underset{\displaystyle R^3}{C}}\!\!\diagdown\!\!N-R^2$
carboxylic acid		$R-\overset{\displaystyle O}{\underset{\displaystyle O-H}{C}}$	$\underset{\displaystyle H-O}{\overset{\displaystyle O}{C}}-R$
ester		$R^1-\overset{\displaystyle O}{\underset{\displaystyle O-R^2}{C}}$	$\underset{\displaystyle R^2-O}{\overset{\displaystyle O}{C}}-R^1$
haloalkane		$R-\boxed{X}$	$\boxed{X}-R$

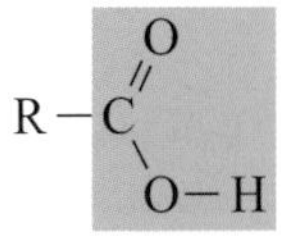

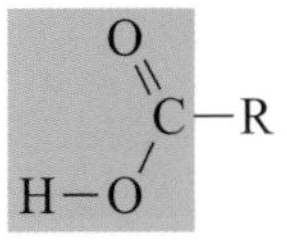

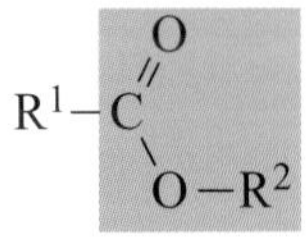

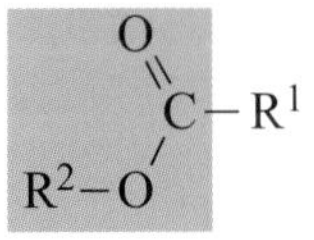

where X is F, Cl, Br or I

Types of reaction

Addition

$$R^1-CH=CH-R^2 \;+\; X-Y \;\longrightarrow\; R^1-\overset{\displaystyle X}{\underset{}{CH}}-\overset{\displaystyle Y}{\underset{}{CH}}-R^2$$

Condensation

$$R^1-\overset{\displaystyle O}{\underset{\displaystyle OH}{C}} \;+\; H-O-R^2 \;\longrightarrow\; R^1-\overset{\displaystyle O}{\underset{\displaystyle O-R^2}{C}} \;+\; H_2O$$

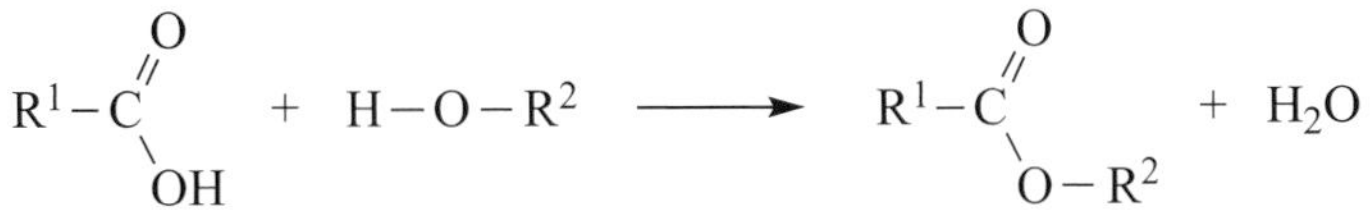

Hydrolysis*

$$R^1-\overset{\displaystyle O}{\underset{\displaystyle O-R^2}{C}} \;+\; H_2O \;\longrightarrow\; R^1-\overset{\displaystyle O}{\underset{\displaystyle OH}{C}} \;+\; H-O-R^2$$

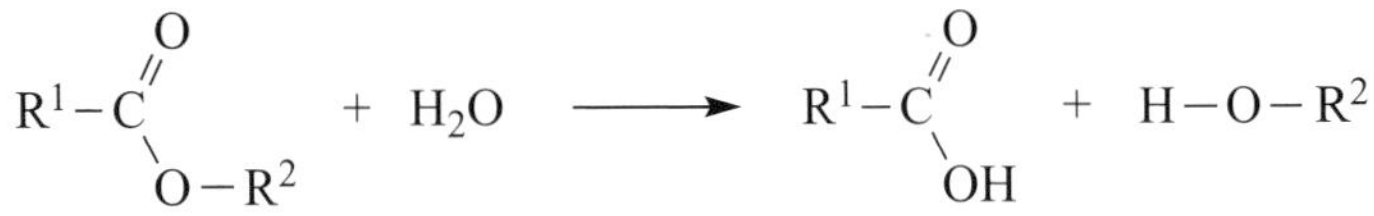

Oxidation

$$R-CH_2-OH \;\xrightarrow[\text{HCl}]{K_2Cr_2O_7}\; R-COOH$$

Reduction

$$R-COOH \;\xrightarrow{H_2/\text{catalyst}}\; R-CH_2-\boxed{OH}$$

Chapter 15
Applying the functional group approach: food chemistry

Food is a complex mixture of a whole range of different compounds. For example, Figure 15.1 reproduces the nutritional information label found on a snack bar.

NUTRITION INFORMATION		
TYPICAL VALUES	PER BAR	PER 100 g
ENERGY	536 kJ 127 kcal	1532 kJ 362 kcal
PROTEIN	1.5 g	4.2 g
CARBOHYDRATE of which sugars	26.3 g 17.2 g	75.0 g 49.0 g
FAT of which saturates	1.8 g 1.1 g	5.0 g 3.2 g
FIBRE	0.6 g	1.8 g
SODIUM	0.1 g	0.3 g
PER BAR 127 CALORIES, 1.8 g FAT, 0.3 g SALT		

Figure 15.1   Nutritional information given on a snack bar.

Terms like **protein**, **carbohydrate** and **fat** have become everyday terms in western countries increasingly concerned about maintaining a healthy diet. The terms refer to classes of organic compound, and you will be able to use the functional group approach outlined in Chapter 14 to explore some of the chemistry of these substances. In Book 5, you will explore the biological roles of these molecules but, after reading this chapter we hope that you will have an appreciation of the way in which an understanding of their underlying chemistry can help. This chapter will concentrate on the three major groups: fats, proteins and carbohydrates.

15.1   Fats and oils

15.1.1   Properties of fats and oils

Fats and oils are the same chemical class of compound; they differ only in their physical properties. Fats are solid or semi-solid at room temperature, whereas oils are liquid. However, the distinction is not at all precise – palm oil is liquid at room temperature in the tropical countries where it is produced, while in the temperate UK it is often a solid.

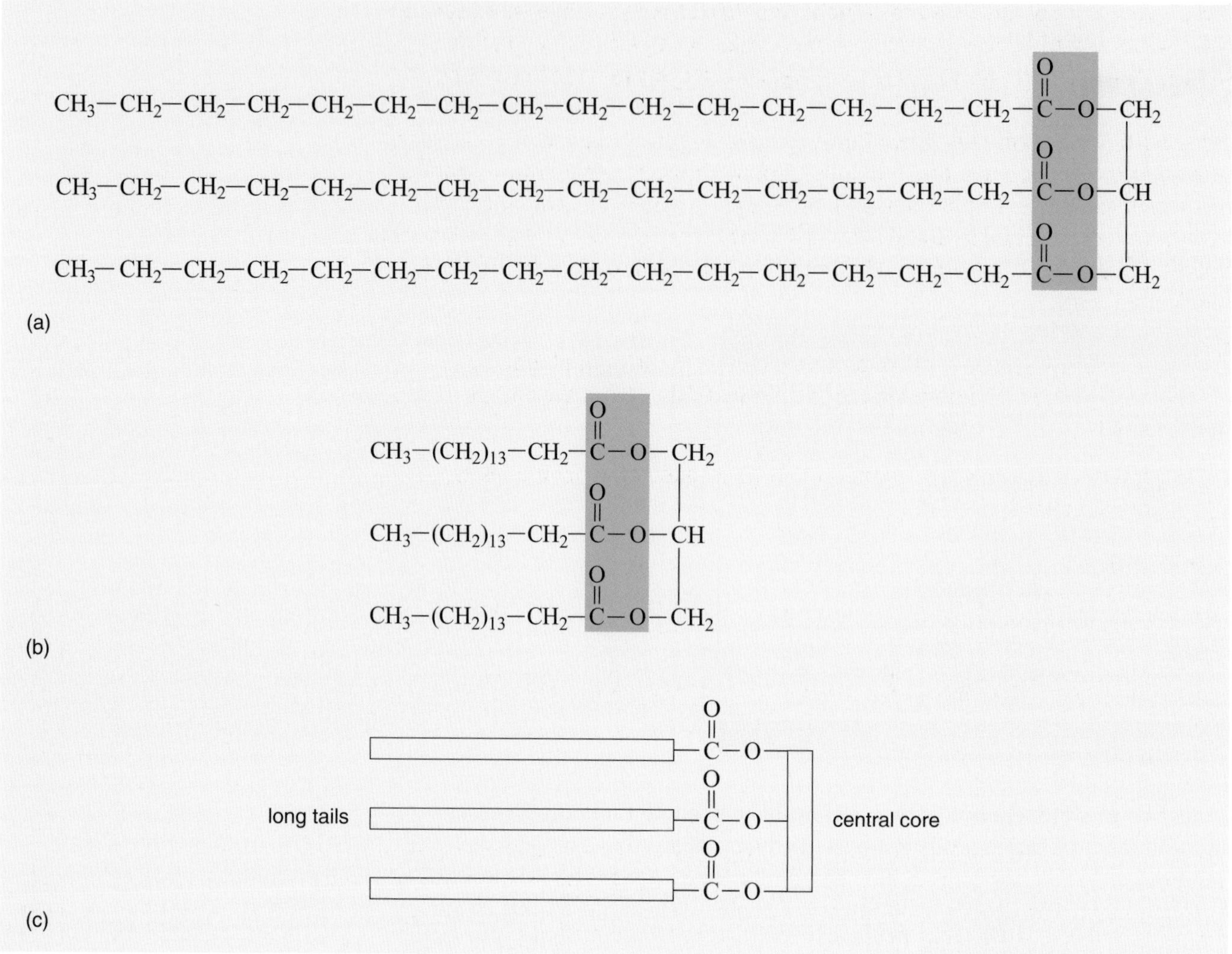

(a)

(b)

long tails

central core

(c)

Figure 15.2   The structure of a triacylglycerol: (a) the abbreviated structural formula in full; (b) the same in a truncated form, using $-(CH_2)_{13}-$ to indicate a chain of 13 carbon atoms; (c) a simplified model.

The most important class of fats is the **triacylglycerols** (pronounced 'tri-ace-isle-gliss-er-rolls') (the abbreviation **TAGs** is sometimes used). These compounds are the main constituents of vegetable oils and animal fats. Triacylglycerols are large molecules, as shown in Figure 15.2a and 15.2b. A simplified schematic representation is shown in Figure 15.2c.

Triacylglycerols consist of three long tails connected to a central core. These long tails are chains of carbon atoms, usually between eight and 20 carbon atoms long with sufficient hydrogen atoms attached to satisfy the valency of each carbon atom. The central core consists of three carbon atoms.

These molecules are a little more complicated than those you have encountered so far, and this will be true for most of the nutrient groups discussed in this chapter. However, you will be able to gain many insights into the behaviour of these molecules if you follow the functional group approach that you met in Chapter 14. Remember that, when thinking about organic molecules, you divide them up into distinct parts: the functional group or groups, which often involve atoms such as oxygen or nitrogen; and the rest of the molecule, which usually involves just carbon and hydrogen atoms. The reason they are divided in this way is because when organic compounds react, only the functional group undergoes chemical change.

■ Identify the functional groups in a triacylglycerol, as highlighted in Figure 15.2a and b. (You may like to refer to Table 14.3 at the end of Chapter 14.)

☐ The functional groups are highlighted in green and correspond to ester functional groups:

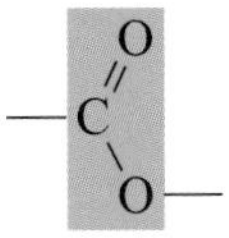

Note that the ester functional group is sometimes represented with the bonds at right angles:

This is for convenience, when drawing rather more crowded structures, as in this case where there are three ester functional groups in close proximity.

These three ester functional groups provide the links by which the three tails are attached to the central core. As well as rationalising its structure, the identification of the functional group helps you to understand how triacylglycerols are manufactured in nature and, as you will see later, how they are broken down in the body. In Section 14.2.1, you saw that esters can be produced by a condensation reaction in which a carboxylic acid and an alcohol react together, producing water as a by-product.

$$ R^1 - C {\overset{O}{\underset{OH}{}}} \quad + \quad H - O - R^2 \quad \longrightarrow \quad R^1 - C {\overset{O}{\underset{O - R^2}{}}} \quad + \quad H_2O \quad (15.1) $$

In triacylglycerols, the core to which the three tails are attached is derived from glycerol, structure **15.1**, more commonly called glycerine, a syrupy liquid that is used in many skin products. This molecule contains three alcohol functional groups, each of which can be converted to an ester.

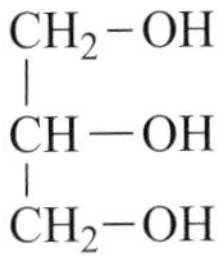

$$ \begin{array}{l} CH_2 - OH \\ | \\ CH - OH \\ | \\ CH_2 - OH \end{array} $$

15.1

■ What does each molecule of glycerol need to react with to create three ester groups, as in a triacylglycerol?

□ Each molecule of glycerol needs to react with three molecules of a carboxylic acid to give three ester groups.

Equations 15.2 to 15.4 show the reaction of each of the three alcohol functional groups with each carboxylic acid molecule.

$$
\begin{array}{l}
CH_2-O-H \\
\ | \\
CH-O-H \\
\ | \\
CH_2-O-H
\end{array}
\ + \
HO-\overset{\overset{O}{\|}}{C}-R
\ \longrightarrow \
\begin{array}{l}
CH_2-O-\overset{\overset{O}{\|}}{C}-R \\
\ | \\
CH-O-H \\
\ | \\
CH_2-O-H
\end{array}
\ + \ H_2O
\qquad (15.2)
$$

$$
\begin{array}{l}
CH_2-O-\overset{\overset{O}{\|}}{C}-R \\
\ | \\
CH-O-H \\
\ | \\
CH_2-O-H
\end{array}
\ + \
HO-\overset{\overset{O}{\|}}{C}-R
\ \longrightarrow \
\begin{array}{l}
CH_2-O-\overset{\overset{O}{\|}}{C}-R \\
\ | \\
CH-O-\overset{\overset{O}{\|}}{C}-R \\
\ | \\
CH_2-O-H
\end{array}
\ + \ H_2O
\qquad (15.3)
$$

$$
\begin{array}{l}
CH_2-O-\overset{\overset{O}{\|}}{C}-R \\
\ | \\
CH-O-\overset{\overset{O}{\|}}{C}-R \\
\ | \\
CH_2-O-H
\end{array}
\ + \
HO-\overset{\overset{O}{\|}}{C}-R
\ \longrightarrow \
\begin{array}{l}
CH_2-O-\overset{\overset{O}{\|}}{C}-R \\
\ | \\
CH-O-\overset{\overset{O}{\|}}{C}-R \\
\ | \\
CH_2-O-\overset{\overset{O}{\|}}{C}-R
\end{array}
\ + \ H_2O
\qquad (15.4)
$$

Note that fat molecules are called triacylglycerols because there are three tails attached to the glycerol core. If two tails are attached, the molecule is called a diacylglyceride and if only one is attached, it is called a monoacylglyceride. The basic structure of a triacylglycerol is the same irrespective of whether the fat comes from animals, for example in meat or dairy products, or from plants, for example in sunflower oil, olive oil or margarine.

■ Figure 15.3 shows the molecular structure of three triacylglycerols: one from an animal, one from a plant and one from an oily fish. What are the similarities and differences between these three molecules?

□ All three consist of a central core connected to three long chains via ester groups. The main difference between the various triacylglycerols is the structure of the three long hydrocarbon chains, more specifically the number of carbons atoms in the chain, and the number of double bonds present.

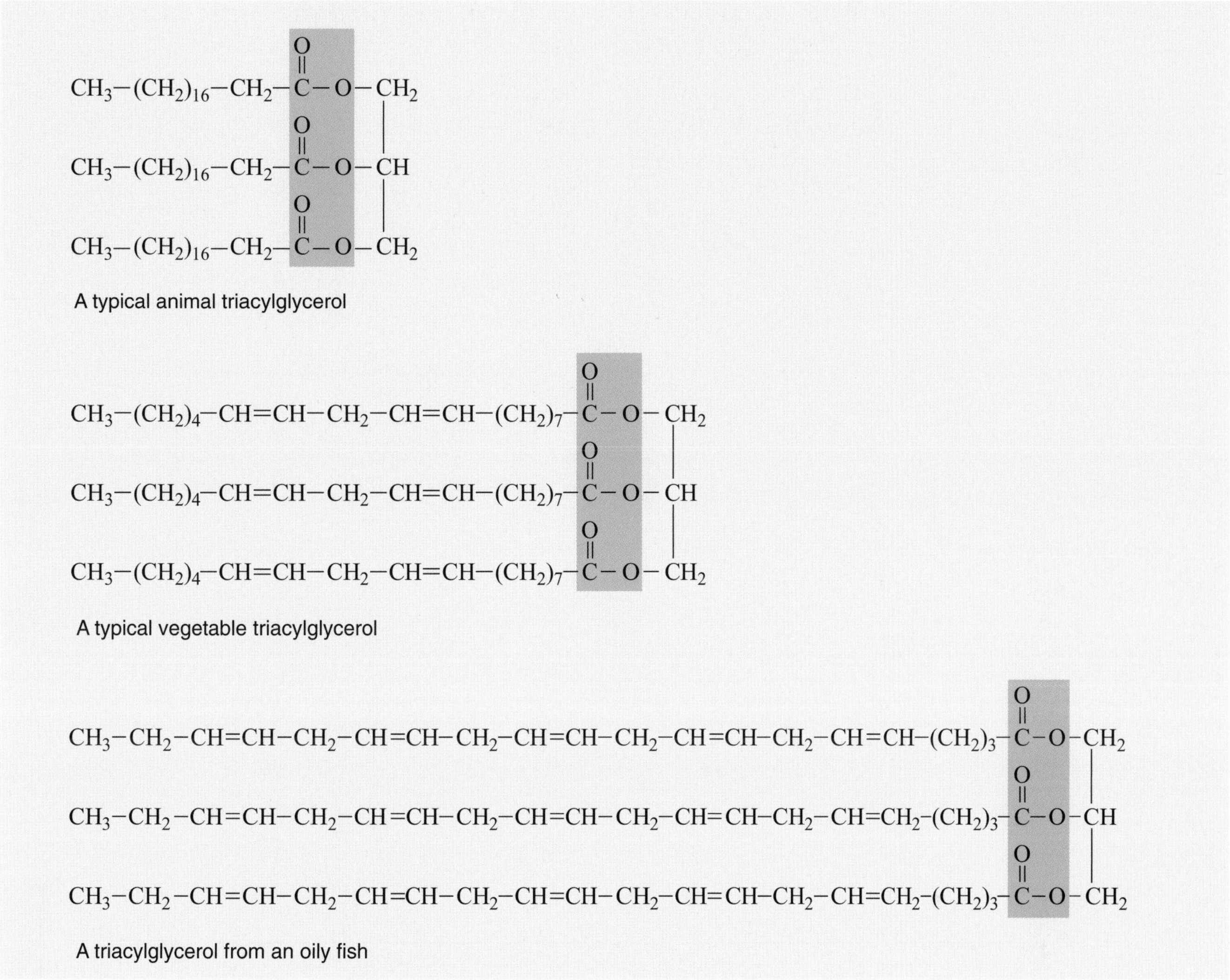

$$CH_3-(CH_2)_{16}-CH_2-\underset{\underset{\displaystyle O}{\|}}{C}-O-CH_2$$

$$CH_3-(CH_2)_{16}-CH_2-\underset{\underset{\displaystyle O}{\|}}{C}-O-CH$$

$$CH_3-(CH_2)_{16}-CH_2-\underset{\underset{\displaystyle O}{\|}}{C}-O-CH_2$$

A typical animal triacylglycerol

$$CH_3-(CH_2)_4-CH=CH-CH_2-CH=CH-(CH_2)_7-\overset{\overset{\displaystyle O}{\|}}{C}-O-CH_2$$

$$CH_3-(CH_2)_4-CH=CH-CH_2-CH=CH-(CH_2)_7-\overset{\overset{\displaystyle O}{\|}}{C}-O-CH$$

$$CH_3-(CH_2)_4-CH=CH-CH_2-CH=CH-(CH_2)_7-\overset{\overset{\displaystyle O}{\|}}{C}-O-CH_2$$

A typical vegetable triacylglycerol

$$CH_3-CH_2-CH=CH-CH_2-CH=CH-CH_2-CH=CH-CH_2-CH=CH-CH_2-CH=CH-(CH_2)_3-\overset{\overset{\displaystyle O}{\|}}{C}-O-CH_2$$

$$CH_3-CH_2-CH=CH-CH_2-CH=CH-CH_2-CH=CH-CH_2-CH=CH-CH_2-CH=CH_2-(CH_2)_3-\overset{\overset{\displaystyle O}{\|}}{C}-O-CH$$

$$CH_3-CH_2-CH=CH-CH_2-CH=CH-CH_2-CH=CH-CH_2-CH=CH-CH_2-CH=CH_2-(CH_2)_3-\overset{\overset{\displaystyle O}{\|}}{C}-O-CH_2$$

A triacylglycerol from an oily fish

Figure 15.3   The molecular structure of three triacylglycerols, one from an animal, one from a vegetable and one from an oily fish.

Since each of the triacylglycerol molecules are formed by reacting glycerol with three carboxylic acids, the difference between the triacylglycerols of the three species results from each organism using different carboxylic acids. Table 15.1 (overleaf) shows the structure of some of the common carboxylic acids, known as **fatty acids**, used in nature to make triacylglycerols, together with their names and origins.

Table 15.1 Structures of some fatty acids together with their traditional names and origins.

Name	C atoms	Structure	Type	Origin of name
butyric	4	$CH_3(CH_2)_2COOH$	saturated	from *butyrium*, Latin for butter
capric	10	$CH_3(CH_2)_8COOH$	saturated	smells of goats, from *caper*, Latin for goat
lauric	12	$CH_3(CH_2)_{10}COOH$	saturated	from laurel
myristic	14	$CH_3(CH_2)_{12}COOH$	saturated	from nutmeg (genus *Myristica*)
palmitic	16	$CH_3(CH_2)_8COOH$	saturated	from palm oil
stearic	18	$CH_3(CH_2)_{16}COOH$	saturated	from *stear*, Greek for fat
oleic	18	$CH_3(CH_2)_7CH=CH(CH_2)_7COOH$	monounsaturated	from *oleum*, Latin for oil
linoleic	18	$CH_3(CH_2)_4CH=CHCH_2CH=CH(CH_2)_7COOH$	polyunsaturated	from linseed oil
linolenic	18	$CH_3CH_2CH=CHCH_2CH=CHCH_2CH=CH(CH_2)_7COOH$	polyunsaturated	also from linseed oil
arachidonic	20	$CH_3(CH_2)_4CH=CHCH_2CH=CHCH_2CH=CHCH_2CH=CH(CH_2)_3COOH$	polyunsaturated	found in peanuts (genus *Arachis*)

■ The fatty acids in Table 15.1 are classified as saturated, **monounsaturated** and **polyunsaturated**. What do these terms mean?

☐ The terms saturated and unsaturated were used in reference to hydrocarbons in Chapter 13. Unsaturated hydrocarbons contain at least one C=C double bond, while saturated hydrocarbons contain none. In the same way, a *mono*unsaturated fatty acid contains one double bond in the hydrocarbon part of the molecule; a *poly*unsaturated fatty acid contains several double bonds; and a saturated fatty acid contains none.

Figure 15.4 shows the range of fatty acids that lead to the triacylglycerol molecules that make up the fat or oil found in a particular food. The data are presented as a series of bar charts where the relative height of a band reflects the percentage composition based on the number of molecules of the different fatty acids that lead to the fat. Fats are an essential part of the diet, and there are many millions of people in the world who do not have enough in their diet. In the western world, overconsumption of fat has led to a number of health problems, contributing to the high levels of obesity and to a high incidence of heart disease. The British Heart Foundation (BHF) argues that in the UK the population needs to eat less fat overall, and to increase the proportion of unsaturated fats. Unsaturated fats can help reduce the amount of cholesterol in the bloodstream.

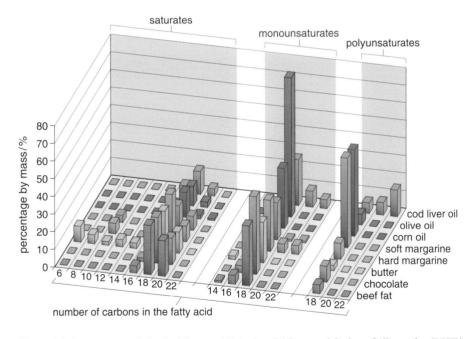

Figure 15.4   Bar chart of the fatty acids content of the fats found in various foods.

■ Which sources of fat in Figure 15.4 should be avoided to follow the BHF's advice and which fats are more acceptable?

☐ Butter, beef fat and chocolate should be consumed in moderation since they contain a high level of triacylglycerols made from saturated fatty acids. Foods containing polyunsaturated fatty acids, such as soft margarine and oily fish, are more acceptable.

Another factor that helps determine the properties of unsaturated fatty acids is the shape of the molecule around the C=C double bond. Often when a compound contains a C=C double bond, it can come in two forms called *cis* (pronounced 'sis') and ***trans***. Note that by convention these terms are always written in italics. As shown in Figure 15.5, *cis* double bonds have the two hydrogen atoms on the same side, while *trans* double bonds have the two hydrogen atoms on opposite sides. You will explore the shape of these molecules in Activity 15.1.

Figure 15.5 (a) Oleic acid can be represented as a simple linear molecule, as shown here, but in fact the molecule can occur in two quite different forms, depending on the arrangement of groups around the C=C double bond.
(b) *cis*-oleic acid is the naturally occurring form, and has the two hydrogen atoms on the same side of the double bond.
(c) *trans*-oleic acid has the two hydrogen atoms on the opposite sides of the double bond; it is not naturally occurring.

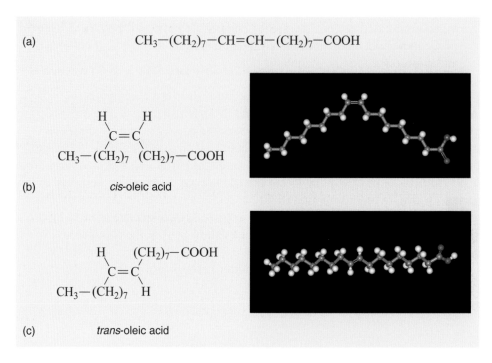

(a) $CH_3-(CH_2)_7-CH=CH-(CH_2)_7-COOH$

(b)   *cis*-oleic acid

(c)   *trans*-oleic acid

Naturally occurring fatty acids tend to be in the *cis* form, and there is some evidence that these are healthier than the *trans* form. The *trans* fatty acids tend to have similar properties to the less healthy unsaturated fats.

Finally in this section, it is important to note that each triacylglycerol molecule is made from three fatty acids and a single molecule of glycerol, but these fatty acids are not always the same. As shown in Figure 15.4, a particular fat or oil is produced from a large range of fatty acids. In fact, rather than being a single compound, a particular fat or oil is made up of a mixture of different triacylglycerol molecules, each derived from different combinations of three fatty acids. While some of the triacylglycerols will be made from three identical fatty acids, the majority of triacylglycerol molecules are derived from two or three different fatty acids, for example structures **15.2** and **15.3**.

15.2   **15.3**

15.1.2 Some reactions of fats

You have seen that saturated fats contain only the ester functional group, while the unsaturated fats contain both the ester and alkene functional groups. Remember that an important part of the functional group approach is that you can assume that the hydrocarbon part of the molecule is unreactive, and acts as a spectator. You can therefore assume that almost all chemical reactions involving fats will involve either the ester or alkene groups.

Table 14.3 introduced a reaction of esters: **hydrolysis**. A hydrolysis reaction is one in which a molecule is split into two or more parts in a reaction with water. The general equation for the hydrolysis of an ester is:

$$R^1-\overset{\displaystyle O}{\underset{\displaystyle O-R^2}{C}} \; + \; H_2O \; \longrightarrow \; R^1-\overset{\displaystyle O}{\underset{\displaystyle OH}{C}} \; + \; HO-R^2 \qquad (15.5)$$

You might notice that this reaction is the reverse of a condensation reaction.

The hydrolysis of triacylgycerides is an extremely important process, and follows the general form in Equation 15.6 for the hydrolysis of a triacylglycerol:

$$
\begin{array}{l}
CH_2-O-\overset{O}{\overset{\|}{C}}-R \\
CH-O-\overset{O}{\overset{\|}{C}}-R \quad + \quad 3H_2O \quad \longrightarrow \\
CH_2-O-\overset{O}{\overset{\|}{C}}-R
\end{array}
\quad
\begin{array}{l}
CH_2-O-H \\
CH-O-H \quad + \quad 3\left(HO-\overset{O}{\overset{\|}{C}}-R\right)(15.6) \\
CH_2-O-H
\end{array}
$$

The hydrolysis of the triacylglycerols is the first step in their digestion and in humans occurs in the small intestine. The process is catalysed by **enzymes** called lipases. Enzymes are biological catalysts, and you will learn much more about enzymes in Book 5.

Hydrolysis is also one of the processes that cause fats and oils go rancid. When butter becomes rancid, its unpleasant taste and smell comes from the short-chain fatty acids that are released. The process is catalysed in this instance by enzymes secreted by various microbes. A similar process is involved in the production of cheeses. Here the fats are hydrolysed by the enzymes from the moulds that develop as the cheese matures. The fatty acids that are released are a major element of the flavour of the cheese.

The fact that saturated hydrocarbon chains are relatively inert to many chemical reactions means that the hydrocarbon chains in saturated fatty acid esters do not undergo many reactions. However, since unsaturated fatty acid esters contain an alkene functional group, these fats can undergo a number of reactions specific to double bonds. The most important reaction, which is characteristic of all double bonds, is an addition reaction, shown in Equation 15.7 (see Table 14.3).

$$R^1-CH=CH-R^2 \; + \; X-Y \; \longrightarrow \; R^1-\overset{\displaystyle X}{\underset{}{CH}}-\overset{\displaystyle Y}{\underset{}{CH}}-R^2 \qquad (15.7)$$

Hydrogenation is the addition of hydrogen across a double bond to give a hydrocarbon. The process requires the presence of a metal catalyst. Using the generalised form of an alkene, the hydrogenation reaction is:

$$R^1-CH=CH-R^2 \quad + \quad H_2 \quad \xrightarrow{\text{catalyst}} \quad R^1-CH_2-CH_2-R^2 \quad (15.8)$$

The terms saturated and unsaturated arise from the fact that unsaturated compounds contain double bonds which can react with reagents such as hydrogen to give saturated compounds. However, saturated compounds do not react – they are full up, or saturated, with hydrogen.

■ Predict the structure of the product obtained from the hydrogenation of an oleic acid ester (see Table 15.1 for the structure of oleic acid).

☐ This reaction converts the oleic acid ester into a stearic acid ester:

$$CH_3(CH_2)_7-CH=CH-(CH_2)_7-\overset{\overset{\displaystyle O}{\displaystyle \|}}{C}-O-R \xrightarrow{H_2/\text{catalyst}} CH_3(CH_2)_7-CH_2-CH_2-(CH_2)_7-\overset{\overset{\displaystyle O}{\displaystyle \|}}{C}-O-R \quad (15.9)$$

The metal catalyst is usually platinum, palladium or nickel.

■ In general terms, how does a catalyst make a reaction go faster?

☐ The catalyst provides an alternative, faster reaction pathway.

This reaction (Equation 15.9) is very important in the manufacture of fats for spreading (Figure 15.6). Margarine is usually made by mixing oils with fat-free milk. Low-fat spreads contain 40–80% fat, whereas hard margarine has a minimum of 80% fat. The rest is water, so if you pay extra for a low-fat spread

Figure 15.6 Flow diagram of margarine production. The process occurs at relatively high temperatures so that the fat is in liquid form. The reaction takes place at temperatures of above 170 °C and at high pressures. While the reaction mixture needs heating at first to get it up to temperature, the reaction is exothermic so further heating is not required.

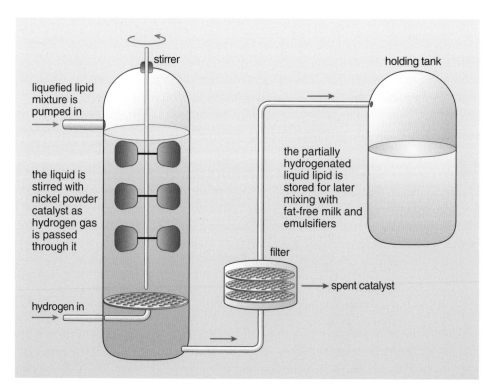

you are paying for more water! Several different types of oil are blended together to get margarine of the right consistency.

In general, saturated fats tend to be relatively solid, while unsaturated fats tend to be liquids. In order to produce a margarine that is relatively solid, but still spreadable, the fat has to be made more saturated, by reducing the proportion of double bonds. Manufacturers do this by carefully hydrogenating unsaturated vegetable oils. In the past, this process also unfortunately converted a proportion of the naturally occurring *cis* fats into less healthy *trans* fats, but modern manufacturers have found ways to minimise this unwanted side-reaction.

Before moving on from this section, it is important to note that, despite their bad reputation, fats are vital to our diet. Some polyunsaturated fatty acids, for example linolenic and arachidonic acids (Table 15.1), are often referred to as the 'essential fatty acids'. Our biochemical systems are incapable of producing these fatty acids, and they have to be present in our diets. After ingestion, they are converted to a group of hormones called the eicosanoids. You will learn more about hormones in Book 5, but for now it is enough to say that these compounds are involved in the control of many biological processes, and play a vital role in our response to infection.

Question 15.1

In Activity 14.2, you analysed the structure of the emulsifier glyceryl monostearate (structure **14.6**), which you should now recognise as a monoacylglyceride. This compound can be formed by the reaction of a fatty acid and glycerol. Draw out the chemical equation by which this molecule can be formed, including the full structural formulas of the molecules involved.

14.6

15.2 Proteins

Most people know what fats or sugar (a carbohydrate) physically look like. However, proteins are more difficult to identify because they occur in so many different forms. Most people might identify protein with eggs, cheese or meat, but even in lean beef there is only 20% protein and in eggs 12%, the rest being water and fat. In fact, low-fat soya flour has one of the highest percentage protein contents at 45%. Some proteins are present in nature as the structural part of tissue, as in muscle, tendons and hair. Others play an important part in cells as the molecules that carry out and control many of the bodily functions.

Proteins are made by joining together smaller compounds called **amino acids**. Alanine, structure **15.4**, is a typical amino acid.

$$H_2N-CH-\overset{\displaystyle O}{\overset{\displaystyle \|}{C}}-OH$$
$$\underset{\displaystyle CH_3}{|}$$

15.4 alanine

■ Using Table 14.3, identify the functional groups in alanine.

☐ The functional groups are highlighted in green and correspond to the carboxylic acid functional group:

$$H_2N-CH-\boxed{\overset{\displaystyle O}{\overset{\displaystyle \|}{C}-OH}}$$
$$\underset{\displaystyle CH_3}{|}$$

☐ and an amino functional group (NH_2):

$$\boxed{H_2N}-CH-\overset{\displaystyle O}{\overset{\displaystyle \|}{C}}-OH$$
$$\underset{\displaystyle CH_3}{|}$$

The amino group is a functional group you have not come across before (at least not in this course). If the amino group is the only functional group in a molecule, the substance will be an example of a class of compounds called amines. The simplest is methylamine, CH_3NH_2, a compound that smells strongly of rotten fish!

There are 20 or so common, naturally occurring amino acids; some of them are shown in Figure 15.7.

Figure 15.7 The structural formulas of the amino acids valine, leucine and isoleucine.

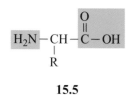

$$H_2N-CH-\overset{O}{\overset{\|}{C}}-OH$$
$$CH-CH_3$$
$$CH_3$$
valine

$$H_2N-CH-\overset{O}{\overset{\|}{C}}-OH$$
$$CH_2$$
$$CH-CH_3$$
$$CH_3$$
leucine

$$H_2N-CH-\overset{O}{\overset{\|}{C}}-OH$$
$$CH-CH_3$$
$$CH_2$$
$$CH_3$$
isoleucine

■ What are the common structural features of these amino acids?

☐ They all contain an amino group and a carboxylic acid group attached to the central carbon atom of an $H_2N-CH-COOH$ group.

Structure **15.5** shows the general formula of all the amino acids. The group R is known as the side-chain and represents a range of different structures.

$$\boxed{H_2N}-CH-\overset{\displaystyle O}{\overset{\displaystyle \|}{C}}-OH$$
$$\underset{\displaystyle R}{|}$$

15.5

■ Identify the R groups in the amino acids in Figure 15.7.

☐   The R groups are shown in blue in Figure 15.8.

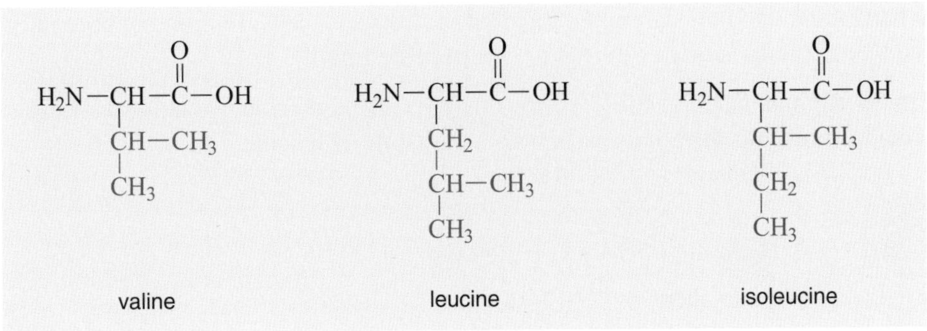

Figure 15.8   The R groups in valine, leucine and isoleucine are shown in blue.

You have seen that alcohols react with carboxylic acids to give esters; amines react with carboxylic acids in a similar way, to give **amides**:

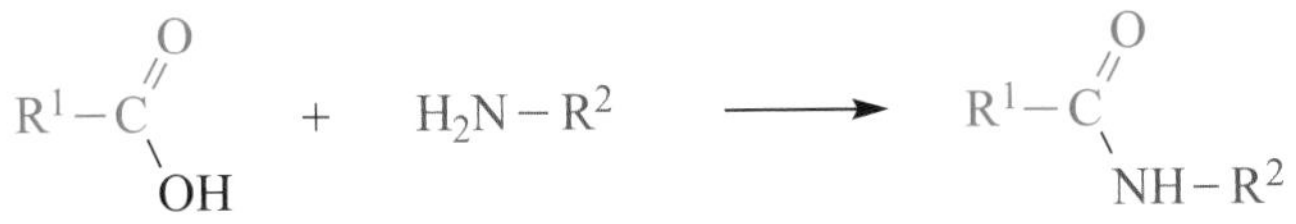

■   Look back at Table 14.3 and identify what type of reaction this is.

☐   It is a condensation reaction. The carboxylic acid and amine molecules react together to form a new larger molecule, together with a molecule of water.

Note that another new class of compounds, the amides, have been introduced, and that these always contain the amide functional group:

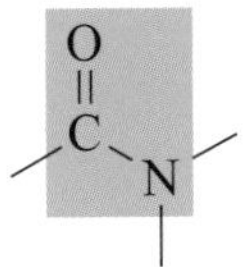

Alternative ways of drawing amides are given in Table 14.3.

Amino acids contain both amine and carboxylic acid functional groups, so they can form amides by undergoing condensation reactions with themselves. Equation 15.11 shows two alanine molecules reacting together:

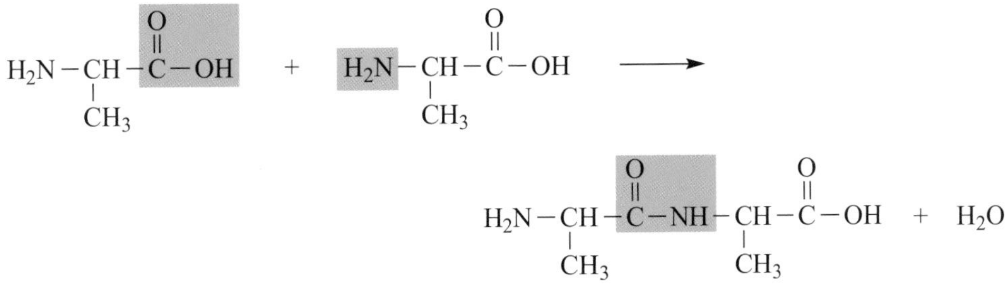

(15.11)

225

The reacting functional groups are highlighted, as is the amide group that is formed.

When two amino acids are liked together in this way, the C—N bond of the amide functional group is often referred to as a **peptide bond**.

The two amino acids reacting together may be different, as in Equation 15.12 in which a molecule of valine reacts with a molecule of leucine:

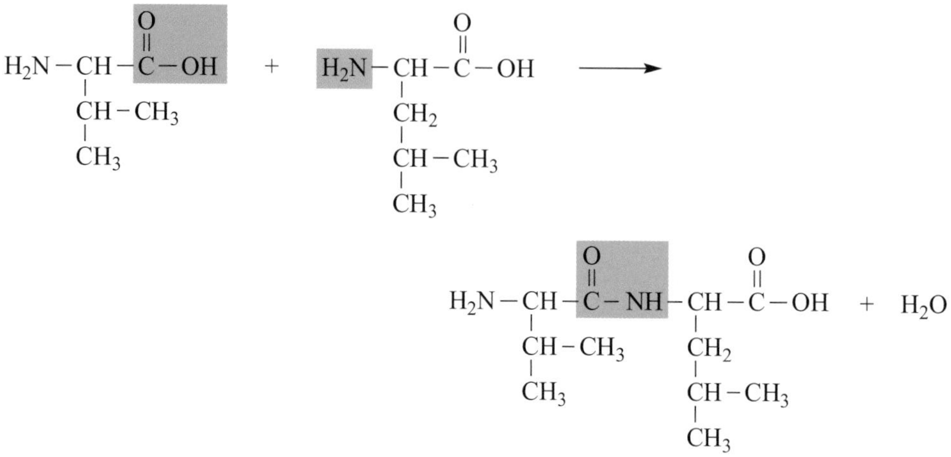

(15.12)

Equations 15.11 and 15.12 show that the product of a condensation reaction between two amino acids will always have a carboxylic acid group at one end and an amino acid group at the other. This means that the product can react with more amino acids. Irrespective of how many amino acids groups are added to the chain, it will always have a carboxylic acid group at one end and an amino group at the other, so very long chains can be built up (Figure 15.9). These very long

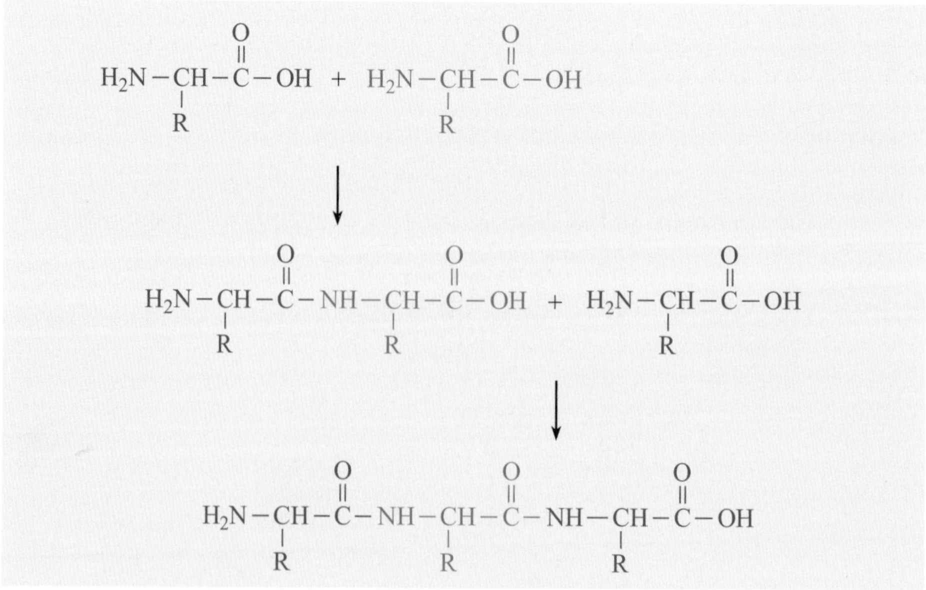

Figure 15.9   Formation of a peptide from amino acids.

chains are called **polypeptides** – a protein is a substance made up of one or more polypeptides. The term **peptide** is often used to refer to smaller chains of amino acids joined together. The terms peptide, polypeptide and protein tend to be used rather loosely; the important point is that you remember that they all refer to chains of amino acids linked together by peptide bonds.

■   What is the name of a long-chain molecule made up of very many smaller units linked together?

☐   A polymer. As proteins are found in biological systems, they are often referred to as **biopolymers**.

Peptides and polypeptides are polymers formed via condensation reactions from amino acid monomers (Section 13.3.1). Polymers formed in this way are called **condensation polymers**. In order to form condensation polymers, the monomers must have two functional groups, one at either end of the molecule, so that each monomer can join to the chain in two places. It may be easier to think of this by using an analogy. If railway carriages have only one coupling each, they can only be joined in pairs. However, if they have two couplings each, one at each end, they can form a long train. The couplings that monomers have are functional groups, which allow them to form at least two covalent bonds to other monomers, thereby building up long chains.

Although the backbone of the peptide polymer has the same repeating unit, there will be a rich diversity in the order of side-chains and this leads to the many different properties and uses of proteins. The structural unit that each amino acid contributes to the biopolymer is known as the **amino acid residue**, as shown in Figure 15.10a. The sequence of amino acid residues in a particular protein is known as the **primary structure** of the protein. When writing out the sequence of amino acid residues, rather than draw out the structure, a three-letter abbreviation is often used to show the order, as shown in Figure 15.10b. The convention used is that the amino end of the chain is always on the left and the carboxylic acid group always on the right.

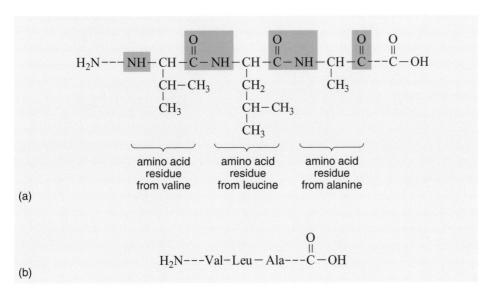

Figure 15.10   Two representations of part of a protein chain: (a) using the structural formulas and (b) using the three-letter abbreviations. (The dotted lines represent the rest of a long chain of atoms.)

With roughly 20 amino acids to choose from, and each chain containing hundreds and sometimes thousands of amino acid residues, it is clear that the number of different possible protein molecules is almost limitless. It can be calculated that for a medium-sized protein containing 288 amino acids residues, using only 12 of the possible 20 amino acids, there are over 10 300 possibilities! However, as you might imagine, in nature nothing is left to chance. When proteins are made in living organisms, the order in which the constituent amino acids are added together is carefully controlled.

15.2.1   Handedness in proteins

It is appropriate at this point to introduce one of the most important properties of biological molecules – their 'handedness'. You may be aware that, except to the finest detail, our hands are mirror images of each other (Figure 15.11). They have the same features and same shape, yet they are not identical. If you put one hand flat on a table and then place the other hand on top, it is obvious that you cannot arrange them such that all of the features of one hand occupy exactly the same positions and space as those of the other. Our hands are therefore not superimposable, and are said to be non-superimposable mirror images.

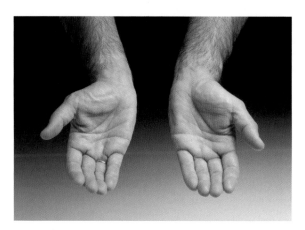

Figure 15.11   Hands are mirror images of each other; they are non-superimposable.

It may come as a surprise to learn that many molecules have 'handedness' too. Molecular handedness arises because of the way four atoms, or groups of atoms, can be arranged around a tetrahedral carbon atom. You will explore this further when you complete Activity 15.1.

For now, examine Figure 15.12a. This shows a carbon atom surrounded by four groups, two of which are identical; they are arranged so that the two models are mirror images of each other. You should be able to see that they are if you manipulate them so that each atom or group occupies exactly the same position in space (Figure 15.12b).

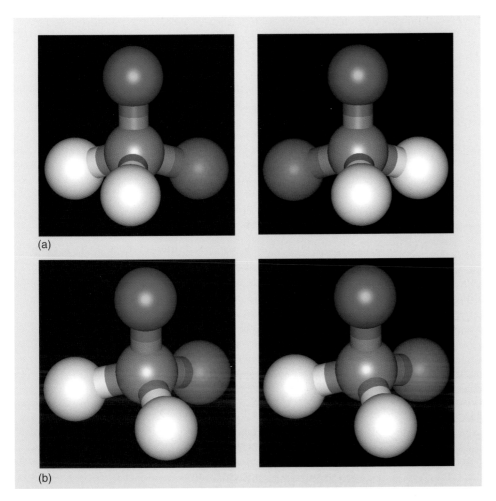

Figure 15.12 (a) Models of a carbon atom surrounded by four groups, two of which are the same. They are arranged to be mirror images of each other. (b) The two models can be manipulated so that all the groups are in identical positions; they are superimposable.

Now examine Figure 15.13a (overleaf). Note that this time all of the groups around the carbon atom are different. Once again the models have been arranged to help you see that they are mirror images of each other. But are they identical? In fact, it is impossible to manipulate the models so that all the groups are in the same position (Figure 15.13b).

This is a general result – whenever a carbon atom is surrounded by four different groups, there are always two ways of arranging the groups around the carbon atom. This means that it is possible to obtain molecules that are, like hands, identical in every respect except that they are mirror images of each other. The Greek word for hand is *chiros* (pronounced 'kye-ros'), so carbon atoms with four different groups around them are said to be **chiral** (pronounced 'kye-ral').

Figure 15.13 (a) Models of a carbon atom surrounded by four different groups. They are arranged to be mirror images of each other. (b) The two models cannot be manipulated so that all the groups are in identical positions; they are non-superimposable.

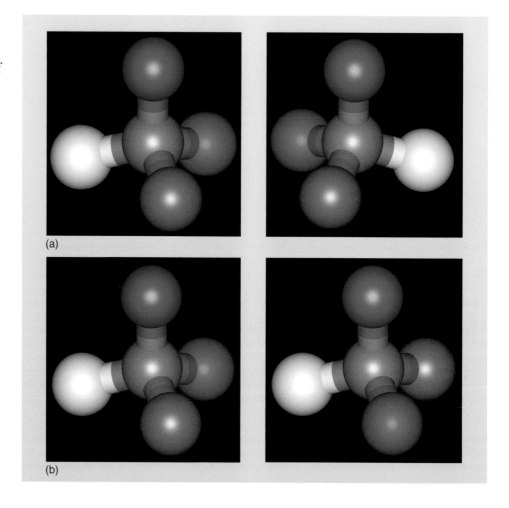

(a)

(b)

If you look again at the general structure of amino acids (structure **15.5**), you should see that the central carbon atom is surrounded by four different groups, and therefore predict that amino acids are chiral.

$$H_2N-CH-\overset{\overset{\displaystyle O}{\|}}{C}-OH$$
$$|$$
$$R$$

15.5

This is indeed the case; with the exception of glycine (where R = H), all amino acids can exist in two chiral forms. In general, only one form of each amino acid is found in nature, the so-called L-form. It seems that all living things have evolved to deal with only one mirror image of the amino acids. Why this should be the case is an area of ongoing research, a question to which there is no conclusive answer at the moment.

15.2.2   Reactions of proteins

This section on proteins concludes by looking at how they are broken down during digestion. In humans, this is a reaction that occurs in the stomach and small intestine.

The long chain of amino acid residues is broken up into its constituent amino acids, by reaction with water:

$$\text{H}_2\text{N}---- \underset{\text{R}^1}{\text{NH}-\text{CH}}-\overset{\text{O}}{\overset{\|}{\text{C}}}-\underset{\text{R}^2}{\text{NH}-\text{CH}}-\overset{\text{O}}{\overset{\|}{\text{C}}}-\underset{\text{R}^3}{\text{NH}-\text{CH}}-\overset{\text{O}}{\overset{\|}{\text{C}}}----\overset{\text{O}}{\overset{\|}{\text{C}}}-\text{OH} \quad + \quad 3\text{H}_2\text{O}$$

(15.13)

$$\underset{\text{R}^1}{\text{H}_2\text{N}-\text{CH}}-\overset{\text{O}}{\overset{\|}{\text{C}}}-\text{OH} \; + \; \underset{\text{R}^2}{\text{H}_2\text{N}-\text{CH}}-\overset{\text{O}}{\overset{\|}{\text{C}}}-\text{OH} \; + \; \underset{\text{R}^3}{\text{H}_2\text{N}-\text{CH}}-\overset{\text{O}}{\overset{\|}{\text{C}}}-\text{OH}$$

Equation 15.13 shows the breakdown of a fragment of protein.

■   What type of reaction is this?

☐   It involves breaking bonds by the addition of water – it is a hydrolysis reaction.

The hydrolysis of amides is not, under normal circumstances, an easy reaction to perform. In the laboratory, you would probably need to boil the protein with strong acid or base for an extended period. The reaction occurs relatively quickly during digestion, because the process is speeded up by enzymes known as peptidases and proteases.

The amino acids produced are absorbed into the bloodstream and used by the body to build new proteins, for energy, or may be processed further to produce other essential biological chemicals.

Question 15.2

A short peptide made of three amino acid residues is described in a biology textbook as Gly–Val–Ala. Draw the full structural formula of this peptide. (Remember that Gly = glycine, Val = valine and Ala = alanine.)

Question 15.3

Which of the following molecules are chiral?

(a) $\underset{\text{H}}{\overset{\text{Br}}{\text{Cl}-\text{C}-\text{Br}}}$

(b) $\underset{\text{NH}_2}{\overset{\text{CH}_3}{\text{H}-\text{C}-\text{COOH}}}$

(c) $\underset{\text{CH}_3}{\overset{\text{COOH}}{\text{H}-\text{C}-\text{CH}_3}}$

(d) $\underset{\text{H}}{\overset{\text{Br}}{\text{CH}_3-\text{C}-\text{Cl}}}$

15.3   Carbohydrates

The simplest carbohydrates are the **sugars**. Household sugar is sucrose, obtained from sugar cane or sugar beet. There is also milk sugar (lactose), malt sugar (maltose), grape sugar (glucose) and fruit sugar (fructose). More complex carbohydrates include cellulose, starch, pectin and glycogen. The carbohydrates are a widespread class of organic compound, with important biological functions, for example providing structural support (cellulose in plants) and as energy stores (glycogen in animals, starch in plants). Nevertheless, despite the variety, they are all based on the same basic unit.

The structures of carbohydrates can seem complicated, but you need not worry too much about them. The important factors will be highlighted. Rather than remember each structure, it is more important that you get a feel for how the structures can differ.

We will start with a simple sugar, glucose, sometimes called dextrose. This is found in grapes (7% by mass) and onions (2%) but the richest source is honey (31%). It plays an essential part in the metabolism of all plants and animals and is the main product of photosynthesis, the process by which plants use light energy from the Sun to convert atmospheric carbon dioxide into useful chemicals. Human blood has about 80–120 mg of glucose in every 100 ml and glucose is the only sugar that can be utilised by the brain. Glucose has the molecular formula $C_6H_{12}O_6$, and its structure is shown in Figure 15.14a.

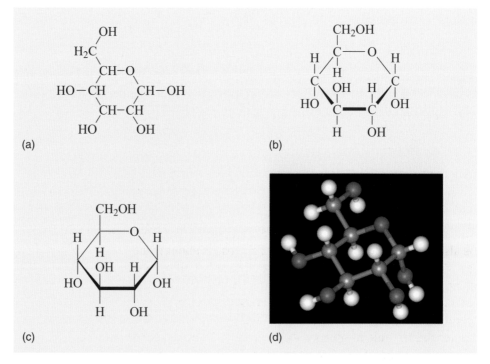

Figure 15.14   Four ways of representing the structure of glucose: (a) the abbreviated structural formula; (b) a perspective view with carbon atoms labelled; (c) a perspective view without carbon atoms labelled (a Haworth projection); (d) a ball-and-stick model for comparison.

Glucose consists of a ring of six atoms – five are carbon atoms and one is an oxygen atom, as shown in Figure 15.14a. Attached to the carbon atoms are four OH groups and one CH_2OH. This structure has a precise three-dimensional shape, which helps to determine its properties. Figures 15.14b and 15.14c show 'sideways-on' perspective views which give some indication of this shape. Figure 15.14c is an example of a Haworth projection – a way of representing sugars developed by the English chemist W. N. Haworth (1883–1950). The Haworth projection is a very useful way of drawing sugars, but it is not particularly accurate, as the ring of six atoms is not flat and each carbon atom is tetrahedral. The ball-and-stick model shown in Figure 15.14d gives a far better indication of the real shape of the molecule. However, it is not convenient to draw a ball-and-stick model every time you want to discuss a sugar molecule. Despite their limitations, either the full structural formula (as in Figure 15.14a) or a Haworth projection (as in Figure 15.14c) will be used to represent sugar molecules here. You will explore more about the shapes of simple carbohydrates in Activity 15.1, at the end of this chapter.

Using the functional group approach, you should notice that there are five hydroxyl (OH) groups in the molecule, and you might expect that this compound will behave something like the alcohols you have explored in Chapter 14. In many ways this is true, but one of the hydroxyl groups behaves slightly differently, due to the proximity of the oxygen in the ring. In fact, this forms part of a different functional group – an **acetal** (Figure 5.15).

The simple acetals you are expected to spot will always contain the group:

R—C—O—
with OH above C and H below C

Alternative ways of drawing acetals are given in Table 14.3. (Note that in many carbohydrates, this functional group forms part of a ring of atoms.)

Let's now look at another simple carbohydrate, fructose, which is also found in honey (about 35%). Fructose is about twice as sweet as household sugar (sucrose). So, only half as much is needed to sweeten a meal. Fructose, therefore, can be part of a calorie-controlled diet. Unlike glucose, it can be used by people with the disease diabetes mellitus. Fructose has the same molecular formula as glucose, but a slightly different structure, as shown in Figure 15.16. One form of fructose has a five-atom ring structure.

■ Identify the one acetal and four alcohol functional groups in fructose (Figure 15.16a).

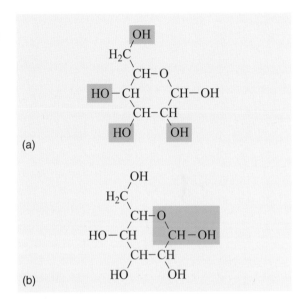

(a)

(b)

Figure 15.15   Structural formula of glucose with (a) alcohol functional groups and (b) acetal functional groups highlighted.

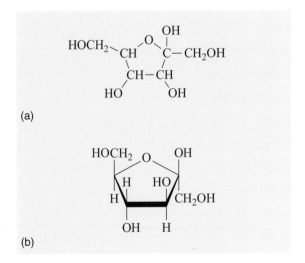

(a)

(b)

Figure 15.16   Simple cyclic structure of fructose: (a) the abbreviated structural formula; (b) a perspective view without carbon atoms labelled (a Haworth projection).

□ The functional groups are identified in Figure 15.17.

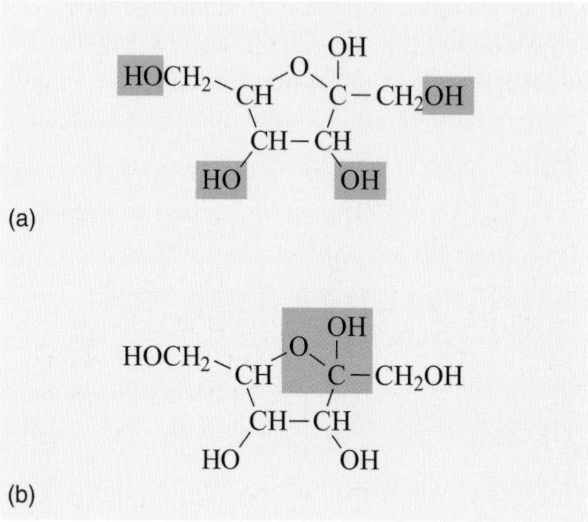

Figure 15.17 Fructose with (a) the alcohol functional groups and (b) the acetal functional group highlighted.

Acetal functional groups can undergo condensation reactions with —OH groups in alcohols or other acetals, so glucose and fructose can react together (Equation 15.14). The product is sucrose, or household sugar. The sugar used in the home has not been made using this reaction, but rather has been extracted from sugar cane or sugar beet. Sucrose is of immense commercial importance – in the early part of this century, worldwide sucrose production was over 130 million tonnes.

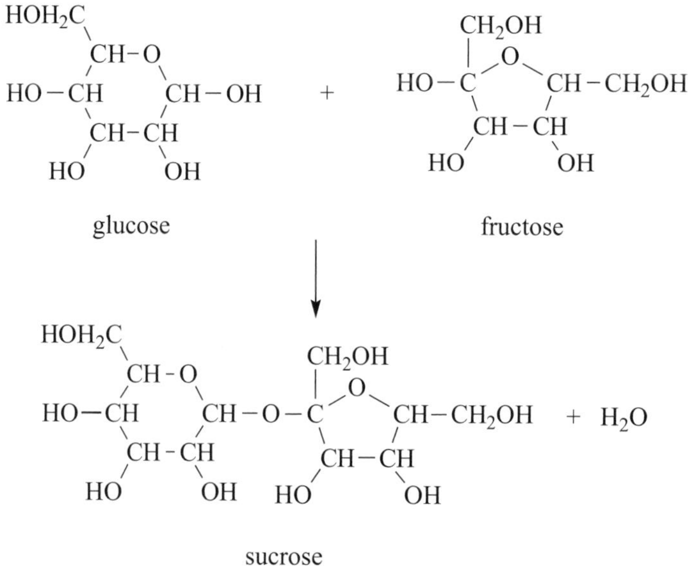

(15.14)

Equation 15.14 shows the formation of sucrose (household sugar) from glucose and fructose.

Carbohydrates such as fructose and glucose that involve only one sugar unit are known as **monosaccharides** (pronounced 'mono-sack-a-rides') from the

Latin for sugar – *saccharum*. Sucrose involves two sugar units, fructose and glucose, and so is known as a **disaccharide** (pronounced 'dye-sack-a-ride'). Other disaccharides are maltose, obtained when starchy material is broken down, and lactose, present in human (5%) and cows' (8%) milk. Maltose is formed by joining two glucose units together and lactose is made from glucose and another sugar, galactose.

Many sugar units can be joined together to form biopolymers called **polysaccharides**, such as cellulose and starch. Cellulose is the main structural carbohydrate of plants and as such is widely distributed from the toughest tree trunk to the softest cotton wool. Cellulose is the most abundant organic compound on Earth, comprising more than half of the organic carbon. 10^{15} kg of cellulose is synthesised and degraded on Earth each year! This polymer is made by joining together glucose units (Figure 15.18); as many as 12 000 units may be linked together in a single cellulose chain.

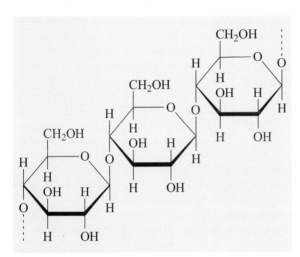

Figure 15.18 Cellulose consists of a series of glucose units linked end-to-end in very long, unbranched chains. This figure shows only three glucose units linked together. In reality many thousands of glucose units will be present in each chain, and a large number of these straight chains will be packed very tightly together.

Although cellulose is the most abundant natural product, humans and most other carnivorous animals cannot digest it. The long flat chains are packed very tightly together, held together by a large number of hydrogen bonds (Section 4.2.3). Our digestive systems cannot break down the strong rigid structure that is formed.

■ Which groups of atoms in the cellulose chain allow it to form hydrogen bonds?

☐ The OH groups.

Cellulose can be used by ruminants such as sheep and cows and by horses and rabbits, which harbour bacteria in their digestive tracts that can breakdown the cellulose into small nutrient molecules that the animal can absorb into its bloodstream.

Cellulose does play an important role in our food as dietary fibre, the importance of which has only recently become apparent. Since it is not digested it passes straight through us. The fibre listed on the food label in Figure 15.1 is likely to be almost exclusively cellulose.

As there are several OH groups in each saccharide unit, there are several ways in which the units can be joined together to form polysaccharides. Many polysaccharides have branched chains and are connected together in such a way that the biopolymer chains cannot pack tightly together. These loosely packed polysaccharides are much easier for humans to digest. Starch is a particularly important example. It is the chief food reserve of all plants, stored in stems, as in the sago palm, or in the tubers as in potatoes and cassava, from which tapioca is made. Under a microscope, starch granules can be seen in the cells of such foodstuffs.

The digestion of starch involves a hydrolysis reaction and, again, it is catalysed by various enzymes. It is easier to picture this process using a simple disaccharide. Equation 15.15 shows the hydrolysis of sucrose (household sugar):

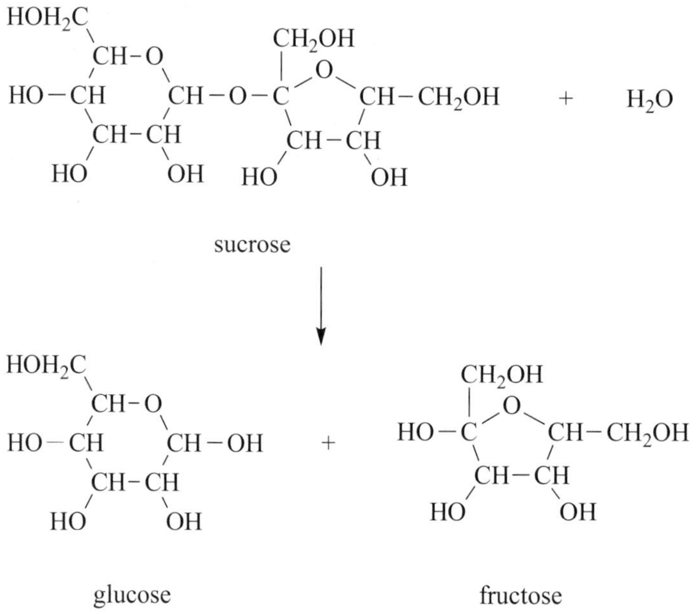

sucrose

(15.15)

glucose   fructose

Industrially, the hydrolysis of sucrose is used to produce syrups – so-called 'golden syrup' is produced in this way. Under the influence of digestive enzymes, a polysaccharide like starch will undergo a similar hydrolysis, to produce glucose molecules.

Finally, this section returns to the concept of 'handedness', more properly called chirality.

■ Look again at the acetal functional group below. Will molecules containing this functional group be superimposable on their mirror images? To put the question in another way, will they be chiral?

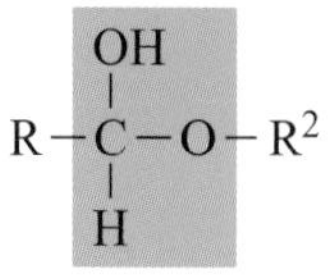

$$R - \overset{\displaystyle OH}{\underset{\displaystyle H}{C}} - O - R^2$$

☐ There are four different groups (R, OH, O—R^2 and H) attached to the central carbon atom, so the molecules will not be superimposable on their mirror images. Acetals, and therefore sugars, are all chiral.

In fact, all sugars contain several chiral carbon atoms and, like proteins, are not superimposable on their mirror images. As you saw in the case of amino acids, only one of the two mirror image forms of sugar tends to be found in nature.

The 'handedness' of sugars has interesting consequences. Our digestive enzymes have evolved to deal with only one of the two mirror images of the sugars – the naturally occurring D-sugars. The alternative unnatural versions – the L-sugars – are indigestible and pass harmlessly through the digestive tract. The labels D and L arise from the way the sugars interact with a particular form of light, but that is a level of detail we don't need to go into here! In tests, panels of subjects have been unable to distinguish between the taste of D- and L-sugars, raising an interesting possibility. Could L-sugars be used as zero-calorie sweeteners? A major problem is that the unnatural sugars are expensive to produce and, at the time of writing, they have not been marketed commercially.

In the 1980s, a group of scientists tested a series of L-sugars for their potential as zero-calorie sweeteners, when they were accidentally sent the wrong batch of tagatose – an obscure sugar found in small quantities in dairy products. They were sent the naturally occurring D-form. They tested it anyway, and found that it was almost as sweet as sucrose, but could only be partially absorbed, and so provided only 25% of the calories of sucrose. Despite initial high hopes, however, D-tagatose has not proved a commercial success as a sweetener.

You may have noticed that a recurring theme in this chapter is the importance of the three-dimensional shape of food molecules in determining how our bodies deal with them. This is a feature of all biological molecules, and this chapter ends with an activity that allows you to visualise some of these molecules using computer graphics.

Question 15.4

Structure **15.6** is the Haworth projection for the monosaccharide galactose. Draw the structural formula for this sugar. Compare both the structural formula and Haworth projection of galactose with the structural formula and Haworth projection of glucose given in Figure 15.14. In what ways are the two sugars similar, and in what ways are they different?

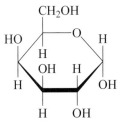

15.6 galactose

Activity 15.1   Viewing food molecules

We expect this activity will take you approximately 30 minutes.

In this activity, you will study a computer-based activity called **Visualising Organic** *Food Molecules*. This will allow you to examine in more detail the shapes of the three classes of food molecules explored in this chapter.

There are no comments on this activity.

15.4   Summary of Chapter 15

In this chapter, you looked at the chemical nature of fats, proteins and carbohydrates.

Fats and oils are mixtures of triacylglycerol molecules. These triacylglycerols are esters made from reacting three fatty acids with glycerol, which contains three —OH groups.

Fats and oils are usually derived from a range of fatty acids. Some contain one or more carbon–carbon double bonds (unsaturated) and some do not (saturated).

Polyunsaturated fatty acids contain more than one double bond.

Naturally occurring fatty acids tend to have a particular orientation of groups around the double bond, in which the hydrogen atoms are on the same side. This is called the *cis* form. Manufacturing processes can result in unnatural *trans* fatty acids, in which the hydrogen atoms are on opposite sides.

Fats and oils are broken down by hydrolysis reactions during digestion.

Unsaturated fats can undergo addition reactions at the alkene functional group. Hydrogenation is an addition reaction used in the manufacture of margarine.

Proteins are biopolymers made from amino acids. There are 20 or so naturally occurring amino acids, of the form:

$$H_2N - CH - \underset{\underset{R}{|}}{C} - OH$$
$$\quad\quad\quad \overset{O}{\overset{||}{}}$$

15.5

Proteins are made by joining amino acids together via peptide bonds. Each amino acid gives rise to an amino acid residue.

Proteins are broken down by hydrolysis during digestion.

Carbohydrates are based on saccharide (sugar) units.

Polysaccharides are chains of saccharide units. These chains can be broken into their constituent units by hydrolysis. Starch is a polysaccharide with an open structure, which is relatively easy to break down. Cellulose is one with a tightly packed structure, which is much more difficult to digest.

Amino acids, sugars, and many other naturally occurring compounds are chiral. The molecules are not superimposable on their mirror images. Usually only one of the two mirror-image forms is found in nature.

The shape of biological molecules is very important in determining their properties.

This chapter has given you the opportunity to develop your skill in interpreting structural formulas.

Chapter 16
Organic molecules in action: pharmaceuticals

Even though proper nutrition and good hygiene go a long way in maintaining a healthy life, our bodies are assailed by a host of biological agents that can cause illness and disease.

■ List some of the biological agents that may cause illness and disease.

☐ Your list may contain such things as viruses, fungi and bacteria.

Degeneration of the body may also be caused by genetic diseases and general breakdown of the system of chemical reactions in the body that maintain life. All of these factors can lead to temporary or long-term health problems. One of the ways of preventing and combating such problems is through the use of pharmaceuticals (drugs) – chemicals useful in the therapeutic treatment of disease.

In this section, you will look at aspects of the chemistry of drug action and some of the thinking that goes into the design of new drugs. Most drugs in common use are organic compounds, often made via a circuitous route from crude oil. You will start by looking at aspirin.

16.1   The discovery of aspirin

Like many drugs, aspirin was developed from a natural remedy. It is very difficult to know when humans first used these natural remedies, but almost 2500 years ago the early physician Hippocrates recommended the use of willow bark for pain control during childbirth. The active ingredient was first isolated from willow bark in 1829; it was salicylic acid (pronounced 'sally-sill-ick'; structure **16.1**).

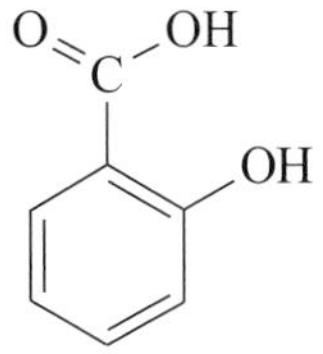

16.1 salicylic acid

Question 16.1

Use the strategy you developed in Activity 14.2 to analyse the structure of salicylic acid. Identify the framework of carbon atoms and the functional groups and their relative positions. For the purposes of this question, assume that the benzene ring is not a functional group, but provides the carbon framework.

■ How is salicylic acid likely to react with sodium hydroxide?

☐ Sodium hydroxide is an alkali, which reacts with acids to give a salt and water. Salicylic acid contains a carboxylic acid functional group that undergoes a neutralisation reaction, as shown in Equation 16.1. Thus salicylic acid reacts with sodium hydroxide to give water and sodium salicylate (pronounced 'sally-sill-ate'), which is a carboxylate salt.

$$\text{(salicylic acid)} + NaOH \longrightarrow \text{(sodium salicylate)} + H_2O \quad (16.1)$$

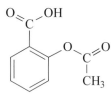

16.2

Sodium salicylate was first used for the treatment of rheumatic fever in 1875. This is a serious illness which causes inflammation of the heart; it is no longer common in developed countries, but is widespread in other parts of the world. Sodium salicylate was an effective treatment, but had the disadvantage of causing severe irritation of the stomach. The Bayer Chemical Company examined a range of compounds derived from the acid, hoping to find a less irritating drug. Acetylsalicylic acid (structure **16.2**) was found to be the best. In 1899, Bayer introduced aspirin, the active component of which is acetylsalicylic acid, as a drug effective against fevers, pain and arthritis. The name aspirin was derived by adding an 'a' for acetyl to 'spirin', which came from the name of the plant, *Spiraea ulmaria*, from which the salicylic acid was prepared. Manufacturers have tried to market the product under other names, but 'aspirin' has stuck (Figure 16.1).

■ Identify the functional groups in acetylsalicylic acid (again assuming that the benzene ring is not a functional group).

☐ Acetylsalicylic acid contains a carboxylic acid functional group and an ester functional group:

■ What is the relationship between acetylsalicylic acid and salicylic acid?

☐ Acetylsalicylic acid is an ester, which is derived from the alcohol functional group of salicylic acid, not from the carboxylic acid group.

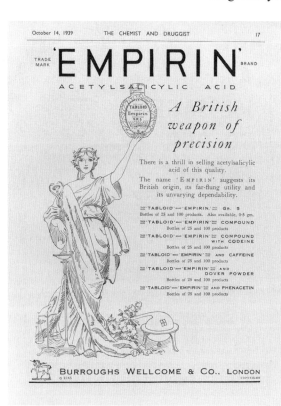

Figure 16.1 Acetylsalicylic acid has appeared under several names. This advertisement was aimed at pharmacists during the Second World War. Despite its discovery by German chemists, the manufacturers marketed Empirin as a uniquely British product.

As you might expect, acetylsalicylic acid can be prepared by the condensation reaction of salicylic acid with acetic acid:

$$(16.2)$$

This story of aspirin demonstrates an important way in which drugs are discovered. Traditional herbal medicines often provide a starting point. The active ingredient can be isolated and then the structure determined. By making a series of slight modifications to the structure of the active compound, a more effective drug can be developed which may have fewer side effects. Some people may be tempted to suggest that the natural compound is 'healthier' than the synthetic compound, but remember that the plant produces salicylic acid for its own purposes, not to cure our headaches. In this instance, the natural compound causes stomach irritation, while its synthetic derivative does not.

16.2 How drugs work

To understand how drugs work, you need to examine, briefly, some of the chemistry that goes on inside an organism. A more thorough understanding will have to wait until you study Book 5. Organisms take in chemicals – like the food they eat or oxygen from the air – which then undergo various transformations to supply materials for building and repairing the organism and to supply energy. These processes are collectively called metabolism, and they are essentially chemical in nature. However, the system of reactions that perform these tasks in the body is very complex, and each reaction or series of reactions is carried out in a controlled and balanced fashion. Illness is often associated with a change in the rate and balance of some of these reactions. Thus, one way of curing the illness is to influence these reactions so they return to their normal state. This is essentially how many drugs work. Put simply, they are chemicals that can influence the reactions that go on in the body. That is why the choice of drug and the dose used are so important. First, the right chemical is needed to influence the right set of reactions that are out of kilter in the body. Second, the right dose must be administered; too little will have no effect, whereas too much may lead to complete shutdown of a particular set of reactions or to unwanted effects on other sets of reactions.

One of the ways in which drugs work is by affecting the properties of enzymes. Enzymes are nature's catalysts, and they are very effective at their job. Like all catalysts, they provide an alternative, faster reaction pathway to that followed by the uncatalysed reaction. They enable reactions to take place in the body that would require quite stringent and extreme conditions in the laboratory. Enzymes are proteins – the biopolymers that were discussed in Chapter 15. More specifically, they are proteins with a particular sequence of amino acids, coiled up in a precise fashion to take up a specific shape.

Figure 16.2 shows two representations of the protease enzyme trypsin, which catalyses the hydrolysis of food protein in the gut (this reaction was discussed in Section 15.2.2). However, the enzyme has a very specific way of working – it does not hydrolyse the amide link between any amino acids, but only where there is a specific sequence of amino acids. As Figure 16.2a shows, the enzyme is an extremely large protein molecule. It contains about 31 000 atoms, mostly carbon, hydrogen, oxygen and nitrogen, and has a relative molecular mass of 231 800. Each molecule of trypsin has this same shape because the sequence of amino acid residues along the chain is the same in every molecule.

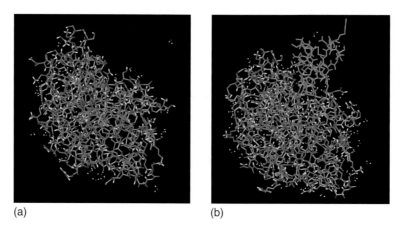

(a) (b)

Figure 16.2   Two representations of the enzyme trypsin: (a) with the active site empty and (b) with the active site occupied by a protein, shown in green at the top right. Note that with complex molecules like this one, it is generally more convenient to use a wire-frame representation in place of a ball-and-stick representation.

You don't need to worry about most of the features of this molecule; you just need to concentrate on a region called the **active site**, which is shown in Figure 16.2b. The active site of an enzyme is the place in the large protein molecule where the chemical reaction actually takes place. It is at this site that the protein in food is converted into smaller molecules. Effectively, a particular segment of the long-chain food protein fits into the active site of the enzyme like a hand into a glove. This site provides the segment of the food protein with the ideal environment for reaction with water, which results in the food protein being broken in two.

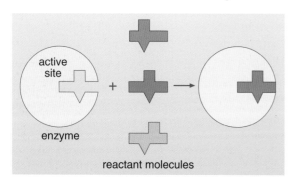

Figure 16.3   Schematic representation of the relationship between the active site of an enzyme and reactant molecules: only one of the three reactants shown has exactly the right shape to fit the active site.

Because reactant molecules have a three-dimensional shape, and because the active site fits like a glove, the active site must have a specifically shaped three-dimensional hole or crevice that will accommodate only a very limited range of reactant molecules (Figure 16.3). As you will see in the next section, this is the key to drug action. This relationship between enzyme and reactant has also been likened to a lock and key. The key fits the lock and will turn it; the reactant fits the active site and reaction occurs.

Enzymes provide one way of controlling the metabolic reactions in an organism. Since enzymes are catalysts, they are not consumed during a reaction. So once an enzyme molecule has catalysed the conversion of one molecule of reactant into product, it is available to catalyse the conversion of more molecules of reactant into product. Thus, only a relatively small amount of an enzyme is needed to catalyse the conversion of a large amount of reactant into product. One of the ways in which an organism 'turns on' a reaction is to supply an active enzyme; the more it provides, the faster the reactant is converted into the product. To slow down or turn off the reaction, the organism simply removes the active enzyme. If the amount of active enzymes in the organism can be controlled, it may then be possible to control the reaction or sets of reactions that are out of kilter. This is one of the ways in which drugs work, by affecting the amount of particular active enzymes. Let's look at an example to make this clearer.

16.2.1   Enzyme action: formation of covalent bonds

Although aspirin has been taken for many years, its mode of action has only relatively recently been discovered. Aspirin has a number of effects: it is

- an analgesic – it reduces pain
- an antipyretic – it lowers the temperature of the body if you have a fever
- an anti-inflammatory drug – it reduces inflammation
- an anticoagulant – it thins the blood and is used long-term to reduce the risk of heart attack.

Some of these effects result from reducing the concentration, in particular parts of the body, of a group of compounds called prostaglandins. You don't need to know the structures of these compounds, which are quite complex, or about their role in controlling body temperature or causing pain, etc. Suffice it to say that aspirin inhibits the production of prostaglandins in the body.

Prostaglandins are all made in a similar way (incidentally from the essential fatty acids you met in Section 15.1). One of the first steps in their production involves an enzyme known as cyclo-oxygenase. Aspirin has the right shape to fit into the active site of the cyclo-oxygenase enzyme, where it reacts with a hydroxyl group attached to one of the amino acid R groups in the enzyme protein, as shown in Figure 16.4.

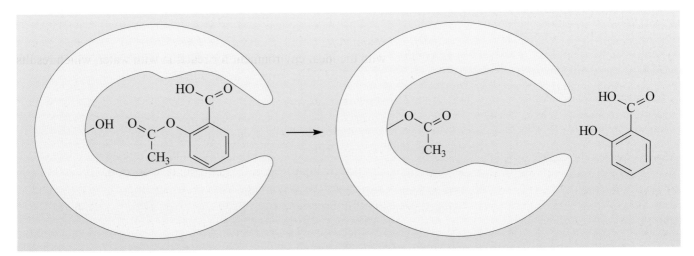

Figure 16.4   Aspirin blocks the active site in cyclo-oxygenase by forming a new covalent bond, to give an ester.

■ The reaction in Figure 16.4 is not one of the reactions in Table 14.3. Look at the functional groups in the reactant and the product, and describe what changes are taking place.

☐ The carboxylic acid group of the aspirin remains unchanged during the reaction. The alcohol group of the amino acid reacts with the ester of the aspirin to give a new ester, which is attached to the enzyme, and salicylic acid.

Once the new ester group is covalently bound to the cyclo-oxygenase enzyme, it blocks the active site, preventing its specific reactant molecules from getting in. Thus, the blocked enzyme can no longer function as a catalyst in the reaction pathway leading to prostaglandins. It is rather like blocking a lock with superglue; the key can no longer get in. The reaction of aspirin with the enzyme reduces the concentration of effective catalyst and so the reaction slows down. This means that, overall, prostaglandin production is reduced and the pain goes away. Only when the body makes unblocked enzyme does prostaglandin production start up again.

So one way for drugs to block enzyme action is through specific covalent bond formation, but drugs can also block enzymes via intermolecular forces.

Question 16.2

Identify the functional groups in paracetamol (structure **16.7**). As before, assume for the purposes of this question that the benzene ring is not a functional group. Would you expect paracetamol to block the cyclo-oxygenase enzyme in the same way that aspirin (structure **16.2**) does?

16.3

16.2.2   Enzyme action: intermolecular forces

Figure 16.5 shows the molecular structures of three related compounds that act on the central nervous system.

* Adrenalin is a molecule found naturally in the body.
* Pseudoephedrine is the active ingredient in medicines, such as Actifed™ and Sudafed™, which are used to relieve nasal and respiratory congestion.
* Salbutamol is used in inhalers for asthma relief, and is sometimes marketed as Ventolin™.

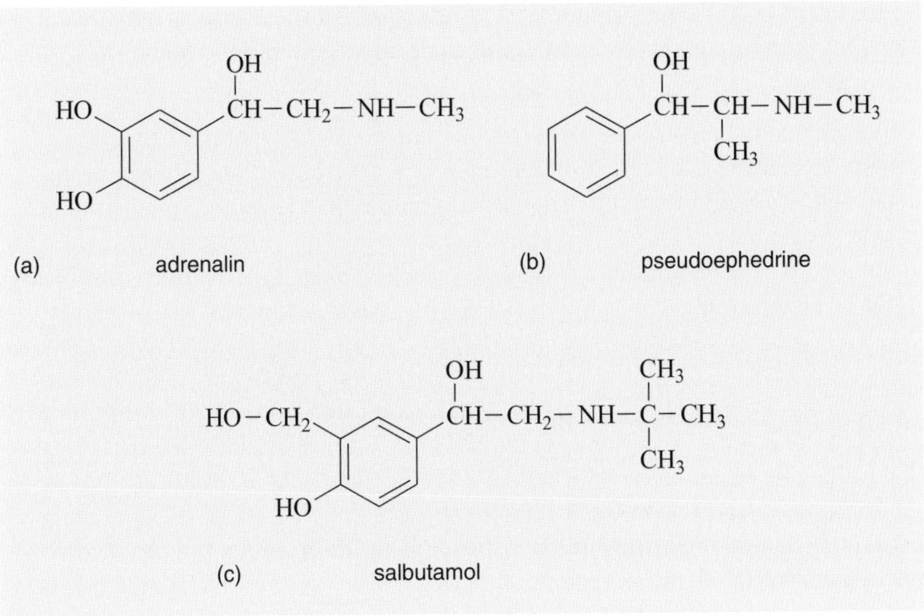

Figure 16.5   The structural formulas of some compounds that act on the central nervous system.

■ Which features are present in all three molecules?

☐ They each contain an alcohol functional group, an amine functional group and a benzene ring, and these three features have the same relative positions in each molecule, as shown in the partial structure **16.4**.

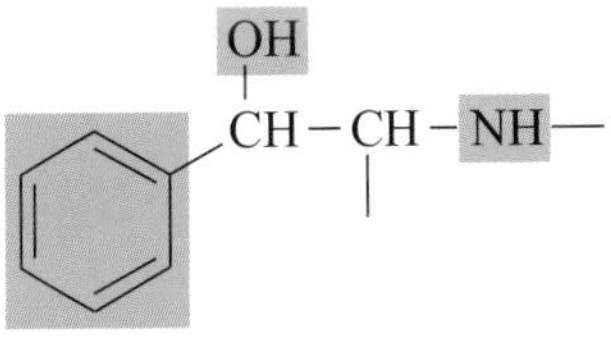

16.4

Despite the different uses to which these compounds are put, they all work in the same way. Unlike aspirin, they do not act on an enzyme but on another type of large protein molecule called a **receptor**. One of the ways in which chemical reactions are controlled in the body is through the use of specific chemicals – **hormones** – that act as 'messengers'. To promote a bodily function, a hormone is made at one site in the body and is then transported in the bloodstream to another site, where it interacts with a receptor, triggering the required response. Like enzymes, receptors have a specific site that will effectively accommodate only one shape and type of molecule. When a hormone binds to a receptor, it stimulates the process it was sent out to initiate, such as the contraction or relaxation of smooth muscle.

All of the compounds in Figure 16.5 act by attaching themselves to receptors. For example, adrenalin is a natural hormone that is released into the bloodstream by the adrenal gland, now known more properly as the suprarenal gland. The gland itself sits above the kidneys, but the adrenalin it releases acts on distant organs such as the heart, lungs and digestive tract. It is sometimes referred to as the 'fight or flight' hormone, and is produced when we are in stressful situations. It promotes rapid heart beat and the release of glucose into the bloodstream. It restricts blood flow to the skin and digestive tract, while increasing the blood supply to the muscles. These actions facilitate an energetic response to the stressful situation – either by responding aggressively (fight) or by running away (flight). Both responses require a good supply of energy to the muscles – hence the increased blood supply and release of glucose. All these effects are a result of adrenalin binding to receptors in the different organs around the body.

Around 10% of the population of developed countries has asthma. During an asthma attack, the airways in the lungs become constricted, and it becomes difficult to breathe. One effect of adrenalin is a widening of the airways in the lungs, and you might imagine that adrenalin could provide some relief from an asthma attack. However, while widening the airways in the lung might relieve the symptoms of an asthma attack, the other aspects of the 'fight or flight' response might be distressing.

Salbutamol (Figure 16.5c) is one of a number of drugs that mimic adrenalin, causing the airways in the lung to widen. However, unlike adrenalin, it does not affect other organs, such as the heart. To understand how salbutamol does this, you need to examine how compounds, such as those in Figure 16.5, bind to receptors.

It is a fairly general rule that, unlike aspirin, most drugs do not bind to receptors by covalent bonds. Covalent bonds, such as C—C, C—O or C—N single bonds, are very strong and would require a large amount of energy to break them once formed. Thus, if a drug is bound to a receptor via a covalent bond it would be difficult to remove and the organ would be continuously stimulated, which is not usually the required response. It is better if drugs are held in the receptor by intermolecular forces of the kinds discussed in Section 4.2. These interactions are much weaker than covalent bonds, and therefore are easier to break. The intermolecular forces allow the drug to bind to the receptor for long enough to have the desired effect. However, because it is held in the receptor by relatively weak interactions, after a while it will leave the receptor and the body will return to its previous state.

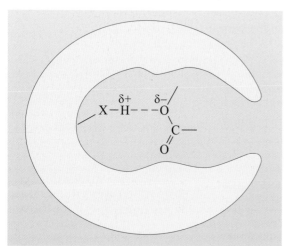

Figure 16.6   Typical hydrogen bonding at a receptor site: X can be a sulfur atom, an oxygen atom or a nitrogen atom.

■ What intermolecular forces have you met that might help bind a molecule to a receptor surface?

☐ Hydrogen bonds and van der Waals forces.

Hydrogen bonds certainly provide suitable interactions for drug binding. For example, if the surface of a receptor site has a hydrogen atom with a $\delta+$ charge, it can form a hydrogen bond to an oxygen atom bearing a $\delta-$ charge in the drug molecule, for example in an ester group. This is shown schematically in Figure 16.6.

Interactions between ions of opposite charge are also significant in the context of drug binding. A suitable pair of functional groups for an ionic interaction are a negatively charged carboxylate ion and a positively charged ammonium ion (Figure 16.7). This is referred to here as an ionic interaction rather than ionic bonding because ionic bonding arises from a network of very many positive and negative charges where ions of opposite charge are small and relatively close to each

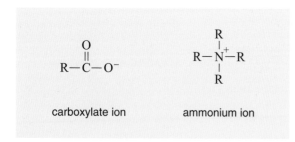

Figure 16.7   A negatively charged carboxylate ion and a positively charged ammonium ion will attract one another.

other. An ionic interaction involves an attraction between isolated positively and negatively charged groups that are usually further apart. As such, ionic interaction, like hydrogen bonding and van der Waals forces, is a much weaker force than a covalent bond.

If there is a receptor molecule with a long hydrocarbon chain, and a drug molecule also with a long hydrocarbon chain, it may well happen that the two chains line up side-by-side, as a result of hydrophobic interactions, as described in Box 16.1. Benzene rings also bind to other benzene rings or hydrocarbon chains by hydrophobic interactions.

Box 16.1 Frightened of water

The reasons why oil and water do not mix are explored in Section 4.6 (see also Figure 16.8). The hydrocarbon chains that make up the oil do not contain any substantially charged atoms that can interact with the $\delta+$ and $\delta-$ charges on the water molecules, and so cannot disrupt the network of hydrogen bonds between the water molecules.

This incompatibility between water and oil means that the oil tries to expose to the water the smallest possible surface, which is a sphere. Such hydrocarbons are said to be hydrophobic, which means 'frightened of water'. This tendency for hydrocarbons to stick together in a charged environment is also observed in biological systems, where hydrocarbon groups try to align themselves next to each other. This is another form of intermolecular interaction, known as hydrophobic interaction, and its importance will become clearer in Book 5.

Figure 16.8 Oil and water not mixing.

16.2.3 Drug specificity

Each of the intermolecular forces described in Section 16.2.2 is relatively weak (from 3 to 10% of the strength of a covalent bond). One such interaction is not enough on its own to bind a messenger molecule to a receptor and stimulate or inhibit a process. However, if a drug is bound to a receptor by more than one intermolecular interaction, it can be held tightly enough to produce the desired effect.

■ Look at the structure of adrenalin in Figure 16.5a. What types of intermolecular interaction would bind adrenalin to a receptor?

☐ The —OH and —NH— groups could bind via hydrogen bonding, and the benzene ring could bind by hydrophobic interaction.

Figure 16.9 shows one way in which adrenalin could bind to its receptor in more than one place. There are two types of interaction: hydrogen bonding and a hydrophobic interaction.

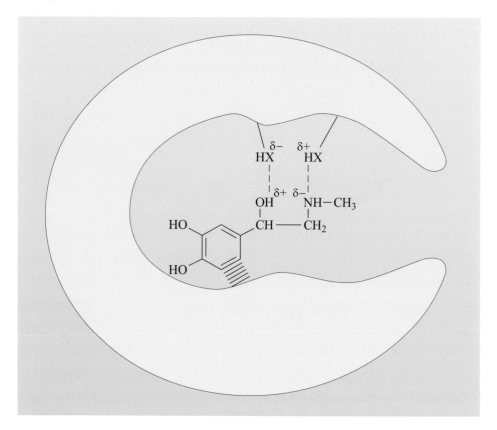

Figure 16.9   Possible binding of adrenalin to a receptor at three places. The dashed lines indicate hydrogen bonds, and there is a hydrophobic interaction between the benzene ring and the receptor surface, indicated by parallel lines.

The requirement for more than one binding site puts very stringent constraints on the composition and shape of drug molecules. First, they must contain functional groups that can undergo the specific types of intermolecular interaction that match the groups on the receptor. Second, the binding points in the receptor occupy defined positions in three-dimensional space, and so the appropriate functional groups on the drug molecule need to match this geometric arrangement. However, the functional groups in a molecule can take up only certain fixed positions relative to each other, and these positions are limited by the overall structure. The net result is that only a few molecules will have the correct functional groups in the correct orientation to bind to a particular receptor.

Binding at more than one place ensures that only molecules with appropriate geometries and functional groups can fit the receptor.

Compounds **16.5**, **16.6** and **16.7** will not bind very well to the receptor in Figure 16.9. Compound **16.5** has only one point for hydrogen bonding – the amine group – rather than the two required. Compound **16.6** has two functional groups in the correct orientation, but one is a chloro group rather than an alcohol. Although the amine group can form a hydrogen bond with the receptor, the chloro group cannot undergo this interaction and so will not bind. Finally, compound **16.7** has the correct three groups but in the wrong positions in space relative to each other. Although one hydrogen bond is possible, say through the —OH group, the other functional group (—NH$_2$) will not be in the right place to form a second hydrogen bond with the receptor.

16.5   **16.6**

16.7

It is no coincidence that the three compounds shown in Figure 16.5 have a common basic structure; after all, they bind to the same type of receptor. However, they do have slightly different structures and this is the source of their specificity. Salbutamol, for example, is similar enough to adrenalin that it binds to the receptors in the airways of the lungs, but it is sufficiently different that it does not stimulate the receptors in the heart.

In this section, you have seen how drugs bind to receptors through intermolecular forces. In general, for a drug to be effective, it must have the correct shape so that it can fit the receptor and it must have appropriate functional groups in the right places (correctly disposed to each other in space) to ensure that it binds to the receptor in more than one place. Drugs can also bind to the active site of enzymes in a similar fashion and block their action. One aspect of the shape of drug molecules not discussed here is their chirality. Often one mirror image of a drug is active, while the other is not. Sometimes the two mirror images can have different effects. One mirror image of the drug thalidomide is a useful treatment for morning sickness during pregnancy; the other causes severe birth defects. The drug was sold as a mixture of the two forms and, between 1956 and 1962, 10 000 children worldwide were born with severe malformities. Partly as a result of this tragedy, much more rigorous testing regimes for new drugs have been introduced.

Discovering drugs with just the right structure may seem a tall order, but an understanding of drug action does allow new drugs to be designed. This latter process demonstrates the true creativity of chemistry. Based on knowledge of a particular receptor or enzyme, a chemist can propose a new drug with a particular structure. Using the functional group approach, the required structure can be built up, bit by bit, from relatively simple starting materials – often derived from crude oil.

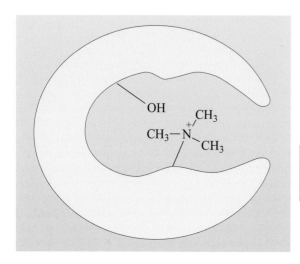

Figure 16.10   An active site on an enzyme.

Question 16.3

An enzyme has an active site with the two functional groups shown in Figure 16.10. Describe the possible interactions between this active site and parts of the ion **16.8**.

$$CH_3-CH_2-CH_2-CH-C\overset{NH_2}{\underset{O^-}{\overset{O}{\diagup}}}$$

16.8

Question 16.4

The ion **16.9** binds to a particular receptor. By looking at the functional groups and their disposition, suggest which of the ions **16.10** to **16.12** are likely to fit the same receptor.

$$CH_3-CH_2-CH_2-CH_2-\underset{\underset{OH}{|}}{CH}-\underset{\underset{C=O}{|}{O^-}}{CH_2}$$

16.9

$$CH_3-CH_2-CH_2-\underset{\underset{OH}{|}}{CH}-\underset{\underset{C=O}{|}{O^-}}{CH_2}$$

16.10

$$CH_2-CH_2-CH_2-CH_2-CH_2-\underset{\underset{OH}{|}}{CH_2}\quad \overset{O^-}{\underset{}{C=O}}$$

16.11

$$CH_3-CH_2-CH_2-CH_2-\underset{\underset{OH}{|}}{CH}-\underset{\underset{N(CH_3)_3}{|}{+}}{CH_2}$$

16.12

16.3   Summary of Chapter 16

Drugs work by affecting the action of enzymes or receptors that control the chemistry that goes on in the body.

Both enzymes and receptors are proteins – biopolymers made from amino acids – and have sites where drugs can bind.

Some drugs react with enzymes or receptors, binding via covalent bonding, and completely blocking their action.

More usually, drugs can bind to enzymes and receptors via weaker intermolecular forces, which have a more temporary effect. Interactions at more than one place in this binding site not only ensure that the drug is bound tightly, but also guarantee that only a few compounds will fit in the site and bind at the correct positions.

Chapter 17
Summary of Book 4

17.1   Sustainable organic chemistry?

In the last few chapters, you have explored organic chemistry – the chemistry of carbon compounds. All the compounds that were discussed have had a biological origin. They may be directly derived from plants and animals, like the nutritional groups discussed in Chapter 15, or be derived from crude oil. You have seen that the petrochemical industry can take crude oil and, through a series a processes of separation and elaboration, convert it into compounds containing a variety of functional groups. Crude oil too has a biological origin – it was formed from organisms that died many millions of years ago.

The fact that we rely on crude oil for both fuel and so many modern materials is problematic. The reserves of crude oil are finite and, when they run out, it will be necessary to find alternative sources of chemical feedstocks.

■   Where do you think the best alternative source of feedstocks for polymers and drugs will be found?

☐   For renewable sources, we will have to depend on plants.

The types of compound in plants are very different from those in crude oil, and so it will be necessary to develop a range of new strategies in order to use these potential new feedstocks. Developing such strategies is one of the fundamental challenges for chemists at the start of the 21st century. One possible new feedstock and fuel is ethanol, derived from the fermentation of sugars using yeast. This is how wine, beer and spirits are made. Distillation of the mixture leads to the isolation of pure ethanol, a good alternative to petrol. The internal combustion engine can be modified to run on almost pure ethanol, while many unmodified cars can run on unleaded petrol containing up to 10% ethanol. In some parts of the world, fuels containing proportions of ethanol derived from biological sources (bioethanol) are becoming commercially available (Figure 17.1).

Ethanol can also be used as a feedstock for the petrochemical industry, because under certain conditions it loses water to give ethene:

$$CH_3-CH_2-OH \longrightarrow CH_2=CH_2 + H_2O \qquad (17.1)$$

Ethene is the simplest alkene, and you have seen that alkenes are the key intermediate in the production of modern materials.

The search for economic, sustainable, alternative feedstocks will no doubt provide many new challenges for chemists over the coming decades but, given the success over recent years in designing a huge variety of molecules for a wide range of applications, there is every reason to believe that this goal will be achieved.

Figure 17.1   A variety of biofuels for use with vehicles have become available. This fuel pump in Santa Fe (New Mexico, USA) allows customers to choose between biodiesel and mixtures containing ethanol.

However, the challenge of moving away from fossil fuels does not simply test the ingenuity of the chemist – it throws up a number of social and political challenges. Deriving chemical feedstocks and fuels from plants might require vast areas of land to be dedicated to the growth of appropriate crops. This in turn poses a problem. Should agricultural land be turned over to the production of crops to replace fossil fuels? This land is desperately needed to produce foodstuffs for a growing global population. The alternative might be to turn wild, uncultivated areas like the rainforests over to agricultural land for this purpose. Are we comfortable with the idea of felling rainforests to produce plastics and fuels? Perhaps the choices will not be so stark, but the potential decline in fossil fuels is a major challenge.

Activity 17.1   Alternatives to oil

We expect this activity will take you approximately 90 minutes.

The need to develop alternatives to products derived from crude oil is a pressing problem for humanity. This activity will allow you to engage with some current ideas about how we might address the issue, and the problems we still face.

You will access a recent article on this subject from a journal in the Open University Library. Having read the article, you will be asked to write a short piece of text that explains for another S104 student some of the issues raised.

This may be the first time you have accessed material from the OU Library. It is a tremendously useful resource, and we hope that this activity will give you the confidence to explore the materials available there. You will find full instructions on the course website.

Now go to Activity 17.1 on the course website.

There are no comments on this activity.

17.2   Looking back at Book 4

The key concepts covered in this book include atomic, ionic and molecular structure; chemical bonding; states of matter: gas, liquid and solid; chemical formulas, structural formulas and chemical equations; the mole and calculations using the mole concept; and the relationship between elements in the Periodic Table. You have also studied energy changes in chemical reactions; chemical equilibrium; acids, bases and pH; rates of chemical reactions and catalysis. In the sections on organic chemistry you have studied the properties and uses of hydrocarbons; simple organic functional groups and their reactions; and organic molecules in food and pharmaceuticals. Wherever possible, in developing these concepts you have referred to the properties of familiar materials – you tested the pH of household substances, and explored the properties of materials like polymers and metals which are especially important in modern life.

As you have progressed through *Exploring science*, you should have found that skills you developed in a particular context can be used, perhaps with some modifications, in a variety of different contexts. This is true of learning skills, mathematical skills, communications skills, and the science skills that you have developed. You will also have discovered that the various areas of science that you have met are connected and interlinked in many different ways. For example, ideas about chemistry in this book are linked to the chemistry of living things in Book 5, to ideas about energy in Book 3 and to the carbon cycle in Book 1. You may think of other links.

You have developed a number of highly varied problem-solving skills in this book. You were introduced to a fairly formal procedure for solving problems in Book 3, where you were mainly concerned with energy calculations. You may have found it helpful to use the approach, possibly modified in some way, to tackle the problems in this book.

You have been asked in some of the activities in this book to note down your technique or strategy for tackling a particular task. For example, you have thought about your strategies for deciding what happens when chemical equilibrium is disturbed, for analysing the structure of organic compounds, and for predicting the products of organic reactions. These strategies relate to specific tasks, but the idea of formulating strategies, so that you have them at your fingertips, ready for use, applies more generally.

While studying the other books, you will have developed techniques and strategies covering numerous areas, ranging from plotting graphs to manipulating algebraic expressions, and from planning a piece of writing to reaching an understanding of a difficult concept. You may find it useful to keep some notes on the strategies you have developed – perhaps as part of your study folder.

In earlier parts of the course, you often had to pull together information from different sections of the book you were studying. As you progress through the course, you will also need to look back to previous books to remind yourself of information introduced earlier. For example, while studying this book you probably needed to refer to Book 3 to remind yourself of ideas about energy introduced there. In doing this, you are developing two important skills: you are transferring scientific information from one context to use it in a different context, and you are *synthesising* – drawing on information from a variety of sources, making connections, and putting it together in a new form to reach a more complete understanding.

There are many places where a system of classification is used in this book. To take two examples from the last few chapters: organic compounds have been classified by their functional groups as alkenes, carboxylic acids, alcohols, esters, and so on; reactions of organic compounds have been classified as addition, condensation, hydrolysis, oxidation and reduction. You should be able to recall other examples of the use of classification in this book and in previous ones.

Scientists often choose to classify things. Classification requires them to pick out key similarities and differences between items, and it can be a very useful technique when there is too much information to comprehend and remember readily. You can make more sense of the information when it is organised in some way. For example, if you remember the reactions of carboxylic acids, you do not have to remember separately how acetic acid, propanoic acid, stearic acid and lots of other organic acids each react.

Classification schemes often make it easier to make sense of new information about the items in the scheme. For example, you already knew about the highly reactive alkali metals and their positions in the Periodic Table, and so learning that they have one electron in their outer shell (electron configuration ns^1) can easily be added to this classification. Indeed, this additional information can then be used to help you to understand and retrieve information on the way in which many elements react.

Moreover, if you can identify an 'item' that you know very little about within a certain class, and you know how that class of things behave, then you can predict the properties of the 'item'. For example, if you knew that decanoic acid is a carboxylic acid, you could predict what reactions it would undergo and what the products would be.

You probably noticed that the summary of this book has taken a slightly different form from the equivalent sections in earlier books. In Books 1, 2 and 3 you were asked to formally record your progress against the course Learning Outcomes, while here you have explored in a general way the skills and knowledge that you have developed in studying this book. It is recommended that you continue to record your progress against Learning Outcomes, even though this is not included as a formal activity here. You may now like to set aside a short time to note the skills from this summary in your study folder, so that you have an ongoing record.

17.3   Looking ahead to Book 5

You have now completed your study of Book 4, but you will find that the chemistry you have learned is crucial to understanding much of the science that is yet to come. This will be particularly true of Book 5, which covers the science of biology. One of the challenges of biology is that it examines the science of living things at every level – it includes the study of the very small, like the chemical reactions in biological systems, and the relatively large, such as whole organisms and even populations of organisms. A significant part of your study of biology will therefore rely on an understanding of the chemistry you have learned here. This will be particularly true of your study of biochemistry – the study of the reactions of the organic chemicals found in living organisms. However, you may be relieved (or possibly disappointed) that your study of biology will not be limited to its chemical aspects.

Answers to questions

Question 2.1

The average abundance of gold in the Earth's crust is $4.0 \times 10^{-7}\%$ by mass, which means that there is an average of 4.0×10^{-7} kg of gold in every 100 kg of the Earth's crust.

1.0 kg of gold would be found in $\dfrac{100 \text{ kg}}{4.0 \times 10^{-7} \text{ kg}}$ kg of rock $= 2.5 \times 10^8$ kg of rock.

Now 20 g represents $\dfrac{20}{1000}$ kg.

So 20 g gold would require $\dfrac{20}{1000}$ kg $\times 2.5 \times 10^8$ kg of rock $= 5.0 \times 10^6$ kg of rock to be extracted.

Question 2.2

The average abundance of carbon in the Universe is 0.3% by mass. In other words, 100 parts by mass of the Universe contain 0.3 parts by mass of carbon.

1 part by mass of the Universe contains $\dfrac{0.3}{100}$ parts by mass of carbon.

One million parts by mass of the Universe contain $\dfrac{0.3}{100} \times 10^6 = 3 \times 10^3$ parts by mass of carbon. So the average abundance of carbon in the Universe is 3×10^3 ppm.

Question 3.1

Assume that the gold leaf is a square sheet of side 1.0 m.

Each side is represented by $\dfrac{1.0 \text{ m}}{2.9 \times 10^{-10} \text{ m}} = 3.45 \times 10^9$ gold atoms.

A layer of area 1.0 m^2 and one atom thick contains $(3.45 \times 10^9)^2 = 1.19 \times 10^{19}$ gold atoms.

In 1.0 g gold, there are $\dfrac{1.0 \times 10^{-3} \text{ kg}}{3.3 \times 10^{-25} \text{ kg}} = 3.03 \times 10^{21}$ atoms.

Therefore, the sheet of gold leaf is $\dfrac{3.03 \times 10^{21}}{1.19 \times 10^{19}} = 2.5 \times 10^2$ atoms thick.

It seems amazing that just by beating pure gold with a hammer, it is possible to get a sheet just 250 atoms thick.

Question 3.2

Subscripts in formulas indicate the number of the atom immediately preceding the subscript (Section 3.3). The formula for ammonia can be written NH_3.

Question 3.3

A hydrogen atom comprises a single proton as the nucleus and an electron. The hydrogen cation is a hydrogen atom that has lost an electron, so is just a proton. A hydrogen cation and a proton are different names for the same thing.

Question 3.4

The atomic number indicates the number of protons in the nucleus. In this case, there are 12 protons together with 12 neutrons which make up the relative atomic mass of 24. There are also 12 electrons in the neutral atom. The charge on the magnesium cation of +2 indicates that there are two fewer electrons than there are protons in the cation, so there are 10 electrons.

Question 4.1

Larger molecules generally have more electrons than smaller molecules. Van der Waals forces are greater in molecules with more electrons so the attractive forces between the molecules are greater for larger molecules. To separate large molecules during boiling, more thermal energy is required, hence higher boiling temperatures.

Question 4.2

The volume of a gas is dependent on its temperature and pressure whereas the volume of a solid tends to vary little with temperature and pressure.

Question 4.3

A key idea is that one mole of a gas occupies a volume of 24.5 dm^3 at 25 °C and one atmosphere pressure.

A volume of 24.5 dm^3 is occupied by 1.00 mol He.

A volume of 1.00 dm^3 is occupied by $\dfrac{1.00}{24.5}$ mol He.

A volume of 2.45 dm^3 is occupied by $2.45 \times \dfrac{1.00}{24.5}$ mol He = 0.100 mol He.

A balloon half the size contains half the number of moles of gas. Note that it does not matter what the gas is; the Avogadro hypothesis applies to any gas. So there will be 0.0500 mol hydrogen, H_2.

Question 4.4

One mole of 'anything' comprises 6.02×10^{23} 'things'. The balloon containing helium has 0.100 moles of helium atoms.

The number of atoms of helium is $(0.100 \times 6.02 \times 10^{23}) = 6.02 \times 10^{22}$. Unlike helium, which exists as atoms, hydrogen forms diatomic molecules, H_2. So 0.0500 moles of hydrogen molecules comprise (2×0.0500) moles of hydrogen atoms, that is 0.100 moles of hydrogen atoms. There are the same numbers of atoms in each of the two balloons. The number of hydrogen atoms in the other balloon is also 6.02×10^{22}.

Question 5.1

Nitrogen has atomic number 7 so has seven protons in the nucleus and seven electrons. Given that the maximum occupancy of s and p subshells is two and six respectively, the electronic configuration for the nitrogen atom can be written $1s^2 2s^2 2p^3$, which in abbreviated form is $[He]2s^2 2p^3$.

Question 5.2

The calcium atom has atomic number 20 and there are 20 electrons in the neutral atom. So the calcium cation has 18 electrons, as the charge of +2 on the ion indicates that there are two more protons in the nucleus than there are electrons around the nucleus. There are 18 electrons to accommodate in the lowest-energy shells, giving an electronic configuration for Ca^{2+} of $1s^2 2s^2 2p^6 3s^2 3p^6$, which in abbreviated form is simply $[Ar]$.

Question 5.3

From Table 5.1, the valency of aluminium is 3 and that of sulfur 2. To satisfy the valency criteria, the formula of aluminium sulfide is $Al_2 S_3$, where there are two aluminium atoms for every three sulfur atoms.

Question 5.4

With six outer electrons each, the two oxygen atoms in the O_2 molecule must form a double bond (two shared electron pairs, structure **5.7**) with each other if each is to attain a noble gas configuration. SCl_2 contains single bonds (structure **5.8**).

5.7   **5.8**

In these Lewis structures, oxygen attains the neon configuration, and sulfur and chlorine the argon configuration. When drawing Lewis structures, shape is unimportant; the important point is to show the correct number of bonds (shared electron pairs) formed by each atom. As either form of structure **5.8** does this, both are acceptable.

Question 5.5

The structural formulas of NH_3 and F_2 are shown as structures **5.9** and **5.10**, and the Lewis structures as structures **5.11** and **5.12**.

5.9   **5.10**   **5.11**   **5.12**

Question 6.1

The balanced equations are as follows.

(a) $FeO + H_2 = Fe + H_2O$

(b) $Fe_2O_3 + 3H_2 = 2Fe + 3H_2O$

(c) $N_2 + 3H_2 = 2NH_3$

(d) $CH_4 + 2Cl_2 = CH_2Cl_2 + 2HCl$

Question 6.2

(a) This is balanced, as there are the same number of atoms or ions of each type on the two sides of the 'equation' and the total charge on each side is the same.

(b) This is not balanced. Even though there are the same number of atoms or ions of each type on the two sides of the 'equation', the charges on each side are different: +4 on the left and 0 on the right.

(c) This is balanced, as there are the same number of atoms or ions of each type on the two sides of the 'equation' and the total charge on each side is the same.

Question 6.3

(a) The molar mass of NaCl is 58.5 g mol^{-1}, so:

$$\text{number of moles of NaCl} = \frac{\text{mass of NaCl}}{\text{molar mass of NaCl}}$$

$$= \frac{20.0 \text{ g}}{58.5 \text{ g mol}^{-1}} = 0.342 \text{ mol}$$

As the solution will have the same number of moles of Na$^+$(aq) ions as there are moles of NaCl, the concentration of Na$^+$(aq) is 0.342 mol dm^{-3}.

(b) The molar mass of CaCl$_2$ is 111.1 g mol^{-1}, so:

$$\text{number of moles of CaCl}_2 = \frac{\text{mass of CaCl}_2}{\text{molar mass of CaCl}_2}$$

$$= \frac{30.0 \text{ g}}{111.1 \text{ g mol}^{-1}} = 0.270 \text{ mol}$$

As the solution will have twice the number of moles of Cl$^-$(aq) as there are moles of CaCl$_2$, the concentration of Cl$^-$(aq) is $2 \times 0.270 = 0.540$ mol dm^{-3}.

(c) The molar mass of glucose is 180.1 g mol^{-1}, so:

$$\text{number of moles of glucose} = \frac{\text{mass of glucose}}{\text{molar mass of glucose}}$$

$$= \frac{25.0 \text{ g}}{180.1 \text{ g mol}^{-1}} = 0.139 \text{ mol}$$

The solution contains 0.139 moles of glucose in 0.5 dm^3 of solution. The number of moles in 1.0 dm^3, and therefore the concentration, will be $2 \times 0.139 = 0.278$ mol dm^{-3}.

Question 7.1

Copper, silver and gold are elements that have been found as the metal rather than as compounds. Although copper is generally found as an ore, it is relatively easy to extract the metal. This information is consistent with the fact that these metals are not very reactive; that is, they do not form compounds when exposed to air very easily. This is an ideal feature for a coinage metal.

Question 7.2

Carbon is used in the smelting of many metals. When heated with an oxide of the metal, carbon is able to remove oxygen from the metal oxide and form carbon monoxide, CO, or carbon dioxide, CO_2, in the process. So at higher temperatures, carbon appears to have a greater affinity for oxygen.

Question 8.1

The key to this question is the activity series. If a metal higher in the series is added to an aqueous solution containing cations of a metal lower in the series, the metal higher in the series will be oxidised to the cation and the cations of the metal lower in the series will be reduced to the element.

(a) Tin is higher in the activity series than copper, so tin will be oxidised to Sn^{2+} and copper cations, Cu^{2+}, reduced to elemental copper. (It is only tin and copper that are involved in the reaction. Chloride ions are present at the beginning and at the end of the reaction and take no part in the reaction.)

$$Sn(s) + Cu^{2+}(aq) = Sn^{2+}(aq) + Cu(s)$$

(b) Copper is lower in the series than lead so there will be no reaction.

(c) Sodium is higher in the series than iron, so sodium metal should be oxidised to the sodium cation, Na^+, and the iron cation, Fe^{2+}, reduced to elemental iron. However, sodium reacts quite violently with water to produce hydrogen gas, so this is the reaction that would take place.

Question 8.2

Both iron and aluminium react with oxygen in the air. The iron oxide produced is porous, allowing air and water to penetrate so the rusting can continue. With aluminium, as soon as the oxide has formed, no further oxidation takes place. Aluminium oxide is not porous and adheres well to the underlying metal, protecting it from further oxidation.

Question 8.3

In principle, any metal above iron in the activity series would do, provided that it does not react significantly with water. Probably the best choices would be zinc or manganese.

Question 9.1

(a) As the question indicates, it is necessary to cool the injury. This can be achieved if an endothermic chemical reaction occurs in the pack; the area of injury becomes part of the surroundings and its temperature is lowered as the reaction absorbs energy in the form of heat. Since the solid is soluble, the chemical reaction that is taking place must be the dissolution of this solid in the water. (A solid that is used in this type of cold pack is ammonium nitrate, NH_4NO_3.)

(b) A possible design for a hot pack would operate along the same lines, but would use a solid that undergoes an exothermic reaction when it dissolves in water. (Of course, the day must not be so cold that the water in the pack freezes before the pack is put into action!) In fact, a hot pack based on calcium chloride, $CaCl_2$, is commercially available.

(It is important to note that the dissolution of solids in water can be either endothermic or exothermic. This is consistent with the idea that internal energy changes can result in the release or the absorption of energy depending on the nature of a particular chemical reaction.)

Question 9.2

In the initial stages of an endothermic reaction, the temperature of the reaction mixture will be lowered. (You saw an example of this in the computer-based Activity 9.1 and in Figure 9.6.) However, with time, energy will flow in from the surroundings until the products of the reaction are at the same temperature as the reactants were at the start. In these circumstances, all of the energy in the form of heat absorbed during the reaction will have been taken from the surroundings. This situation is then the same as if the reaction had occurred at constant temperature.

Question 9.3

As indicated in the question, first it is necessary to work out the mass of one mole of water molecules. Thus, you add together the relative atomic masses of the atoms in the formula unit and follow the number that is obtained by the symbol for the gram. For H_2O, adding the relative atomic masses gives: $[(2 \times 1.0) + 16.0]$ which equals 18.0 (to three significant figures). The mass of one mole of water molecules is thus 18.0 g.

You are told that $\Delta H_{vap} = +2260 \ kJ \ kg^{-1}$.

For 1 g of water, the magnitude of the enthalpy change is $\dfrac{2260}{1000} \ kJ$.

Thus for 18.0 g of water, the magnitude of the enthalpy change is

$\dfrac{2260 \times 18.0}{1000} \ kJ = 40.7 \ kJ.$

Hence, for one mole of water molecules, the magnitude of the enthalpy of vaporisation is 40.7 kJ.

Question 9.4

When steam comes into contact with (relatively cold) skin, it will condense. This process is exothermic and so it will release heat (over 2 kJ per gram of condensed water). This heat will raise the temperature of the skin. In addition, the condensed water, initially at 100 °C, will cool by transferring heat to the skin. There are thus two contributions that raise the temperature of the skin, and this results in (painful) damage to the skin tissue.

Question 9.5

To carry out the calculation, first it is necessary to find the molar mass of ethanol, C_2H_5OH: there are two carbon atoms, six hydrogen atoms and one oxygen atom. Adding the relative atomic masses gives: $[(2 \times 12.0) + (6 \times 1.01) + 16.0]$, which is 46.1 (to three significant figures). The molar mass is thus 46.1 g mol^{-1}. According to the thermochemical equation, the reaction of one mole of ethanol molecules, i.e. 46.1 g of ethanol, results in the release of 1238 kJ of energy in the form of heat. So 1 g of ethanol will release $\dfrac{1238}{46.1}$ kJ.

If 1 kg (1000 g) of liquid ethanol is fully burned in oxygen, the energy released in the form of heat will be:

$$\frac{1238 \times 1000}{46.1}\ kJ = 27\ 000\ kJ$$

(The answer has been rounded to the nearest thousand kilojoules.)

A value of 27 000 can thus be entered in the final column of Table 9.4 as the energy released (in kJ) per kg of ethanol.

Question 9.6

The reaction can be viewed as a two-step process.

Step 1: $H_2(g) + Cl_2(g) \longrightarrow 2H(g) + 2Cl(g)$

Step 2: $2H(g) + 2Cl(g) \longrightarrow 2HCl(g)$

Considering the bonds broken in step 1, there are 'one mole of hydrogen–hydrogen bonds' and 'one mole of chlorine-chlorine bonds'. Hence:

$\Delta H(\text{step 1}) = 436\ kJ + 242\ kJ = +678\ kJ$

Considering the bonds formed in step 2, there are 'two moles of hydrogen–chlorine bonds'. Hence:

$\Delta H(\text{step 2}) = 2 \times (-431\ kJ) = -862\ kJ$

Thus, for the overall reaction:

$\Delta H = \Delta H(\text{step 1}) + \Delta H(\text{step 2})$

$= +678\ kJ + (-862\ kJ)$

$= +678\ kJ - 862\ kJ$

$= -184\ kJ\ mol^{-1}$

The enthalpy change is negative, so the formation of HCl gas from hydrogen and chlorine gas is exothermic.

Question 10.1

The energy diagram is shown in Figure 10.23. As the reaction is exothermic (ΔH is negative), the internal energy of the products is lower than that of the reactants.

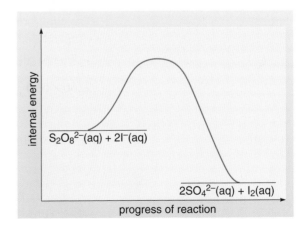

Figure 10.23 Schematic representation of how the internal energy changes during the reaction in Equation 10.3.

Question 10.2

(a) For the reaction of 1 mole of nitrogen and 3 moles of hydrogen gas giving 2 moles of ammonia, the equilibrium expression is:

$$K = \frac{[NH_3(g)]^2}{[N_2(g)] \times [H_2(g)]^3}$$

(b) For the reaction of 2 moles of nitrogen monoxide and 1 mole of oxygen gas giving 2 moles of nitrogen dioxide, the equilibrium expression is:

$$K = \frac{[NO_2(g)]^2}{[NO(g)]^2 \times [O_2(g)]}$$

(c) For the reaction of 2 moles of hydrogen iodide giving 1 mole of hydrogen and 1 mole of iodine gas, the equilibrium expression is:

$$K = \frac{[H_2(g)] \times [I_2(g)]}{[HI(g)]^2}$$

Question 10.3

For the reaction, the equilibrium expression will be:

$$K = \frac{[H^+(aq)] \times [NO_2^-(aq)]}{[HNO_2(aq)]}$$

The equilibrium constant at 25 °C can be calculated for all three solutions. Thus, for example, for solution 1:

$$K = \frac{(6.2 \times 10^{-3} \text{ mol dm}^{-3}) \times (6.2 \times 10^{-3} \text{ mol dm}^{-3})}{0.090 \text{ mol dm}^{-3}} = 4.3 \times 10^{-4} \text{ mol dm}^{-3}$$

Similar calculations for solutions 2 and 3 in Table 10.1 give the same value of K. The value for the equilibrium constant at 25 °C is 4.3×10^{-4} mol dm^{-3}. The magnitude of this quantity is clearly the same for all three equilibrium mixtures.

Question 10.4

The equilibrium yield of nitrogen monoxide will increase with increasing temperature because the reaction in the forward direction is endothermic. Thus, the yield will be greater at 500 °C than at room temperature.

Question 10.5

For the reaction in Equation 10.33, you are told that $\Delta H = -57$ kJ mol^{-1}.

$$2NO_2(g) \rightleftharpoons N_2O_4(g) \quad \Delta H = -57 \text{ kJ mol}^{-1} \tag{10.33}$$

This implies that the reaction is exothermic (having a negative value of ΔH). If the temperature of the equilibrium mixture of these gases is reduced, the forward reaction is favoured, so the concentration of $N_2O_4(g)$ will increase. The nitrogen dioxide is a brown gas and the dinitrogen tetroxide is colourless. Therefore, as the temperature of the reaction vessel is reduced, the intensity of the brown colour of the mixture will diminish as more $N_2O_4(g)$ is produced and more $NO_2(g)$ is used up in the process.

Question 10.6

(a) A suitable diagram for the changes in internal energy is shown in Figure 10.24.

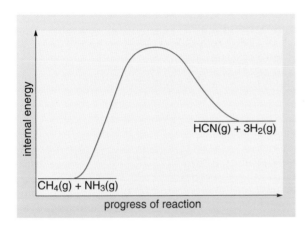

Figure 10.24 Schematic representation of how the internal energy changes during the production of hydrogen cyanide from methane and ammonia.

(b) (i) Raising the temperature would increase the yield because the reaction is endothermic in the forward direction (Section 10.8.2).

(ii) There are four moles of product molecules and two moles of reactant molecules, and therefore increasing the pressure would decrease the yield (Section 10.8.1).

(iii) Using a catalyst will lower the energy barrier of the reaction, but does not affect the yield of hydrogen cyanide.

Question 10.7

(a) The reaction in Equation 10.36 is exothermic in the forward direction, and so increasing the temperature of the exhaust gases will decrease the *equilibrium yield* of nitrogen and carbon dioxide.

(b) Both the raised temperature and a catalyst increase the *rate* of the reaction in Equation 10.36.

(c) The catalyst increases the rate of the reaction in Equation 10.36, so that by the time the exhaust gases reach the atmosphere, the reaction is virtually complete. The concentration of $NO(g)$ in the exhaust is therefore minimised – minimising the amount of $NO_2(g)$ formed via Equation 10.38.

Question 11.1

(a) The balanced equation that includes all the ions in solution is:

$$Mg^{2+}(aq) + 2OH^-(aq) + 2H^+(aq) + SO_4{}^{2-}(aq) = Mg^{2+}(aq) + SO_4{}^{2-}(aq) + 2H_2O(l) \qquad (11.20)$$

(b) The general balanced equation is:

$$Mg(OH)_2(aq) + H_2SO_4(aq) = MgSO_4(aq) + 2H_2O(l) \qquad (11.21)$$

1 mole of magnesium hydroxide reacts with 1 mole of sulfuric acid to give 1 mole of magnesium sulfate and 2 moles of water.

Question 11.2

Dissolving 10 g of sulfuric acid (H_2SO_4) would give the following reaction:

$$H_2SO_4(aq) = 2H^+(aq) + SO_4{}^{2-}(aq) \qquad (11.22)$$

The molar mass of H_2SO_4 is 98.1 g mol^{-1}, so 10.0 g of sulfuric acid is

$$\frac{10.0 \text{ g}}{98.1 \text{ g mol}^{-1}} = 0.102 \text{ mol}$$

This amount is contained in 1 dm^{-3} of solution, so the concentration of the sulfuric acid is 0.102 mol dm^{-3}. According to Equation 11.22, sulfuric acid dissolves in water to give two hydrogen ions and one sulfate ion for every formula unit of dissolved H_2SO_4, and so the hydrogen ion concentration is 2×0.102 mol dm$^{-3} = 0.204$ mol dm^{-3}.

Question 11.3

(a) For the dissociation of iodic acid in water, the equilibrium expression for K_a can be written in the form of Equation 11.13:

$$K_a = \frac{[H^+(aq)] \times [IO_3{}^-(aq)]}{[HIO_3(aq)]} \qquad (11.23)$$

To calculate K_a at 25 °C and 45 °C, you simply substitute the concentrations given for the species $HIO_3(aq)$, $H^+(aq)$ and $IO_3{}^-(aq)$ into Equation 11.23 for each temperature:

At 25 °C:

$$K_a = \frac{0.071 \text{ mol dm}^{-3} \times 0.071 \text{ mol dm}^{-3}}{0.029 \text{ mol dm}^{-3}} = 0.17 \text{ mol dm}^{-3}$$

At 45 °C:

$$K_a = \frac{0.066 \text{ mol dm}^{-3} \times 0.066 \text{ mol dm}^{-3}}{0.034 \text{ mol dm}^{-3}} = 0.13 \text{ mol dm}^{-3}$$

In general, from the answer it seems that K_a is reduced as the temperature of the solution is increased from 25 to 45 °C. This is indicated in the data in the table by the reduction in the concentration of products and increase in the concentration of reactant as the temperature increases.

(b) You have calculated the equilibrium constant for the dissociation of iodic acid at two temperatures in part (a). You have also seen that the value of K_a decreases as the temperature rises, which indicates that the equilibrium is shifted to the reactants, $HIO_3(aq)$, rather than the products, as the temperature increases. This is the way in which the K_a will change for an exothermic reaction. So the dissociation of iodic acid is an exothermic reaction. This answer can be checked to see whether it is consistent with Le Chatelier's principle. The data in the table indicates that the equilibrium position moves to the left as the temperature is raised. According to Le Chatelier's principle, this would be consistent with the dissociation reaction being exothermic in the forward direction, as K_a is reduced as the temperature is increased.

Question 11.4

(a) Sodium hydroxide dissociates completely in water to give $Na^+(aq)$ and $OH^-(aq)$ ions. Thus, in an NaOH solution of concentration 1.0×10^{-2} mol dm^{-3}, it follows that $[OH^-(aq)] = 1.0 \times 10^{-2}$ mol dm^{-3}. At 25 °C, the corresponding hydrogen ion concentration will be $[H^+(aq)] = 1.0 \times 10^{-12}$ mol dm^{-3}. The solution, as expected, is basic because the hydrogen ion concentration is less than 1.0×10^{-7} mol dm^{-3} (Figure 11.7).

(b) Hydrochloric acid is a strong acid. Thus, a 1.0×10^{-5} mol dm^{-3} solution of HCl will have $[H^+(aq)] = 1.0 \times 10^{-5}$ mol dm^{-3}. The solution is acidic because the hydrogen ion concentration is greater than 1.0×10^{-7} mol dm^{-3} at 25 °C.

(c) NaCl dissolves to give only $Na^+(aq)$ and $Cl^-(aq)$ ions. Thus the concentration of hydrogen ions will not be affected and will remain at that for neutral water, i.e. $[H^+(aq)] = [OH^-(aq)] = 1.0 \times 10^{-7}$ mol dm^{-3} at 25 °C.

(d) Acetic acid is a weak acid and will only partially dissociate into ions in water. Thus a 1.0 mol dm^{-3} solution of HAc will have a hydrogen ion concentration greater than $[H^+(aq)] = 1.0 \times 10^{-7}$ mol dm^{-3} but very much less than 1.0 mol dm^{-3}.

Question 11.5

(a) Mixing 1.00 dm^3 of a 1.0 mol dm^{-3} hydrochloric acid solution with 1.00 dm^3 of a 1.0 mol dm^{-3} sodium hydroxide solution is effectively carrying out a neutralisation reaction:

$$HCl(aq) + NaOH(aq) \rightleftharpoons NaCl(aq) + H_2O(l)$$

or

$$H^+(aq) + OH^-(aq) \rightleftharpoons H_2O(l)$$

The hydrogen ion concentration that results will be that for pure water, i.e. $[H^+(aq)] = 1.0 \times 10^{-7}$ mol dm^{-3} at 25 °C.

(b) Mixing 2.00 dm^3 of a 1.0 mol dm^{-3} hydrochloric acid solution with 1.00 dm^3 of a 1.0 mol dm^{-3} solution of sodium hydroxide is effectively mixing 2.0 moles of $H^+(aq)$ with 1.0 mole of $OH^-(aq)$. Neutralisation occurs, but 1.0 mole of $H^+(aq)$ is 'left over'. The total volume after mixing is expected to be 3.00 dm^3 and so the final hydrogen ion concentration is 1.0 mol in 3.00 dm^3, i.e. 0.33 mol dm^{-3}.

Question 11.6

(a) (i) A 0.01 mol dm^{-3} solution of nitric acid is completely dissociated as it is a strong acid:

$$HNO_3(aq) = H^+(aq) + NO_3^-(aq)$$

Therefore, for the dissociation of every one formula unit of nitric acid one $H^+(aq)$ is produced, so the hydrogen ion concentration is 0.01 mol dm^{-3}, and this can be related to the pH as $pH = -\log([H^+(aq)]/mol\ dm^{-3})$, so:

$$pH = -\log 0.01 = 2$$

The pH of a 0.01 mol dm^{-3} solution of nitric acid is 2.

(ii) A 0.05 mol dm^{-3} solution of sulfuric acid is also a strong acid so it is completely dissociated:

$$H_2SO_4(aq) = 2H^+(aq) + SO_4^{2-}(aq)$$

The dissociation of every one formula unit of sulfuric acid now results in 2 moles of $H^+(aq)$ and so the hydrogen ion concentration is 2×0.05 mol dm$^{-3} = 0.1$ mol dm^{-3}. The pH of the solution is:

$$pH = -\log 0.1 = 1$$

The pH of a 0.05 mol dm^{-3} solution of sulfuric acid is 1.

(b) A nitric acid solution with a pH of 2.5 will be completely dissociated and the pH can be related to the hydrogen ion concentration by the formula $[H^+(aq)] = 10^{-pH}$ mol dm^{-3}. Therefore, the hydrogen ion concentration is:

$$[H^+(aq)] = 10^{-2.5}\ mol\ dm^{-3} = 0.0032\ mol\ dm^{-3}$$

A solution of nitric acid with a pH of 2.5 will have a hydrogen ion concentration of 0.0032 mol dm^{-3}.

Question 11.7

A sample of seawater has a pH of 7.9 at 25 °C, so you can calculate the hydrogen ion concentration from this, as you know that:

$$[H^+(aq)] = 10^{-7.9}\ mol\ dm^{-3} = 1.26 \times 10^{-8}\ mol\ dm^{-3}$$

You can calculate $[OH^-(aq)]$ using the ion product of water, which is 1.0×10^{-14} mol^2 dm^{-6}:

$$K_w = [H^+(aq)] \times [OH^-(aq)] = 1.0 \times 10^{-14}\ mol^2\ dm^{-6}$$

Substituting the value of $[H^+(aq)]$ you have calculated and rearranging the equation:

$$[OH^-(aq)] = \frac{1.0 \times 10^{-14}\ mol^2\ dm^{-6}}{1.26 \times 10^{-8}\ mol\ dm^{-3}} = 7.9 \times 10^{-7}\ mol\ dm^{-3}$$

The concentration of hydroxide ions in a solution of seawater with a pH of 7.9 at 25 °C is 7.9×10^{-7} mol dm^{-3}.

Question 11.8

Nitric acid is strong and every mole dissociates to give one mole of [H⁺(aq)]. Assuming that the final volume of the solution is 10 dm³, the dissociation of the HNO_3 in solution will yield:

$$[H^+(aq)] = \frac{0.001 \text{ mol}}{10 \text{ dm}^3} = 1 \times 10^{-4} \text{ mol dm}^{-3}$$

This is far greater than the [H⁺(aq)] in pure water (1×10^{-7} mol dm⁻³), so you can ignore any contribution from the solvent and take 1×10^{-4} mol dm⁻³ to be the real value of [H⁺(aq)]. Then the pH = $-\log(1 \times 10^{-4}) = 4$. Now, using the ion product of water, you can calculate the hydroxide ion concentration:

$$[OH^-(aq)] = \frac{1.0 \times 10^{-14} \text{ mol}^2 \text{ dm}^{-6}}{1 \times 10^{-4} \text{ mol dm}^{-3}} = 1 \times 10^{-10} \text{ mol dm}^{-3}$$

Therefore, the hydroxide ion concentration in the 1×10^{-4} mol dm⁻³ nitric acid solution is 1×10^{-10} mol dm⁻³.

Question 12.1

Figure 12.11 shows the stages in drawing the structural formulas of ethane and pentane. The carbon chain is drawn first, then bonds are added so that each carbon has four (to satisfy its valency), and finally hydrogen atoms are added.

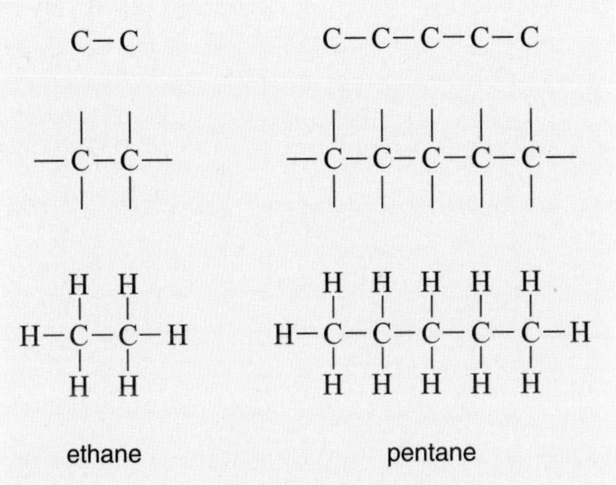

Figure 12.11   The three stages in drawing the structural formulas of ethane and pentane.

Question 12.2

Figure 12.12 shows how you might approach drawing the structural formula of propane. This shows that propane has the molecular formula C_3H_8.

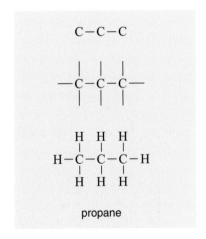

Figure 12.12   The three stages in drawing the structural formula of propane.

Question 12.3

12.9 is a linear-chain alkane. There is a linear chain of six carbon atoms.

12.10 is a cycloalkane. The chain of four carbon atoms is arranged in a ring.

12.11 is a branched-chain alkane. There is a linear chain of six carbon atoms, with a one-carbon branch attached to the third carbon from the left.

12.12 is not an alkane. As well as hydrogen and carbon atoms, it contains a fluorine atom.

Question 12.4

12.14 is a linear-chain alkane. The carbons are joined to each other by single bonds, in a linear fashion.

12.15 is an aromatic compound. It contains a ring of six carbon atoms joined by alternating single and double bonds.

12.16 is another linear-chain alkane. Even though it is drawn in a bent fashion, the carbons are joined to each other by single bonds, one after the other.

12.17 is a branched-chain alkane. There is a row of linked carbon atoms with a branch attached to the second carbon from the right.

Question 12.5

12.18 and **12.20** have correct structural formulas. Each carbon has four bonds attached to it and each hydrogen atom is attached by one bond. Thus all the valencies are satisfied.

12.19 has an incorrect structural formula: the central carbon has only three bonds attached to it. To satisfy the valency of this carbon, another hydrogen (or other atom with a valency of one) must be attached.

Question 12.6

(a) The structural formula of a linear-chain alkane C_8H_{18} is:

$$\begin{array}{c} \text{H}\ \ \text{H}\ \ \text{H}\ \ \text{H}\ \ \text{H}\ \ \text{H}\ \ \text{H}\ \ \text{H} \\ |\ \ \ |\ \ \ |\ \ \ |\ \ \ |\ \ \ |\ \ \ |\ \ \ | \\ \text{H}-\text{C}-\text{C}-\text{C}-\text{C}-\text{C}-\text{C}-\text{C}-\text{C}-\text{H} \\ |\ \ \ |\ \ \ |\ \ \ |\ \ \ |\ \ \ |\ \ \ |\ \ \ | \\ \text{H}\ \ \text{H}\ \ \text{H}\ \ \text{H}\ \ \text{H}\ \ \text{H}\ \ \text{H}\ \ \text{H} \end{array}$$

The abbreviated structural formula is:

$$CH_3-CH_2-CH_2-CH_2-CH_2-CH_2-CH_2-CH_3$$

(b) The structural formula of the cycloalkane C_4H_8 which contains a ring of four carbon atoms is:

$$\begin{array}{c} \text{H}\ \ \text{H} \\ |\ \ \ | \\ \text{H}-\text{C}-\text{C}-\text{H} \\ |\ \ \ | \\ \text{H}-\text{C}-\text{C}-\text{H} \\ |\ \ \ | \\ \text{H}\ \ \text{H} \end{array}$$

The abbreviated structural formula is:

$$\begin{array}{c} CH_2-CH_2 \\ |\qquad | \\ CH_2-CH_2 \end{array}$$

(c) The structural formula for the branched-chain alkane C_4H_{10} is:

$$\begin{array}{c} \text{H} \\ | \\ \text{H}-\text{C}-\text{H} \\ \text{H}\ \ \ |\ \ \ \text{H} \\ |\ \ \ \ |\ \ \ \ | \\ \text{H}-\text{C}-\text{C}-\text{C}-\text{H} \\ |\ \ \ \ |\ \ \ \ | \\ \text{H}\ \ \text{H}\ \ \text{H} \end{array}$$

Drawing the abbreviated structural formula for C_4H_{10} may have given you some problems if you did not realise that bonds in abbreviated structural formulas can go in any direction, including up or down if there is no other place to draw them. The important point is to have the right number of bonds to each carbon, i.e. four:

$$\begin{array}{c} CH_3 \\ | \\ CH_3-CH-CH_3 \end{array}$$

(d) If the molecule contains a ring of four carbons, the molecular formula indicates there must be another carbon atom outside the ring as a one-carbon branch. It can come off any of the four carbons in the ring because they are all equivalent. Two equally correct ways of drawing the structural formula are (there are several others):

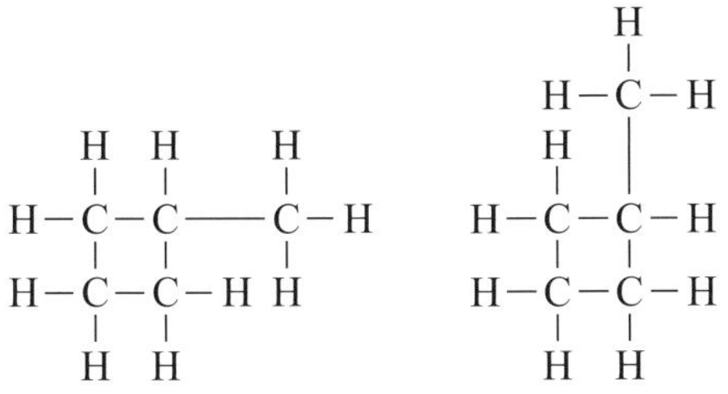

The equivalent two ways of drawing the abbreviated structural formula are:

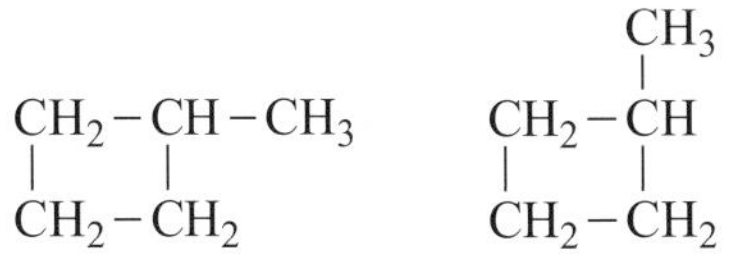

Question 12.7

Isomerisation implies a process in which the product is an isomer of the reactant. For example, hexane can be converted into a branched-chain alkane with the same molecular formula. You may have come up with a different example but, in order to be correct, your answer must be a compound that has a branched chain and six carbon atoms with 14 hydrogen atoms.

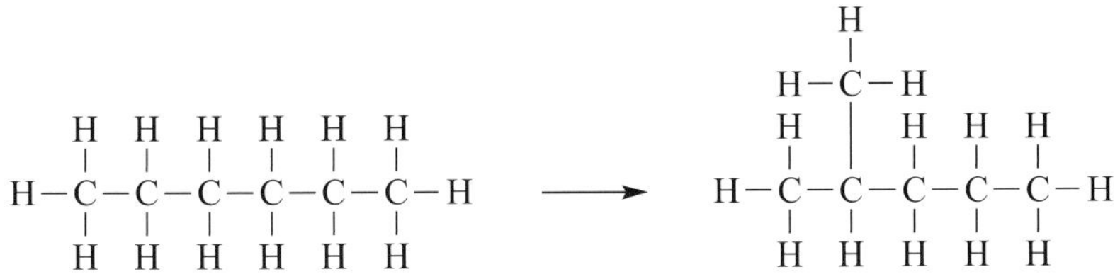

12.23

Table 12.4 shows that branched-chain alkanes have much higher octane numbers than linear-chain alkanes. In fact, a range of branched-chain isomers of pentane and hexane can be formed. (This process is carried out at 100–200 °C using a platinum catalyst.)

Question 13.1

The reactions involved are as follows.

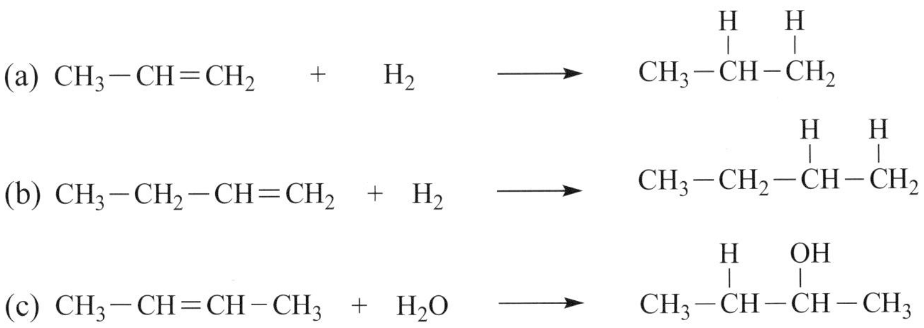

(a) $CH_3-CH=CH_2 + H_2 \longrightarrow CH_3-CH-CH_2$ (with H, H)

(b) $CH_3-CH_2-CH=CH_2 + H_2 \longrightarrow CH_3-CH_2-CH-CH_2$ (with H, H)

(c) $CH_3-CH=CH-CH_3 + H_2O \longrightarrow CH_3-CH-CH-CH_3$ (with H, OH)

269

Question 13.2

The alkene monomers are:

(a) chloroethene

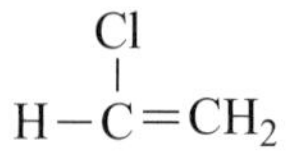

$$H-\underset{\underset{\displaystyle Cl}{|}}{C}=CH_2$$

(b) propene

$$H-\underset{\underset{\displaystyle CH_3}{|}}{C}=CH_2$$

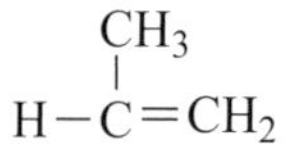

Question 13.3

The polymer formed by linking together tetrafluoroethene monomers is:

$$\cdots\cdots CF_2-CF_2-CF_2-CF_2-CF_2-CF_2-CF_2-CF_2-CF_2-CF_2\cdots\cdots$$

Question 14.1

(a) This molecule contains an alcohol group, written as HO—, and a carboxylic acid group, —COOH.

$$\boxed{HO}-CH_2-CH_2-CH_2-CH_2-CH_2-\boxed{COOH}$$

alcohol   carboxylic acid

(b) This molecule contains a carbon–carbon double bond, so it is an alkene. It also contains an ester group.

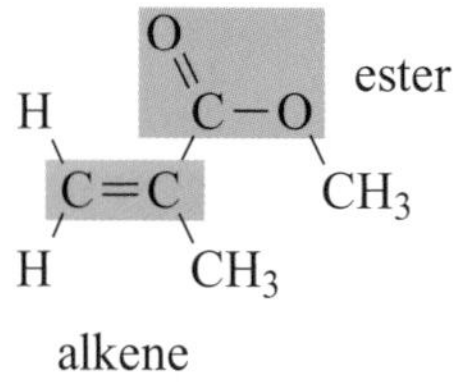

Question 14.2

If you replace the CH_3 by an R group in Equation 14.13, you get the generalised reaction for the reduction of a carboxylic acid to an alcohol:

$$R-\boxed{COOH} \xrightarrow{H_2/\text{catalyst}} R-CH_2-\boxed{OH}$$

This reflects the fact that only the functional group undergoes change in the reaction and not the hydrocarbon group. In benzoic acid, R is a benzene ring; thus replacement of the R group by a benzene ring in the generalised equation gives:

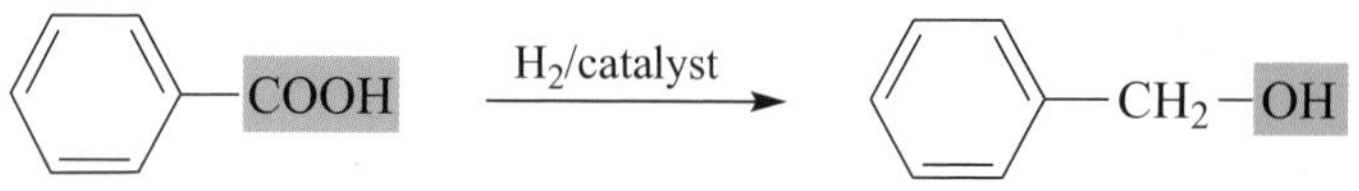

Question 14.3

The strategy developed in Activity 14.3 was:

1 identify the functional group

2 look up the reactions of this functional group

3 identify the hydrocarbon portions of the reactants that do not change and copy them to give the product.

(a) The reactant is an alcohol. Potassium dichromate ($K_2Cr_2O_7$) in hydrochloric acid oxidises an alcohol to give a carboxylic acid. The generalised equation for this is given by Equation 14.13. In this case, the R group in the reactant alcohol is CH_3-CH_2-; thus substituting this for R in the product in Equation 14.13 gives:

$$CH_3-CH_2-\overset{\displaystyle O}{\underset{\displaystyle O-H}{C}}$$

(b) In this reaction there are two reactants: a carboxylic acid and an alcohol. The only way in which these two groups react together is via a condensation reaction to give an ester. The generalised equation is given in Table 14.3. Because there are two reactants, you have to make sure you do not get the R groups mixed up, so you label them R^1 and R^2. R^1 comes from the carboxylic acid, so it is CH_3-CH_2-; R^2 comes from the alcohol, so it is $CH_3-CH_2-CH_2-CH_2-$. Substituting these groups in the generalised equation gives the product:

$$CH_3-CH_2-\overset{\displaystyle O}{\underset{\displaystyle O-CH_2-CH_2-CH_2-CH_3}{C}}$$

(c) The third reaction involves an alkene. The only reaction you have learned for alkenes is an addition reaction. In this case, water is added across the double bond. In terms of the general addition reaction given in Table 14.3, $X = H$ and $Y = OH$, and R^1 is CH_3- and R^2 is $-CH_3$, giving the product:

$$\overset{\displaystyle OH}{\underset{\displaystyle }{CH_3-CH-CH_2-CH_3}}$$

Question 14.4

Leaf alcohol contains two functional groups – an alkene functional group and an alcohol functional group:

$$CH_3-CH_2-\underset{\text{alkene}}{CH=CH}-CH_2-CH_2-\underset{\text{alcohol}}{OH}$$

Each functional group will undergo characteristic reactions. Alcohols undergo oxidation to carboxylic acids or react with a carboxylic acid to give an ester. Alkenes undergo addition reactions.

(a) This reaction is a condensation reaction between the alcohol functional group of leaf alcohol and the carboxylic acid to give an ester. The generalised reaction is given in Table 14.3. Here R^1 comes from the carboxylic acid, so it is CH_3, and R^2 comes from leaf alcohol, so it is $CH_3-CH_2-CH=CH-CH_2-CH_2-$. Substituting these groups in the generalised equation gives the product:

$$CH_3-C\begin{matrix}O\\\|\end{matrix}\quad O-CH_2-CH_2-CH=CH-CH_2-CH_3$$

(b) This reaction is an addition reaction. Equation 13.4 shows that bromine adds across the double bond. The generalised addition reaction is given in Table 14.3, and in this case X and Y are both Br. Also, R^1 is CH_3-CH_2- and R^2 is $-CH_2-CH_2-OH$, so the product is:

$$CH_3-CH_2-\overset{Br}{\underset{}{CH}}-\overset{Br}{\underset{}{CH}}-CH_2-CH_2-OH$$

[Note that R^2 contains another functional group, OH, which does not react; in this case, R^2 represents 'the rest of the molecule'.]

Question 14.5

(a) In this reaction, the alcohol gains oxygen and loses hydrogen. It is oxidised.

(b) In this reaction, which is an addition reaction, the alkene gains hydrogen so is reduced. In this case, there is no accompanying loss of oxygen.

Question 15.1

Applying the strategy developed in Activity 14.2, you should identify that glyceryl monostearate (structure **14.6**) contains a single ester group.

14.6

Esters are formed by condensation reactions between appropriate carboxylic acids and alcohols. From Table 14.3, the general equation is:

$$R^1-C\begin{matrix}O\\\|\end{matrix}\backslash OH \;+\; HO-R^2 \longrightarrow R^1-C\begin{matrix}O\\\|\end{matrix}\backslash O-R^2 \;+\; H_2O$$

In this case, the R^1 group is derived from a fatty acid containing 18 carbon atoms (stearic acid), while the R^2 group comes from glycerol:

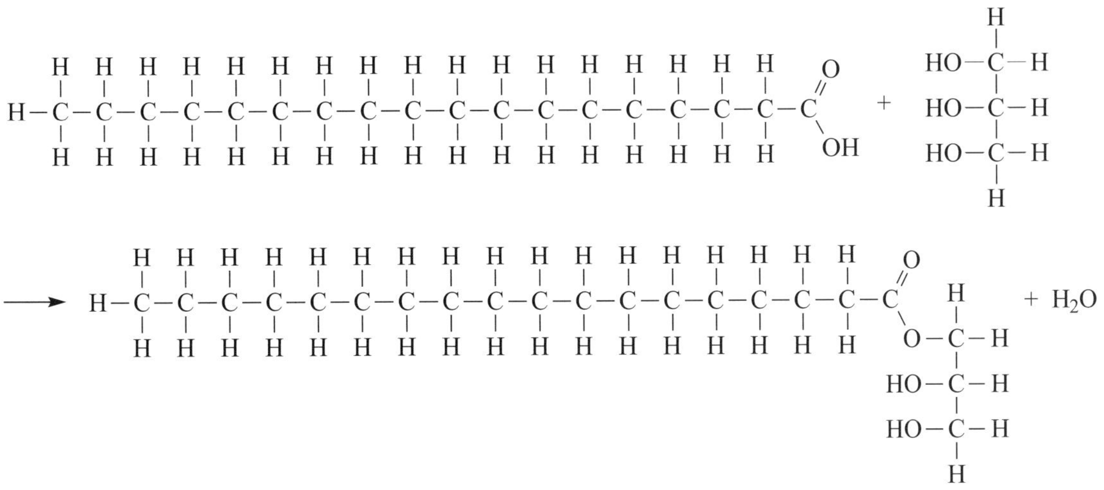

Question 15.2

It is important to remember that by convention the amino end of the chain is always drawn to the left, and the carboxylic acid to the right. The structural formula of the peptide Gly–Val–Ala is:

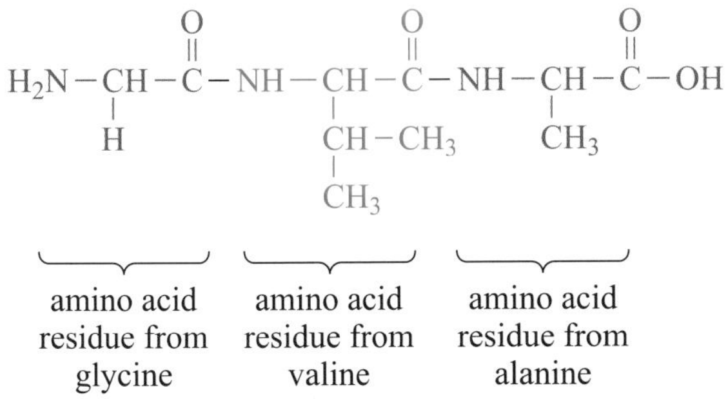

amino acid residue from glycine   amino acid residue from valine   amino acid residue from alanine

Question 15.3

Chiral molecules all have four *different* groups attached to a central carbon atom. Only structures (b) and (d) satisfy this criterion, so only (b) and (d) are chiral. In structure (a) there are two bromine atoms attached to the central carbon atom, and in structure (c) there are two methyl (CH_3) groups attached to the central carbon atom.

Question 15.4

Below are the structural formula and Haworth projection of galactose.

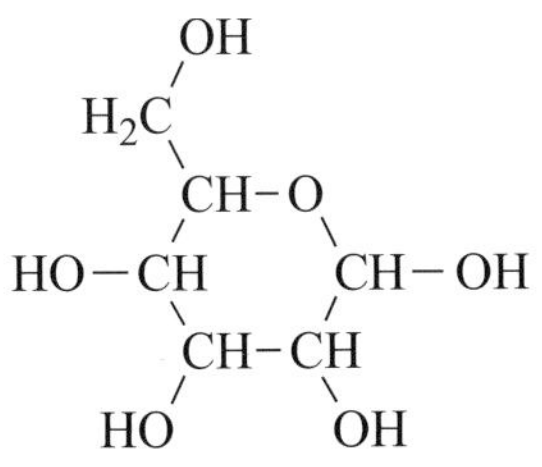

structural formula of galactose 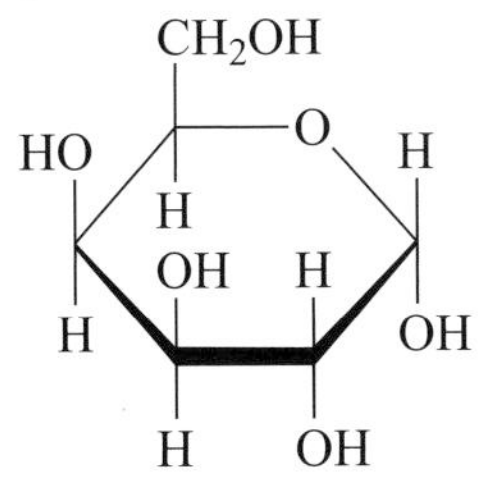   Haworth projection of galactose

Below are the structural formula and Haworth projection of glucose.

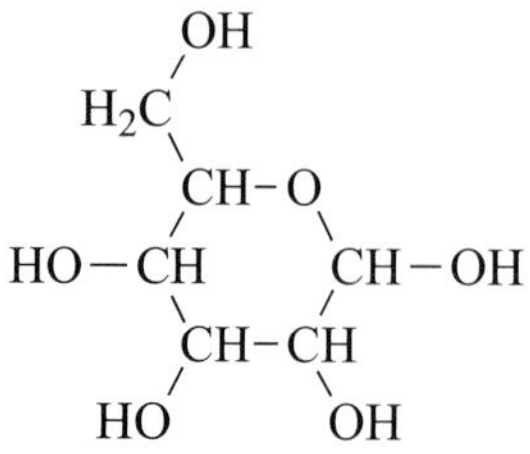

structural formula of glucose 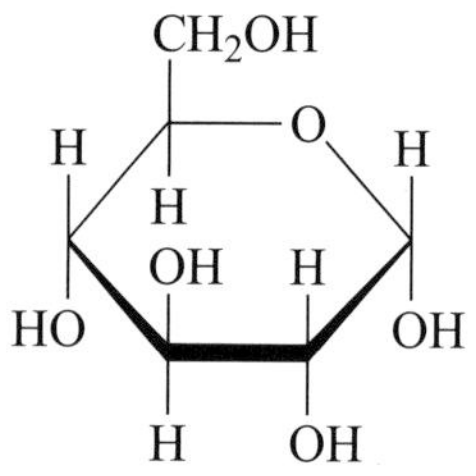   Haworth projection of glucose

You should note that the two structural formulas are identical: glucose and galactose are isomers. The two monosaccharides differ only in the orientation of one of the hydroxyl (OH) groups.

Question 16.1

In salicylic acid you can identify an alcohol and a carboxylic acid functional group:

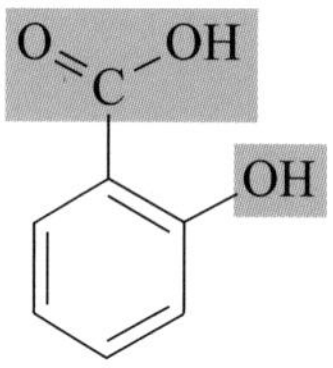

In this compound there are no linear chains of carbon atoms. However, the benzene ring provides the framework on which to hang the other functional groups. In salicylic acid, the alcohol and carboxylic acid groups are attached to adjacent carbon atoms.

Question 16.2

The functional groups in paracetamol are highlighted below – an alcohol group and an amide group.

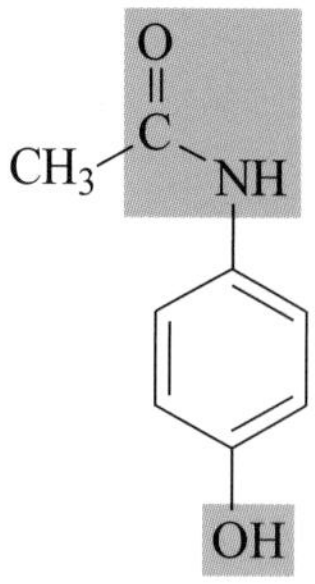

The shape of the paracetamol molecule is very different from that of the aspirin molecule, and it does not contain an ester group that could react with an —OH group in the active site. Hence, you would not expect it to block the cyclo-oxygenase enzyme in the same way that aspirin does. [Paracetamol binds to another part of the cyclo-oxygenase enzyme via intermolecular forces and thus blocks its action. This is why paracetamol has a similar effect to that of aspirin.]

Question 16.3

The first step is to look for particular functional groups; you can split the ion **16.8** into a number of imaginary parts – an amino group, a carboxylate group and a saturated hydrocarbon chain:

$$CH_3 - CH_2 - CH_2 - \underset{\underset{\displaystyle NH_2}{|}}{CH} - C \overset{\displaystyle O}{\underset{\displaystyle O^-}{\diagup}}$$

The nitrogen of the amino group, NH_2, is able to form a hydrogen bond with a hydrogen atom attached to another nitrogen or an oxygen atom, such as that found in the alcohol group at the enzyme active site. Alternatively, the hydrogen attached to the nitrogen of the amino group can form a hydrogen bond with the oxygen of the alcohol group.

The carboxylate group bears a full negative charge and is therefore likely to form an ionic interaction with the positively charged ammonium group at the active site.

Question 16.4

First, you need to identify the types of binding that **16.9** would undergo. The hydrocarbon chain could be attracted by hydrophobic interactions, the alcohol group could form a hydrogen bond, and the negatively charged carboxylate group could undergo an ionic interaction with a positively charged group. But, remember, the groups need to be in the correct places.

The ion **16.10** has one $-CH_2-$ group fewer than the ion **16.9**, but it would be expected to bind to the same receptor because it contains the same functional groups in the same places. The loss of one $-CH_2-$ group would have only a minor effect on the hydrophobic interactions of the hydrocarbon group.

The ion **16.11** will not bind. Although it has the correct groups, they are not in the right spatial orientation; in **16.9** they are close together whereas in **16.11** they are far apart.

The ion **16.12** will not bind. The functional groups are in the correct places, but the negatively charged group has been replaced by a positively charged one. The negatively charged group in the ion **16.9** would bind with a positively charged group on the receptor, but the latter group would repel the positively charged group in **16.12**.

Comments on activities

Activity 3.1

Task 1

Nearly every grain is a tiny cube with perfectly flat sides: a crystal of sodium chloride. The few grains that are not perfect cubes are either broken grains or several cubes joined together.

Task 2

The large grain of sea or rock salt is probably more irregular than the grains of table salt, being a fragment broken from a larger crystalline mass. You should be able to see that breakage has produced flat facets arranged in steps. Note how the facets are always at right angles to each other.

After crushing the large grain, you will see that each fragment has fractured along sharp facets at right angles. In fact, even if you had ground the salt very finely, a microscope would have revealed that, no matter how small the grains, they all break in this very regular way. Sodium chloride crystals break along extremely closely spaced planes of cleavage that run all the way through the solid.

Figure 3.6 shows how the sodium, Na^+, and chloride, Cl^-, ions are packed together in a regular array. Note how the ions are arranged in three sets of planes at right angles. This regularity controls the cubic shape of salt crystals, and accounts for the way the salt cleaves into cubic fragments. Observing the way in which crystals of natural minerals fracture is often a simple clue to the crystal structure of each mineral.

Activity 4.1

Task 1

Like common salt, quartz also has a number of flat facets, but in quartz they are not at right angles. These crystal faces are at angles that allow them to come together in a point. If you look down on the point, the specimen shows a clear, six-sided (hexagonal) cross-section, whereas salt crystals are square in cross-section. The opposite end of the quartz specimen is broken, yet quite differently from the breakage of common salt or halite (Activity 3.1).

Task 2

Quartz is harder than glass, and scratches it. A salt grain has no effect on glass or quartz and is very much softer.

Task 3

The broken surface of quartz consists of many curved surfaces, but none that are perfectly flat. The quartz structure (Figure 4.11) contains no planar arrangements of weaknesses to produce regular cleavage: that absence confers strength on the crystal.

Task 4

You should have noticed that the quartz crystal from the Kit is imperfect, and so are the examples given in the computer-based resource. You should have found that natural quartz varies in colour, depending on very small concentrations of elements other than silicon and oxygen. Only an extremely pure form is colourless, and then often 'milky' because of minute fractures within the crystal. Natural minerals are both imperfect and slightly variable in composition, so identifying them depends on features such as crystal shape and cleavage, which depend on their structural chemistry.

You might have examined the 'single SiO_4 group'. This shows in ball-and-stick form how a single silicon atom is covalently bonded to four oxygen atoms, equivalent to Figure 4.11b. To be strictly accurate, the SiO_4 group would not exist as an independent molecule: each oxygen atom is involved in a covalent bond to another silicon atom at the core of another SiO_4 group. The whole quartz structure is thus built from this simple group. In different ways, so too are all other silicate minerals, as you will discover in Book 6.

You might have discovered that the angles between the Si—O bonds force the three-dimensional structure to have an in-built spiral geometry. Viewed from end on, each of these spirals defines a hexagon that underpins the six-sided cross-section of *every* quartz crystal.

Overall, you should have noted the most important point: quartz is held together by an extended framework of strong covalent bonds, which explains both the hardness of the material, and the fact that it does not cleave easily.

Activity 4.2

Task 1

Your completed table should match Table 4.2.

Table 4.2 Completed Table 4.1.

Substance	Mass of flask containing fixed volume of gas/g	Mass of evacuated flask/g	Mass of gas/g	Relative molecular mass of substance
hydrogen, H_2	144.174	144.162	0.012	2
nitrogen, N_2	144.330	144.162	0.168	28
oxygen, O_2	144.354	144.162	0.192	32
fluorine, F_2	144.390	144.162	0.228	38
carbon dioxide, CO_2	144.425	144.162	0.263	44

Your graph should look something like the one in Figure 4.17 – the straight-line relationship suggests that the data support Avogadro's hypothesis.

Any minor deviations from an exact straight line could be due to two possible factors: (a) the Avogadro hypothesis is only approximately true, or (b) they are experimental errors. Given the rough-and-ready method of carrying out the experiment, the latter seems most likely.

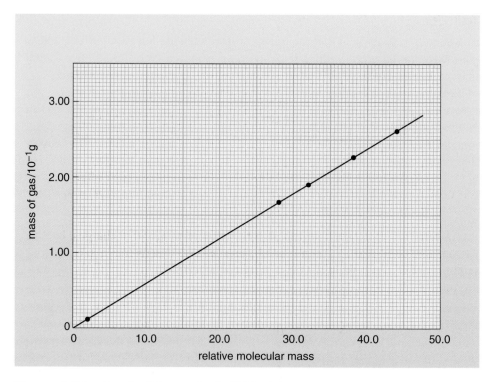

Figure 4.17   Graph of the results in Table 4.2.

Task 2

(a) The empirical formula is the simplest possible ratio of the types of atom present. As you have been told that the ratio of carbon atoms to hydrogen atoms is 1 : 1, the empirical formula is simply CH. You might have written C_1H_1; strictly speaking this is correct, but the standard practice is to omit 'ones' when they appear in formulas.

(b) The molecular formula gives the ratio of the types of atom in each individual molecule in a substance. For any given empirical formula there is an infinite number of possible molecular formulas. For Q, the simplest four will be CH, C_2H_2, C_3H_3 and C_4H_4. For each possible molecule, you can calculate the relative molecular mass (RMM) by adding the relative atomic masses (RAMs) of the atoms present:

$$RMM(CH) \quad = RAM(C) + RAM(H) \qquad\qquad = 12 + 1 \qquad\qquad = 13$$
$$RMM(C_2H_2) = [2 \times RAM(C)] + [2 \times RAM(H)] = [2 \times 12] + [2 \times 1] = 26$$
$$RMM(C_3H_3) = [3 \times RAM(C)] + [3 \times RAM(H)] = [3 \times 12] + [3 \times 1] = 39$$
$$RMM(C_4H_4) = [4 \times RAM(C)] + [4 \times RAM(H)] = [4 \times 12] + [4 \times 1] = 52$$

(c) When the flask was filled with Q, the total mass was 144.314 g. Therefore, the mass of Q in the flask is:

$$\text{mass of Q} = 144.314 \text{ g} - 144.162 \text{ g} = 0.152 \text{ g}$$

Reading across from 0.152 g on the y-axis of your graph (Figure 4.17) to your straight line and then extending down to the x-axis gives a relative molecular mass of approximately 25.5. This is very close to the value for C_2H_2 and, as there may be a number of small experimental errors, you can assume that this is the correct molecular formula of Q.

Activity 6.1

Task 1

K^+, Ca^{2+}, Al^{3+}, S^{2-}, F^- and Br^-.

Task 2

(a) K^+ carries a single positive charge; F^- carries a single negative charge. In order for the charges to balance, they must be present in a 1 : 1 ratio, so the chemical formula is KF.

(b) Ca^{2+} carries two positive charges; Br^- carries a single negative charge. In order for the charges to balance, there must be two bromide ions for each calcium ion, so the chemical formula is $CaBr_2$.

(c) K^+ carries a single positive charge; O^{2-} carries two negative charges. In order for the charges to balance, there must be two potassium ions for each oxide ion, so the chemical formula is K_2O.

(d) Al^{3+} carries three positive charges; Br^- carries a single negative charge. In order for the charges to balance, there must be three bromide ions for each aluminium ion, so the chemical formula is $AlBr_3$.

(e) This one is slightly more complex. Al^{3+} carries three positive charges; O^{2-} carries two negative charges. The simplest way for the charges to balance is that there must be three oxide ions for every two aluminium ions, so the chemical formula is Al_2O_3.

Task 3

Following the approach of balancing the charges given in part (b), and remembering that where there is more than one ionic group it will appear in brackets, you should arrive at the following answers.

(a) KOH

(b) K_2SO_4

(c) $Ca(NO_3)_2$

(d) NH_4F

(e) $(NH_4)_2SO_4$

Activity 6.2

Part 1, Task 1

To do these calculations, you will need to use Equation 6.5:

$$\text{number of moles of a substance} = \frac{\text{mass of a substance}}{\text{molar mass of substance}} \qquad (6.5)$$

(a) The relative atomic mass of He is 4.00, therefore the molar mass of He is 4.00 g mol^{-1}:

$$\text{number of moles of He} = \frac{10.0 \text{ g}}{4.00 \text{ g mol}^{-1}}$$

$$= 2.50 \text{ mol}$$

(b) The relative molecular mass of H_2O is 18.0, therefore the molar mass of H_2O is 18.0 g mol^{-1}.

$$\text{number of moles of } H_2O = \frac{54.0 \text{ g}}{18.0 \text{ g mol}^{-1}}$$

$$= 3.00 \text{ mol}$$

(c) The relative formula mass of NaCl is 58.5, therefore the molar mass of NaCl is 58.5 g mol^{-1}.

$$\text{number of moles of NaCl} = \frac{85.5 \text{ g}}{58.5 \text{ g mol}^{-1}}$$

$$= 1.46 \text{ mol}$$

(d) The relative formula mass of CaF_2 is 78.1, therefore the molar mass of CaF_2 is 78.1 g mol^{-1}.

$$\text{number of moles of } CaF_2 = \frac{0.769 \text{ g}}{78.1 \text{ g mol}^{-1}}$$

$$= 9.85 \times 10^{-3} \text{ mol}$$

(e) The relative formula mass of H_2SO_4 is 98.1, therefore the molar mass of H_2SO_4 is 98.1 g mol^{-1}.

$$\text{number of moles of } H_2SO_4 = \frac{26.5 \text{ g}}{98.1 \text{ g mol}^{-1}}$$

$$= 0.270 \text{ mol}$$

Part 1, Task 2

To do these calculations, you will need to use Equation 6.4:

$$\text{mass of a substance} = (\text{number of moles of substance}) \times (\text{molar mass of substance}) \qquad (6.4)$$

(a) Ar has molar mass 39.9 g mol^{-1}, so:

$$\text{mass of Ar} = 0.350 \text{ mol} \times 39.9 \text{ g mol}^{-1}$$

$$= 14.0 \text{ g}$$

(b) KF has molar mass 58.1 g mol^{-1}, so:

$$\text{mass of KF} = 6.90 \text{ mol} \times 58.1 \text{ g mol}^{-1}$$

$$= 401 \text{ g}$$

(c) Na_2O has molar mass 62.0 g mol^{-1}, so:

$$\text{mass of } Na_2O = 1.55 \text{ mol} \times 62.0 \text{ g mol}^{-1}$$

$$= 96.1 \text{ g}$$

(d) SnI_4 has molar mass 627 g mol^{-1}, so:

$$\text{mass of } SnI_4 = 0.320 \text{ mol} \times 627 \text{ g mol}^{-1}$$

$$= 201 \text{ g}$$

(e) $C_6H_{12}O_6$ has molar mass 180.1 g mol^{-1}, so:

$$\text{mass of } C_6H_{12}O_6 = 0.140 \text{ mol} \times 180.1 \text{ g mol}^{-1}$$

$$= 25.2 \text{ g}$$

Part 2, Task 1

You have seen that each mole of carbon dioxide reacts with 2 moles of the metal hydroxide. You need to know the mass of 2 moles of each metal hydroxide, so you will have to use Equation 6.4:

$$\text{mass of a substance} = (\text{number of moles of substance}) \times (\text{molar mass of substance}) \qquad (6.4)$$

From the relative atomic masses given in the Periodic Table (Figure 5.3), you can calculate that the relative formula masses of LiOH and NaOH are:

(a) relative formula mass of NaOH = RAM(Na) + RAM(O) + RAM(H)

$$= 23.0 + 16.0 + 1.01 = 40.0$$

(b) relative formula mass of LiOH = RAM(Li) + RAM(O) + RAM(H)

$$= 6.94 + 16.0 + 1.01 = 23.9$$

This means that the molar formula masses of LiOH and NaOH are 23.9 g mol^{-1} and 40.0 g mol^{-1} respectively.

Given that, in both cases, 2 moles of the metal hydroxide are required to absorb one mole of CO_2, you can insert these values into your equation:

(a) mass of NaOH required $= 2 \text{ mol} \times 40.0 \text{ g mol}^{-1} = 80.0 \text{ g}$

(b) mass of LiOH required $= 2 \text{ mol} \times 23.9 \text{ g mol}^{-1} = 47.8 \text{ g}$

In order to ease the launch of a spacecraft, equipment should be as light as possible, so it is not surprising that the US space programs use LiOH, which also happens to absorb the CO_2 at a faster rate.

Part 2, Task 2

You know that each mole of CO_2 requires 47.8 g of LiOH, but you are told that each astronaut emits 1.0 kg of CO_2 per day. One mole of CO_2 has a mass of 44.0 g (this is the relative molecular mass expressed in grams, found by adding together the relative atomic masses).

If 44.0 g of CO_2 react with 47.8 g of LiOH, 1 g of CO_2 will react with $\frac{47.8}{44.0}$ g or 1.0864 g of LiOH. Thus for each kilogram of CO_2, 1.0864 kg of LiOH is required. (Note that an increased number of significant figures has been used in this intermediate answer, to avoid rounding errors in the final answer.)

If you have three crew members on a ten-day mission:

$$\text{minimum LiOH required} = 30 \times 1.0864 \text{ kg}$$

$$= 32.6 \text{ kg}$$

Obviously, it might be sensible to include a little more than this.

Activity 7.1

The completed Table 7.2 is shown in Table 7.4.

Table 7.4 Completed Table 7.2.

Property	High										Low
abundance in Earth's crust	Al	Fe	Mg	S	Cr	Zn	Cu	Pb	Sn	Ag	Au
cost	Au	Ag	Sn	Cr	Cu	Zn	Al	Mg	Pb	Fe	S
annual world production	Fe	S	Al	Cr	Cu	Zn	Pb	Mg	Sn	Ag	Au
melting temperature	Cr	Fe	Cu	Au	Ag	Al	Mg	Zn	Pb	Sn	S
density	Au	Pb	Ag	Cu	Fe	Sn	Cr	Zn	Al	S	Mg
heat conduction	Ag	Cu	Au	Al	Mg	Zn	Cr	Fe	Sn	Pb	S
electrical conduction	Ag	Cu	Au	Al	Mg	Zn	Fe	Sn	Cr	Pb	S

(a) Silver, copper and gold are the best conductors of electricity, but silver and gold are both high-cost metals. It is copper therefore that is the metal most often used as an electrical conductor.

(b) Aluminium is not a particularly costly metal and its low density makes it ideal for the construction of aeroplanes, where weight is important.

(c) Tin has a much lower melting temperature than iron. The can would remain intact if it were dipped into a bath of molten tin which would coat the surface of the can.

(d) Generally, the higher the abundance of the metal in the Earth's crust, the lower the cost. However, this is not an exact relationship, and the cost of a metal will also depend on a number of other factors, including:

*   the proportion of metal in the ores
*   the ease with which it can be extracted
*   the cost of the process by which the metal is extracted from its ores.

Activity 8.1

A definitive list of the reactivity of a representative set of metals is given in Table 8.6. You should compare the table you have constructed with this one. Don't be concerned if some of the detail in your table is different, as this table is based on a much larger number of observations than those you have made. For example, from the information you have, it is not possible to decide where manganese should come relative to calcium and magnesium.

This reactivity order holds quite well for all the reactions of metals. Your observations were based on the reactions of metals with water and acids, but the same order of reactivity would apply for reactions with oxygen, sulfur, chlorine and several other elements. For example, calcium reacts violently with chlorine, but the reaction of chlorine with copper is much less vigorous.

Table 8.6 Reactivity of some metals in decreasing order.

Metal	Reactivity
potassium	most reactive
sodium	↑
lithium	
calcium	
magnesium	
manganese	
iron	
tin	
copper	
silver	↓
gold	least reactive

While the order of reactivity given here is a useful guide, it has to be used with some caution. There are several factors that affect whether or not a reaction occurs, and also how quickly it occurs. These factors are explored in Chapters 9–11.

Activity 9.1

In the tables below, summaries are given for the observations you should have made from the video sequence.

Task 1   Observing the energy changes in chemical reactions

Table 9.5 Completed Table 9.1.

Reaction number	Observation
1	When oxygen is bubbled through the solution, it changes from yellow to red to green. When the oxygen source is removed, the solution changes back from green to red to yellow.
2	When the liquid is added to the beaker, the solution emits light.
3	When the chemicals are mixed, the solution in the cylinder changes from colourless to orange to black. The same colour change occurs when the solutions in the beakers are mixed, but at different speeds.
Reaction number	**Energy changes observed**
4	When the reactants were mixed, light was given out. The temperatures of the reactants and products were the same (about 18 °C), thus little heat was generated.
5	When the aluminium was dipped in the solution in the pot, the electric motor started up. A gas was given off at the surface of the aluminium. When the copper ring was removed from the solution, the motor stopped.
6	When the two solids were mixed, they reacted to form a liquid. The solution cooled down (to −20 °C) so that the pool of water around the bottom of the beaker solidified.

Task 2   What effects do temperature and concentration have on a chemical reaction?

Table 9.6 Completed Table 9.2.

Conditions	Colour at start	Chemicals present at start	Colour at end	Chemicals present at end
beaker of ice	violet	reactant and product	pink	reactant
beaker of hot water	violet	reactant and product	blue	product
test tubes are then swapped over				
beaker of ice	blue	product	pink	reactant
beaker of hot water	pink	reactant	blue	product

Table 9.7 Completed Table 9.3.

Beaker	Concentration of reactants	Time/s
left-hand	highest	5
2nd from the left	high	8
centre	intermediate	13
2nd from the right	low	23
right-hand	lowest	54

Speed of reaction

Towards the end of the video sequence, you examined the effect of temperature and concentration on the speed of a chemical reaction. The reaction used was that of iodide ions, I^-, with peroxodisulfate ions, $S_2O_8^{2-}$, often called the iodine 'clock' reaction:

$$S_2O_8^{2-}(aq) + 2I^-(aq) = 2SO_4^{2-}(aq) + I_2(aq) \tag{9.20}$$

A fixed amount of another compound was added to all the flasks; this compound removed the iodine, I_2, as it was formed. However, the added compound was itself consumed in this process. As soon as sufficient iodine was formed to remove all of the added compound, then the iodine concentration built up to give the black coloration. Thus the colour change marked the time taken for the reactions in each flask to form the same fixed amount of iodine. Faster reactions will form this amount of iodine in less time than slower reactions.

In these experiments, the solution went from colourless to black after different periods of time (Table 9.7). The results confirm that when the concentration of the reactants is reduced the reaction is slower and thus takes a longer time to form sufficient iodine for the colour change.

Task 3   What effect does a catalyst have on a chemical reaction?

Finally, the effect of a catalyst on the breakdown of hydrogen peroxide to give oxygen and water was demonstrated. Lead oxide and manganese dioxide were the best catalysts, i.e. they produced the fastest reaction; liver also produced a reaction, but potato and iron oxide were very poor catalysts.

Important points demonstrated in the video sequence Features of Reactions:

1   The majority of chemical reactions involve energy being released or taken in.

2   Some reactions are essentially irreversible and give only products.

3   Some reactions are reversible and can give a mixture of reactants and products.

4   Reactions occur at different speeds.

5   The speed of a reaction is dependent on temperature and can also depend on the initial concentration of reactants.

6   A catalyst speeds up a reaction without itself being consumed.

Activity 10.1

Your observations should allow you to draw the following conclusions.

Part 1

Introduction

1   A reaction occurring in a closed container at constant temperature and pressure eventually reaches a fixed composition known as the equilibrium composition.

2   At equilibrium, the proportions of the various chemicals present are fixed but individual molecules are continually undergoing chemical change from reactants to products and back.

3   For the same temperature, pressure and proportions of the chemicals involved, the equilibrium mixture for a given reaction is the same whether you start with the compounds on the left of the equation (as written), or those on the right, or a mixture of chemicals from each side.

Effect of pressure

4   For reactions involving gaseous molecules, it is possible to alter the pressure without adding or removing any chemicals. If there are more moles of product molecules than reactant molecules in the equation of the reaction, increasing the pressure in this way will decrease the proportion of product in the equilibrium mixture (set B).

5   If there are more moles of reactant molecules than product molecules in the equation of a reaction involving gaseous molecules, increasing the pressure will increase the proportion of product in the equilibrium mixture (set A). Where the number of moles of reactant and product molecules are the same, increasing the pressure will not affect the composition at equilibrium (set C).

6   The effects of changing pressure are examples of a more general principle known as Le Chatelier's principle, which states that: when a system in equilibrium is subject to an external constraint, the system responds in a way that tends to oppose the effect of the constraint.

Effect of temperature

7   If heat is released into the surroundings when a reaction takes place (i.e. the reaction is exothermic), performing the reaction at an increased temperature decreases the proportion of product in the equilibrium mixture (set A).

8   If heat is absorbed from the surroundings when a reaction takes place (i.e. the reaction is endothermic), increasing the temperature at which the reaction takes place increases the proportion of product in the equilibrium mixture (set B).

9   The effects of changing temperature are also examples of Le Chatelier's principle.

Part 2

Effect of concentration

10   For reactions involving ions in solution, increasing the concentration of a reactant will cause there to be more product in the equilibrium mixture.

11   Conversely, if the concentration of a product is increased, there will be an increase of reactant in the equilibrium mixture.

12   The effects of changing concentration are further examples of Le Chatelier's principle.

13   A graph of the concentrations of products multiplied together plotted against the concentrations of reactants multiplied together gives a straight line. The gradient of the line is known as the equilibrium constant K, and is different for different reactions.

Activity 11.1

Task 1

Here are a student's comments on this task.

> I need to decide what substances I'm going to test, what bits of equipment I'm going to use, how I'll carry out the tests, and how I'm going to record my results.

What substances shall I use?

> The activity instructions give quite a few suggestions. I've got all of the things listed, except for sparkling mineral water and bicarbonate of soda, so I'll test all of those I've got. That certainly gives me some solutions that are fairly acid – lemon juice and vinegar – and I think that washing soda is quite alkaline, so I should have quite a range. I'll also try cola, and I've got an opened bottle of white wine in the fridge so I'll try that too.

What equipment shall I use?

> The indicator papers are the vital things; there aren't many of them, so I'll take the advice in the notes to cut them in half lengthwise. I've got plenty of yoghurt pots saved for recycling, so I'll use them to put the substances or solutions in. I probably ought to wash them out first, since I'm not usually very careful about washing the things that I recycle. And I'll use a permanent marker pen to note the contents on each pot. The only other things that I can think of that I need are a few teaspoons, and some paper towels or rags for mopping up drips and spills, and drying the pots and spoons. And that makes me think that the draining board in the kitchen is the best place to do this work.

How will I do the tests?

> For the liquids, I can just pour a very small amount into a pot and dip a pH paper into it. What about soap and washing soda, which are solids? I'll have to dissolve them in water, but how much water? I guess the best thing to do is to make a saturated solution of each of the solids – put a teaspoonful in a pot and add a few spoonfuls of water, and stir it around for a while; as long as there's still some solid there the solution will be saturated. But does the amount of water make any difference? Presumably it must – the more water I add, the less concentrated the substance will be, so presumably the smaller the concentration of hydrogen ions. It would be worth checking this by measuring some of the solutions and then diluting them and measuring them again to see if there is a change in hydrogen ion concentration.

How will I record the results?

Table 11.2 is the obvious way, with columns for material tested, pH read from the cover of the indicator paper book, and hydrogen ion concentration from Table 11.1. And it will be useful to have a column for comments.

Task 2

Some of the hydrogen ion concentrations measured by a member of the course team are given in Tables 11.9 and 11.10. Do bear in mind that your solutions may not have the same concentrations as these and so you may have different values (although not too different). Also, you probably found that often the colour did not match any of those in the key exactly and you had to make a judgement as to which one or two it was closest to. This subjective element would mean that people testing identical solutions with identical papers may still come up with slightly different values.

Table 11.9 Completed Table 11.2.

Solution	pH	Approximate concentration of hydrogen ions/mol dm^{-3}	Comments
tap water	7–8	1×10^{-8} to 1×10^{-7}	
freshly boiled tap water	7	1×10^{-7}	
sparkling mineral water	5–6	1×10^{-6} to 1×10^{-5}	
lemon juice	2	1×10^{-2}	
vinegar	3–4	1×10^{-4} to 1×10^{-3}	
bicarbonate of soda	9–10	1×10^{-10} to 1×10^{-9}	
washing soda	10–11	1×10^{-11} to 1×10^{-10}	
household bleach	9	1×10^{-9}	difficult to tell; took colour out of paper
washing-up liquid	8	1×10^{-8}	paper colour masked by liquid colour
hair shampoo	5	1×10^{-5}	paper colour masked by liquid colour
floor cleaner liquid	8–9	1×10^{-9} to 1×10^{-8}	

Table 11.10 Completed Table 11.3.

Substance	Undiluted sample		Diluted 10-fold		Diluted 100-fold	
	pH	Hydrogen ion concentration/ mol dm^{-3}	pH	Hydrogen ion concentration/ mol dm^{-3}	pH	Hydrogen ion concentration/ mol dm^{-3}
washing soda	10–11	1×10^{-11} to 1×10^{-10}	10	1×10^{-10}	9	1×10^{-9}
washing-up liquid	8	1×10^{-8}	7	1×10^{-7}	7	1×10^{-7}
lemon juice	2	1×10^{-2}	3	1×10^{-3}	4	1×10^{-4}

Task 3

(a) The higher the hydrogen ion concentration, the more acidic the substance. For example, you know that lemon juice and vinegar are acidic and these have the highest (least negative powers of ten) hydrogen ion concentrations. Interestingly, 'caustic' substances, such as washing soda, have very low hydrogen ion concentrations.

(b) Most personal washing materials which involve skin contact, such as soaps and shampoos, have hydrogen ion concentrations in the range 1×10^{-6} mol dm^{-3} to 1×10^{-8} mol dm^{-3}. Household cleaners and dishwasher liquids have lower hydrogen ion concentrations in the range 1×10^{-8} mol dm^{-3} to 1×10^{-11} mol dm^{-3}. If you tried fabric conditioner, you probably found it has a relatively high hydrogen ion concentration.

(c) With the acidic solutions, dilution by a factor of 10 reduces the hydrogen ion concentration of the solution by up to a factor of 10. Dilution by a factor of 100 again reduces the hydrogen ion concentration. Dilution of the solutions with low hydrogen ion concentrations actually increases the hydrogen ion concentration, because of the contribution of the added hydrogen ion concentration from the dissociation of water.

Task 4

Here are the comments from a student after completing the investigation.

> My ideas in Task 1 were pretty much the same as the instructions, except I didn't think about making saturated solutions from all of the solids – I would have just dissolved an arbitrary amount in water. Also I didn't think about investigating what happens when more water is added to the solutions, though that seemed an obvious next step once it was suggested!

> For some of the liquids, I used their lids to pour a little liquid into for testing, which saved me a lot of fussing with yoghurt pots, though I still had to rinse the lid afterwards. In the dilution tests, I knew that a teaspoon was about 5 ml so I did all the dilutions in a measuring jug – 1 teaspoonful diluted to 50 ml – then tested. Then I diluted this solution to 500 ml and tested. This again saved time.

> After I'd finished the tests, I thought of several other things to test, and I wished that I had thought more carefully about what I was going to use. I wonder whether the liquid that I use for cleaning silver is very acidic, and I also wonder about fabric conditioner. The other thing that I now want to know is what the hydrogen ion concentration of distilled water is.

> So I guess that I was quite pleased with how the experiment worked out. I think that I did well to think of using the bottle lids, and of the method of diluting the liquids. The only minus points were that I should have thought a bit more about the experiment initially – could probably have thought of the dilution experiment myself – but time was short, and I wanted to get going! So the lessons I'm taking away from this are that it's worth looking for my own ways to improve on the instructions for the experiment – I don't need to assume that the OU has specified the best way – and that it would be useful to devote a bit more time to the initial 'thinking' stage.

Note that we gave you detailed instructions in Task 2 so that you would not waste any of your valuable time and because the number of indicator strips was limited. If we had not done so, you would probably have achieved the same results, but it may have taken somewhat longer. Also note that when you are evaluating your performance, it is as important to notice what you did well and why it was done well, as to identify what you can improve on another time.

Activity 12.1

(a) All the names end in -ane.

(b) As you progress from the top to the bottom of the second column, the numbers of carbon and hydrogen atoms in the molecular formula increase. In particular, there is a difference of one carbon atom and two hydrogen atoms between adjacent molecules. The next two columns show the same trend. As you go down the third column, each structure has an extra

$$-\overset{\displaystyle H}{\underset{\displaystyle H}{\overset{\displaystyle |}{\underset{\displaystyle |}{C}}}}-$$

in the structural formula, in comparison with the one above it. Similarly, the abbreviated structural formula contains an extra $-CH_2-$.

(c) As you go down the fifth column, the boiling temperature increases. However, it does not increase by the same amount each time; the difference between the boiling temperatures of adjacent molecules gets smaller and smaller. The increase in boiling temperature is due to the fact that van der Waals forces between molecules become stronger as the size of the molecules increases (Section 4.3).

(d) The next member after octane has a molecular formula with one extra carbon atom and two extra hydrogen atoms, thus the molecular formula is C_9H_{20}. The structural formula has an extra $-CH_2-$, giving:

$$H-\overset{H}{\underset{H}{C}}-\overset{H}{\underset{H}{C}}-\overset{H}{\underset{H}{C}}-\overset{H}{\underset{H}{C}}-\overset{H}{\underset{H}{C}}-\overset{H}{\underset{H}{C}}-\overset{H}{\underset{H}{C}}-\overset{H}{\underset{H}{C}}-\overset{H}{\underset{H}{C}}-H$$

and the abbreviated structural formula has an extra $-CH_2-$ giving:

$$CH_3-CH_2-CH_2-CH_2-CH_2-CH_2-CH_2-CH_2-CH_3.$$

This linear-chain hydrocarbon is called nonane.

Because the boiling temperatures increased by 29 and 28 °C in going from hexane to heptane and from heptane to octane, respectively, it would be reasonable to predict an increase of 27 °C to 153 °C for nonane. The measured value is actually 151 °C, so this is quite an accurate prediction.

Activity 13.1

(i) Hydrocracking involves the breaking down of hydrocarbons into smaller fragments. Hydrogen is supplied to ensure that alkanes are obtained. The atoms are also rearranged to give mainly branched-chain hydrocarbons. For example:

$$C_{16}H_{34}(g) + H_2(g) \longrightarrow 2C_8H_{18}(g)$$

(ii) Catalytic cracking involves heating an alkane strongly *without added hydrogen*, in the presence of a zeolite catalyst, to give alkenes. A typical transformation for catalytic cracking is:

$$CH_3-CH_2-CH_2-CH_2-CH_2-CH_2-CH_2-CH_2-CH_3$$

$$H_2 \; + \; CH_2{=}CH_2 \; + \; CH_3-CH{=}CH_2 \; + \; CH_3-CH_2-CH{=}CH_2$$

One of the products is hydrogen, which can be used in hydrocracking.

(iii) Catalytic reforming involves converting the linear-chain alkanes in crude oil into aromatic compounds, cycloalkanes and branched-chain alkanes. For example:

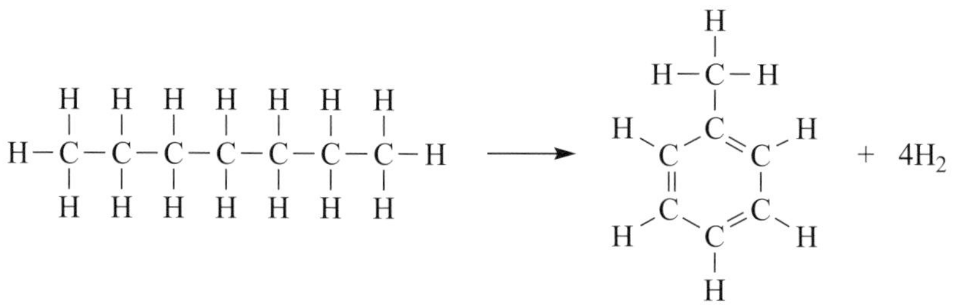

(iv) Isomerisation is carried out at 100–200 °C, using a platinum catalyst, and involves converting a compound into its isomer. For example:

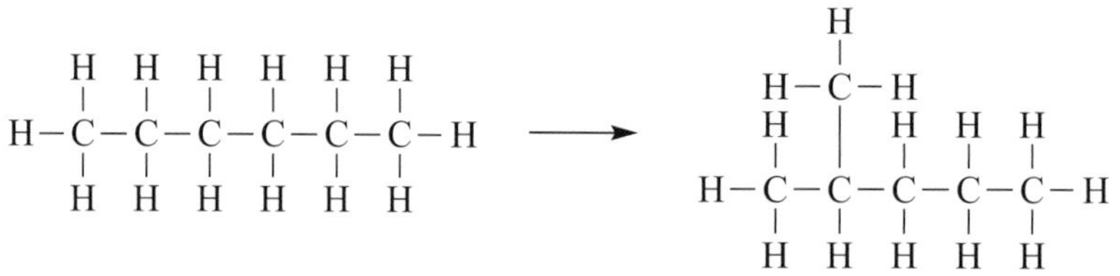

Hydrocracking and catalytic cracking are similar in that they are processes that involve large molecules being broken down into smaller ones. However, hydrocracking produces alkanes, which are saturated hydrocarbons, whereas catalytic cracking produces alkenes, which are unsaturated hydrocarbons. Both catalytic reforming and isomerisation convert alkanes into compounds with similar relative molecular masses to the starting compounds. The processes differ in that hydrocracking uses hydrogen to give alkanes, whereas isomerisation does not use hydrogen, and catalytic cracking and reforming actually form hydrogen. All of the processes require high pressure, high temperature and a catalyst, although this may not be stated explicitly in the text in each case.

Activity 14.2

Task 1

The glyceryl monostearate molecule contains an ester group and two alcohol groups:

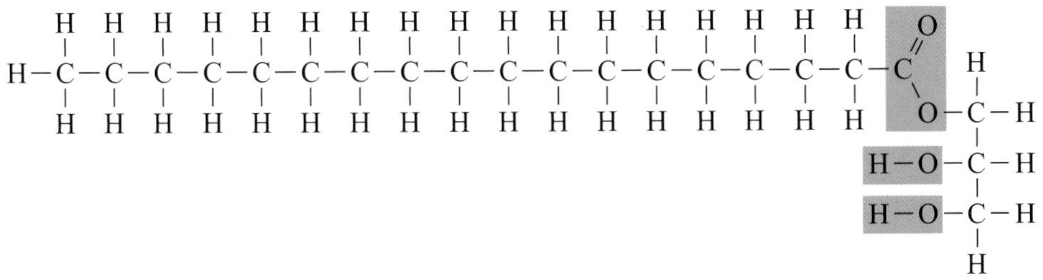

The molecule has a linear chain of 17 carbons attached to the ester group, and it also has a chain of three carbon atoms with an oxygen attached to each:

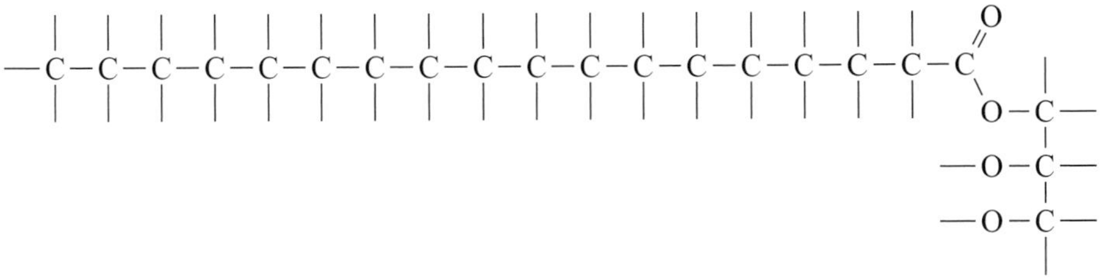

Note that the carbon that is part of the ester functional group is not counted as part of the linear chain of carbon atoms.

Task 2

When an S104 tutor was asked how she analysed the structure of this molecule she responded as follows.

> When I look at a structure, I first focus on the functional groups. The way to spot functional groups is to look for double bonds, or atoms other than hydrogen and carbon. The functional groups that are important for S104 are in Table 14.3. It's important to make sure you've spotted all the atoms in a functional group. For example, an —OH could be an alcohol group, but it could also be part of a carboxylic acid, so I check to see if there is a double bond to oxygen on the carbon connected to the —OH group. Another possible confusion is between a carboxylic acid, which has a hydrogen atom attached to one of the oxygens, and an ester, where the corresponding oxygen is attached to another carbon atom. I usually circle the functional groups, or shade over them, to avoid counting them twice.
>
> Having identified the functional groups, the next thing I do is to focus on the carbon atoms, and identify how many chains, or rings, of carbons are present, how many carbons are in each chain, and whether the chains are linear or branched. Glyceryl monostearate has a linear chain of 17 carbons attached to the ester group, and it also has a chain of three carbon atoms with an oxygen attached to each. Then, if there is more

than one chain of carbon atoms in the molecule, I establish how the chains are joined together and how the groups are sited on the carbon chains. In glyceryl monostearate, the two chains are joined together by an ester group. The —OH groups are on adjacent atoms of the three-carbon chain, next to the ester group.

One final thing that I often do is to check that the remaining valencies on the carbons are satisfied with hydrogens. This helps to confirm that there are no other functional groups that I've missed.

Here is a summary of this tutor's strategy.

1   Identify which functional groups are present.

2   Identify the saturated carbon chains.

3   Establish how the functional groups and chains are joined together.

Your strategy may have been different from this – there is no unique way of analysing the structure of an organic molecule – but you should carefully compare your strategy with the tutor's, and modify your strategy if necessary.

Please attempt Task 3 before reading the following comments.

Task 3

You can use the three steps of the tutor's strategy, summarised at the end of Task 2, to analyse the structure of linoleic acid.

1   Identify which functional groups are present.

Here you can identify two carbon–carbon double bonds and a carboxylic acid group:

$$H-\overset{\overset{\displaystyle H}{|}}{\underset{\underset{\displaystyle H}{|}}{C}}-\overset{\overset{\displaystyle H}{|}}{\underset{\underset{\displaystyle H}{|}}{C}}-\overset{\overset{\displaystyle H}{|}}{\underset{\underset{\displaystyle H}{|}}{C}}-\overset{\overset{\displaystyle H}{|}}{\underset{\underset{\displaystyle H}{|}}{C}}-\overset{\overset{\displaystyle H}{|}}{\underset{\underset{\displaystyle H}{|}}{C}}-\boxed{CH=CH}-\overset{\overset{\displaystyle H}{|}}{\underset{\underset{\displaystyle H}{|}}{C}}-\boxed{CH=CH}-\overset{\overset{\displaystyle H}{|}}{\underset{\underset{\displaystyle H}{|}}{C}}-\overset{\overset{\displaystyle H}{|}}{\underset{\underset{\displaystyle H}{|}}{C}}-\overset{\overset{\displaystyle H}{|}}{\underset{\underset{\displaystyle H}{|}}{C}}-\overset{\overset{\displaystyle H}{|}}{\underset{\underset{\displaystyle H}{|}}{C}}-\overset{\overset{\displaystyle H}{|}}{\underset{\underset{\displaystyle H}{|}}{C}}-\overset{\overset{\displaystyle H}{|}}{\underset{\underset{\displaystyle H}{|}}{C}}-\overset{\overset{\displaystyle H}{|}}{\underset{\underset{\displaystyle H}{|}}{C}}-\boxed{\overset{\overset{\displaystyle O}{\|}}{C}\diagdown_{O-H}}$$

2   Identify the saturated carbon chains.

In **14.7**, there are three sets of saturated carbon atoms: a linear chain of five carbon atoms attached to the carbon–carbon double bond on the left; a linear chain of seven carbon atoms between the carboxylic acid and the carbon–carbon double bond on the right; and a single carbon atom between the two carbon–carbon double bonds:

$$-\overset{|}{\underset{|}{C}}-\overset{|}{\underset{|}{C}}-\overset{|}{\underset{|}{C}}-\overset{|}{\underset{|}{C}}-\overset{|}{\underset{|}{C}}-\overset{|}{C}=\overset{|}{C}-\overset{|}{\underset{|}{C}}-\overset{|}{C}=\overset{|}{C}-\overset{|}{\underset{|}{C}}-\overset{|}{\underset{|}{C}}-\overset{|}{\underset{|}{C}}-\overset{|}{\underset{|}{C}}-\overset{|}{\underset{|}{C}}-\overset{|}{\underset{|}{C}}-\overset{\overset{\displaystyle O}{\|}}{C}\diagdown_{O-H}$$

3   Establish how the functional groups and chains are joined together.

The carboxylic acid group is attached to the end of the chain of seven carbon atoms, and the sets of carbon atoms are joined to each other via the carbon–carbon double bonds. All the other atoms are hydrogen atoms.

$$H-\overset{\overset{\displaystyle H}{|}}{\underset{\underset{\displaystyle H}{|}}{C}}-\overset{\overset{\displaystyle H}{|}}{\underset{\underset{\displaystyle H}{|}}{C}}-\overset{\overset{\displaystyle H}{|}}{\underset{\underset{\displaystyle H}{|}}{C}}-\overset{\overset{\displaystyle H}{|}}{\underset{\underset{\displaystyle H}{|}}{C}}-\overset{\overset{\displaystyle H}{|}}{\underset{\underset{\displaystyle H}{|}}{C}}-\overset{\overset{\displaystyle H}{|}}{C}=\overset{|}{C}-\overset{\overset{\displaystyle H}{|}}{\underset{\underset{\displaystyle H}{|}}{C}}-\overset{\overset{\displaystyle H}{|}}{C}=\overset{|}{C}-\overset{\overset{\displaystyle H}{|}}{\underset{\underset{\displaystyle H}{|}}{C}}-\overset{\overset{\displaystyle H}{|}}{\underset{\underset{\displaystyle H}{|}}{C}}-\overset{\overset{\displaystyle H}{|}}{\underset{\underset{\displaystyle H}{|}}{C}}-\overset{\overset{\displaystyle H}{|}}{\underset{\underset{\displaystyle H}{|}}{C}}-\overset{\overset{\displaystyle H}{|}}{\underset{\underset{\displaystyle H}{|}}{C}}-\overset{\overset{\displaystyle H}{|}}{\underset{\underset{\displaystyle H}{|}}{C}}-\overset{\overset{\displaystyle O}{\|}}{C}\diagdown_{O-H}$$

Please attempt Task 4 before reading the following comments.

Task 4

Again you can use the three-step strategy from Task 2 to decide whether **14.8** is linoleic acid.

1   Identify which functional groups are present.

Here you can identify two carbon–carbon double bonds and a carboxylic acid functional group:

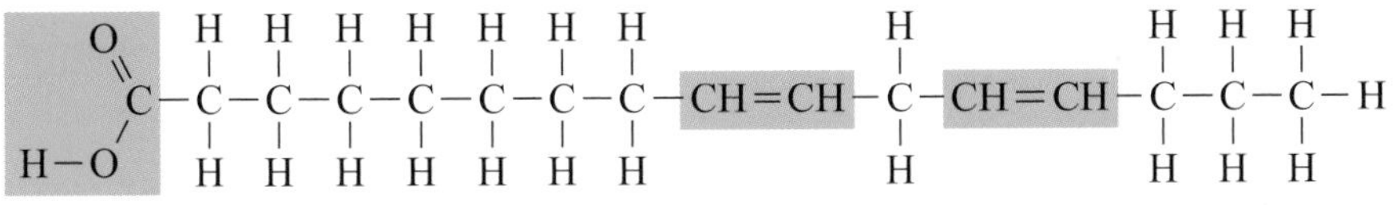

2   Identify the saturated carbon chains.

In **14.8**, there are three sets of saturated carbon atoms: there is a linear chain of three carbon atoms attached to the carbon–carbon double bond on the right of the molecule; and a linear chain of seven carbon atoms between the carboxylic acid on the left of the molecule and the leftmost carbon–carbon double bond; there is also a single carbon atom between the two carbon–carbon double bonds.

3   Establish how the functional groups and chains are joined together.

The carboxylic acid group is again attached to the end of the chain of seven carbon atoms, and the sets of carbon atoms are joined to each other via the carbon–carbon double bonds.

14.8 looks more like the linoleic acid structure in **14.7** if it is rotated through 180°:

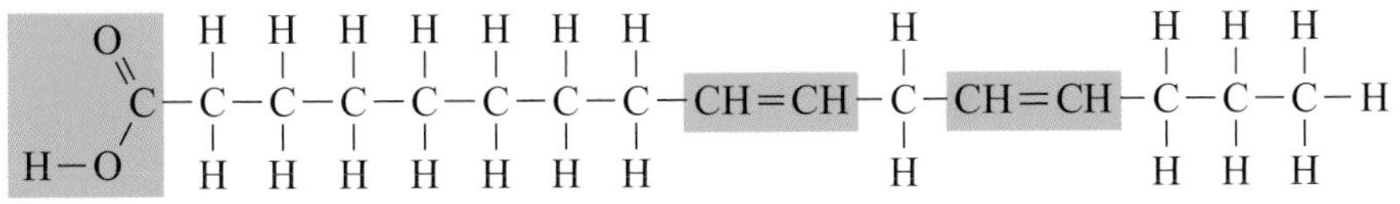

Both **14.8** and linoleic acid have a carboxylic acid group attached to a chain of seven carbon atoms, which is attached to a carbon–carbon double bond, which is attached to a single carbon, which is attached to another carbon–carbon double bond. However, linoleic acid then has a chain of five carbon atoms, whereas **14.8** has a chain of only three carbon atoms, so the two are not identical.

Activity 14.3

Task 1

This is an oxidation reaction, and the product is a carboxylic acid:

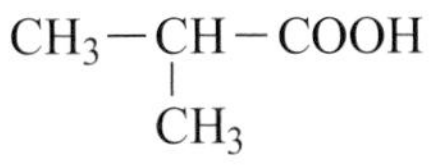

$$CH_3-CH-COOH$$
$$|$$
$$CH_3$$

Task 2

The strategy used by a member of the course team is as follows.

1   Identify the functional group(s) in the organic molecule(s).

In this case, you have an organic molecule containing an alcohol functional group.

2   Next look up the reactions of the functional group(s).

Table 14.3 is a useful source of reference for the important reactions. So far, you have learned that alcohols undergo condensation reactions and oxidation reactions. Condensations reactions involve reaction with a carboxylic acid, which you don't have here. However, the oxidation reaction shown in Table 14.3 indicates that $K_2Cr_2O_7$ oxidises alcohols to carboxylic acids, so this is the appropriate reaction:

$$R-CH_2-OH \xrightarrow[HCl]{K_2Cr_2O_7} R-COOH$$

3   Finally, identify the hydrocarbon portions of the reactant(s), and copy them to give the product.

Comparing the alcohol in the question with $R-CH_2-OH$, you can see that in this case R is

$$\begin{array}{c} CH_3 \\ \diagdown \\ CH- \\ \diagup \\ CH_3 \end{array}$$

so you draw the product by replacing R, to give:

$$CH_3-\underset{\underset{CH_3}{|}}{CH}-CH_2-OH \xrightarrow[HCl]{K_2Cr_2O_7} CH_3-\underset{\underset{CH_3}{|}}{CH}-COOH$$

Compare your strategy with the one outlined above. It may be different – as usual, there is more than one way to tackle a problem! You may want to combine the best points of the two approaches.

Please attempt Task 3 before reading the following comments.

Task 3

Again you can use the three-step strategy outlined in Task 2.

1   Identify the functional group(s) in the organic molecule(s).

In this case, the organic molecule contains an alkene functional group.

2   Next look up the reactions of the functional group(s).

The only reaction of alkenes that you have learned about so far is an addition reaction and, as shown in Table 14.3, this has the general form:

$$R^1-CH=CH-R^2 + X-Y \longrightarrow R^1-\underset{\underset{X}{|}}{CH}-\underset{\underset{Y}{|}}{CH}-R^2$$

In this case, the reaction involves addition of bromine, so X and Y are both Br.

$$R^1-CH=CH-R^2 + Br_2 \longrightarrow R^1-\underset{\underset{Br}{|}}{CH}-\underset{\underset{Br}{|}}{CH}-R^2$$

3   Finally, identify the hydrocarbon portions of the reactant(s), and copy them to give the product.

Comparing the alkene in the question with the general formula $R^1-CH=CH-R^2$, in this case R^1 and R^2 are both CH_3-CH_2-. So the product is drawn by replacing R^1 and R^2 with CH_3-CH_2-:

$$CH_3-CH_2-CH=CH-CH_2-CH_3 + Br_2 \longrightarrow CH_3-CH_2-\underset{\underset{Br}{|}}{CH}-\underset{\underset{Br}{|}}{CH}-CH_2-CH_3$$

Please attempt Task 4 before reading the following comments.

Task 4

The same strategy works for this slightly more complicated reaction.

1   Identify the functional group(s) in the organic molecule(s).

In this case, there are two organic molecules – an alcohol and a carboxylic acid:

$$CH_3-CH_2-C \overset{O}{\underset{OH}{\lt}} \qquad HO-\overset{\overset{CH_3}{|}}{\underset{\underset{CH_3}{|}}{C}}-H$$

carboxylic acid   alcohol

2   Next look up the reactions of the functional group(s).

Table 14.3 shows that alcohols undergo condensation reactions with carboxylic acids:

$$R^1-C\overset{O}{\underset{OH}{\lt}} \quad + \quad HO-R^2 \qquad R^1-C\overset{O}{\underset{O-R^2}{\lt}} \quad + \quad H_2O$$

3   Finally, identify the hydrocarbon portions of the reactant(s), and copy them to give the product.

This is a little more complex because there are two hydrocarbon chains and two different places to put them. The general equation in Table 14.3 shows that the hydrocarbon portion of the carboxylic acid ends up attached to the carbon of the ester group and that the hydrocarbon portion of the alcohol ends up attached to the oxygen of the ester. Another way of looking at this is that the $RC{=}O$ comes from the acid and the $-O-R^2$ comes from the alcohol:

$$\underset{\text{carboxylic acid}}{\text{from}} \quad R^1-C\overset{O}{\underset{O-R^2}{\lt}} \quad \text{from alcohol}$$

Since the hydrocarbon portion does not change during the reaction, once you have identified which hydrocarbon goes where, it is just a question of copying them down correctly. In this case, R^1 is CH_3-CH_2- and R^2 is $CH_3-CH-CH_3$. So the reaction is:

$$CH_3-CH_2-C\overset{O}{\underset{OH}{\lt}} \quad + \quad HO-\overset{\overset{CH_3}{|}}{\underset{\underset{CH_3}{|}}{C}}-H \quad \longrightarrow \quad CH_3-CH_2-C\overset{O}{\underset{O-\overset{\underset{CH_3}{|}}{\underset{|}{C}}-H}{\lt}}\overset{CH_3}{}$$

At various points during the rest of the book you will be asked to predict reactants or products, and it is recommended that you use a similar strategy whenever possible. You will find that this strategy, and also your strategy for analysing the structure of organic molecules, will be useful when you meet functional groups during your study of Book 5.

References

US Geological Survey (2007) *Mineral Commodity Summaries 2007*, Washington, US Geological Survey; also available online at http://minerals.usgs.gov/minerals/pubs/mcs/2007/mcs2007.pdf (Accessed 26 October 2007).

Acknowledgements

The S104 course team gratefully acknowledges the contributions of the S103 *Discovering science* course team and of its predecessors, and the contributions of Stuart Bennett and the ST240 *Our chemical environment* course team.

Grateful acknowledgement is made to the following sources for permission to reproduce material in this book.

Figures

Cover: Eric Heller/Science Photo Library;

Figures 1.1, 1.2, 1.4, 1.5 and 1.9: Courtesy of Stuart Bennett; Figure 1.3: NASA; Figure 1.7: © bpk/Gemäldegalerie, SMB/Jörg P. Anders; Figure 1.8: Mary Evans Picture Library;

Figure 2.4: Publisher unknown;

Figure 3.2: Courtesy of TopoMetrix Corporation;

Figure 4.9: Scott Camazine/Science Photo Library; Figure 4.11: Courtesy of Stuart Bennett;

Figures 7.1 and 7.2: © The Trustees of the British Museum; Figures 7.3, 7.7 and 7.17: Courtesy of Stuart Bennett; Figure 7.5: Peter Newark American Pictures/The Bridgeman Art Library; Figure 7.12: Courtesy of Billiton International Metals; Figure 7.13: Courtesy of Wardown Park Museum, Luton, Bedfordshire, UK; Figure 7.16: Michael Holford; Figure 7.18: Courtesy of Weald and Downland Open Air Museum;

Figures 8.5 and 8.6: Courtesy of Stuart Bennett;

Figure 9.3: FreeFoto.com; Figure 9.9: © Return to Fitness Ltd; Figure 9.12: Petrucci, R.H., Harwood, W.S. and Herring, G., (2002) *General Chemistry: Principles and Modern Applications* (8th edn), p.9, © 2002, reprinted by permission of Pearson Education Inc, Upper Saddle River, NJ;

Figure 10.1a: Roger Courthold; Figure 10.1b: A Room with Views/Alamy; Figure 10.5: Richard Sheppard/Alamy; Figure 10.14b: Lee Hacker/Alamy;

Figure 11.6a: © Mark Edwards/Still Pictures; Figure 11.6b: Building Research Establishment;

Figure 12.1: Martyn F. Chillmaid/Science Photo Library; Figures 12.3 and 12.4: Courtesy of Minton Treharne & Davies Ltd;

Figure 13.3: Robert Brook/Science Photo Library;

Figure 14.1: Science Photo Library;

Figure 15.11: Steve Percival/Science Photo Library;

Figure 16.1: Wellcome Library, London; Figure 16.8: Charles D. Winters/Science Photo Library;

Figure 17.1: Charles Bensinger, Renewable Energy Partners of New Mexico;

Every effort has been made to contact copyright holders. If any have been inadvertently overlooked the publishers will be pleased to make the necessary arrangements at the first opportunity.

Index

Entries and page numbers in **bold type** refer to key words that are printed in **bold** in the text and that are defined in the Glossary. Where the page number is given in *italics*, the index information is carried mainly or wholly in an illustration, table or box.

A

abbreviated structural formula 171, *172, 173*

acetal *210,* **233**–4, 236

acetate ions 150–1, 153–4

acetic (ethanoic) acid 144, 150–5, *155,* 198

    formation 205

    reactions 202–3, 241

acetylene 103

acetylsalicylic acid 240–1

acid rain *156*

acidic solution 159, *160*

acids 83, 143, 144

    equilibrium constant for acid dissociation 153–5

    hydrogen ion concentration 144–53

    measuring acidity 160–4

    reactions of metals with 81, 83–5

    see also individual acids

active site 242–4, 249, *250*

activity series 82, 83–6, 90

addition reactions 189–90, *208, 211,* 221

adrenal (suprarenal) gland 245

adrenalin 244–6, 247–8, 249

aircraft 1, 70, 90

alanine 224, 225, *227*

alcohols 197, *208, 210*

    oxidation 205–6, 207

    reactions 201–3, 215–16

    see also ethanol

alkanes 177–83, *208*

    haloalkanes 196, *208, 211*

    see also methane

alkenes 188, *192,* 195, *208, 210*

    reactions of 189–90, 221–3

allotropes 76

alloys 45, 69, 78, 92–3

aluminium *70,* 86, 87

    reactions 93, 95

    uses 70, 90

aluminium bromide 95

aluminium oxide 86, 90, 93

amides *211,* **225**–6, 231

amines *210,* 224–5

amino acid residue 227–8, 231

amino acids 224–8, 230–1

amino group *210,* 224, 225–7

ammonia 152

    production 124, 136, *137*

ammonium chloride 124

ammonium dichromate *99*

anaesthetics *196*

anions 19, *20,* 58

    charges on *88, 90*

anode 33, 87

aqueous solution 34–5, 61, 81–2

A$_r$ **16**

arachidonic acid *218,* 223

argon 43, 50, 51–2

aromatics 177–9, *181,* 182

Arrhenius, Svante 83, 84

aspirin 239–41, 243–4

Association for the Study of Peak Oil 209

asthma 244, 246

atomic nucleus 17, 43

atomic number 15, *48*

atoms 13–17, 43–4

    in crystals 28–30

    electronic configuration 44–7, 49–52

    in molecules 17–19

Avogadro constant 40

Avogadro hypothesis 37–40

B

balanced chemical equation 60–2, 95–6

ball-and-stick model *18, 24, 28, 175, 232, 233*

barbituric acid 176

barium nitrate 57

base number 161

bases 84, 143, 144–53

basic solution 159, *160*

benzene 178, *181*

benzoic acid 203

beryllium 93

biofuels *251*

biopolymers 227

bitumen *169, 185*

blast furnace 80, 86

blister copper 75, 87

blood, pH 163, *164*

boiling temperature 36, 167, 168, *169*

    hydrocarbons *172, 173,* 174

bond angle 18, *28*

bond length 17, *28*

bonding electrons 25–6

branched-chain hydrocarbons 173–5

    alkanes *177,* 178, *181,* 182

brass 45, *93*

bromine 95, 189–90

bronze 45, 76–8, 92–3

Bronze Age *3,* 4, 69, 77, 78, 79

butane 170, 171, *172,* 174, *185*

butanoic acid 198

butyric acid *218*

C

caesium 82

calcium 82

calcium carbide 103

calcium hydroxide 143

calcium nitrate 143

capric acid *218*

carbohydrates *109,* **213,** 232–7

carbon

    allotropes 76

    bonding 29–30, 170

    burning *109*

    handedness 228–30

    in iron and steel 79–80, 93

valence electrons 53
see also double bonds
carbon dioxide 32, *39, 55*
from burning fuels 62, 109
concentration in the air 64–5
as reaction product 59–61
carbon monoxide 141
carboxylic acids 198, 203–4, *208, 211*
functional group 224, 225–7, 240
reactions 206, 215–17, 225
see also acetic (ethanoic) acid
cars
exhausts 141
fuels for 180–2, 251
cassiterite *75, 76*
catalysts 98, 123–4, 140, 182, 222
see also **enzymes**
catalytic converters 141
catalytic cracking 188, *208*
catalytic reforming 182
cathode 33, 87
cations 19, *20,* 58
in aqueous solution 81–2
charges on *88,* 90
metallic *73, 74*
cellulose 235
CFCs 186, 196
changes of state 104–8
charcoal 79
chemical bonds 17, 112
see also **covalent bonds;** double
bonds; **hydrogen bonds; ionic
bonding;** single bonds
chemical energy 99
chemical equations 59–62
balanced 60–2, 95–6
calculating quantities from 62–5
ionic 61, 83–5
thermochemical 104–9
chemical equilibrium 115, 124
computer-based activity 133–4, 140–1
Le Chatelier's principle 133–41
quantitative approach 127–32
reversible reactions and dynamic
equilibrium 124–7
see also equilibrium constant;
equilibrium dissociation
chemical formula 18, 29, 57–8
chemical kinetics 115–17

changing the energy barrier 123–4
molecular collisions and energy 119–23
varying the reaction rate 118–19
chemical reactions
effect of concentration on 98, 116–20
and enthalpy 102–4, 110–13
exothermic and endothermic 100–2
observing properties of 97–8
thermochemical equations 104–9
see also **chemical equilibrium;
chemical kinetics**
chemical symbols 14
chiral 229–31, 236–7, 249
chlorine 16, 19, *20, 35*
atom 25, 51–2
gas molecule 54–5
production 33–4
chloroform (trichloromethane) *196*
cholesterol 219
chromium *70,* 93
cis **220**–1
citric acid 144, 176
classification 253–4
compounds in crude oil *177, 179, 181*
elements 45
organic compounds 195
'clock' reaction 116, *117,* 118–19
coke 80, *185*
cold pack *102*
compounds 18
compressibility 32, 37
computer-based activities 5
chemical equilibrium 133–4, 140–1
Features of Reactions 97, 99, 116,
117, 123
*Functional Groups of Organic
Molecules* 195
Minerals Gallery 20, 22, 30–1
Reactivity of Metals 81
The Shapes of Molecules 176
Viewing Food Molecules 237
concentration 65–6, 152
and acid dissociation 153–4
and chemical equilibrium 127–9,
139–41
effect on a chemical reaction 98,
116–20
and equilibrium constant 131–2
condensation 106, 167

condensation polymers 227
condensation reactions 201, 202–4,
208, 211
acetals 234
amino acids 225–6
salicylic acid 241
triacylglycerols 215–16
copper *70,* 74–5
alloys 76–8, 92–3
cations in solution 81–2
electrolytic purification 87
occurrence and extraction *81,* 86
reactions 78, 85, 86
copper oxide 75, 85
copper sulfate 87
corrosion *78,* 90–2
resistance to 92, 93
see also rust
covalent bonds 17, 54–6, 189
in crystals 28–9
formation from enzymes 243–4
cracking 187, 188, *208*
hydrocracking 181–2, 186, 187
crude oil 167–9, 171, 251
activity on alternatives to 252
compounds in 176–9
functional groups and 208–9
further uses of 185–93
hydrocarbons in *173, 177*
as a source of fuel 180–3
crystals 19–20, 23, 27–9
examining quartz 30–1
phase change 31, 32
cycloalkanes 177, 178, *181,* 182
cyclohexane 177, 180, *181*
cyclo-oxygenase 243–4

D

D-sugars 237
Δ*H* 103–4
density *70,* 72
desalination *168*
detergents 83
diacylglyceride 216
diamond 76
diesel *169, 185*
digestion 221, 230–1, 235–7
dilute 152

dinitrogen tetroxide 139–40

dipole 24–6, 29–30, *35*

dipole–dipole forces 25–6

disaccharides 235, 236

displacement reactions 82, 85, 90

dissociation 111, 132

    acids 150–2, 204

    equilibrium constant for 153–5

    equilibrium dissociation of water 156–60

distillation 167–9, 181

double bonds 55, 178, 187–8, 189, *210*

    cis and *trans* forms 219–20

dry cleaning 35, 196

dry ice 32

dynamic equilibrium 124–7

E

Earth

    crust 7, *8*, 9–10, *70*

    distribution of elements *8*, 9–10

    distribution of metals *70*

    energy consumption *97*

    water cycle 156

eicosanoids 223

electrical charge 15, 16, 17, 19–20

electrical circuit *151*

electrical conductivity 33, *70*, 71, 73–4, 87

    acids 150, *151*

electrodes 33, 87

electrolysis 33–4, 86–7

electron shells 43–5, 47, *49*, 50–2

electronic configuration 44–7, 49–52

electrons 15–17

    bonding electrons 25–6

    dipole and 24–5

    loss and gain in chemical reactions 46–7, 205

    in metal structures 73–4

    sharing 54–5

    valence electrons 50, 53

elements 7, *8*, 9–10

    atoms in 15–16

    classification of 45

    and the Periodic Table 47, *48*, *49*, 50–2

    valency values *53*

empirical formula 29

emulsifiers 200, 223

endothermic 100

    and chemical equilibrium 137–**8**

    energy barriers and *122*

endothermic reaction 101, *104*, 105

energy barrier 121–4

energy changes 95–113

energy consumption, global *97*

energy profiles *123, 124*

enthalpy 102, 103, 104

enthalpy change 103, *109*, 110–13

    changes of state and 104–8

enthalpy of vaporisation 105–6

enzymes 124, 221, 231, 236–7

    active site *250*

    effect of drugs on 241–3

    formation of covalent bonds 243–4

    intermolecular forces 244–7

equilibrium constant 128, *140*

    for acid dissociation 153–5

    magnitude of 132, 157

    units for 130–2

equilibrium dissociation *155*, 156–60

equilibrium expression 127–31

equilibrium yield 135

essential fatty acids 223

esters 199–200, *208, 211*

    formation 202–3, 244

    functional groups 215–16, 240

    hydrolysis 221

ethane *172*

ethanol *109*, 197, 202

    as alternative feedstock 251

    water solution 34–5

ethene 187, *188*, 189, 192, 251

ethyl acetate 199

ethylene glycol 197

exothermic 100, *122*, 137–8

exothermic reaction 101, 102, 103, *104*

experimental design 146, 147

F

fats 213

    manufacture *222*, 223

    properties 213–20

    reactions *109*, 221–3

fatty acids 188, 201, **217**–20

Features of Reactions 97, 99, 116, *117*, 123

fibre, dietary 235

'fight or flight' hormone 245–6

fluorine *39*, 102, 108

fluoromethane 196

food 83, 118, 200, *213*

    cans 70, 76

    functional groups in food chemistry 213–38

formula mass 75

forward reaction 124–5, 127

fossil fuels 96, *97*, 209, 252

    see also **crude oil**; fuels

fractional distillation 167–9

fractions (distillation) 168, *169*, 181

freezing 31, 35, **107**

freons 196

fructose 232–6

fuels

    burning in oxygen 108, *109*

    for cars 180–2, 251

    crude oil as a source of 180–3

    fuel filling station 2–3

    see also fossil fuels

functional groups 190

    approach 195–201

    in aspirin 239–41, 244

    characteristic reactions of 201–8

    crude oil and 208–9

    in drugs 245, 248–50

    in food chemistry 213–38

    key functional groups *210*–11

    in triacylglycerol 215–16

Functional Groups of Organic Molecules 195

fusion 107–8

G

galactose 235, 237

galvanising 91–2

gases 37–40

    chemical equilibrium and 135–6, *137*

    enthalpy changes between 110–13

    see also individual gases

gasoline (petrol) *169*, 180–2, *185*

gastric juice 163, *164*

geraniol 197

glucose 232–6

    reaction with oxygen 60–1

glycerol (glycerine) 215–17

glyceryl monostearite (E471) 200, 223

gold 9, *10, 70,* 71–3

    atoms in 13, *14*

    jewellery *71,* 72, 78

    occurrence and extraction *81*

    reactivity 46, 47, 72–3, 78

graphite 76

'grey tin' 76

ground state 45

group 47

group 1 52, *88,* 90

group 2 52, *88,* 90

group 13 *88,* 90

group 16 *88,* 90

group 17 *88,* 90

H

H 103

Haber–Bosch process 136

halite 22

haloalkanes 196, *208, 211*

handedness 228–30, 236–7

hardness 77–9, 92, 93

Haworth projection *232,* 233, 237

heat 99, *109*

    conductivity *70, 71*

    release and absorption of 100–2, 103

helium 18, 44–5, 49

    in the Universe 7, *8*

heptan-2-ol 197

heptane *172,* 180, *181,* 182

hexane *172, 181,* 183

hexanoic acid 198

Hindenburg disaster 109

history 3–5, 7

hormones 245–6

household solutions

    hydrogen ion concentration 146–9

    pH 162–3, *164*

hydrocarbons 170–9

    see also **alkanes; aromatics**

hydrochloric acid 83, 84, 85, 143, 152

    concentration of hydroxide ions in 158

conductivity 150, *151*

    equilibrium constant *155*

    as reagent 205–6, 207

hydrocracking 181–2, 186, 187

hydroelectric power *97*

hydrogen 18, 44–5, 170, 171

    burning in air 108, 109

    production 128, 136, 138

    reactions 110–12, 125–31, 139, 189, 190

    relative molecular mass 38, *39,* 40

    in the Universe 7, *8,* 9

hydrogen bonds 26–**7,** 28, 31, 106–7

    in drugs *246,* 247–8

    in solutions *34,* 35

hydrogen chloride 25–6, 83, 150, 152

hydrogen iodide 125–31, 139

hydrogen ion concentration 144–53

    measuring 160–4

    from water 156–60

hydrogen ions 83, 84–5, 143, 204

hydrogen peroxide 123

hydrogen sulfide 26

hydrogenation 222–3

hydrolysis *211,* **221,** 231, 236, 242–3

hydrophobic interactions 247, 248

hydroxide ions 84–5, 143, 152

    concentration 144, *145,* 156–60

hydroxyl groups **197,** 201–2, *210,* 233–5

hypochlorous acid *155*

I

ice *27,* 28, 29, *105*

    melting 31, 33

indicator papers 146–9

Industrial Revolution 5, 69, 78

inorganic chemistry 187

insulators 71

intermolecular forces 23–7, 244–9

internal energy 99–103

    and energy barriers *121,* 123–4

intramolecular forces 23

iodic acid *155*

iodine

    'clock' reaction 116, *117,* 118–19

    molecules 24–5, 27

    reaction with hydrogen 125–31, 139

ion product of water 157, 158

ionic bonding 20, 32

    in drugs 246–7

    valency and chemical formulas 57–8

ionic equations 61, 83–5

ionic groups *58*

ionic solids 20–2, 27, 32, 33, 35

ions 19–20, 58, 61

    metal ions 81–2, 88, 90

    see also **anions; cations**

iron *8,* 9, *70,* 82

    occurrence and extraction 73, 79, *81,* 86

    reactivity 72, 86

    rusting of 46, 72, 78, 82, 90–2, 101, *115*

    uses of 78, 93

Iron Age *71,* 78, 79–80

iron oxide 79, 80, 86

isoelectronic 51

isoleucine *224, 225*

isomeric 174

isomerisation 183

isomers 174

iso-octane 180, *181*

isopentyl acetate 199

isotopes 16

K

K_w 157–9

kerosene *169, 185*

kinetic energy 99

knocking 180–1

krypton 50

L

L-sugars 237

lactose 232, 235

latent heat of vaporisation *105*

lauric acid *218*

law of conservation of energy 99

law of mass action 127

Le Chatelier's principle 133, *134,* **135**–41

lead *70,* 93

leaded petrol 181

leucine *224, 225,* 226, *227*

Lewis structure 54–5, *170*

linear-chain hydrocarbons 170–1, *172, 191*

    alkanes *177,* 178, 180–3

linoleic acid 201, *218*

linolenic acid *218,* 223

lipases 221

liquids 32–6

    see also water

lithium 44–5, 50–1

lithium hydroxide 64–5

logarithms 160–2

lubricating oils *169,* 181, *185*

M

M_r **18**

magnesium 58, *70*

    reactions 46, 47, 83–4, 102, 108

    as sacrificial metal 92

magnets *24*

malachite *74,* 75

maltose 232, 235

manganese 86

margarine production *222,* 223

mass

    formula mass 75

    molar mass 63, 66

    see also **relative atomic mass; relative formula mass; relative molecular mass**

melting 31–2, 33

melting temperature *70, 77,* 93

Mendeléev, Dmitri 45, 47

metabolism 232, 241–2, 243

metal ions 81–2, 88, 90

metals 45–7, 69–80, *70*

    atomic model of 73–4

    modifying 92–4

    occurrence and extraction *81*

    oxidation and reduction 85–8

    in the Periodic Table 88, *89,* 90

    properties 69–71, 90–2

    reactions 81, 83–5

    through history 7, 69, 71–2, 75–7

    see also individual metals

methane 53, 55, *170, 172*

burning in oxygen 59–60, 62, 108, *109, 115*

    production of hydrogen from 136, 138

methanol *109,* 197, 202, 203

methyl butanoate 199

methyl group 173

methyl salicylate 199

2-methylbutane *173,* 176

2-methylpentane *173,* 176

2-methylpropane *173,* 174, 176

Minerals Gallery 20, 22, 30–1

mirror images *228, 229, 230,* 236–7, *249*

molar bond enthalpy 111–12

molar mass 63, 66

mole 40–1, 95

    calculations from chemical equations 62–5

    and concentration of solution 65–6

    enthalpy changes and 105–6

    practicing calculations using 63–5

molecular crystals 27, *28,* 30–1

molecular formula 29

    hydrocarbons *172, 173,* 174, *175*

    organic compounds 196

molecules 17–19

    forces between 23–7

    in gases 37–40

    handedness 228

    in liquids 32–5

    molecular collisions and energy 119–23

    and vaporisation 36

monoacylglyceride 216, 223

monomers 192–3, 227

monosaccharides 234–5

monounsaturated fatty acids *218,* 219

myristic acid *218*

N

natural gas 59, 62, 96, *97, 109*

    see also methane

neon 50

neutral solution 158, *160*

neutralisation 84–5, 143–4, 240

neutrons 15–17

nickel 93, *222*

nitrate group 57, 58

nitric acid *83,* 143, *155*

nitrogen 27, *39,* 40, 55

    forming ammonia 124, 136, *137*

nitrogen dioxide 139–40

nitrogen monoxide 138, 141

nitrogen trichloride 55

nitrous acid 132

noble gases 47, 49–50

non-metals 45

    in the Periodic Table 88, *89,* 90

nuclear bombardment 45

nuclear power *97*

nutritional information *213*

O

obesity 219

octane *109, 172,* 180–1

octane number 180–2, 183

oils 35, 247

    energy consumption 96, *97*

    properties of 213–20

    see also **crude oil**

oleic acid *218,* 220

Open University Library 252

organic chemistry 186

organic compounds 167, 187

    analysing the structure of 200–1

    classification 195

    names of 175–6

    predicting products of organic reactions 207–8

    see also **crude oil; functional groups; hydrocarbons**

Organic Molecules 176, 195

osmium *124*

oxalic acid 198

oxidation 85–8

    and corrosion 90–2

    functional groups and 204–8, *211*

oxides 46

oxygen *8,* 9, 10, 18

    fuels burning in 108, *109*

    hydrogen bonding 27, *34, 35*

    reaction with methane 59–60, 62, 108, *109, 115*

    reactions 46, 60–1, 110–12, 130

    relative molecular mass 38, *39,* 40

ozone layer 186, 196

P

paint 91

palmitic acid *218*

paracetamol 244

peak oil 209

pentane *172, 175,* 183

peptidases 231

peptide bond 226–7

peptides *226,* **227**

period 47

Periodic Table 47, *48, 49,* 50–4
   and ion formation 58
   metal ions and 88, *89,* 90

permanent dipole 26

peroxodisulfate ions 116, 118

pesticides 186

petrochemicals 185–8, 209
   alternative sources of 251–2

pewter 45

pH 144–9
   common solutions 162–3, *164*

pH scale 144–7, **160**–4

pharmaceuticals 239–50

phase change 31, 32

phosphoric acid *83*

photosynthesis 232

plants, feedstocks from 251–2

platinum *124*

polar bonds 26

polarised 25, 35

polymerisation 192–3, *208*

polymers 2, **190**–3, *208,* 227

polypeptides 227

polypropylene *192*

polysaccharides 235–6

polystyrene *192*

polythene 29, 32, *191,* 192

polyunsaturated fatty acids 188, 201, *218,* 219, 223

polyvinyl chloride *192*

potassium 45, 82

potassium chloride 23

potassium dichromate 205–6, 207

potassium hydroxide 84–5, 143

potential energy 99

practical activities 5–6
   examining quartz 30–1
   examining salt 20–2
   hydrogen ion concentration household solutions 146–9
   verifying the Avogadro hypothesis 38–39

pressure, chemical equilibrium and 133–6, *137*

pressure cooker 36

primary structure 227

principal quantum number 43–5

problem-solving skills 6, 253

products 59–61, 95–6, 98
   calculating quantities of 62–5
   energy changes and *101*
   enthalpy change 103, *104*
   and equilibrium constant 132
   rate of formation 119–22
   temperature and pressure effects 133, *134*

propane *172,* 185

propene *188, 192*

proportionality 127–8

prostaglandins 243–4

proteases 231, 242

proteins 213, 223–31
   hydrolysis 242–3
   see also **enzymes**

protons 15–17

pseudoephedrine 244, *245*

PTFE 193

Q

quantum numbers 43–5

quartz *20, 28, 29,* 30–1

R

R groups 203, 224–5

RAM 16

rates of chemical reactions *see* **chemical kinetics**

reactants 59–61, 95–6, 98, 242–3
   see also **products**

Reactivity of Metals 81

reagents 205–6, 207

receptors 245–9

red cabbage 144, *145*

reduction 85–8, 204–8, *211*

relative atomic mass 16, *48,* 63, 64, 66, 75

relative formula mass 62, 63

relative molecular mass 18, 37–40, 62, 63, 75

residual fuel oil *185*

reversible reactions 124–7

rheumatic fever 240

RMM 18

rock salt 20–2, 30–1

rubidium 82

rust 46, 72, 78, 82, 90–2, 101, *115*

S

sacrificial metal 92

safety precautions 21, 146

salbutamol 244, *245, 246,* 249

salicylic acid 239–41, 244

salt *see* sodium chloride

salts, formation 143, *144*

saturated compounds 188, *191*

saturated fatty acids *218,* 219, 221–3

scanning tunnelling microscopy 14

sea salt 20–1, 30–1

seawater 164, *168*

semi-metals *89*

The Shapes of Molecules 176

silicon *8, 9, 10, 28, 29*

silver *70,* 71–3, 78, *81*

single bonds 55, 170, 177–8, 187–8

smelting 92

sodium 19, *20, 35,* 50–1
   production 33–4
   properties 46, 47

sodium chloride 19–20, 29
   activity examining 20–2
   electrolysis 33–4
   solubility in water 23, *35,* 65–6

sodium hydroxide 64–5, 84, 85, 152
   hydrogen and hydroxide ions 159
   reactions 204, 240

sodium salicylate 240

solder 93

solids 27–32
solubility 23, *35*, **65**–6
solute 65
solutions 34–5, 158–60
    aqueous 34–5, 61, 81–2
    working with 65–6
solvation 35
solvents 34–35, 65, 196
space-filling model *18, 24, 175*
space travel 1, *2*
    calculation 64–5
spectator ions 140
stainless steel 45, 93
starch 236
stearic acid *218*
steel 45, 46, 70, 79–80, 93
    corrosion *78*
    prevention of rusting 91–2
Stone Age 75, 76
strong acids 152, 155
strong bases 152
structural formula 55, 170–1, *174, 175*
    abbreviated 171, *172, 173*
    drawing 195
    key functional groups *210–11*
study timetable 5–6
styrene (phenylethene) *192*
sublimation 31, 32, **107**–8, 124
subshells 43–5, 47, *49,* 50–2
sucrose 232, 234–5, 236
sugars 232–7, 251
sulfur *70,* 71
sulfur dioxide 135, 138
sulfur trioxide 61, 135–6, 138
sulfuric acid 83, 84–5, 143, 144
    production of 135–6
surroundings 100
sustainability 251–2
sweeteners 237
synthetic polymers 2, 191
syrups 236
system 100, *101*

T

TAGs *see* **triacylglycerols**
temperature
    and chemical equilibrium 131, *134,*
    137–9
    effect on a chemical reaction 98,
    118–22
    melting temperature 70, *77,* 93
    and solubility 23, 65
    and vaporisation 36
    see also **boiling temperature**
tetrachloromethane 196
tetraethyl-lead 181
tetrafluorethene 193
tetrahedron *28,* 228, 233
thalidomide 186, 249
thermal decomposition 124
thermochemical equations 104–5,
106, 107–9
tin 32, *70,* 75–8, *81*
    alloys 92–3, 93
    reactivity 83–4
'tin pest' 76
toluene *181,* 182
trans 220
transient dipole 25, 29–30
triacylglycerols 214–17, 219–21
triple bonds 55
trypsin *242*
tungsten *124*

U

undissociated acid 151, 152
universal indicator 144, *145*
unsaturated compounds 188
unsaturated fatty acids *218,* 219–23
urine 80

V

valence electrons 50, 53
valence shell 50, 51, 52

valency 53, 55, 170
    in benzene 178
    functional groups and 195–6
    in ionic compounds 57–8
valine *224, 225,* 226, *227*
van der Waals forces 25, 169
vaporisation 36, 168
    water 104–8
vapour deposition 107
Viewing Food Molecules 237
vinegar 150, *151*
vinyl chloride (chloroethene) *192*

W

water 17–18, 29, 57, 143
    bonding in 27, 28, 55
    changes of state 104–8
    equilibrium dissociation of 156–60
    properties 31, 35, 36, 247
    reaction with alkenes 189, *208*
    reactivity of metals with 46
    solubility of sodium chloride in 23,
    35, 65–6
    see also aqueous solution
water cycle 156
'water-gas shift' reaction 128
waxes *169*
weak acids 152, 154–5
weak bases 152
'white tin' 76
willow bark 239

X

xenon 50

Z

Z **15**
zeolites 182, 188
zinc *70,* 83, 84, 91–2
zinc oxide 92